AD Biography
Rasputin Gri 1990

O9-BTN-069

Myles, Douglas. Rasputin : satyr, saint, or Satan
9000680964

9000680964

DISCARDED BY
MEAD PUBLIC LIBRARY
OK
9/90

DO NOT REMOVE CARD FROM POCKET

A

Mead Public Library
Sheboygan, Wisconsin

Each borrower is held responsible for all library
materials drawn on his card and for all fines
accruing on same.

DEMCO

RASPUTIN

also by the author

THE GREAT WAVES
PRINCE DRACULA

RASPUTIN

Satyr, Saint, or Satan

Douglas Myles

McGRAW-HILL PUBLISHING COMPANY

New York   St. Louis   San Francisco
Hamburg   Mexico   Toronto

Copyright © 1990 by Douglas Myles. All rights reserved. Printed in the United States of America. Except as permitted under the Copyright Act of 1976, no part of this publication may be reproduced or distributed in any form or by any means or stored in a data base or retrieval system without the prior written permission of the publisher.

1 2 3 4 5 6 7 8 9 DOC DOC 9 5 4 3 2 1 0

ISBN 0-07-044239-8

Library of Congress Cataloging-in-Publication Data

Myles, Douglas.
  Rasputin : satyr, saint, or satan / Douglas Myles.
    p.   cm.
  Includes bibliographical references.
  ISBN 0-07-044239-8
  1. Rasputin, Grigori Efimovich, ca. 1870–1916.   2. Soviet Union—
Court and courtiers—Biography.   3. Soviet Union—History—Nicholas
II, 1894–1917.   I. Title.
DK254.R3M95   1990
947.08′3′092—dc20
[B]   90-30019
                                                                  CIP

B
R184m
c.1

680964

*For Elizabeth Myles
and Isabel Nibecker*

680064

R.184m
c.1

CONTENTS

Introduction   1

1.   The Origins of a Prophet   7
2.   The Light   21
3.   The Khlisti   39
4.   The Starets of Pokrovskoye   60
5.   Ferocious Fermentations   80
6.   "The Tsarevich Will Live"   102
7.   Enter Iliodor   126
8.   Enter Yussupov   154
9.   The Miracle   182
10.   Prelude to Holocaust   202
11.   "Would You Be Tsar?"   227
12.   The Lethal Conspiracy   249
13.   And Farewell   275

Epilogue   287
Glossary of Foreign Words and Guide to Pronunciation   307
Bibliography   309
Index   311

Introduction

This is the story of one of the strangest and most enigmatic figures in history. He was Grigori Efimovich Rasputin, the Russian holy man who searched for God but instead found power, who prayed for chastity but succumbed to lust, who was uncanny prophet, mysterious divine, astounding faith-healer, and who during an incredibly bizarre interlude ruled Russia through control of its Empress.

Try as one will, it is all but impossible to find an historical personage who is more compelling or memorable than Rasputin. An illiterate carter from the frozen wastes of western Siberia, he knew very little of politics and still less of war. Yet a day was to come when both statesmen and generals were to fear his influence, when some would go into enforced retirement because of him, when the hatred he aroused was such that people of the very highest order of nobility would look with favor on any serious plot, however treacherous or ignoble, to assassinate him.

Almost from the time of his death in the winter of 1916 an overwhelming mass of material has been published about him: tracts, articles, memoranda, over a hundred books in several languages, primarily Russian, German, and English. Unfortunately for the veracity of the historical record, the earliest outpourings were those which took their "facts" from the carefully manufactured Soviet archives, one of whose chief purposes was to justify the Bolshevik "politics of terror" by branding the Russian Royal Family and those connected with it as heinous and debauched. Rasputin was not only associated with that family but stood unofficially as its chief advisor and protector. It therefore became politically expedient to denigrate him to whatever extent possible.

This book is not a defense of Rasputin. Indeed, so far as his sexual activities were concerned much that was said about him was true. It is, however, extremely doubtful that he ever raped a woman as alleged. On the contrary, they very nearly raped him, at least figuratively, scores of them over the years, all flocking to go to bed with this man many of whose followers considered him to be a reincarnated Jesus, albeit a very liberal manifestation. The truth is that he needs no "whitewashing" to stand firmly as a remarkable figure. He had incredible gifts and several serious weaknesses. His character was multifaceted, complicated in the extreme, and some of what he possessed remains inexplicable to this day. Science cannot understand it—but then the same human beings who reach for the stars cannot create a single blade of grass. Parapsychologists have studied it—but what this man had is far beyond their ken. In all truth, the world may not see his like again in a thousand years.

In the 1930s, before a successful lawsuit caused all copies of the film *Rasputin and the Empress* to be withdrawn, it was still possible to watch the entire Barrymore clan perform splendidly in a story dealing with the final years of tsarism in Holy Russia. It was an extraordinary film, sombre, deeply moving, and some of its more vivid sequences may still be etched in public memory. No longer is the musical score recalled. Yet often in imagination, when in his mind's eye the filmgoer remembers the bloody climactic scene, he may possibly accompany it in thought with the infinitely powerful score of Modeste Moussorgsky's *A Night on Bald Mountain*, the Russian composer's titanic conception (possibly drug induced) of the Witches' Sabbath—*Walpurgisnacht*. The inexorable unfolding of the tragedy invites the sonorous tones, from the gathering of the damned and the furious dancing of the devil's disciples, to the sudden clanging of the church bell that heralds the dawn, to the muted, forced slinking away of the demonic revelers who must go to their dark abodes before the rising of the sun.

Rasputin and the Empress

Glittering light and all-enfolding shadow. *A Night on Bald Mountain*. In memory the observer is enthralled and held spellbound, for the story of Rasputin speaks of the amazing contrasts in humanity, not only of the mind but of the far deeper reaches of the soul. Is this obscure? In his introduction to Stevenson's great classic, *Dr. Jekyll and Mr. Hyde*, B. Allen Bentley writes

> What is the reality that Stevenson re-creates in *Jekyll and Hyde*? It is the dual nature of the personality of man—the co-existence within the human body and soul of goodness, morality, and idealism in equilibrium with an equal energy of evil, depravity, and sadism. Stevenson's analysis of this psychological structure results in the total separation of the two fields into isolated characters, marshaled at every point into pure contrast and yet, inevitably, synthesized into one human being at once agonized and glorious. . . .

> The captivating power of *Dr. Jekyll and Mr. Hyde* lies largely in the truth that it arose from the author's profound conviction of the dualism at the root of the nature of man, as that conviction arose, not merely from the observations of other men, but as it broke from his own soul, in dream, in thought, and in every episode of his glorious and tormented life.

Glorious and tormented. Yes, Stevenson was both. And how many humans on the face of planet Earth have been that? History has seen them before. Go back as far as you like, into ancient times if you wish. Witness Mary Magdalen, who whored but found grace at last; Saul of Tarsus, who killed the followers of the Christ but became Saint Paul; Marcus Junius Brutus, who could be at once the slayer of his friend Caesar and "a noble Roman"; Justinian I, who blinded Belisarius, the man who had saved his throne, yet codified Roman law and built the great church of Hagia Sophia; Innocent III, "the Gray Eminence," master of war and dark intrigue, yet the pope who made possible the miracles of Saint Francis; Tsar Peter I, a ruler who could behead men with his own hand, yet who laid down his life to rescue a common sailor.

The Dual Nature of the Personality of Man

Let us take on the one hand the Venetian adventurer and rake, Casanova de Seingalt, a man whose dissolute life landed him in prison, whose personal memoirs detailing his many seductions of women are well known to literature. Then let us add another notorious individual, Italy's Alesandro Cagliostro, mesmerist, necromancer, mystic, and alchemist, a "miracle worker" who died in a Roman dungeon where he had been imprisoned on a charge of heresy and sorcery. Does the brew begin to ferment? Of course. Finally, by way of extreme contrast, there comes to mind Father Damien de Veuster, the Belgian priest who went to the island of Molokai to minister to the lepers, who knew he would contract the dread disease, yet who willingly made the supreme sacrifice to serve them to the end and call attention to their plight. A saint in all but name.

Casanova, Cagliostro, Father Damien. Individuals so disparate could never be combined in *the same human being*, could they? Yet in Rasputin there were, to an amazing degree, the outstanding characteristics of all three. An adventurer and seducer of many women he certainly was. That he had the miraculous power to heal by faith made more devastating by an astounding clairvoyance is also beyond dispute. And the grace of the martyr who knowingly embraces his self-destructive course? Rasputin knew he risked violent extinction. He predicted his own death. Rather than desert the Tsar and Tsaritsa of Russia, he repeatedly returned to St. Petersburg, the city that he knew for him was fatal, and was slaughtered at his post. *Here* is the dualism of man. Here, schizophrenia, if you will. But here, also, in the much maligned person of an illiterate Siberian peasant—greatness.

Siberia. Vast. Brooding. Hiding many mysteries. In the nineteenth century a land of almost limitless distances half-forgotten by time. Along the great rivers that drain into the Arctic Ocean, the Ob, the Yenesei, the Lena; along the Amur that empties into the Sea of Okhotsk; along their numberless tributaries, too, there lived and still lives today a hardy people whose thousands of villages seem dwarfed and isolated in the profound immensity of it all. What challenges have they faced? The winters have always been one. The birds freeze solid in the trees and drop out of them lifeless. Humans who are exposed fall asleep (the beginning of the freezing process) and are dead before they can be awakened. No other inhabited land has seen such temperatures. In February of 1892, in the town of Verkhoyansk in the north central Yakutsk Republic on the right bank of the Yana River, they experienced the greatest cold ever recorded on planet Earth. Ninety degrees below zero.

War. Rapine. Conquest. Siberia has known them repeatedly. Long before the Cossack Yermak crossed the Urals in 1582 to conquer the Tatar Khanate of Sibir, the Mongols under Batu Khan (a grandson of the mighty Genghis) had established their invincible Golden Horde at Sarai on the Volga. The religion they brought from the Gobi Desert was shamanism, the belief of the Ural-Altaic peoples in an invisible spirit world of gods, demons, and ancestral shades with whom only the *shaman* or priest could communicate. The religion was very old. Its original practitioners, the Tungus, a Mongoloid people of eastern Siberia, had spread it to the south and west. Genghis Khan had believed in it. It is said that when he ordered the death of a treacherous *shaman*, Tebtengri (he had three powerful wrestlers break his back), he caused his own yurt to be moved over the body, the entrance flap to be secured, and the corpse to be lifted through the smoke hole in the dead of night. He then explained to his people that the wizard had transgressed Mongol law and simply vanished, claimed by "the spirits of Heaven."

From the ancient Byzantine Empire, Russia acquired much of its architecture (the characteristically Byzantine "onion" domes of its churches, for example) and the Cyrillic alphabet, the latter from the monk Kyril, "Apostle to the Slavs," who journeyed to heathen Rus from Constantinople in A.D. 869. And it gained something else from the same source, the all-powerful Orthodox religion. None were more staunch supporters of it than the peasants, of which class Rasputin was one. But if the monks, priests, archimandrites, and bishops were held in great respect, a yet older tradition made another kind of religious devotee even more revered. This was the *starets*, or "holy man," metamorphosed from the Tungusic *shaman*, the wandering beggar-pilgrim who first sought divine enlightenment in the windswept Siberian steppes. Even outside Siberia his counterpart was to be found in much of Asia, among the itinerant lamas of distant Tibet, for instance, and the severely self-castigating *sadhus* of Hindu India. The latter have often been commemorated in literature. One thinks of Kim's long-haired *bairagi* in Kipling's famous novel, of the sinister Ram Gwar in Max Ehrlich's *Shaitan*. In Russia prior to Rasputin, not many lines had ever been penned about any *starets*. They simply existed. They *were*. Perhaps it was because they were almost exclusively a peasant phenomenon and very few people born to that level of life could read or write.

Now consider: The scene is St. Petersburg in the opening years of the twentieth century, the imperial capital of Holy Russia on the Baltic, a city which in some respects was the strangest and most degenerate in the world. It was the seat of the throne of the Romanovs. In one of its palaces dwelt Tsar Nikolai II (Nicholas), last of his line, and the Tsaritsa Aleksandra. Isolated, condemned to loneliness and fear both by their natures and their position, aware of the smoldering menace of impending revolution all around them, they turned away from untrustworthy, scheming courtiers and, in desperation, put their faith and their hope in soothsayers, practitioners of the occult arts, and unscrupulous charlatans intent on personal gain.

It was in the midst of this fated mélange that the dark-robed figure of Rasputin appeared like a god-sent wind from the far Siberian steppes. He would save the lives of royalty. Inadvertently, he also would help to precipitate the holocaust that would destroy them. Once he had set his foot upon the stage nothing was ever to be the same again. Nothing. Destiny resided in him, fixed and inexorable. So did Nemesis.

CHAPTER 1

The Origins of a Prophet

Under the shimmering starlight he walked rapidly with his companion. As they went from the back of the tall, old-fashioned house to the street in front, he was surprised to see the prince still held him by the arm as he had done when they came down the stairs together. The young noble seemed in a hurry. As their boots broke through the hard-packed snow, the crackling sounds of their footfalls appeared unnaturally loud in the silence of the night. It reminded him of artillery fire on the Eastern Front, the German guns that were killing Russians, though he had never heard it.

Gorokhovaya Street was empty, not surprisingly considering it was after midnight. At the curb a black limousine awaited them, one of the prince's cars. And now a noticeable oddity occurred. Normally, the chauffeur would have alighted to open the back door. But the man in front with his turned up collar and pulled down cap, as muffled in fur as his employer, made no move. The Prince opened the door and got in last. He closed the door. The car moved away at unusual speed, tire chains screeching as its rear wheels spun on the ice.

Rasputin was not alarmed. As he had done more often than he cared to admit to people who might question his sanity, he was at that moment spiritually separated. It was not a phenomenon unique to himself. He knew it had been done in India and Tibet for centuries by Hindu and Buddhist avatars, the incarnated deities of Asia who claimed to leave their bodies in absolute physical detachment. He was never sure he had this capability but he could detach *his mind* utterly. He could and often did wander far and away on a stream of consciousness that seemed to isolate him from the confines of self, returning at will. He was doing so now. For the moment he had the sense of being an entity other than the bearded man called Father Grigori. He stood aloof and gazed down on himself: the large, powerful hands, gloved now; the rugged face with its high cheekbones and prominent, fleshy nose; the eyes of an intense blue, capable of assuming an expression which no one who saw it would ever forget.

Just now those eyes were closed. In the chill of this winter night he was remembering, his mind traveling back over a life which so far had endured some forty-five years, but which the remnant of his prophetic powers told him was drawing to a conclusion. There were scenes from his early youth, an unhappy childhood in the main, spent mostly alone because he had willed it so, influenced in strange ways by an obsessive quest which even now he had not entirely fulfilled.

He had few regrets, he decided. Indeed, if he had it all to do over, he suspected he would conduct himself much as before, love the same women, confront the same events in much the same manner, make the same enemies, come to the same grim finality. There was but one circumstance that gnawed at him and would not give him peace. He had failed the Tsar and Tsaritsa, the four princesses, in the end even the Tsarevich, whose life he had saved repeatedly. They would not long outlive him. He had told the Little Father that. Peasant though he was, he was their bulwark, their strength in adversity, their only hope for survival. And now he rode through the dark streets of frozen St. Petersburg—he didn't much care for the name of Petrograd—and admitted to himself, rather pitifully he thought, that he was played out because God had ordained it.

He opened his eyes suddenly as a question came to him. Would he make his mark in history? He had been ambitious. No denying that. He had flown very high, considering his origins. But would he leave any trace at all of his passing? Russia was at war. Perhaps he would end as a mere footnote to that ghastly feast of blood. *Russian* blood. *Peasant* blood, most of it. And he the hated and despised because he opposed it, because he had done all in his power to stop it and save what was left. *German sympathizer*, they called him. *Traitor. Tool of the Kaiser* and the war party in Berlin. If only they knew how much he loved this land and its people. If only. . . .

⁀ His thoughts were arrested in midcareer. How had Protopopov been so *sure* they would try to kill him? What a look he'd had on his face when he had come to his benefactor's lodgings this very night and pleaded with him not to go out, speaking darkly of a rumored plot to assassinate him. The little man had been so intense, so earnest, so fearful. Was it gratitude because he, Rasputin, had raised him into prominence, made him Minister of the Interior when most people thought he was a fool or worse? Or was it more than that? Did Protopopov love him then? Was his foreboding based on whispered utterances, a casually dropped word here, a look or gesture there? Did the poor fellow give undue credence to some Okhrana report? Or was it something deeper, the product of that mysticism in which he was said to dabble? Something deeper. A fleeting glimpse into the infinite, the power of augury, that divine gift of *déjà vue* which he himself had known. What a shame. Since coming to this humanity-engorged cesspool where all his vices were magnified, he had the gift only at intervals. The dread of losing it entirely was tinged with infinite sadness.

He was trying to give his thoughts shape and cohesion—and failing. Where had he been? Ah yes. Protopopov might have the power now, fleetingly. It was possible. It was also probable that deep in his bourgeois soul the little minister distrusted all aristocrats, none more so than Prince Yussupov.

He turned his head slightly to look at the latter, descending to the here and now. All furs in the cold. Muffled to the eyes behind the fogged windows. Silent. For a brief moment he watched him intently. *There* was a pretty lad, for other lads. Delicately handsome, elegant, essentially vain and purse-proud, yet somehow fascinating. The fact was that he, the *starets*, had taken a fancy to the Prince. Nothing physical. He knew of the man's reputation as a homosexual and found it the least attractive part of him. He really couldn't put his finger on it, the feeling he had. Yussupov sang well and played the guitar, and shared his love of Gypsy music. That was part of it. Perhaps the other part was his wife, the reputedly beautiful Princess Irina Aleksandrovna, a woman whom he, Rasputin, had never seen. Were her recurring headaches real? Was it true she longed for the healing grace of the *starets*? Why had Yussupov married her when his primary interest was men? But then the Prince was capable of enjoying her voyeuristically, a common enough thing in the St. Petersburg demimonde. The fact that her sex partner would be a crude and uncouth *muzhik* (a peasant) would make her seduction by a stranger all the more exciting to watch. Titillating, as Yussupov might put it.

He settled deeper into the seat. He tried to see out the window but the heavy frost made it impossible. He had a burgeoning sense of speed, a dangerous thing in these icy conditions, especially at night. Why was Yussupov hurrying? Then he remembered another warning he'd been given, that of his frightened daughter Maria, tearful-eyed, disheveled, encountered in the hallway of his flat less than an hour ago. He had taken her in his arms. "Don't go, Papa." He had kissed her cheeks and her eyes, trying to soothe and reassure. "Don't *go*, Papa!" What was it that *she* was feeling? What did she *sense*? The reasoned advice of a mere man was one thing, the God-given premonition of a young girl who adored her father something else.

Suddenly, he knew he was a fool not to have listened to her. Worse than a fool. Possibly suicidal. He recalled how he had kissed her sleeping sister Varya, rejecting the same plea of his maid who was also his mistress, the loving and intense Katya. Feminine intuition? All had tried to stop him. All had failed. Somewhere he had heard of a man called Caesar in ancient Rome, a would-be tsar in that land. He'd had a wife named Calpurnia, a woman of vision who had warned her husband as these, his loved ones, had tried to warn him. It was said that Caesar would not listen either. He turned his head and looked directly at Yussupov.

"Why the hurry?" he asked.

Yussupov appeared to hesitate. "My wife is having a party," he said, "but the guests will be leaving very soon, I'm sure. We'll go to the game room and wait for her there."[1]

Rasputin said nothing. That a woman with a chronic sick headache would throw a party was highly implausible. Seeming to realize this, Yussupov tried to explain.

"She insisted I bring you tonight. She somehow manages to get through even though her headaches are painful."[2]

Rasputin straightened his back. He was feeling unwell. He had not been right for two and a half years, ever since the summer of 1914 when the fanatic Chionya Guseva had buried her knife in his abdomen and nearly disemboweled him. Make love to Princess Irina? He'd be lucky if he could *walk*. He thought of Pokrovskoye, his home village where Guseva had done the deed. His wife Praskovia was there now. So was his other devoted love, Dunia. Siberia. . . . People who cared. . . . Love for Rasputin. . . . No one knew how much he needed love. No one had ever known.

But the Tsar and Tsaritsa of Russia needed him, too!

He put one hand to his lower belly and suppressed a moan. Improperly healed lesions, the doctor had said. And who was he, Grigori Efimovich, to go to such a man? Could he not heal himself as he had healed others? No, he could do nothing. He had not the grace anymore, was no longer the child of God. Tonight he would forget it. Even the pain he would forget, for pain could be controlled by the mind. Irina Aleksandrovna Yussupova would meet her *starets*, receive his ministrations, and Fate would decide.

He scarcely knew where they were. Trying to see out the frosted window, he could barely discern the long line of the Moika River, a dark, undulant thread in a world of otherwise unrelieved whiteness. More minutes passed. When they finally reached their destination and the car slowed and stopped, he vaguely discerned through a light fall of sleet the great building itself, the imposing massiveness of the Palace Yussupov hard by the river. Here it was—and whatever awaited him. They had arrived at a side entrance. Yussupov got out. Again no help from the unknown driver. Rasputin followed him. *God's will be done* was his silent thought. *So be it.*

At the Gorokhovaya flat her father had recently left, Maria Rasputin had watched him being driven away. Desperately she had tried to open her upstairs bedroom window, hoping to call out to him, but had found it frozen fast. Almost in a frenzy she had rubbed the pane with her hand until enough frost had been cleared to see. Then, the car gone, she'd said something she had never said before, something she was to remember for well over half a century. At all their many partings it had always been *"Dosvidaniya*, Papa"—*So long*. Now, as her father was engulfed in the darkness, from the dire agony of her prophetic soul there was wrung another word: *"Proshchaitye*, Papa"— *Farewell.*[3]

On her bed she prayed for her father's return, and prayed and prayed until at last claimed by sleep.

Historians and biographers often differ in the matter of dates, never more so than concerns the one ascribed as the year of Rasputin's birth. In *Nicholas and Alexandra*, Robert K. Massie says he was born in 1872 (p. 194). In *Rasputin and the Fall of Imperial Russia*, Heinz Liepman writes: "The closest one can come with any certainty is sometime between the years 1863 and 1873" (p. 21). In *Rasputin, The Holy Devil*, René Fülöp-Miller, often reputed to be the foremost of Rasputin's biographers, gives no date for his birth whatever. Then there is Colin Wilson, one of the most intellectual of those who have dealt with the subject. In his *Rasputin and the Fall of the Romanovs* we read the following: "The exact date of Rasputin's birth is not certain, but it is convenient to assume that it took place in the late 1860s . . ." (p. 23).

Actually, using logic after a careful study of her work, there is very little reason to doubt the word of Rasputin's oldest daughter, Maria. In her book, *Rasputin, The Man Behind the Myth*, she is precise, saying her father's birth occurred "on the night of January 23, 1871 . . ." (p. 17).

The village of his birth is Pokrovskoye in western Siberia. It is seldom found on ordinary maps, therefore often imperfectly located in historical accounts. However, the National Geographic Society's map of the Union of Soviet Socialist Republics printed in December 1944 pinpoints it exactly. Pokrovskoye is on the north shore of the Tura River, a branch of the Tobol, itself a tributary of the mighty Ob. The nearest city of any size is Tyumen, about fifty miles to the west as the crow flies; the second nearest trading center Tobolsk at the confluence of the Tobol and Irtysh, a Cossack-founded emporium for furs and fish some ninety crow-flown miles to the northeast. In his self-apologia, *Rasputin* (originally with the subtitle *His Malignant Influence and His Assassination*), Yussupov says Pokrovskoye was on a hill, prosperous, surrounded by groves of birch (p. 28). He might have added that the vast steppe to the north and east, in addition to its nearly limitless stands of evergreens, contained some of the most extensive marshlands on earth, a beautiful but essentially hostile environment for the unwary.

Like almost all Siberians of the time, Rasputin was born into a peasant household. His father, Efim Akovlevich, was well enough off to own several horses and a fertile plot of land. He was industrious and God-fearing. In seeming contradiction, he was also from the time of his marriage reputedly something of a drinker who had once been arrested for horse stealing.

Rasputin's mother, Anna Egorovna, appears to have come from very strong stock. No wine dependency for her. One is reminded of enduring, largely uncomplaining pioneer women in many of the world's harsh regions in the nineteenth century, stalwart breeders who took each day as it came, often raised large families, many of whose children died young, and faced their difficult lives with a hardihood and resolution the equal of any man's. Such, apparently, was she.

A majority of those who have written about Rasputin have stated that his name means "dissolute" or "lewd," and many have regarded it as a sobriquet attached to him in condemnation of his character. This is taking much for granted. The Russian word *rasputse* has another meaning as well, that of "crossroads." The village of Pokrovskoye is on such a crossroads between Tyumen and Tobolsk. Maria Rasputin tells us that more than half its population shared her family name as a result of this circumstance.

From his daughter, too, we learn that the boy Rasputin was a precocious child, for so his mother had described him to her. Not starting to talk until nearly two and a half years of age, he was behind his older brother Mischa (Mikhail) in this respect. However, when he did begin speaking, he progressed rapidly in the art, and his ability to walk was well in advance of his brother's earlier efforts. Rasputin had a lively imagination, and even as a small child sometimes startled people with it. His mother related how he told her of seeing a beautiful lady once when he was sick, how she sat beside his bed until her soft, sweet voice took his fever away. Thinking about her grandmother's words in later years, Maria was less than certain that this vision of her father's boyhood had been unreal.

While still very young, Grischa, as his family called him, was already giving evidence of something extremely unusual, the power to heal sick animals by *sound* and *touch* alone. A horse would be restless or even unmanageable. The boy would calm him immediately with a few soft words and gentle strokings of the hand. A cow would refuse to be milked, but Grischa's mere entry into the barn would quiet her at once, after which she readily submitted. It was Efim Akovlevich who told of the horse with the strained leg tendon. He mentioned the animal's condition at the dining table, speaking only of a pulled hamstring. The boy heard it and went out. Prompted by curiosity, his father followed him. What he saw left a permanent impression. Grischa was standing by the horse. At first he did nothing and seemed lost in a sort of reverie, the very state of mind Efim deplored when he thought his son was shirking his work. The youth went to the injured hind leg, immediately found the hamstring (he had never heard of the term *podkolenaya djila*), and cupped it with the warmth of his hand. For a short interval he stood in silent concentration. Ultimately, releasing the leg and straightening his body, he spoke soothingly to the horse, pronouncing a completed cure. Then he left.

The father was puzzled at first, uncomprehending. Once his son returned to the house, he decided to test what he had seen. Outside the stable he walked the horse for a considerable time, round and round. The injured leg carried its share of the weight. It was no longer lame. Efim Akovlevich was proud, though still a little incredulous. His son seemed to have proved himself. From that day forward the lad was given other animals to cure and he always did so. In time, a day came when his reputation as a near-miraculous healer of livestock had spread throughout the village, and inevitably his healing art began to be applied to human ills. What kind of a boy was this, the villagers asked themselves. Legend spoke of such children but no one in living memory had ever seen one. Until now.

Although some writers say he was older (Wilson, for example, says he was twelve), Maria Rasputin claims her father was only eight when tragedy struck the family for the first time. Withdrawn by nature, the boy Grischa took very little part in the communal life of the village, his only companion being his brother Mischa, two years his senior. The pair were very close. On those occasions when they found themselves briefly free of their farm labors, they would often walk in the forest together to considerable distances from the house or go down to the Tura River to swim or fish. On this fateful day they decided that a swim was the thing but went farther downstream than usual. The current was strong and swift here, faster than they realized. Mischa was first in, and was immediately knocked off his feet and caught in the water's grip. In panic, he shouted for help. When Grischa seized his arm he lost his footing and was himself pulled in as both boys were dragged under.

We are told they were saved from drowning by a peasant who saw their desperate plight. He must have been a powerful man. As one lad clung to the other he dragged them both out by brute strength. They were chilled to the bone. Back home once again, they each came down with pneumonia very quickly. No one knew what to do about it. Doctors were a rarity, and the nearest one lived in the city of Tyumen. Mortality rates were high. Even mothers during childbirth were nearly always attended by midwives, not physicians, and deaths from puerperal infection (childbed fever) were extremely common. In the case of the two boys, who wheezed and groaned as they struggled for breath, there was nothing much the helpless adults could do but pray. Grischa, who in later years repeatedly gave evidence of an iron constitution, recovered after a time. His brother, however, steadily lost strength until at last he succumbed to the dreaded asphyxiation attending this malady. According to the woman who would have become his niece had he lived, Mikhail Efimovich departed this life at the tender age of ten.

The effect of his brother's death on Rasputin was profound and long lasting. His own convalescence was lengthy. Although he eventually regained his physical health, psychologically he was much altered. Becoming more introverted than ever, subject to unexpected changes of mood that ran the gamut from deep depression to heights of near elation, he began to display some of the characteristic symptoms of the manic-depressive personality. Such persons usually antagonize other people and often frighten them. In the case of the frequently morose and always unpredictable youth who had lost his only companion and solace in life, the effect was to cause him to withdraw still further from social activity with his peers. This caused other problems. Children in his age group, retaliating against what they considered the strange boy's snobbery, ostracized or verbally abused him as the occasion suited.

It was at about this time, when he was slowly and very painfully recuperating from the loss of his brother after a prolonged lapse, that Rasputin began to manifest more of those powers which were to cause even greater amazement than his healing by touch. These were his clairvoyance and precognition. Although possibly present together in a single individual, they are not the same. Webster defines *clairvoyance* as "the professed power of discerning objects not present to the senses"; *precognition* as "clairvoyance relating to an event or state not yet experienced." Maria Rasputin gives a fascinating example of the former, citing an event that occurred in St. Petersburg when her father's ESP (extrasensory perception) was in the full strength of its maturity. A woman he had never seen paid a visit to his flat and was admitted. Her hands were concealed in a fur muff, a fairly common accessory to feminine cold weather apparel. The moment Rasputin saw her he shouted "Drop that!", then made a grab for the muff and knocked it to the floor. A loaded revolver fell out. Terribly shaken by what she apparently thought was black magic, the would-be assassin collapsed as her strength dissolved.

As curious and wonderful as is this gift of the *sixth sense*, perhaps even more remarkable is that of *second sight*, the precognitive phenomenon of actually being able to see into the future. This also was noted early in Rasputin. Often he would announce the coming of a stranger to the house, a not unusual thing in a land of many solitary wanderers. Occasionally, the man would show up within a short while, but sometimes hours would pass before his arrival. Whichever way it transpired, he always came as the boy had said he would. Rasputin's reputation as a seer, in his case literally as a child prophet, grew apace.

Easily the best known of the occult phenomena associated with his boyhood is the incident of the stolen horse. The owner was one of the poorer peasants. When the animal was found to be missing, the adult males of Prokovskoye met at the house of Rasputin's father because he was the head man of the village (he had reformed his drinking somewhat) and there discussed the loss. As it happened, the boy Rasputin was ill with fever at the time and a bed had been prepared for him in the room where the meeting was held. He listened for a while, then sat up abruptly and made a clear identification. "Here is the thief."

His father was embarrassed and angry. The accused man was a prominent village elder, virtually above reproach, so much so that only the lad's illness saved him from severe paternal punishment. Nonetheless, the suspicions of two of the villagers caused them to follow the man to his house. There they waited in concealment. When darkness fell, they saw him lead the stolen animal out of his barn and release it. They leaped on the culprit and soundly thrashed him. The horse was restored to the owner. Once again the genuineness of the young Rasputin's "peculiar gift" had been vindicated.

The recollections of family members were in general agreement as to when the youth first turned to religion. He was fourteen years old. Because reading and writing were not considered important in the average peasant community, he had not learned these arts. However, his memory was nearly as phenomenal as that of the young Mozart in the preceding century, who at thirteen wrote down the entire hours' long score of Allegri's *Miserere*, correcting it only slightly after a second hearing. Rasputin's subject for memorization was biblical scripture. He went to church with his family. He listened intently to the priest. Afterward, whenever the mood was upon him, he would quote long passages from the Bible, chapter and verse, page after page, with scarcely a mistake. This feat alone would have singled him out as the possessor of a remarkable intellect.

For generations, authors, behavioral psychologists, sociologists, and theologians have written and talked about the "Russian soul." In eighteenth-century Russian novels, the theme recurs incessantly. Writers such as Gogol, Turgenev, Chekhov, and Tolstoy have expounded on it. Berdyaev has philosophized well into this century. Perhaps Dostoevski has gone further than any to lay it bare. Writing in *The Sabres of Paradise*, her life of the Murid emir Shamyl, "Lion of Daghestan," Lesley Blanch says that the Russians ran (and still run) to extremes in everything, that possibly their chief character trait (and the one least understood by the West) is excess. In his life of Rasputin,

Colin Wilson refers to the Russians as full of contradictions, something few who know them will dispute. However, after comparing them to the heroic but emotionally unstable Arabs of England's famed T. E. Lawrence, then citing John Gunther's comparative analysis based on character traits inherited from the invading Mongols ("cruelty, fatalism, and sloth"), he makes the following interesting statement about religion in Russia: "But there is another characteristic of the Russian that must be understood: when he is religious he takes God for granted. God is an external force. George Fox's concept of God as the 'inner light' is completely foreign to a Russian."

Maria Rasputin tends to differ. In her full biography of her father completed in Los Angeles in 1976 (after a lapse of decades had given her much time to consider), she wrote of Rasputin's spiritual transcendence at the age of fourteen. It was a Sunday. He had gone to church with his parents. There he heard Otyets Pavel (Father Paul) preach a sermon which to him was new and startling. "The kingdom of God cometh not with observation: Neither shall they say, Lo here! or, Lo there! for, behold, the kingdom of God is within you."

The boy took the words very seriously. That afternoon, as the family was preparing for dinner, he slipped out of the house and entered the forest which flanked the village on its opposite side from the river, seeking solitude and contemplation. God was not a thing apart nor unreachable. He was *within*. Eventually he came to an area of dense, verdant woodland that seemed to offer peace and he sat down. Gone were the sights and sounds of Pokrovskoye. Here the only sounds were the twittering of birds, the hooting of an owl, the chattering of squirrels. He tried to concentrate his mind. With every fiber of his being he struggled to turn it inward, to leave the known world and enter that spiritual nirvana the yogis of India seek by what they call "transcendental meditation." In the end he began to lose himself as the world faded. His daughter writes: "As he did so, a glimmer of light arose in his mind's eye, that 'third eye' of which the mystics speak; a scintilla, a faint gleam that began to expand even as he watched it. And as it grew, it approached, nearer and nearer, brightening as it came, until what had been a soft golden glow suddenly erupted in a blinding white flash."

This, of course, was how Rasputin described the remarkable incident to Maria many years later. He had been afraid, he told her, and his fear had prevented his full acceptance of the incredible revelation, causing him to recoil from the very edge of the "Great Unknown." Immediately afterwards, he had prayed that his reluctance to step across the wondrous threshold be forgiven, prayed that the light and its golden invitation be restored to him. All to no avail. He saw nothing further. By the time he had made his way home it was already growing dark. The vision of something he was sure had been sent to him straight from God had passed from his ken.

The experience left the boy shaken. Henceforth, introspection became even more his way of life as the process of withdrawal continued and his social isolation increased. In the weeks and months that followed, a coldness developed between father and son, for in Grischa's odd behavior Efim Akovlevich saw only a stubborn and rather worthless youth given to idleness and cant. In fact, it was possible the boy might be a bit *touched*. Then the unexpected occurred. Heretofore, Rasputin had always been of a peaceful nature, ignoring insults, turning away from heated disputes no matter what the provocation of certain pugnacious peers. But a day came when the most aggressive of the village bullies carried things too far. Approaching Rasputin with two of his friends in tow, he accosted him with violence in mind and called him *malodushni* (coward). Rasputin declined to fight. Backed by his eager cohorts the bully insisted. Finally, provoked by his would-be victim's reluctance and sure of his own power, the young ruffian let fly with a blow aimed at the head. Rasputin blocked it and struck back with all his force. The bully went down—and out. In face-saving desperation the other two then attacked Rasputin and were themselves soundly beaten.

The word quickly spread through the village: Grigori Efimovich is not to be taken lightly. He may *look* peaceful but he has a punch like the kick of a mule and is not afraid to use it. This is no *malodushni*. Give him a wide birth. This from the boys. Of course, the reaction of the *girls* of Pokrovskoye was exactly the opposite. The powerful Grischa had defeated three tough attackers at once and was a hero to them, fair game romantically, and a newly coveted prize for the clever *devochka* (girl) who could capture him.

But their efforts were all in vain then. At fourteen, Rasputin was able to control his natural desires, to sublimate them to the thing which ever since his experience in the forest had become an obsession to him, his search for the renewal of the light. He was sure it had been from God, and he *must* find God again. At that time, for the fulfillment of this single, all-pervasive goal he would have given his life. It was a soul-engaging preoccupation and terribly demanding. It called for sacrifice. Although he did not know it there was within it, in spirit at least, something of the sublime grandeur of the greatest epic of Dark Age Britain, Galahad's quest for the Holy Grail.

NOTES

1. Maria Rasputin and Patte Barham, *Rasputin: The Man Behind the Myth*, Warner Books, New York, 1977. (Published by arrangement with Prentice-Hall, Inc.)
2. *Ibid*.
3. *Ibid*.

CHAPTER 2

The Light

The girl who had danced with her Gypsy partner in the firelight was extremely beautiful. Now, with her flaring dark blue skirt and low-cut scarlet blouse, her long hair as black as her sparkling eyes, she sang in the night as a violinist played, sang the love songs of old Russia in their haunting minor key. Plaintive. Haunting. Full of the yearning soul of Russia, yet somehow thrillingly romantic and terribly sensual.

At first Rasputin was almost unaware of her. Closed out of his senses, too, was the large crowd of people who watched and listened, some dozens of her own tribe bedecked as she was in their Gypsy finery, and the many villagers of Pokrovskoye, here to welcome this band of strolling players encamped on the settlement's outskirts.

He heard her voice but did not see her. Seated with several others on a fallen tree trunk, his booted ankles crossed, he gazed into the flickering camp fire as into some ever-receding unknown, his mind on the past. He had changed very much in two years. At sixteen he had been a shy and innocent boy, a male virgin who knew very little of life and love. Yet now he had the reputation of one of the worst rakes in the village. People watched their daughters carefully when he was about, and no young girls were allowed near him if their parents knew of it. But two years ago? There had been a girl in Tyumen. Would he ever forget her name? Irina Danilova Kubasova, wife of General Kubasov, a retired and very wealthy officer old enough to be her grandfather. Using her feminine wiles to the utmost, she had lured the youthful and utterly naive carter to her home. There she had made a perfect fool of him, had five of her maidservants overwhelm and rape and humiliate him as a sixth girl, the only one who held back from the sport, was forced to watch. Then she'd had his unconscious body removed from the estate grounds and left naked on a public road.

He picked up a clod of soil and threw it at the fire, aimlessly, not seeing its flight. She had drawn the line of class against him, that ripe, promiscuous bitch. He had been mad about her, drunk with the beauty of her, but in her eyes he was only a dirty *muzhik*, a peasant unfit for anything but to wipe her feet on. He had heard the word somewhere. It was the word *cynic*, and that was what she had made of him. No longer was he the wide-eyed innocent. No longer were females something to adore and respect. He used them now as things of pleasure and little else. He had no scruples about it and very little conscience, only his ever-present need. It amused him to walk in the streets of the village while taking note of the girls he had had, like a hunter counting his trophies. They took note of him, too. He could imagine their whispered confidences, was sure they compared notes on his genital size and prowess. Let them. They were only so much grist for his mill, the willing playthings of desire.

He uncrossed his legs and crossed them again. The dark-eyed Gypsy girl was still singing. She seemed closer now, an animated fleshly trap advancing and receding on the edges of his consciousness. He knew it more by feeling than thought. Did she sing to *him* now? She was fading . . . fading. . . .

His soul was not all black. The thought penetrated his brain like a knife. Suddenly. Probing deep. There had been another after Kubasova. Another failure, yet in a way she was a sort of victory, too. Names. What lay in a name? Hers was Natalya Petrovna Stepanova and he thought of her as his second carnal frustration. Yet he had saved her. There was no doubt of that. She it was who revealed his father's weakness of character to him, the old man's cruelty and sexual hypocrisy. Because she was young and attractive and took a lover now and then she was accused by one of the village's female gossips of prostitution, a charge laid before Efim Akovlevich as Pokrovskoye's headman. The moral code of the village was strict. He had shown little inclination to mercy. Father Paul, the village priest, had shown even less. It was the churchman who decreed that she should be stripped naked, her head shaved, then tied to a horse and whipped out of town never to be allowed to return. So much for the charity and compassion of Orthodox clergy. So much for the sexual "purity" of her accusers and judges, the villagers who had first disrobed her, then leered at her exposure with what lewd thoughts only God could know.

And he, Rasputin? What had the boy he had been then done? He had gone into the forest and found her torn and bleeding and near death, and his healing hands and prayers and tender kindness had brought her back to life. He had built a shelter for her and kept her in it, telling no one, visiting her daily to bring food and help her in every way he could. Then, when she was well enough to travel, like the *durak* (fool) he had always been, he got drunk with two other youths and took them out to her, promising them pleasure of her, repenting at the last moment and driving them off. And the outcome? He could have had her himself. That much she would have given in gratitude if nothing else. But he couldn't accept her gift. Overcome with remorse for the outrage he had nearly committed, he had fled away, praying in desperation for forgiveness. And something had happened. He had found his light again, though dimmer than before. He could not find it now.

The music seemed to diminish. The alluring voice of the Gypsy girl was blending with the softness of Natalya Petrovna's vividly re-membered charms as he had ministered to her bleeding injuries, clean-sing her wounds, dirt-encrusted from being dragged, healing them rapidly by the God-given miracle of his touch. Natalya disappeared from his dream. In her place was the lovely Gypsy standing close to him, her arms extended palms out as though in supplication, her voice vibrant with passion, her dark eyes seeking, inviting. . . .

He returned her gaze. Would one of her Gypsy lovers try to kill him if he accepted her offer? Perhaps the fiddler with the scar on his face or he who had danced with her earlier. He could imagine their hidden knives. But what did it matter? In her burning glance was the promise of Paradise. *She* was not Kubasova, not his social superior above him and looking down on him, nor smiling falsely with a heart full of malice. No. No, she would thrill to his calloused hands and even harder body, a body ripe with honest sweat, not feminized with perfume like those of many tsarist officers. If a knife were pulled on him, he would make its owner eat it—literally. He got to his feet. He caught her by her waist and one beringed hand and began to dance with her as the audience clapped to keep time to the rhythm and her jingling bangles flashed.

Abandoned gaiety. A headlong flight of the senses akin to madness. Her eyes were deep, he noted, as deep and as black as the night itself but glittering like jewels. Yet it was *his* eyes whose blue depths dominated her, and he saw this, sensed it with every lithe movement of their whirling bodies as more violins joined and the wild Gypsy air moved into crescendo. Only eighteen? He was a *man* now and all the folk in Pokrovskoye knew it; the Gypsies too, and this *Djipsaya* more than any of them. He was a man and he would take her like one, show her the bold, winning ways of men like Taras Bulba and Stenka Razin, the sons of the soil and the steppe. By the time the music stopped and the dance ended it was only a question of walking away with her to seek seclusion.

Although Rasputin was a peasant, although the Cossacks, an elite warrior caste, despised the peasants, it is not unlikely that at this stage of his life he might have felt a strong affinity with such storied leaders as Bulba and Razin, both known to peasant folklore, for Cossacks were frequently in rebellion and so was he. Pokrovskoye was not big enough for him. He sensed that very early. Like all peasant communities it stifled ambition and was a road that led nowhere. Its symbol was the *isba*—the peasant's hut; its customs and superstitions those imposed on a helpless and hopeless people by untold centuries of poverty and ignorance and dumb, resigned acceptance of a miserable lot in life. He knew there must be more "out there," much, much more, a whole vast world of adventure and experience which lay untouched by youths like himself. He did not know what he wanted from that world—only that he wanted *something*. He did not know how he could earn a living in it, or even if it were possible to do so, only that some day he must try. As he moved into his late teens he felt the increasing pangs of a persistent dissatisfaction. He felt wasted. The prospect of a lifetime of it appalled him. Instinctively, he knew he could not forever ignore his growing frustration.

Because Maria Rasputin did not choose to reveal the "Kubasova incident" until later years, this all-important causal effect in the formation of her father's character went unmentioned for decades even in the better researched biographies. The truth seems to be that it played a very important role in the formation of the man. His attitude toward women largely derived from it, at least in the days before they became his spiritual as well as his sexual partners. Even when in later years he had lost his bitterness and sense of inferiority, indeed when his many conquests made him aware of his mastery over women, the facts give evidence that some vestige of a desire to degrade them through an utter and obsessive sexual dominance remained. So did an intense resentment of an enforced inferiority based on class. Again and again we see the marks of this in his later life. Always it fueled his ambition, forcing him to *prove* himself repeatedly if only in his own eyes, driving him onward and upward until he became at last the despotically oriented power behind the Russian throne, a figure of light for its close adherents, of darkness for many who stood outside it or mistakenly sought to defend it against him.

But in Pokrovskoye in 1889, Rasputin's eighteenth year, political preeminence, tarnished glory, and stark tragedy for him lay still in the unfathomed future. Irina Kubasova had drawn him like a moth to a flame, betrayed his trust, and made a pitiful ass of him. Natalya Stepanova had increased his faith in his God-given power to heal but made clear the dark curse of peasant cruelty and hypocrisy that hung over all such as he, a curse that he knew could not be broken except by moving away from it—and out of it. Increasingly, he waited for his day of liberation.

Curiously enough, in him there developed quite early a sharply opposed emotional dichotomy. On the one hand, he was strongly, even fanatically drawn to spiritual matters and the contemplative life. On the other, before he was out of his teens he found himself more and more the half-unwilling victim of persistent sexual desire, gripped and controlled by urges so strong that ultimately they were to take on the characteristics of a full-fledged, immutable obsession. These seemingly irreconcilable tendencies warred in him relentlessly and endlessly, causing him much suffering through the bitter remorse of repeated self-condemnation. How could he become a man of God if he lacked the strength to resist temptation? How could he serve God and save his soul if he repeatedly fell from grace by surrendering to lust? He was deeply divided within himself, and this apparently insoluble problem brought him again and again to the edge of despair, for in his own mind he was a helpless penitent who forever offended. Fortunately for his sanity it was not a condition that was to endure. In the course of time its solution, strange to the point of incredibility, would come from the most unexpected of all possible sources.

Since his brief romantic interlude with the Gypsy girl only weeks had passed. Walking slowly in the bright sunshine, his hands on the shafts of the plough and the horse's reins around his neck, Rasputin found himself trying hard to keep his mind on his work. The field was even enough. It had lain fallow for a year and now with the coming of spring was to be planted again. And that was the whole trouble. A broken field or one less level would have forced him to concentrate on what he was doing, keeping him bent to his task. But here, with a well-trained animal endlessly turning the soil in straight, evenly spaced furrows, his mind tended to wander far away, as though to prove his father's opinion that he was lazy, unsuited to farm life, and of little credit to the family.

Doggedly he tried to settle down and do the work assigned to him. He did not have to plow all year round. That was a comfort. At other seasons, when the soil yielded of its ripeness or surplus produce was to be sold, he was the one who hauled it to market. Then it was mile after endless mile of slow, steady driving in the cart, in rain or storm at times, to be sure, but pleasant for the most part, amid the wild and beautiful scenery of the steppe he had always loved. He liked being a carter when he had the chance. He did not like the task of ploughman. His body was tied to it as sure as the crupper was buckled to the saddle of a riding horse, and he accepted that. But why should his mind not be free, he was thinking now? Why should it, too, be a prisoner to this infinitely boring toil when he could escape from it all through marvelous flights of fancy? Could he not find God again? If he concentrated every fiber of his being on that one single goal, could he not summon forth that divine manifestation which as a boy of fourteen had so enthralled him?

As often happened to him, he began to think of the past. In the four years that had come and gone since then he had seen it but once. It was when he had brought the other two boys to Natalya in her forest lean-to; then retreated from his own overwhelming sense of wrong and unworthiness, begging for absolution with tears in his eyes. He had seen it, but it had been dim, not like the day it was first revealed to him. Yet its second appearance in his life had given him hope, a renewed sense that all was not yet lost, that the Almighty might somehow know of his existence, might somehow care. The light was with him always but only barely visible, like some great shining truth hanging veiled in a mist, infinite, unfathomable, shrouded in unseen splendor. Where *was* this truth, he asked himself? Was it of this earth? Could he take it unto himself and know it as he knew the rain and the wind and the gentle balm of birdsong at evening? It was a *living* thing, was it not? And living things could be seen, felt, heard.

Suddenly he halted. The light that was always there was brighter. He hung on the reins to stop the horse, which responded instantly to the bit's pressure. Was it a dream? No, he was wide awake, and what he saw was reality; not everyone's reality, maybe, but his reality. *His.* He went to the ground between the shafts, driving them downward. He was on his knees now but looking straight ahead, his gaze riveted on a point in the air above the horse. Light. It was blinding him. *Blinding him.* He felt his mouth go dry. He trembled in every limb but was determined that this time he would see it through. Could he bear it? Could he bear the sheer ecstasy of it? The strangely glittering effulgence seemed to grow larger in size, then larger still as it brightened to a white heat. Now it filled his world and his universe. *There was nothing else but light.* Yet, incredibly, he felt no fear, only a vast, all-encompassing curiosity mixed with overwhelming wonder.

He felt chilled, shaking in every limb. He caught his breath. Then out of the light, seemingly a part of it yet somehow shining distinctly in a radiance of its own, he saw a human figure. It was that of a woman. Beautiful. Ethereal. Existing yet not existing. Despite her magnificently jeweled, sparkling white robe, he recognized her. She was the one to whom he had prayed all his life, the one to whom most of the villagers prayed, the Virgin of Kazan. He stared, helpless. He wanted to cry out, to fall on his face in adoration, yet the vision held him spellbound and rigid. It was really the Virgin Maria he saw, the Holy Mother of Christ. He did not know how he knew it, only that it was so. She was crowned in gold, enhaloed in glory, enshrouded in shimmering, diaphanous garments not of this world. Her pale hand lifted above him in thrilling, mind-benumbing benediction even as he felt her divine acceptance of him. The heavenly rapture for which he had prayed so long was his at last.

Later, he was not sure how long his nearly unbearable sensations had endured or when the vision had departed like a drifting mist. He had a sense of having traveled far out in the universe among the stars, but when he returned to his own confined realm of terrestrial life the fresh-plowed earth was once again beneath him and he found himself on his knees behind his waiting horse. Had he experienced reality or was it simply a particularly vivid dream? He had heard music. He remembered it now. A choir of a thousand voices, ten thousand, all singing a rhapsody of heavenly praise as he had never heard it sung —a vast, sonorous glorification of the Diety. And he thought he had heard a voice, an infinitely resounding male voice bidding him keep silent about what he had seen and heard—the voice of God.

When he fully regained his senses he could do no more plowing. Filled with a nearly overpowering knowledge of having experienced Divine Revelation, still weak with a feeling of having been totally, wondrously possessed, he abandoned his plow in the field and slowly led his horse away.

Many years were to pass before Rasputin, divining perhaps his own approaching death, finally put aside the admonition of He whom he believed to be the Creator and told his daughter Maria of his miraculous illumination. She tells us he referred to it as his "Awakening" or "Spiritual Rebirth" and regarded it as the great turning point in his life.[1] There is something very poignant about this imagined scene in the St. Petersburg of a later year, when the man who was possibly the most hated in Russia spoke to his teenage child of the day of his longed-for enlightenment. What he really saw in that field will never be known. That he firmly believed it was the Mother of God is beyond question.

Did this day of his *awakening* at Pokrovskoye mark the moment of Rasputin's calling? He was to backslide many times. Concerning his preordained mission in life, he had yearned to receive some word or overt sign from the Virgin, but there had been nothing tangible. She had not spoken to him in words, he explained, only to his heart and spirit in communion that was not the less eloquent for being soundless. We are reminded of the calling of other religious devotees, some of them of incalculable worldwide influence down the centuries. One thinks of Siddhartha Gautama, the Lord Buddha, a prince of the Kshatryia caste who relinquished his high position and all his wealth to become first a hermit and ultimately a penniless wanderer. What is called in Buddhist scripture the "Great Enlightenment" is said to have occurred at Buddh Gaya, a village in central Bihar Province, northeast India, where the Master sat under a pipal tree to receive the principles of Buddhism through a miracle of God. There is much in this to remind us of Rasputin. Ultimately, he too became a *strannik* (a religious mendicant or wanderer) and a *starets* (a holy man).

Are there other comparisons? A great many, for all religious enlightenment invariably has points in common. Witness the conversion of Saint Augustine at age thirty-three, said to have been the result of divine revelation; Saint Jerome's miraculous vision at age thirty-one; the calling of Mohammed at age forty, surely one of the most significant events in the history of humanity. In their ultimate effect, such supernatural occurrences, whether real or imagined, are not always benign. Lost in the dim antiquity of ancient India is the origin of the worship of Siva's many-armed consort Kali, Goddess of Blood and Death, progenitor of the age-old Cult of Thugee, its professional stranglers, and tens of thousands of ritual murders through the dusty millenia. And in medieval Persia, the otherworldly choosing of Omar Khayyam's boyhood friend Hasan ben Sabbáh led to the formation of the dreaded Cult of the Assassins of Alamút, whose daggers likewise put thousands to death. In the time of the First World War in Europe there were many in Russia who would have sworn that Rasputin was an inheritor of the latter tradition, his purpose infinitely sinister, his power diabolical. As to what he really was, as to his character in all its multifaceted manifestations, the reader may be the judge.

With irrefutable logic, Maria Rasputin turns to the eternal verities of Hindu scripture in her attempts to solve the riddle of her father's religiosity: the Bhagavad Gita, the Upanishads, the Vedas. During this early period of Rasputin's life, Maria refers to him as a fallen saint, defining this in Vedic terminology as one who has attempted to achieve *samadhi* (illumination) but failed. She says Rasputin again lost his inner light, and when constant prayer was of no avail, he gradually fell back into his old ways as a frequenter of taverns and devotee of women and dalliance.

Yet Rasputin himself had referred to those wondrous moments in the sunlit field as his "spiritual rebirth." Of endless fascination is the incredible variety of ways in which such experiences may come to human beings. In his truly remarkable autobiography, *The Lives of a Bengal Lancer*, the English soldier and mystic Francis Yeats-Brown writes of how he too experienced the partial withdrawal of the veil of life. He had been seeking a *yogi* (theistic philosopher) named Sivanand who would point the way to his predestined *guru* (spiritual guide and teacher). Finding himself near the city of Agra and the bank of the Jumna River, he gazed across the dark predawn water toward the Taj Mahal, the tomb of an empress, perhaps the most beautiful edifice ever created. He recorded his thoughts thus:

I knew that if I did not find Sivanand Joshi here, I should find another. I was under sway of the sanctuary and the hour. I felt a rightness in the time and place—and a growing exaltation. Destiny had led me here: not eyes, nor ears, nor nose told me this, but the skin, through millions of avenues. My fate had been built up day by day out of a thousand actions and reactions. It was for this moment that I had waited and worked.

On the crescent that crowns the dome of Mumtaz's tomb, the heralds of the morning had come. Where I stood it was dark, but the dome had begun to glow like a pearl, like a monstrance above an altar. For me it was a symbol of the unity of worlds visible and invisible. One greater than Mumtaz was there, Unity itself. . . .

The sense-world slid away, and I sat no longer by the river, but by an ocean of bliss. It was a glimpse, a gathering-up, a heightening of the senses on every plane, not least the physical—an effulgence of eternity. I think that this was a turning-point in my life: the sharpest turn.

Later, after he had found his *guru*, he wrote: "What could be more natural than the fruition of my hopes? For six years I had desired this meeting. Now it had happened. Time is nothing in India. *Karma* rules all, and the belief in its influence is infectious. . . . This talk was planned before my birth: I had chosen the womb that should give me the ears to hear it."

In some of us the sense of predestination is deeply laid, and even authors of fiction have recorded it. Thus, in Herman Melville's classic, *Moby Dick*, Captain Ahab addresses his second-in-command shortly before they are joined in death: "Starbuck, of late I've felt strangely moved to thee; ever since that hour we both saw—thou know'st what, in one another's eyes. But in this matter of the whale, be the front of thy face to me as the palm of this hand—a lipless, unfeatured blank. Ahab is for ever Ahab, man. This whole act's immutably decreed. 'Twas rehearsed by thee and me a billion years before this ocean rolled."

The changelessness of Fate. The immutability of celestial decree —or of Satanic curse, for that matter. Yes, Rasputin returned to the taverns, but always in the back of his youthful mind, deep in the very core of his being, there must have been the knowledge that some day, somewhere, he would find his God. This compulsion drove him relentlessly. Like a weary traveler bearing a load too heavy for his back, he would on occasion lay his burden down, falling from grace at such times even more in his own eyes than in the eyes of those who condemned him. But always his obsession reappeared and drove him on; like King Sisyphus of Corinth, who legend says was sentenced to Hades, there to forever roll a great stone up a steep hill and forever see it roll down again.

Who among us is master of his or her own destiny?

He had been to many dances. At this moment, the recent one in his memory was the first that was to have any significance in his life. He sensed this very strongly. It was in the alluring figure of the tall blonde girl who stood at his side, the feline grace of her walk, the arousing warmth of her hand in his when they danced together. More than anything, it was in the intense expression that filled her eyes when she looked at him and the languid, velvety smoothness of her voice, so different from the others, like nothing he had ever heard before.

Her name was Praskovia Feodorovna Dubrovina, and she was three years older than he. From their opening dance he had called her *milochka* (my dear), something he had never done with any other "nice" girl at any time.[2] And they had walked together afterward, and he had seen her home. During that walk, in a pause so pregnant with meaning he would never forget it, he had taken her in his arms as they kissed each other passionately.

These things he thought about as they stood together before Father Paul and listened to the memorable words of the Orthodox marriage ceremony. The little village church was packed with peasants wearing their best. The liturgy of the sacrament of holy wedlock was long and impressive. Ultimately, there came the moment when the priest removed his stole with its brocaded Byzantine crosses and wrapped it three times around the joined hands of the couple. Everything was in threes in the name of the Holy Trinity. About the narrow central aisle that formed the nave of the small building they walked three times very slowly, while the parishioners sang the well-known hymns and every eye was riveted on them. Rasputin wondered why he had waited until he was almost out of his teens for this. Beauty he had had many times, but not love. Sensual gratification was easy to find, but not devotion. He now realized that Praskovia Feodorovna would fill a great void in his life, and that for the first time he would know the blessings of domesticity and stability. This was the true happiness.

As for the villagers, if any of them wondered if this notorious violator of the moral laws of God would take his marriage vows seriously, they kept it to themselves. There was something about him that may have warned them off. There were those strange eyes of his and that look; the muscular physique; the big, horny hands; his hard-won reputation for physical prowess against heavy odds. From all they knew of him, he was almost certainly an ill man to cross. It wasn't only physical. His reputation as a faith healer and clairvoyant had grown over the years. They did not understand his spiritual side, could never hope to do so. To many, the awe in which he was held had something of the *starets* about it, something of long dead supernatural *shamans* and an Asiatic tribe their folklore still remembered as Tungus.

So they watched and listened and sang on cue, and as long as the men among them remained sober, they kept their own counsel. He was Grigori Efimovich Rasputin. He was a rake, to be sure, and an uneducated carter. He was the son of a man once convicted of horse stealing, and he himself was not above suspicion of it. Yet for all his faults, for all his admitted oddness and inner rebellion, it was entirely possible that he had been touched by divine fire. Could they go up against that kind of power? Their many superstitions were deeply laid, as much a part of their peasant psyche as the ancestor worship of the Chinese or the Greek veneration of the gods of Olympus or the Papuan belief in evil demons.

Stated plainly, they feared him. Recalling his easy victory over three of the toughest bullies in the village, some of them wondered if his personal covenant were not with God at all—but with Satan.

Rasputin married his girl and largely ignored them. He was capable of loving those who loved him. As for those who did not, he did not greatly value their opinions. In the back of his mind was always the same conviction. Peasant-born though he was, some other fate awaited him than this, some other life, possibly *another world entirely*, even though it lay within the confines of what humans called Earth. How would he know when his day had come? He wasn't sure. He knew only that he must seek his vision again, search endlessly for the return of his light, pray and pray and struggle ever upward even though to do so might mean to sacrifice everything. Meanwhile, there was Praskovia and her warmth and softness. She would not stand in his path if he got the call. She loved him very much—he was sure of that—but even more, in her own quiet way, she loved the Supreme Being whom her natural inclination and many centuries of Christian tradition induced her to worship. Automatically she would harken to the celestial command. He was certain of that, too. When it was his time, and from the golden heights of Paradise the Almighty beckoned for him to take up his staff and follow in the path of the prophets of old,

Praskovia Feodorovna Rasputina would say only, "My love, my ever-adored one, go ye forth."

The years passed, and life at the farm changed very little. Rasputin did what he had always done. Part of the year he was a cultivator of the soil, heavy labor that grew the more tedious as advancing age sapped his father's strength and the son took over more and more of the load. For the rest of the time he was a carrier who with horse and wagon took surplus produce to various markets, some of them as far away as Tyumen of evil memory and even as distant as Tobolsk.

His wife proved to be fertile. Early in their marriage a son was born, but died in infancy. Rasputin was greatly hurt by the tragedy. Not only did it freshen his memory of his lost brother, Mischa, but according to peasant superstition the death of a firstborn son could be an evil omen, tangible evidence of the Creator's displeasure with serious parental transgression. Plagued by the guilt of his own recent past, Rasputin was not free of such beliefs. Full of doubt about himself, wondering if the baby had succumbed because of something he had done, he resumed his old habit of intense and frequent prayer, sometimes even engaging in it late at night when his wife had long been asleep. He received no sign. He was close to despair. How great was his pleasure and relief when Praskovia Feodorovna quickly became pregnant again and nine months later presented him with another boy whom they named Dmitri.

In the course of time they had a third and fourth child, both of them girls, born about two years apart. The eldest, christened Matriona, came to be called Maria and was destined to mitigate with her writings some of the accusations hurled against her father by his many enemies. The other, Varya, was to live with her father and sister in the great city of St. Petersburg and, like Maria, to be with Rasputin to the end.

The days went on. With the changing of the seasons and the hard work that seemed never to lessen, Rasputin grew ever more physically powerful but ever more spiritually bereft. Yet he worked as though pursued by furies. Some authors say that the two-story house he built, the largest and highest in the village, was constructed in later life with the proceeds of government preferment. But his daughter tells us it was put up with his own hands during the early years of his marriage. Her last book contains a photo of it. Considering the time, the place, and the materials available to its creator it is a remarkable structure in every way, as foursquare as any product of modern architecture, solid appearing, plumb in every line, with contrasting black and white vertical scantlings on the outer walls and high, ornately framed windows that must have seemed quite out of place in as humble a setting as Pokrovskoye. What may have been added in later years were some of the embellishments of the decorative motif, almost baroque in style, their cost and fashioning presumably beyond the means and skill of the youthful carter of those days. Yet the prodigious accomplishment tells us much of Rasputin's character, his drive to excel, his unflagging industry, his perseverance and rather remarkable taste. This was no ordinary being even then.

The day that was to prove one of the most meaningful in his life dawned as had all the others. There was nothing unusual about it, no overt sign that unseen forces had at last determined to take a hand in the molding of his very singular destiny. Fate came to him in the form of a young man named Mileti Saborevski. About him there seemed nothing unusual either. He stood in the road. Rasputin, having left a wagonload of grain at the mill, was on his return trip. He offered a ride. The youth gladly accepted. During the ensuing conversation Saborevski stated that he was a novitiate at Verkhoture Monastery, some two hundred and fifty miles up the Tura River to the north northwest. Rasputin's interest quickened. Did he sense the hand of Destiny? Before many minutes passed, he revealed himself to the other for what he was, a seeker after truth and the Divine Mysteries, a frustrated, soul-searching sinner who had once found The Way but had lost it. Now it was the divinity student's turn to be excited. He told Rasputin he was wasted in this place. He advised him to go to the monastery to find himself again, but not to wait too long lest he lose what might be his last chance. In the end, he offered to introduce him to the monks there, and even to the abbot himself.

By the time Rasputin arrived home he knew that something within himself had changed. He was no longer exactly as he had been. He must fight against it. He knew that, too. For if he did not fight he would lose his wife and children. He would lose *everything*. His home was a happy one, was it not? Yes, he was unfulfilled spiritually but he had always been that. Would this nebulous quest to which he seemed impelled prove worth the terrible sacrifice he envisaged? In the end, were such things as this *ever* worth it? He did not know. He knew only that his unending search for God gave him no peace and never offered compromise. It simply existed. It was there. Steadily and mercilessly it ate away at his soul.

Because at this period of his life he was still illiterate, he had no particular facility with language and could not express his thoughts with any marked coherence. But the thoughts were there, and so were the deep, all-pervasive emotions. For a long time he had suffered from a sometimes vague, almost amorphous sense of unfulfilled purpose. Now he felt a burgeoning within himself like the preflowering expansion of a long-dormant plant and was aware of exhilaration. *Could* he suppress it? Did he *wish* to do so? Yes, he would pray for blessed relief from it. For the sake of Praskovia. For the sake of the children. He must not give in to this. It could lead to self-imposed exile, the *lost* life of the typical *strannik*, in the end even to divorce.

That night he prayed harder than he had ever done, begging for divine guidance. He felt betrayed by his own sense of destiny. He had never been so alone. He was full of fear.

In the bedroom that Rasputin shared with Praskovia the ikon of the Virgin of Kazan was mounted in one corner, and on this night, as always, a single candle burned before it. Rasputin was on his knees, his hands clasped in adoration, his lips murmuring silently in prayer. He prayed for enlightenment and an end to the terrible dilemma that racked him without surcease. Above all he prayed to be shown the way and to find his light again, and so great was his emotional involvement his eyes were filled with tears.

It was in this condition and in this act that Praskovia found him when she awakened before dawn. She was shocked by his state of mind and stricken by his tears. For a long time she had known that something was wrong, that her husband carried within him some heavy burden she could never share, perhaps not even understand. Now she went to him and took him in her arms, begging him to tell her of his plight, to allow her to help him. Like a boy confessing his transgressions to a loving mother, as when a dam suddenly breaks he poured it all out to her, revealing depths of his mind and heart he had never intended to expose to anyone, baring his soul to this woman who shared his life, attempting to describe the indescribable. He was torn by agonizing conflict, he told her: on the one hand rooted to his present life by his great love for her and the children; on the other, drawn away from them as by an irresistible magnet, compelled to answer the call of the visions he had had and seek his spiritual destiny.

His wife was all compassion, all understanding, all love and de-votion and self-sacrifice. To his great surprise, for despite his earlier confidence he had expected an opposite reaction, she told him he must obey the will of God, must follow the divine summons wherever it led. She would help him. Though her heart might break, she would do all in her power to smooth the path he must take and place no obstacle in his way. Were not such voyages into the spiritual unknown deeply-laid in the Russian tradition? He would come back to her. She was sure of that. Then she too wept and was comforted by him in turn. She asked him if it had all come about as a result of her guilt, if she had failed him as a wife, failed to satisfy him in bed, neglected any of her conjugal duties. To Rasputin, who despite the charges of those who hated him in later life was basically a kind man, her misery was heartbreaking. With all the persuasive powers he possessed he reassured her that none of it was her fault, that she had been a very good wife, the best that any man ever had. It was just *Uchast* (Destiny), a thing preordained, the dictates of a cosmic force beyond resistance to either of them. *Could* she bear it if she knew he would return? She said she thought she could.

He slept after that. But Maria Rasputin tells us that her mother could not sleep, so filled was she with sadness, with the bitter self-recrimination of believing she had made a fearful mistake. To what would it all lead? Would her husband be claimed by another life and lost to her forever? To the young mother of three the question was unanswerable. Only Fate would decide it.

NOTES

1. Maria Rasputin and Patte Barham, *Rasputin: The Man Behind the Myth*, Warner Books, New York, 1977. (Published by arrangement with Prentice-Hall, Inc.)
    2. *Ibid.*

CHAPTER 3

The Khlisti

As he stood by the small barred window of the monk's cell he inhabited, Rasputin could see that the full moon had turned night almost into day. He held back the sackcloth curtain the better to observe the scene. Fortunately, his was one of the outer rooms, its single aperture set into the high stone wall that surrounded the monastery. Fortunately, too, it was located on the same side of the building as the Tura River, a beautiful thing in the night's radiance, flowing silently like a glittering silver dream toward its confluence with the waters of the Tobol.

He found that his thoughts were inconstant, that try as he would he could not concentrate them on any single aspect of what now seemed to be a multifaceted existence. His mind was like this huge ecclesiastical compound in a way. What at first glance appeared to be monolithic solidity and strength, with Byzantine domes and soaring church spires, an edifice for the ages supported by Orthodox power, was seen in reality to be quite another thing. For there was schism here, unhealable division, and that malady made the place as fragile as half-shattered glass. How could it be otherwise when divided against itself? It had not taken him long to make the discovery. At least half the monks were sectarians, deviationists accused of heresy, sent here almost as prisoners to be reindoctrinated and disciplined in the dogma of Mother Church. The rest of the clerics were their goalers, so to speak. The castigated ones *appeared* contrite, but he doubted their sincerity. They *seemed* to have recanted, but under their veneer of humble acquiescence he thought he detected something else, the ferment of smoldering rebellion.

Slowly his eyes surveyed the dreamlike panorama. Cultivated fields that appeared to stretch almost to the nearby Urals. Interspersed forest. Low, rolling foothills hazy in the moonlight, a verdant setting for Verkhoture itself. Although it was well above the river, the town was below him, for the monastery graced the highest of the hills. He could see the church in the settlement's center, that of Saint Simeon the Just. In a silver reliquary there it was said that his venerated bones rested, the most precious relic in this part of Siberia. And the monks tilled the fields, and the heretical half were ostensibly recalled to grace, and all the time he had the feeling that the heresy continued in this place under the very noses of the Orthodox, all-pervasive and unquenchable. Indeed, he suspected that even some of the reproving fathers were sectarians themselves.

He had first heard of the sect called the Khlisti when as a boy his father had spoken of them. There was the common village gossip, too, a few wild rumors, the smoldering ashes always fanned to renewed heat by the lurid tales of some wandering *strannik*. Still later there was Mileti Saborevski, the divinity student to whom he had given the ride. The youth had dropped a few hints, an occasional tantalizing phrase or two, but had revealed nothing specific. And now he, Rasputin, was here at Verkhoture Monastery itself, had been here for four months as a neophyte, had *felt* it all around him but could not reach out and grasp any of it, so secretive were they.

He drew a deep breath of anger. Damn them for a lot of close-mouthed fools. Or worse. They taught salvation through sin. He knew that much. They believed that sin, especially *carnal* sin, was necessary to the saving of the soul, for without it there could be neither forgiveness nor redemption. And he *needed* this doctrine as his very life's blood. He *thirsted* for it. But all his efforts to contact members of the sect had failed. The Khlisti? Oh Ivan knew very little of them. He was here for something else, a simple matter of doctrinal misunderstanding. The Brethren of the Free Spirit? They were called that, too. Oh yes, Dmitri had heard of them. They were an old heresy and no longer existed. All their leaders had been crucified ages ago. No, there were no latent survivors here. How could there be? The tsars had stamped them out completely, nailed them to crosses like the Christ they blasphemed. God bless Nikolai II and Holy Mother Russia.

It was Russian duplicity, he believed. It was Russian cunning, and all Europe knew there was none more devious, none more capable of giving the *appearance* of one thing while practicing another.

Far up the river, he thought he could see moving lights. Purse seiners fishing for sturgeon, probably. Torchlit boats drawing their great nets around some unwary school, the roe of the females to be made into caviar for the wealthy who could afford it. In a way, he was like those hapless fish. From the beginning he had not felt entirely at home here, and his nervous tension seemed daily to increase. There was the fat little monk, Father Iosif, with his soft, feminine hands and womanly features. The trap *he* would set if not curbed would be worse than the seining of the fish. He recalled the man's approach, so open and confident, so brazenly homosexual. The would-be seducer had been rejected and had resented it bitterly. And he, Rasputin, had not heard the last of him, he was sure of that. He wondered how many of them were here. Wasn't it common knowledge that monasteries the world over were full of them? A refuge for sectarians was one thing, but a sanctuary for deviates like that was something else. He could not stomach effeminate males. Thus he was bound to make enemies.

He turned to his rope-woven cot with its comfortless mat and sat down on it, staring at the single candle that burned on the tiny table. These brothers were all sworn to poverty. Yet somehow he knew that vast riches were here if he could uncover them, riches of the mind and spirit that far outweighed the worldly wealth men coveted. There was the holy man in the forest, for example, the *starets* Makari who lived alone in his hut and made the noblest of virtues out of utmost want. He had been to visit the recluse once, not long after Iosif had tried to seduce him. What a revelation it had been. By his own will, Makari was in chains with iron fetters on his wrists. They had talked at length. His eyes shining with an inner fire, the old and feeble ascetic had explained that he too had once been the slave of passion,

as susceptible to the sins of the flesh as any man living. But he had
fought against it, praying endlessly for strength, and one day God
had heard him. He had gradually changed after that, a long and bitter
struggle but with victory at the end. The world of sexual craving had
slowly diminished. Whenever the persistent pangs of lust racked him
he had disciplined his mind and emotions through self-torture, enduring the agony in silence. In the end he had won out. In the end,
there was only deep spiritual serenity and a peace such as he had
never known.

Rasputin got up and began to pace, feeling the damp chill of the
room more than before, starting to tremble. Verily, Makari was one
of the blessed, a true *starets*, selected by God for certain salvation.
But what of poor sinners like himself? If he found the Khlisti before
it was too late, his soul might survive, for surely they would show
him the way. But he must leave this place soon. He sensed that
strongly. He had only one friend here, Father Feliks, a kindred spirit
who understood him. But there were children of darkness, too, an
undercurrent of hostility generated by the one he had scorned, the
vindictive Iosif. That one had no intention of leaving him be, a message
to be read in the watery little eyes every time he looked at him. And
the Bible condemned it. The divine law of the Holy Scriptures would
not tolerate it.

He stopped pacing and stood quite still in the middle of the tiny
cell. He was not a self-purified hermit. He knew that Makari's body
was covered with scars, some of which he had seen when the man's
robe fell open. He'd had acolytes lash him with whips, brawny youths
some of them, who must have nearly killed him. That was not for
the carter Grigori. He must pray as he had never prayed before, beg
God to let him find acceptance within the Khlisti before it was too
late. He fell to his knees on the ice cold floor.

What was it Makari had said? He had told him that God would
find him no matter where he was; that his vision of the Virgin was
real, not a fantasy; that no matter what he did or where he wandered
he would find her again in the appointed time and place, though
probably not at Verkhoture. As he prayed, Rasputin was overcome
with emotion. He prostrated himself. He was trembling harder than
ever. As though a long-resistant dam within him had suddenly broken,
he wept silently.

*　　　*　　　*

As events transpired, the thing he had feared happened all too soon. Going back many years to her conversations with him, his daughter Maria relates that Father Iosif came to him again, this time invading his cell with a like-minded confederate, one Father Sergius, and awakening the sleeping youth. Showing stubborn insistence, they solicited Rasputin to surrender to their lust. It was late at night. When he protested vigorously they warned him to be quiet, for what they intended to accomplish was very private. Seeing at once that argument was useless, in the end he was forced to take action, catching Iosif by the throat and threatening to strangle him. That had its effect. The two men departed, but not until Iosif had made threats of his own, vowing revenge, giving voice to what Rasputin already knew. "There are many of us here."[1]

It was then that the young man decided to leave that very night. Fearing they might be watching for him, he allowed some time to pass. Then, putting his meager possessions into his battered carpetbag, he fled quietly from this corrupt cloister and left the monastery forever.

When one of the world's established religions, powerful and ravenous for converts, is superimposed over the spiritual beliefs of a pagan people, numerous societal or tribal dislocations are bound to occur, some of them of deep psychological significance. Of no aspect is this more true than that of sexual restrictions first introduced by the invading faith, then rigorously enforced, often with various forms of violence. It was evangelical Christianity which struck the hardest, by which is meant not the sublime teachings of Jesus but the unnatural parody of them disseminated by fanatical and often hypocritical practitioners of Catholicism, Protestantism, and the Russian and Greek Orthodox Churches. To the zealous advocates of these faiths the creeds they espoused were everything. In many cases (among the Catholics the gentle Franciscans were an exception) they forgot humanitarian concerns and thereby incurred stubborn opposition. They embraced their own stern dogma with unflinching determination and ever-righteous wrath, but forgot people.

But were there not priestly restrictions on human behavior among non-Christian cultures? Most assuredly. Throughout the ages, all this planet's major religions have been restrictive, for without a tight hegemony over the mind and activities of the believer there was no way for a priesthood to maintain its power. Whether it was the followers of the divine Osiris and Isis in the dusty Egypt of the pharaohs, the fertility cults of ancient Mesipotamia who worshiped the phallic Baal, the devotees of amorous Shiva in India, or those of the Druid oligarchy in Dark Age Celtic Britain, all were rigidly controlled by the priests. So were the Dionysian revels of Hellenic Greece and the equally licentious Bacchanalia of Imperial Rome. So, in Mexico, were the Aztec worshipers of Quetzalcoatl, whose priests stood on high-raised temple altars of the sun to cut out the hearts of their living victims. Why then was Christianity different? One of its chief distinctions is easily seen. It was the only creed of all whose dogma maintained that the *sole* purpose of sex was reproduction, that to engage in it for pleasure was therefore a grievous sin.

How far were Christian zealots willing to go to advance their doctrines? Certainly as far as anyone else. To them, the letter of Scripture was all, the meaning nothing, and reactionaries must be crushed. Thus, in the Spain of the Inquisition, heretics were burned alive in *autos-da-fé* (acts of faith) with crosses held before their eyes, and the punishment was regarded as "merciful" and "soul saving." Thus in fallen Cuzco, Atahualpa, last of the Sapa Incas of Peru, was forcibly baptized by orders of the *conquistador* Pizarro, then strangled by the cord the Spaniards called the *garrote*. Before his eyes, too, as he died, a priest held a cross, and the murder was blasphemously committed in the name of Jesus.

In a more enlightened age, it is frequently accepted that the pleasures of the flesh are natural, God-given, and meant to be enjoyed. Very often, the greatest proof of this is taken to be the female clitoris, an organ existing solely for the woman's delectation, having no reproductive function whatever. Even in ancient times, many of the world's primal creeds had no difficulty accepting such a premise. In Christianity, however, the belief was held that humans had been put on this earth to suffer because Christ had suffered, that indeed all this life was but a preparation for the next, and that happiness had no part in it. Sex outside the generative process was therefore evil, a thing to be scarcely more than tolerated even in marriage.

To understand Rasputin it is necessary to examine the sectarianism that produced him. To grasp the implication of that, something must be said of the origin and nature of the Russian religious dissent that generated it. In the seventeenth century, there lived in western Russia a peasant named Nikon Mordvinov. He was a remarkable man. In an oil portrait of him dating from around 1660, we see him in the robes and mitre of the office he eventually held, that of Patriarch of the Russian Orthodox Church. Framed in long black hair and a heavy beard, it is a strong face that looks out of the canvas. There is a sadness in the eyes. This was a man who lost three children to plague and became a *strannik* because of it, whose wanderings led him ultimately to Moscow, where his reputation for holiness caught the attention of the second Romanov Tsar, the deeply pious Aleksei. It was the beginning of a fateful career. Recognition as a *starets* brought ordainment as a priest. Royal patronage played its vital role. Rising rapidly through ecclesiastical ranks, Nikon was invested as Patriarch in Moscow in 1652 when only 47 years old.

As it happened, over a considerable period of time small changes had crept into Orthodox religious practice which Nikon, a rigid conformist, strongly opposed. He had accepted the Patriarchate with the understanding that his fiat would be law within the Church. He therefore immediately set about eradicating those "accretions" he felt to be harmful to ritual and discipline, with a view toward restoring in their exactitude the ancient "rites of Byzantium." His work proceeded apace. Several of his reforms were quite petty: the liturgical utterance of "hallelujah" three times instead of two, the making of the Sign of the Cross with three fingers rather than two, a single-letter alteration in the spelling of the name of Jesus. In 1654, two years after elevation to his high office, he made his first costly mistake when he introduced a revised version of the Orthodox Prayer Book. It was the signal for revolt. As though the masses of the faithful felt that a virulent poison was being spread among them, it galvanized them into violent action.

The factions that now banded together against Nikon, enraged and ready for anything, called themselves collectively the *Raskolniki*

or Old Believers. They had their facts twisted. Ironically, it was
Nikon, accused of being an iconoclast, who was seeking to restore the
old, not the Raskolniki. On the contrary, they were the ones who
stood for the *status quo*, never realizing that it was based on the insid-
iously established changes of recent decades. What seems so unimportant today was hardly trivial to them. They regarded Nikon's
regressive changes as heretical and blasphemous. Inflamed by the
many fanatics among them, men who hated the determined Patriarch,
they actually believed his "innovations" came from the Antichrist and
were satanically inspired, that to condone them meant certain damnation. Very soon, numerous members of the merchant middle class
joined the peasants, and ultimately many nobles. The unrest spread
across Russia. Revolt threatened to become revolution.

Warned by his spy apparatus of what was afoot, warned by his
generals that it could lead to his overthrow, Tsar Aleksei I took vigorous action to crush the insurrection. Units of the army were de-
ployed, including crack Cossack regiments. Centers of rebel strength
were surrounded and destroyed. From one end of European Russia
to the other, "deviationists" were rooted out, hanged, beheaded, and
massacred by massed cannonade. Punitive actions against various
pockets of resistance went on for years. Although Nikon's claim of
clerical supremacy over the state had early alienated the Tsar, Church
and Crown temporarily formed a united front against the common
threat to both, and in 1677 Nikon's successor (Nikon had been deposed
the year before) pronounced the anathema of God against the Old
Believers. They were excommunicated. Outcast. With their movement much enfeebled by the tsarist purges and already dying, many
of the survivors now deserted the cause in the conviction that God
had abandoned them. In 1681, their most electrifying leader and skillful orator, the priest-zealot Avvakum, was burned alive. Mass suicide
of hundreds of his supporters followed.

In Modeste Moussorgski's five-act opera *Khovantschina*, the final
scene of horror is given a poignant grandeur by the sheer magnitude
of human self-sacrifice. In a moonlit forest outside Moscow, the defeated Old Believers have gathered in solemn conclave. They say
goodbye to one another. The former lovers Martha and Andrei are
reunited. As Andrei, who is not a Raskolnik, mounts the great pyre

with all the others, it is Martha who sets it ablaze before she joins him in self-immolation. The flames rise. The orchestra plays its final sonorous chords. The curtain falls. Students of Russian history will recall that this stark pathos was based on fact.

Prior to the violent schism during the patriarchate of Nikon, the Russian Orthodox religion had been more or less monolithic, a ponderous and unyielding creed having no serious rivals within the Empire. But as Luther and Calvin in Western Europe had shattered the solidarity of Catholicism, bringing on the Protestant Reformation, so the limited revolt in Russia opened the first cracks in the massive bastions of Orthodoxy. The result was a rapidly spreading dissent which, though not glaringly apparent at first, was ultimately to have far-reaching effect.

As discontent grew it became general. The original complaints were largely forgotten. In their place there developed a powerful opposition to the entire structure of Church hierarchical power. Anticlerical organizing was secret. The sects were flagrantly heretical. That they were usually carnal as well was one invariable response to tyrannical sexual repression. Regardless of the locale or ethnic background, the more people are told they cannot have a thing the more they desire it. The more they are punished for certain practices, sexual or otherwise, the more determined they are to indulge in them. It does not matter whether it is a Catholic priest attacking native incest in nineteenth-century Tahiti, a Protestant minister preaching against child marriage and *suttee* (widow burning) in what was then British India, or an invading pastor in the American "Kingdom of the Saints" attacking the Mormons in Illinois or Utah for polygamy, all persecution has ever led to historically is hatred and vengefulness even when its aim of eradication eventually succeeds. From Aleister Crowley and the Order of the Golden Dawn in Britain to the 913 disciples of the American Jim Jones and their forced mass suicide in Guyana, efforts to control or stifle "deviationism" have spawned secret societies worldwide, more than a few of historical significance. In Russia, two of the most curious were the Khlisti sect and its even more bizarre offspring, the Skoptzi, each of them proof of just how far reaction could go, of fanaticism engendering fanaticism.

They were proof of something else as well: that the practices of unregenerate societal outcasts, clandestine, ritualistic, proscribed by law, could and often did descend into hidden and grotesque fastnesses of the human soul.

On the rough-hewn bench by the wall, Rasputin sat with the others and was very still. His face with its light brown beard was expressionless. His pale blue eyes were almost closed and he seemed half-asleep. Yet somewhere deep in the core of him his entire being was vibrant with alertness. He knew, for example, that in this peasant domicile with its large family room and huge tiled oven there were seven others beside himself, four of them women. He sat with the men on the right, the women opposite them on the left, the usual arrangement. In the center was a small table, equally crude, and two chairs, both presently unoccupied. There was only one window. Soon, the door of the dwelling would open and more people would enter, each taking a seat as quietly as he had done and saying nothing.

His mind slipped continuously from one thought to another. He was aware of the women staring at him. The men would do so, too, but they were on the same bench as he and not positioned for it. Both those already present and those yet to come were all of this village, but he was a visiting *strannik* and therefore a curiosity. Perhaps they had heard of him. Since leaving Verkhoture, he had visited Pokrovskoye only briefly, spending mere days with his wife and children before beginning his wanderings. That was nearly two years ago now. As the months passed and he traveled endlessly through western Siberia, living the life of a homeless pilgrim, he sometimes wondered if his growing reputation as a holy man preceded him. He sensed that it did. At first, he had been amazed by the number of peasant villages that were secret havens for sectarians, virtual hotbeds of Khlistism, but now it was a matter of common acceptance. He had become one of them long ago. All he needed to be received at the next point of refuge, and the next and the next, was the utterance of the secret words. Then it all opened for him. All was acknowledged and all given, and his soul was refreshed anew in the balm of spiritual ecstasy.

He tried to relax his stiff shoulder muscles. He could proclaim himself a *starets* if he wished. That thought had recurred frequently of late, and he knew he was ready for it. They would accept it without question. There wasn't a hidden Khlisti sanctuary in all Russia that would not accept it. But what of the cities, those vast metropolises of which he had dreamed, the strongholds of the proud and the mighty? Would they, too, spread a carpet of welcoming veneration or reject him with haughty disdain? He bit at his lower lip. What did it matter? This was the world he knew about, the one that knew him, and in *this* world he could rule if he chose, be as truly a monarch as the Little Father in St. Petersburg, the Tsar of All the Russias. Yes, the time was fast approaching. The *strannik* Rasputin was a Khlist and would soon be a *starets*. And a day would come—he was sure of it—when this greatest and holiest of all the sects in Russia would proclaim him one of its many-times-reborn Sons of God, the newly arisen Christ.

As he sat thus plunged in thought, several men entered the room carrying more benches and aligned them with the others along the walls. The light was failing, the shadows lengthening, as more people entered and took their seats. Again there were both sexes, but no recognizable couples. Like himself, some of the devout were married he was sure, but not to each other within this gathering and not by Khlisti recognition, for such arrangements sanctioned by the Orthodox Church were null and void. Occasionally, natural brothers and sisters attended these meetings, fathers and daughters, mothers and sons. Their blood relationships were unimportant, their indiscriminate couplings meaningless in the sense of sin, for the joining of the whole into one was like the mingling of the waters of the sea, and all were the People of God.

He saw that the room was nearly full. There was a strong smell of peasant sweat, something he had always found arousing in females. Now candles were lighted, exactly twelve of them, six on either side, and someone closed the single pair of curtains with the traditional intonement, "The red sun has set." He realized he must have momentarily drifted away in a sort of reverie, for now, too, the chairs with the table between them were occupied by a man and woman, exactly as he knew would happen.

All at once he felt a slight chill, and this too he had experienced before. Someone locked the door and barred it. The village was outside and utterly excluded, far, far away, and here was another universe. The oven seemed to be putting out heat but he hadn't seen them light it. All eyes were fastened on the couple at the table. The man reached out and held the hands of the woman. As though it came from out of nowhere, in the center of the floor a great metal basin of water made its appearance. Fire, air, and earth for the meetings in the forest. Water, air, and earth for those indoors, the basic elements of the physical universe.

The chanting had begun and Rasputin chanted with them, softly at first. The dark-eyed girl he was watching was watching him. She had a Gypsy cast to her features, raven hair to the waist that reminded him of a night years ago in Pokrovskoye, of wanton, trembling flesh that enfolded him and the plaintive sobbing of violins. This girl had a breathtaking figure and he longed for her to reveal it. But that would come. All he had to do was to hold her gaze. If it drifted away he must recapture it at once, weld her to him with bonds of the spirit, make her subservient and pliable. She wanted him. He *knew* that. He locked onto her gaze with his own and held her as in a vise. He sang with the others, as did she. Gradually, the voices grew louder. He knew without looking that all eyes but his and hers were on the couple at the table. They were the "annointed" for this particular meeting, symbolic of Jesus and the Virgin Mother. When he knew the girl was his beyond all chance of withdrawal he would look at them as well.

The minutes passed. At such covert assemblies he was never fully aware of the drifting away of time, for reality was increasingly blurred. He knew that psalms had been sung, and hymns. Now it was songs of the people, very old, more secular than holy. The girl's shining eyes never left his face. There was a growing rapture in them. Now the people were rising and shedding their upper garments, beginning to mill about, spoiling his view of her as he did the same. Even their heavy boots were discarded as groping hands pulled the inevitable long shirts from a pile of linen, the white garment of the holy spirits departed.

He worked hurriedly. Everything was symbolism, he knew, as he drew on the vestment provided. Ivan Suslov, the greatest of the Christs, had been flayed alive. Three times they had crucified him and three times he had been resurrected. On his rising from his final execution, a virgin came to him bearing his skin and draped it over his arms, and he donned it and rose to Heaven without blemish. Now they adored him in this way, symbolically emulating him, casting aside their physical nature to enter the realm of the purely spiritual. Again Rasputin felt the familiar tingling. Already the air in the room was highly charged. He sought the girl's eyes and found them again. Could he dominate her at this distance, ensure her possession by will alone? Oh yes. Surrender was in every line of her.

The singing grew louder, more impassioned. Then one young man with a burly physique stepped to the center of the room and began to gyrate, turning in circles as Rasputin had heard was done by the dervishes of North Africa. Round and round he went, his eyes beginning to close. Was his purpose to enter a trance? Of course. They would all be doing that soon. Already others were joining him, the males pairing with the females as the singing continued and the entire movement of the mass became a round, dancer following dancer, individuals circling independently within the whole.

Watching carefully, Rasputin waited for the progressive motion to bring the girl to him, then stepped in behind her and joined the slow whirling of the others. Instantly she became aware of him. He sensed it at once. They were the disciples dancing around Jesus. That was the meaning of it. They were the stars of the firmament, including the Sun of Earth, orbiting the Lamb of God, the Lord Jesus in his human manifestation. The men put their hands on the hips of the women and clutched them possessively, firmness and strength into incredible softness. And never were hips more soft than hers. The Christ still sat in the center of the room, "showing himself within the circle" as Khlisti scripture required. There came the sound of a blown-upon conch shell, the "golden trumpet" announcing the forgiveness of sins and universal cleansing.

The intensity of the action redoubled. Motions quickened. Rapidly and with unerring lightness of foot the dancers repeatedly crossed the room, their arms uplifted, voices wailing in rising rapture as the spirit of the Holy Ghost was called upon in desperate entreaty. Rasputin called out with the others, moving as they moved, sensing the beat of the great wings overhead as all that was earthly began to dissolve and he became aware of the first transports of ecstasy. It was redemption, the brethren and their sisters being led by Jesus and the Blessed Virgin into Paradise. It was *redemption*, renewal, the miracle of the Almighty become flesh, become man, and now was heard the cry that some claimed the Khlisti had intoned over five glorious centuries of time, a proclamation of unspeakable joy: "The Holy Ghost is among us!"

Over and over they repeated it, on and on until some became hoarse and the melodiousness of the sound turned to dissonance. They stopped dancing then. A quiet fell upon them. The symbolic Christ came to his feet and addressed them. Rasputin knew what to expect and was never disappointed. The risen Jesus spoke in three aspects revealing three faces. He was man as a child, tender, innocent, unsure of himself to the point of stammering; man grown, but full of sin and bowed with guilt; and man redeemed, liberated by the grace of God and purified by the Holy Spirit.

When the dancing was resumed the exaltation of the faithful was as nothing yet seen. Wild they were now, pagan in their triumph, as emotions soared to a fever pitch and worship moved toward frenzy. Rasputin saw that the water in the basin was boiling, giving off curling wisps of steam, though no fire was visible. In the mad whirl of it all he was aware of the girl as before, yet not in the same way. They were no longer simple humans but exalted expressions of the godhead, no longer merely uplifted but gloriously transfigured. In his mind's eye was a vision of the Son of Man in Judea ascending to Heaven from Mount Hermon. But it was time. He sensed strongly that it was *time.*

Suddenly, as though his very thought had triggered the action itself, the sweat-dripping, furiously dancing People of God threw off their white garments, exposing themselves to the waist, offering their bodies as willing flagellants to the "warders of souls" preordained to exact penance. The instruments of holy chastisement were leather-bound switches of willow carefully cured to prevent premature shredding. He saw the girl step up to be whipped. Her sacrifice, like all their sacrifices, symbolized fecundity, the portals of chastity opening to admit the renewal of life. She offered her bare back. Fearing her beautiful breasts would be bruised or lacerated, he took the switch from the chosen one and struck her lightly, almost lovingly across the shoulders, wincing as someone at his rear lashed at him vigorously and repeatedly.

The moments passed. Time seemed to hang suspended as the rods rose and fell on the vulnerable flesh of one and all. The dancing began again. But now the Imitation of Christ must be fulfilled. As the Lord had shuffled off His mortal cloak that His spirit might know resurrection, so all the celebrants divested themselves of the last of their clothes, falling on one another in naked, unashamed embrace. Straw was scattered on the floor. The twelve candles were snuffed. In varying states of sexually induced euphoria the couples *knew* each other in the primal biblical sense.

Rasputin possessed the girl at last, joining her in that same indescribable bliss he had known with so many. That rebirth in the spirit could be achieved through sin he firmly believed. Her loving tenderness was an enchantment, her passion all-consuming, her appetite nearly insatiable. As she lay in his arms and they basked together in the warmth of love's afterglow, the exegete in him, master of Holy Writ, might have quoted softly from The Song of Solomon:

> How fair is thy love, my sister, my spouse! How much better is thy love than wine, and the smell of thine ointments than all spices! Thy lips, O my spouse, drop as the honeycomb: honey and milk are under thy tongue; and the smell of thy garments is like the smell of Lebanon.

Once again, as in the Book of Isaiah, and those of Jeremiah, Ezekiel, and Hosea, the marital love between God and Israel had been consummated.

Down through the ages, religious asceticism has taken many strange forms. Briefly mentioned was the self-immolation of Hindu widows who, in the days before the British stamped it out, became *suttee*, voluntarily burning themselves alive on the same funeral pyres that consumed the bodies of their dead husbands. Closely reminiscent of this (and of the self-destruction of the Old Believers at Moscow) was an event famous in the history of India, that of the Rajput women who burned themselves *en mass* at Chittor (1303) at the time of a ruinous Rajput defeat.

For some, war is a religion, too, where the ruler or the country is worshiped symbolically. Examples of martial self-sacrifice in antiquity include defeated military leaders committing suicide: King Saul after Mount Gilboa, Sardanapalus after the taking of Nineveh by the Medes, Brutus and Cassius after Philippi, Cleopatra and Marc Anthony after Actium, and even in modern times, the French Admiral Villeneuve after Trafalgar and the Russian General Samsonov after Tannenberg. And in feudal Japan, century after century, there were the countless acts of *hara-kiri* (self-evisceration with a consecrated knife) by *samurai* who had lost face, acts strictly ritualized to conform to the Code of Bushido (literally, the "Way of the Warrior"), itself an adjunct of the all-pervasive Shinto faith.

A less fatal yet still brutal means of religious sacrifice is flagellation or other forms of self-inflicted torment. The fifth-century ascetic Saint Simeon Stylites was an example. For thirty-five years he sat on the top of a tall pillar in the Syrian desert. Very early, his eyes were burned out from staring at the sun.

There was England's King Henry II. After the murder of Thomas-á-Becket by four of his knights, this Plantagenet monarch, the father of Richard the Lion-Heart, did penance for the rest of his life by having himself flogged on every anniversary of his martyred friend's death.

And Fray Junipero Serra is familiar to Americans. The revered founder of seven California missions, cofounder with Gaspar de Portolá of the cities of San Diego and Monterey, the benevolent Franciscan friar was also a flagellant who had himself whipped nearly to insensibility by his Indians.

To what extremes will the religiously possessed carry their sacrificial forms of devotion? To any and all extremes. After touching on the excesses of the "Great Awakening" in mideighteenth-century America (but omitting the earlier Salem witch trials) and the "great revivals" of the first half of the nineteenth century, author Marcus Bach writes memorably of the still existing *Hermanos Penitentes* (Brothers Penitent), a Mexican religious cult tracing its ancestry back to the

Third Order of St. Francis (responsible in 1598 for the introduction of flagellation to America's southwest) and the *conquistador* Don Juan de Onate.[2] He tells us how *El Cristo* is flogged as Jesus was, how he carries his 300-pound cross in one of the dusty towns along the Rio Grande—"between Santa Fe and Taos"—how, bleeding and exhausted, he struggles up the hill of *Calvario* (Calvary) amid the chanting and "Hail Marys" of the many faithful. Three times he falls just as Jesus did. Then, the summit having been reached at last,

> Members of the Brothers Penitent now gather around "the chosen one." Strong men pick him up and lay him on the cross, stretching out his arms and making straight his legs. Although he may plead to be nailed, his wish is seldom granted. Wordlessly the crowd watches, transfixed, while *El Cristo's* hands and feet are tied to the roughhewn cross with buckskin thongs which are laced so tightly his hands stand out like claws. As the cross is partially lifted up, a crown of cactus thorns, pressed down on the young sufferer's head, causes a shudder to convulse his already tortured body. The cross with its human sacrifice is raised high, but only for a moment, for it is then let fall into the hole with a sickening thud. *El Cristo* hangs by his wrists, a living corpus on an American *Calvario*.

The Russian Skoptzi has been noted, a sect that practiced mutilation. Founded in 1770 by a separatist Khlist named Kondrati Ivanov, this sect believed in both male and female castration (theoretically, the clitoris was to be removed) and even in the removal of the female breasts, but were not always consistent in going to these extremes. It was the ideal, the ultimate for which to strive, for Ivanov himself had set the example. Shortly after proclaiming his revelation and assuming his status of semidivinity, he used a hot iron to burn away his own genitals. His sect slowly grew. When the Orlov brothers made Tsaritsa Catherine a widow by murdering her insane husband, one of several men who claimed to actually *be* the resurrected Tsar Pyotr III was Ivanov. He did not succeed in his pretense. Another, who very nearly did, was the illiterate Don Cossack Yemelyan Pugachev, who led a serf uprising against Catherine II in 1773–1775. Pugachev was defeated and captured by the great Aleksandr Suvarov. Then Pugachev was executed with typical brutality by dismemberment alive and decapitation, Ivanov being committed to a mental institution.

When Ivanov was released at the beginning of the next reign (that of Aleksandr I opening in 1801), he changed his name to Selivanov and his reputation for holiness grew.

The sinister quality of the Skoptzi grew with it. Many were the tales of members who tried to leave the cult only to be ruthlessly murdered by its assassins. Selivanov lived to reach the century mark, dying in a religious house of detention in Suzdal in 1830. His sect lived on. As late as the Bolshevik Revolution of 1917, it has been estimated that it still thrived nearly unabated on both sides of the Urals. He will come back says Skoptzi prophecy. A day will come when he will make his reappearance at Irkutsk near the northwest shore of Lake Baikal.

The Khlisti was another matter entirely. The parent organization of the Skoptzi which sprang from it, the sect is believed by some modern historians to have been founded in 1363, a time when Moscow was ruled by a dynasty of princes, the rest of divided European Russia by the Golden Horde of the Mongols and the Grand Dukes of Lithuania. It was a signal year in Russian history. The organizing of the first Khlisti cells probably passed unnoticed, but in this year a hero came to the throne as Grand Duke of Moscow. He was Dmitri Donskoy, determined, formidable, and warlike. In 1380 at Kulikovo he would win the victory over Khan Mamai that was to presage the end of Mongol domination.

The Khlisti, among whose ranks in Rasputin's time were many Old Believers, had a violent and incredible past. Very little was heard of them in the fifteenth and sixteenth centuries, so little they may well have come close to dying out. Then, in the seventeenth century, the schismatic religious movement of the Raskolniki and the fracturing of Orthodox solidarity seem to have revitalized them.

Certain things about them had a compelling magnetism for initiates. The life of the Russian peasant was nothing but grueling and unremitting labor and the attendant boredom that could approach madness. The Khlisti offered intense excitement. In the villages, the cold Orthodox morality, austere, puerile, and unbending, was brutally enforced. The Khlisti not only offered an escape from it, but like the Muslim vision of a fleshly Paradise, an open door into undreamed-of sexual abandonment. As for the equality of man, the peasants were not deceived by this hypocritical credo. Everywhere they looked was rigid class distinction, Church, Crown, and nobility at the very top of a huge, immovable pyramid of which they, the downtrodden masses, formed the bottom. But the Khlisti said there were no human differences in the eyes of God once a state of grace had been reached, and they *meant* it.

The cardinal Khlisti belief had enormous appeal and one that held the believers spellbound. It was the article of faith claiming that Christ's resurrection was not a single event but multiple and endless, that again and again down the centuries He had returned to dwell among men in various incarnations, very often in the guise of a simple Russian peasant. What could offer a more profound spiritual uplifting, a more scintillating, soul-searing ecstasy? But the sect's leadership went one doctrinal step further. Every one of these Christs came from the ranks of the Khlisti itself and had always done so, and what male member among them might not be called to this Divine glory, his true nature unknown even to himself until revealed by God? The possibilities were intoxicating, staggering. In the light of them, what man young enough to fulfill this awesome prophecy would ever voluntarily withdraw?

Khlisti history was red with blood. Given the sheer magnitude of the earth-shaking miracles and their devastating effects on the membership, there was no way the incarnations could fail to become known to the authorities. When this happened their fate was sealed. Donskoy himself was the first to act against them. Having defeated the Tatar army at Kulikovo, he then sullied the victory with a heartless murder. A Khlist named Averzhan was brought before him and denounced, for the man claimed to be Jesus. Donskoy demanded he recant and confess his lie. When the zealot refused, he was immediately crucified on the corpse-strewn battlefield.

Subsequent "Christs" met with similar fates. In the reign of the savage and half-mad Ivan IV (Ivan the Terrible), a man named Yemeljan was deified by the Khlisti, then arrested and tortured to death by order of the Tsar. Others followed. According to Khlisti tradition, the army deserter Danila Filipich, a peasant who joined the Old Believers and opposed Patriarch Nikon, was incarnated as Christ in 1645. He vigorously preached the folly of marriage, the abandonment of

wife and children, and the holiness of "spiritual wedlock" within the
sect. When he achieved his own "state of divinity," he abruptly denounced carnality and stressed the blessedness of celibacy, but there
were others with different ideas.

Divine manifestations multiplied. Khlisti annals relate that Filipich, God the Father, begot a celestial offspring, the peasant Ivan
Suslov, whose natural parents were said to be a hundred years old at
the time of his conception. Suslov, therefore, was God the Son and
Christ Incarnate. But the inevitable happened. Tsar Alexei Mihailovich had them both seized and imprisoned in Moscow, whereupon
Suslov was crucified on the Kremlin's wall. Three days later, he rose
in resurrection. Again they crucified him and again he rose. Once
more he was condemned. On the day named for his third execution,
a royal heir, the future Pyotr Veliki (Peter the Great) was born to
Tsaritsa Natalya amid general rejoicing. Suslov was released by the
jubilant monarch. According to the Khlisti, the Tsar had no choice.
Another failure to kill his holy victim would have made him look
ridiculous.

There were successors. Every generation produced a new "Christ":
Prokopi Lupkin, Andrei Petrov, for the most part, names of little
renown known chiefly to the Khlisti. It was the "Christ" called by
the single name Radaev who most influenced Rasputin. Of this Fülöp-
Miller writes:

> But the story of God's advent in the form of the prophet Radaev came
> to Rasputin as an illumination. For Radaev, who had wandered among
> men but a few decades past, was, according to the standards of earthly
> reason, a depraved and wicked sinner, whose licentiousness was far
> greater and more serious than anything of which Rasputin himself had
> ever been guilty. Radaev had practised every kind of carnal sin, and had
> lived with thirteen women at once in open intercourse. Nevertheless, he
> had been a great prophet, and, in spite of all his sinful deeds, the Holy
> Spirit had spoken from his mouth.[3]

Given these circumstances and influences in his background, it
becomes less difficult to comprehend Rasputin. Very soon, being still
possessed by his dream of serving God in some glorious capacity, he
would launch on that course of action destined to bring him to uni-

magined heights. He would do great things. Calling upon the God of Hosts in unending supplication, he would even perform miracles. But his power, ever expanding, evet intensifying, would shake Holy Russia to its foundations.

NOTES

1. Maria Rasputin and Patte Barham, *Rasputin: The Man Behind the Myth*, Warner Books, New York, 1977. (Published by arrangement with Prentice-Hall, Inc.)
2. Marcus Bach, *Strange Sects and Curious Cults*, Dodd, Mead & Company, New York, 1961.
3. Rene Fülöp-Miller, *Rasputin: The Holy Devil*, Viking Press, New York, 1928.

CHAPTER 4

The Starets
of Pokrovskoye

Dunia Bekyeshova was not a beautiful woman, yet she possessed a sensuality of face and figure which she knew would have won her a husband long ago had she chosen to flaunt her attractions. She had not so chosen. Instead, by her own will she was here in Pokrovskoye rather than Tyumen; no longer a servant to wealth yet a servant still; no longer able to travel to such cities as St. Petersburg or Moscow or Paris as before; yet tasting of happiness now, if still with unsatisfied yearning; aware of some measure of fulfillment, if only the merest shred of what might have been.

As she sat in her chair she rocked very slowly, vaguely aware of the details surrounding her within her small downstairs room. It was nearly dark with the sun so low as this. Soon it would set. Fifty miles to the west lay Tyumen, and it would fall right down behind that city, just suddenly as it always did in Siberia, but whether the Kubasovs were there or on one of their frequent trips it wouldn't make any difference. The old general would be as badly deceived as before, ever the cuckold, as the still young Irina Danilova Kubasova was ever the heartless flirt, the dissembler, the adulteress. Oh God, how many times that *zlaya zhenshina* (vixen) had put the horns on her husband's head, with she, Dunia, as one of her accomplices. But never again. All that was finished. Kubasov would die soon and Kubasova would find someone else, probably a bigger fool than her elderly retired spouse and even richer. And if history mentioned that bitch at all it would be because she had maltreated a sixteen-year-old boy, an innocent and love-sick carter named Rasputin.

She stopped her rocking and sat very still. Had it really happened all those years ago in Tyumen? Six maid servants had been thrust upon the youth he had been then, and five of them had obeyed their cruel mistress and abused him shamelessly. Kubasova had never entirely forgiven her for refusing to join them; indeed, had always been somewhat cold to her ever since. But the peculiar irony of it was this: Irina Danilova did not know why her one time favorite maid had left her service and come here, and would not have believed it had she been told. She had forgotten that bygone incident. Undoubtedly, she'd forgotten even the name of Rasputin, the *muzhik* she so despised. And would she believe it possible in any case? Would *anyone* believe it?

Dunia smiled wanly. She only half believed it herself. It was the stuff of fairy tales, wasn't it? The occasion of his painful ordeal was the only time she had ever seen him, yet even in those brief moments she knew that she loved him. Never a day had passed that she had stopped thinking of him. From one of the buyers of his grain she had discovered where he lived. She had made a vow. If ever she had the opportunity she would find him again. If God would only direct her steps to his door she would go to him and be with him. And now? For nearly two years she had worked in the home he no longer occupied; worked for his wife Praskovia in a sort of partnership with the other maid servant, Katya Ivanova; cared for Rasputin's three children and his widowed, ailing father; shared growing confidences with his lonely wife; washed the floors he had trod, made the bed he had slept in, and sensed Praskovia's pain because no warming pan could ever compensate for the lost warmth of her husband's body.

She started to rock again, her eyes opening wider to catch what remained of the dying light. She enjoyed Sundays. In obedience to the scriptural injunction against toiling on the Sabbath, no one did any work save the getting of meals and the farm abode in peace on this day. The children would be coming in now, half-exhausted from their play. Matriona, who she always called Maria, would be looking for her, for they were very close. And then she would see again the haunted look in Praskovia's eyes, and wonder if God would forgive her this love, if her failure ever to consummate it would be enough to win His forgiveness.

She couldn't help it, she told herself. Love was like a disease and could not be fought against at all, let alone successfully resisted. Getting to her feet, she walked to a narrow chest of drawers and withdrew from concealment her two most precious possessions. Her lips moved in prayer as she held them in her hands. Actually, they were not hers at all. They were only things she periodically borrowed from the room of her mistress, things she would have to return covertly, always anxiously wondering if she would be caught.

She gazed at the photo but could barely make it out in the semi-darkness. He had been so young then. They had taken the picture shortly after Varya was born, and Maria's baby sister was cradled in his arms. In memory, she picked out his dimly seen features, longing for him. Then the other item, the silver ring that was bound with the spiraling strands of his light brown hair. As she had done so many times she placed it to her lips, kissing those strands, imagining she held his face to her breasts and offered him everything. A few of the villagers said he was a saint now, the great healer and prophet known only as "the Starets," one whose name was beginning to be mentioned in hushed tones throughout western Siberia. Praskovia believed this. What she would not believe was the other thing, the tales that said he was a member of the Khlisti; indeed, a leader among them with countless females subject to his sexual mastery. And how could his wife question him about it even if she wished? He had never learned to read and write.

She put the beloved mementos back in the drawer and covered them. It was so important to Praskovia not to believe this, for her love for her mate was possessive and nonsharing. But his devoted servant Dunia did not feel this way. She knew something of the Khlisti tradition, things they spoke of openly in Tyumen. He was probably a saint, as some said, even a greater man than the hallowed Radaev, and so above sin, *superior* to sin and untouched by it no matter what he did.

She caught her breath. Beyond her closed door she could hear the entering children shouting, the voices of Praskovia and Katya, even the infirm accents of the aging Efim Akovlevich aroused from his sleep to partake of the evening meal. *Superior to sin.* Above all earthly reproach. Was *that* what she believed about Rasputin? But then what did that *mean?* She began to shiver uncontrollably, her mouth going suddenly dry. If he could not sin, if he was not even subject to the moral laws of humanity, the awesome rumor about him must be true. And she was devoted to him. She had adored him for years from a distance, almost literally worshiping the ground on which he walked. The implication staggered her and she felt weak, robbed of strength. It wasn't possible, was it? It was not veneration in the pure sense. There was nothing sacred about it, nothing that could ever be condoned in the eyes of God. It was profane, this passion of hers. Carnal. She could not be deceived about the nature of what she felt, about the fantasies, her demanding flesh, the dull ache of her persistent longing. She was beyond all hope of redemption and knew it. Oh God. Oh dear God. *She was in love with Christ.*

During the years that saw the turn of the century, of all the rumors reaching Pokrovskoye of a great *strannik*, a miraculous *starets* who healed by the laying on of hands, none could identify this nameless wanderer as Rasputin except by inference. Nonetheless, the mounting evidence was impressive and undeniable. At times, the physical descriptions fit so well that Praskovia and Dunia thrilled to what they were certain were positive identifications, suspicions made all the more poignant by signs that at least once he had been fairly near his home, as when it was said he taught the Gospel to the fishermen on the Tura, appearing among them as Jesus had done on the shore of Galilee.

If so inclined, a persuasive theologian might have strengthened the growing belief among the peasants that this itinerant holy man was indeed the Christ. There was only one description of Jesus ever left to humanity, that contained in a letter to Tiberius Caesar from Publius Lentulus, Procurator of Judea. Speaking of a bearded young Nazarene, "his eyes bright and blue, clear and serene, his look innocent, dignified, manly and mature," the missive informed the dissolute Emperor: "He calls back the dead from the grave and heals all sorts of diseases with a word or touch. . . . Oftentimes, however, just before he reveals his divine powers, his eyelids are gently closed in reverential silence. . . . He rebukes with majesty, counsels with mildness, his whole address whether in word or deed being eloquent and grave. No man has seen him laugh, yet his manners are exceedingly pleasant, but he has wept frequently in the presence of men. He is temperate, modest, and wise."[1]

So might Rasputin have been described in his platonic aspect. He was completely sincere in it. There is little reason to doubt that when he prayed over this world's helpless and injured victims, he had no other purpose than to cure by the power he believed God had given him, to give peace of mind and respite from pain to the afflicted. But his other side was always there, never far beneath the surface of his multifaceted personality. The rumors of Khlisti orgies were based on fact. So were those that spoke of the *strannik's* "harem," large numbers of females, some of them very young, who were often seen in his company.

As concerns the region where he functioned during these years, most of the cities and towns from which the tales emanated were, quite logically, located on or near rivers, for river barges were one of his chief means of transportation: Nizhni Novgorod, Kazan, Kuibyshev, and Saratov near the Volga; Turinsk on the Tura; Tobolsk on the Irtysh. Today it is impossible to tell how much of this hearsay was accurate. Yet one report was persistent enough to eventually appear in the files of the Okhrana, the tsarist secret police. It placed Rasputin more than once in the city of Kazan, Tatar capital of the Khanate of the Golden Horde since the decline of Sarai in the fifteenth century, captured and reduced by Ivan the Terrible in the sixteenth century. What could have been more logical? Was the *starets* not the inheritor of the Tatar tradition of shamanism? Was Kazan not still teeming with their descendants? One biographer writes of a miracle performed there, of a cripple who got up and walked because Rasputin asked him to do so, of large crowds who kissed his hand and the hem of his robe, and showered their blessings upon him as upon a savior.[2] Although only a decade later Feodor Chaliapin might sing of Kazan at war in Moussorgski's opera *Boris Godunov*, to the ancient site of so much bloodshed Rasputin brought only peace and love.[3]

Of all the many incidents related concerning Rasputin's activities, one was so awe inspiring that it found its way into native folklore and is spoken of to this day. It happened because the effect of what the Church termed the debauchery of the *starets* and his followers was cumulative. When he told simple fishermen he was the emissary of God he was believed by most, but a few did not believe. When he raised his hand in benediction and said that through the power of the Almighty it had been given to him to perform miracles, the vast majority of his peasant audience believed that too, but on several occasions a handful slunk away and went to the priests, sure of the clerical denunciation that was never long in coming. The wretch was a fornicator. That had been "proved" repeatedly. If he fornicated he broke God's law and was therefore subject to anathema and excommunication by the Church, a matter of course in any case if the accusation of Khlistism was ever substantiated. As the *starets* moved on, the numbers of malcontents and accusers increased, until a point was reached where they and not his supporters were in the majority.

As it happened, he gave them the ammunition they needed. Always the basis for their hatred was sexual. Despite his miraculous cures and the general adulation of the multitude, the stigma of the whispered imaginings concerning the Khlisti hung over Rasputin like a thickening pall, a fine thread of corruption which seemed to grow broader and more visible as he progressed. It is said to have occurred outside the city of Kazan, in a field where a large gathering of his enemies confronted him. They were in an ugly mood. Led by a local priest, they flung accusation after accusation. Rasputin had *not* exorcized a demon that had possessed a nun. That was a proven lie. He had *never* cured a cripple in the city, restored speech to the dumb or sight to the blind. All lies. What they really saw in him was a blasphemer, an instrument of Antichrist sent among them by Satan, a purveyor of vicious lust who had left a trail of fallen women from one end of the Urals to the other. No, they would not listen to his falsehoods nor succumb to his devil-spawned cleverness. Instead they called down curses on his head. If nothing else availed, they would seal his mouth with dirt.

At length Rasputin could stand no more of it. He stood almost alone, his frightened disciples having drawn back in dismay. No longer was his arm lifted in benediction but in inexorable wrath. These were farming people, many of them related to his female followers, even husbands and fathers among them. Their living came from the soil. His voice fell upon them in stentorian denunciation: "Let there be no rain for three months!"[4]

And so it befell. Week followed week and no drop appeared. The parched land cracked under a burning sun, a condition virtually unknown in this area. The crops withered. Ruin for many was a certainty. Nor could the man of miracles be found and pleaded with to lift the ruinous curse. Long since, having gathered his flock as a shepherd gathers his sheep, he and they had disappeared into the green density of the forest.

The barn was very large, drafty, and uncomfortable, and the night was cold, a starless night with a half moon riding the heavens and often obscured by drifting cloud. As he sat on one of the benches with the others Rasputin's eyes were closed. He was not sure why he closed them. He knew that more and more people were coming in, most of them women, so many that the *vozhd* (leader) with whom he had discussed this meeting beforehand would probably achieve his goal of a hundred celebrants.

As he had done on request, so did all the others. On entering, they all stripped naked immediately, an unheard of thing for the Khlisti. The robes they then donned were black rather than white, and that too was unheard of. Maybe this was why he closed his eyes, he thought, to blot out a scene about which there was something wrong, preparations he instinctively recognized as false to Khlisti tradition, clearly heretical, setting an ominous pattern that could lead to almost anything. He reminded himself that he was a *vozhd* now, too, that he had agreed to let this priest preside only because the man was senior to him within the sect. But what was the fellow's intention? What sort of rite had he planned that called for nudity at once and vestments as black as sin? He hadn't said a word about anything like this, not a word.

Rasputin leaned back against the wall, pulling the robe tighter about his shivering body, still with closed eyes. They *must* light a fire soon. There were stacked bales of hay and much of it scattered on the floor, and they obviously feared the flames. But how could they conduct the rite with flesh as chilled as this? There were dozens in the barn already, all of them sitting silently, all of them waiting. He felt strangely touched by foreboding. More and more troubled in his mind, he found himself seeking diversion, snatching at any random thought that might lessen the fears that were rising in him.

Memories intruded. He went back almost four years to when it all started, nearly to the beginning of his pilgrimage. He had stopped to ask a night's lodging at an *isba*, a peasant's hut no different from all the others in the same village. There was sickness, a father and mother with their faces drawn in despair for their stricken daughter. They had begged the *starets* to help her, and he had done so, asking to be left alone with the girl, praying at her bedside hour after hour in one of the most intensely devout vigils he had ever mounted. The sick one had been unconscious, racked with fever, her breathing shallow and her pulse almost gone. But God had heard him. While still he prayed, she regained her senses, spoke, even summoned the strength to raise her pale hand. Though still weak on the following day, she was already well on her way to recovery.

And that was how he had found the elusive sect at last. Both parents were Khlists, something he discovered only gradually when in the course of conversation he revealed his own broadmindedness and deep interest. They were amazed by what he had done, boundlessly grateful, though he reminded them that the credit lay not with him. They introduced him to their *vozhd*, he remembered, a strongly built man with blond hair and beard and blue eyes, a scholar such as he had never seen who spoke not only of the Khlisti's past but of the sect's place in history; of the god Krishna, also, India's Khristos (Christ), the phallic *lingam* the Hindus worshiped; even of Christianity's sex-ridden past before the advent of its ironbound restrictive dogma. They had won him over easily, for the golden promise they held out to him was one he had long sought. That very night he attended his first sectarian meeting and participated in his first orgy. The fact that the girl's mother was one of his sex partners, that she gave herself freely in her husband's presence yet acted on Rasputin's departure as though nothing had happened, was a revelation to him. So was the fact that he felt no guilt at all afterward, only a great flowing enlightenment and peace. The entire thrilling experience had exceeded his wildest dreams. He *wanted* to be one of them. He knew that the course of his future was set at last, seemingly ordained by the Almighty.

But *this*. He opened his eyes and glanced about. They *had* built a fire, albeit a small one. Some men had swept the center of the earthen floor clean. Small logs were being kindled. Looking up, he saw only darkness but assumed there must be a vent of some sort in the lofty roof, an escape for rising sparks that might otherwise ignite the structure. He waited for the heat to reach him. He saw the flames leap up and heard the sounds of their crackling but the longed-for warmth seemed never to come. And there was the *vozhd*. Seeing him now it was hard to believe he was actually an Orthodox priest, ordained and sanctified, not altogether a rarity among the Khlisti. The cope he wore was as black a garment as any of them and had no cross upon it, no Christian device of any kind. Instead, there was a small emblem of some sort centered at the chest. Rasputin struggled to focus his eyes on it. It was an embroidered five-pointed star, what he believed was called a pentacle. There was something he had heard about such things, but memory eluded him. Did it have religious significance? Was it—?

Then he saw the girl and caught his breath. She was behind the standing *vozhd*. In the uncertain light of the dancing fire she was barely visible, yet she was there. She was naked and lying on her back. For a long moment she seemed to be suspended in midair. But there was something under her, a raised structure draped with a black cloth, the altar of God such as he had never seen it, black, the color of night, the color of darkness and death, with a nude female where the cross should have been. But *what* god was this? Instantly his feeling of unease was heightened. The altar cloth, too, was decorated with pentacles at the corners. No crosses. No crosses anywhere. Against its ebony expanse the exposed flesh of the girl was gleaming white. He laughed silently, trying to break the increasing tension within him. White? It was the color of purity and virginity, but the Mass about to be held was black. It was *black*.

What happened afterwards was only partly retained by his memory, for his shocked senses caused his mind to reject large parts of it and drive the infernal scene deep into the subconscious. It was a phantasmagoria, an unimagined dream not to be fully credited, in some ways almost a nightmare in which heaven and hell played equal roles. In relating portions of it in later years he spoke of the unbelievable, of a leader of the Khlisti who unashamedly and joyously performed the rites of Satan—for such he knew them to be—amid a throng of peasant disciples as abandoned and fanatical as himself. It was blasphemy of the worst possible form, desecration of all that was holy and sacrosanct, sin heaped upon sin and all of them mortal, with no sign whatever among the celebrants of any aim or purpose other than the most lascivious gratification of the flesh and the worship of the Prince of Darkness.

Rasputin participated because he could not help himself. Never had the air been so charged with sexual power, the vibrations of lust so overmastering and insistent, the acts engaged in so monstrously liberating and breathtakingly sensual. Fearing damnation, dreading that what he did this night could mean surrender to the eternal flames, like a drunkard plunged into forbidden revel from which there is no exit he wallowed in the insensate depravity of it all, immersed to the eyes in a diabolical madness over which he seemed to have no control

Nonetheless, it was this soul-shriveling experience, terrifying and vividly illuminating, that in his fourth year as a *strannik* turned his steps at last toward home.

Rasputin's experience with the Black Mass stands as evidence of how easily satanism may infiltrate any secret cult, particularly a religious one much of whose creed and practice is based on sexual indulgence. Speaking of this meeting of diabolists, his daughter writes:

> In the first place, there was no preliminary prayer, nor the usual procedures of the normal church service, such as Grischa had learned and employed, but the celebrant launched directly into a type of black mass that he had devised for himself. All the participants were unclad from the start, and the prettiest of the women was chosen to serve as the altar

itself, not to mention the chalice. The sacramental wine was poured into her navel, from which the priest drank; he recited the Lord's Prayer in reverse, and began performing acts of perversion with his female "altar" before Grischa's horrified eyes. Here was not a gradual buildup of the fervor of the congregation, but a frontal attack upon their basest natures. And yet, the scene held a certain fascination for Grischa, once he had become entrapped by the lust that began stealing over him, and he found himself engaging in the general debauchery despite his initial revulsion.[5]

The rite was of course very old. Such a scene in sixteenth-century France describes the defilement of the host or eucharistic bread, often represented by devil worshipers as a turnip, carrot, or other vegetable:

> Every time during the course of the mass when the priest had to kiss the altar, instead he kissed the body of the girl. He consecrated the host over her private parts, into which he inserted a small portion of the host. At last the mass was finished, and the priest went into the woman, and, with his hands dipped in the chalice, washed all her genital areas.[6]

Intromission was not restricted to the female sexual organ. In his notorious novel *Justine*, the Marquis de Sade wrote of similar rites involving *coitus per anum* preceded by the insertion of the host in the same orifice. Nor is the Black Mass an obsolete observance that has passed into history. On the contrary, the practices of witchcraft, black magic, and satanism are more common today than ever and are prevalent throughout the world. One expert calculates that in Britain alone there were in 1971 about 4000 witches, "a number which is increasing daily."[7]

Writing in the early 1970s, the biographer of Anton Szandor LaVey, California's "Black Pope," describes how it is done in the Church of Satan near the cliffs of San Francisco Bay:

> . . . Anton was ready for his Friday night rituals. At first they were basically the traditional Black Mass of profanation. The altar for the service was a naked woman. The music was a series of corruptions of hymnals. The cross was turned upside down. Whiskey was used as the alternative to Christ's blood, seminal fluid in milk as the substitute for holy water. The Lord's Prayer was recited backwards. Mock holy wafers

were consecrated by insertion in a naked woman's vagina. The names of the infernal deities were invoked in lieu of the Christian God.[8]

Ostensibly, Rasputin escaped the possible dire consequences of all this when he indulged himself but once and then hastily withdrew. Yet even stranger things were to happen to him. In the meanwhile, turning at last toward Pokrovskoye and home, searching for the re-assurance of God's grace in what he considered the sexually normal, he had intercourse with a more than willing peasant housewife in her *isba* while her husband was away, a liaison that she solicited. He did it joyously, almost in the spirit of an equinoctial rite of spring, a pagan fertility ceremony he believed would cleanse him of diabolical con-tamination. Yet he must have wondered what awaited him. He was fairly sure his reputation had preceded him. But which aspect was uppermost now, his miraculous power or what some called his in-iquities? How would they receive him in the village where he was born? Would Proskovia open her arms to him or turn away?

He felt he could achieve spiritual mastery over all Siberia if he willed it, and he was growing more ambitious. Yet of what account was he in the eyes of the Almighty? On the long trek home he prayed more than ever, humbled himself on his knees more times than he could remember. What was it the Bible said? "Vanity. Vanity. All is vanity." He must remember who he was and to whom his life was dedicated. Nothing temporal must deprive him of that. Some day, he felt intuitively, he would be like Samson at Gaza, blind, helplessly exposed to his enemies, and terribly, even mortally in need. "If I forget thee, O Jerusalem. . . ."

But he would not forget. He was a sinner; aye, many times over. Perhaps he would be damned in the end. But he was still the same person who had seen the Mother of God in the field that was bathed with light.

The event that was to prove the most significant in the history of Pokrovskoye took place on an evening which outwardly at least was much like any other. The shadows of dusk were lengthening. Pra-skovia Feodorovna, head of the Rasputin household since the onset of her elderly father-in-law's debility, had just called the family to supper, and all were around the table ready to be seated. No knock was heard at the door. It simply opened and a man came into the kitchen, a bearded stranger in a ragged cloak with long, unkempt hair that reached below his shoulders.

He spoke no word. It may be imagined with what misgivings Praskovia questioned this intrusion as she looked sharply at the slovenly fellow and waited for him to explain himself. His gaze swept the others, lingering fondly on old Efim Akovlevich and the three children. Momentarily, it was arrested by Dunia's startled countenance as though she had touched something in his memory. Then again the intense blue eyes seemed to consume Praskovia. He approached her with a loving smile on his face and stood looking down at her. She returned his gaze. There was no mistaking those eyes of his, and in a moment of breathless wonder, she recognized him. "Grischa!" she cried, and flung herself into his arms. "Oh Bozheh moi! [Oh my God!] Oh Grischa!"

The reunion after four seemingly interminable years was doubtlessly the most joyous event the Rasputins had ever experienced. Long did the *starets* cling to his wife, as starved for her as she was for him. And Mitya, his little son, was swept off his feet by his bearlike father, then Maria and Varya each in turn, held aloft by his powerful hands, clutched to his bosom, kissed on their foreheads, eyes, and cheeks until all were nearly breathless with gladness and long awaited fulfillment. For the man who had given him life he had the warmest of greetings, the wrinkled hands held lovingly in both his own, the traditional Russian kiss on both cheeks, words of more kindness than Efim Akovlevich had ever before received from his son. Then, as though the repeated outbursts of joy reminded him of another duty, Rasputin made the Sign of the Cross and raised his hand in benediction. All went to their knees before him. It was as though they had forgotten that this man was more than husband and father to them, and were now reminded of it. He blessed them all, then said a special prayer for the soul of his deceased mother, Anna Egorovna, lost to them so recently of a fever.

In recalling the event long afterwards, Maria writes of how her father ate with relish, how they questioned him eagerly and endlessly, how Praskovia told him first of her life in his absence, then he of his "after some careful editing," omitting all reference to the Khlisti and their activities of which the daughter was to learn only years later.

News of the prodigal's return quickly spread through the village. A few peasants came to the door; then many more, all being admitted, until the house was full of the sounds of celebration, laughter, and unrestrained good fellowship. Before long, an accordionist began to play as Rasputin and a rejuvenated, sparkling Praskovia started to dance. Other couples joined them. In minutes, Dunia and Katya had lighted many candles until the entire ground floor of the dwelling resounded with the festivities, and only then did Maria remember the look in Dunia's eyes as she gazed at Rasputin, an expression whose meaning the little girl was still too young to interpret.

For long the revel continued, Rasputin repeating the exotic tales of his travels as new arrivals joined the celebrants. When it was over and the uninvited guests departed it was late. Little Dmitri and Varya were long since in bed. Maria had fallen asleep in a chair, and was lifted bodily into Dunia's arms and taken upstairs. The *strannik* who had fulfilled the cardinal precept of Russian mysticism, *uiti v stranstvo* or wandering, had come home at last.

Joyful had been Rasputin's return, the loving relationship he re-established with his family as "normal" as that of any other spouse and parent under the circumstances. At this point the villagers remembered him simply as the same high-spirited, rather flamboyant Grischa who had departed years before, many of them nodding their heads in private conversation as they speculated on when he would make his first romantic overtures to Pokrovskoye's more receptive females. Although previously a handful had thought differently, now scarcely a soul associated him with the wonder worker spoken of in reverence as "the Starets," the fabled Siberian saint whose fame had spread so widely. The returned father of three was simply Grischa and nothing more. But this was soon to change. Few men in history have more typified the dual personality than he. He was a *podpol'nik* or "underground man," so-called because the village refuges of many a wandering *strannik* were cellars, monks' retreats where they stayed the night. Within days, he was hard at work on the construction of one. He did it with only a few men to help him. Choosing an outlying farm building as the site, he pursued the task with the phenomenal energy that had always characterized him, devoting himself to it from sunrise to sundown day after day as he labored with shovel and spade. They would *see* who he was. Steeped in the Khlisti tradition of endlessly reincarnated Christs, he could not have been entirely forgetful of the words of Jesus: "Who do men say that I am?"

In a matter of a few short days the underground chapel was completed. Rasputin furnished it with benches ordered from a local carpenter; then filled its hand-cut wall niches with holy ikons collected on his travels. Now there occurred an unexpected and wondrous metamorphosis. His first step was to move an iron cot into the deep candlelit interior and separate himself from his wife. When she feebly protested, he explained he would spend three weeks in meditation and devotion to God, then return to her as before. He had no choice, for as a *starets*, all that he did was preordained, his life course as irrevocably committed to a certain path as the stars and planets to their orbits. Praskovia could do nothing but agree. When the two were alone, Efim Akovlevich tried to comfort her, saying that all this was by divine decree. When he realized he was simply rephrasing Rasputin's words, he grew silent.

It was some hours after the descent of the *strannik* into his newly constructed sanctuary that the first wailing was heard, a strange singsong lamentation the words of which, if indeed there were any, were unintelligible. No one in the village had ever heard chanting precisely like this. There was suffering in it. It went on and on. At times it rose to an astounding cacophonous falsetto that hung shrilly in the upper levels of sound, then descended in diminuendo, ultimately to change still again into something almost like the Latin *Dies Irae* sung at Catholic requiem masses, the spellbinding funereal hymn that spoke of the Day of Judgement.

Listening to this evident pain, knowing it bespoke a deep and heartrending penitence, Praskovia and Efim Akovlevich could only look at the gathering crowd of the silent curious outside their house and pray for Rasputin's merciful relief, meanwhile ordering Dunia and Katya to keep the children indoors. The night had passed and the morning was well advanced before they dared go down to the sufferer. When they did so, they were shocked by what they saw.

Before the candlelighted altar Rasputin was kneeling on the cold earth. He seemed to be trembling visibly. Endlessly he raised his clasped hands to the cross he had affixed, then let them fall. Unceasingly he repeated the Greek supplication which so often he had intoned during his wanderings. *"Kyrie eleison. Kyrie eleison"*—*Lord have mercy.*

After an hour of this and uncounted repetitions, there were many who might have doubted the efficacy of the words. They were like the eternal Buddhist prayer of the Tibetan lamas in far distant Lhasa: *"Om mane padme hum"*—*The jewel in the heart of the lotus.* Only a few initiates comprehended why it had to go on and on. The penitent's wife and father did not understand either. Yet soon they found themselves on their knees near him, sharing in his devotions, feeling something of what he felt, at last abandoning themselves altogether to this most abject form of total self-denial and denunciation. As Rasputin wept, their tears fell also. As he prostrated himself full length on the chapel floor so they also became prone, a difficult task for the rheumatoid sire whose loins had bred the penitent. At last, Rasputin began to sing a hymn that was one of triumph and exhilaration, one of victory over evil and the soul ascendant over vice. In this the other two also joined, gripped now by the charged atmosphere of intense sanctity and this man of God who was so close to them and yet so distant.

As it continued day after day it became the talk and wonder of the entire village, indeed virtually the only subject of discussion as the rumor began to spread that Rasputin *must* be "the Starets" of whom all had heard, the sainted "man of miracles" sent to Siberians from God. In greater and greater numbers they invaded his property as though such things as individual ownership had become meaningless, standing in speechless silence before the entrance to the enchanted crypt, hearing the alternating wails of near despair and paeans of joy. When the penitent suffered they suffered with him, many of them weeping openly. When he exulted in praise of God they too felt a surge of exhilaration, a few so gripped by religious ecstasy they unknowingly emulated the man in the cellar by throwing themselves to the ground.

But none dared go down to him. Even the examples of his wife and father did not move them to do that, for most instinctively felt that what they witnessed was nothing less than a divine manifestation, the entire place being under a celestial spell and touched by the hand of the Almighty.

Eventually an old peasant did go down, a village church councilman who had been a scoffer but who now was wondering if there might not be some truth in the circulating rumors. He was escorted to the entrance by Efim Akovlevich, who did not accompany him farther. He spent some minutes in the vault as those who waited outside listened to the supplicant's heartrending lament. Once again there arose from the depths a hymn of joy and splendor. Again the massed listeners were half-entranced, scarcely believing what they heard. Then there was silence. The superstitious villagers crossed themselves repeatedly—and waited. Was it the Diety who had stilled that voice? What had happened to the curious councilman? When the old man came out he was changed. Pale was his face and rigid his expression. No one thought to try to question him. Few would have had the courage. Seemingly almost in a comatose state, he walked quietly and rather stiffly out of the yard, leaving an impression of someone who had gazed on Eternity.

As he had promised Praskovia, on the twenty-first day after the beginning of his holy vigil Rasputin himself emerged. He was pale and thin and haggard, yet in his eyes was something no one had seen in them before, a kind of otherworldly expression which more often than not looked right through an observer as though he or she wasn't really there. He returned to his wife. He slept with her again and was seen with his children. Yet the most casual examination would reveal that he had changed profoundly. He began to hold services in the little chapel; then, because there wasn't room for the increasing multitude, in the courtyard of his house. People came and listened and quickly fell under his thrall. They neglected the village church services, their household duties, even their filial obligations. He *was* a saint; they knew it now, and the Lord had given him to Pokrovskoye.

In less than a month after his completion of the chapel he had conquered them more totally than another might have done by force of arms. His resurgent fame spread more quickly than before, moving far beyond Pokrovskoye like the rings spreading in a pond from a flung stone. This time there was a name to be linked with his deeds. The "Great Starets" of the cities and forests, the saint who had set

all of western Siberia aflame with his holy manifestations, was known
to the people at last. He was that same carter, Grischa, who as a boy
had plied these dusty roads with his horse and wagon. A simple man
of the people. Unlettered. Unanointed. Grigori Efimovich Rasputin.

There was one individual hurt by these remarkable events, even
stunned by them. He was the village priest, Otyets Pyotr (Father
Peter), Pokrovskoye's resident clergyman since the death some years
ago of Otyets Pavel (Father Paul). A venal little man, very jealous of
his clerical prerogatives, he had stood by helplessly, not only to watch
his church emptying out as his parishioners flocked to hear the new
sensation, but also in the certainty that he would soon be losing money.
Like all Russian priests, his main source of income was the government
in the nation's capital. There was his basic salary. There were also
perquisites paid for his many services, the sacraments of weddings,
baptisms, funerals, and all the rest. These were payable only as long
as he had a viable congregation, not empty pews. And he knew who
Rasputin *really* was, a dog of a Khlisti heretic and a servant of Antichrist. For reasons both divine and secular he resolved to smash him.
His first step was a blistering denunciation from the pulpit, a dire
warning to "all true believers" in which he attacked Rasputin directly
as Satan's emissary. It had no visible effect and attendance in the small
church fell off even more. He ranted feverishly, threatening hell fire
and certain damnation. Loyalty to him flagged quickly, and the holy
precincts became nearly deserted. Growing desperate in the end, he
decided there was only one thing to do. Locking his house of worship,
he left for the city of Tyumen to lay very serious charges before the
Bishop himself. He met with the imposing prelate and presented his
case. The man Rasputin had returned to Pokrovskoye and was de-
bauching its inhabitants. He had never been ordained by the Church.
As though he wore cassock and mitre, he had the effrontery to conduct
services of his own, rites of damned heresy that were clearly Satanic
and almost certainly of Khlisti origin.
The Bishop was both shocked and amazed. He was angry, too,
for heresy of this sort was the very devil to root out and it frightened
him. Wasting no time, he quickly gathered members of his personal

staff and a few police, and returned with the priest to Pokrovskoye. He was prepared to see Rasputin arrested and tried, ready if necessary to place the entire village under the ban of anathema. Invite heretical doctrines into their midst, would they? Sanction diabolism and spit upon God's holy name, would they? When the journey by coach had ended and the Bishop had reached his destination, he was already in a state of outrage and prepared literally for anything.

He found nothing. Though the police disguised themselves as visiting peasants from another village and infiltrated Rasputin's services, not a word did he utter that seemed in the least offensive. Though the churchmen interrogated numerous villagers of both sexes, plying them with carefully phrased questions intended to make them give themselves away, not one revealed a thing that could be construed as heretical. This went on for days. A lengthy written report was compiled. At the end of it all, at a conference held in the parish house, the Bishop stated plainly that the accusations brought by Otyets Pyotr could not be upheld. The secret tribunal, convened without the knowledge of the accused or of any villager, found him innocent *in absentia* and the charges against him groundless. Otyets Pyotr was in trouble. Though he apologized abjectly, admitting grievous fault, he was told that a vote of censure would undoubtedly be positive and the result could hurt his career.

And that was all. Though the priest's hatred of Rasputin had redoubled and he continued to nurse it, he was helpless. Rasputin was unconcerned about him. Of late he had had disturbing thoughts of another kind and visions stranger than any in the past. There was a cloud over Russia. He felt it, a blackness that grew steadily larger with the passage of time and ever more threatening. He prayed incessantly. He spoke of it to Praskovia. She asked if he had again seen the Virgin of Kazan but he replied in the negative. The only thing of which he was sure was that the roiling center of the cloud hung now over the city of St. Petersburg, that God was calling him there, that he had no choice but to go. His devoted wife tearfully acquiesced.

In less than a fortnight after he first revealed this to her, his family prayed with him at length, hugged and kissed him each in turn, then gathered by the post road to watch him walk away as he slowly faded from sight.

Praskovia went to their room and fell on her knees. It seemed scarcely possible that it could all be happening again. Like the forlorn Penelope two thousand years before, she begged the Lord to save her husband, to spare them both the agony of this, to restore to her bosom one last time her wandering Ulysses. She prayed until she was exhausted and her knees rubbed raw. Then she went outside again and gazed for many minutes in the direction her loved one had taken. But the birds did not sing for her now. The green of the enveloping woods seemed suddenly black. The long road to St. Petersburg was empty.

NOTES

1. The eleventh-century English translation from the Latin was by Anselm, Archbishop of Canterbury, the Italian-born prelate (1034–1109) most esteemed by William the Conqueror.

2. Heinz Liepman, *Rasputin and the Fall of Imperial Russia*, Rolton House, New York, 1959.

3. The reference is to the aria "In the Town of Kazan" in Act II. The premier performance of *Boris Godunov* in the United States was at New York's Metropolitan Opera House on November 19, 1913.

4. Rene Fülöp-Miller, *Rasputin: The Holy Devil*, Viking Press, New York, 1928.

5. Maria Rasputin and Patte Barham, *Rasputin: The Man Behind the Myth*, Warner Books, 1977. (Published by arrangement with Prentice-Hall, Inc.)

6. Rossell Hope Robbins, *The Encyclopedia of Witchcraft and Demonology*, Crown Publishers, New York, 1959.

7. Interview with British magician and hereditary witch Alex Sanders in *Man, Myth, & Magic Magazine*, BPC Publishing, Ltd., Great Britain, 1971.

8. Burton H. Wolfe, *The Devil's Avenger: A Biography of Anton Szandor LaVey*, Pyramid Communications, New York, 1974.

CHAPTER 5

Ferocious Fermentations

Though it was already March, the waters of the eastern Baltic were still bound in ice, as they always were for five months of the year. From the high bell tower of the basilica Rasputin could see it all. He liked it up here. Because it was open on four sides it was terribly cold, and if this onshore wind increased he knew he would have to go down. It was no worse than Siberia, he told himself. Indeed, he had seen worse many times, been closer to freezing than most people ever came, yet survived. God wanted him to see this. God had prepared this frozen landscape for him because the vast expanse of gleaming whiteness seen at such a height refreshed the soul, and the Lord knew his was in need of refreshing. He would ignore the elements and stay awhile, for the chill he felt was only in the mind. It was not real. He was sure he could control it inwardly and stop the shivering of his all-too-mortal flesh with the God-given power of his will.

As his gaze slowly shifted he embraced the entire panorama. This small island of Kotlin, with its town and fortress of Kronstadt founded by Pyotr Veliki (Peter the Great), its religious academy and ice-locked harbor, lay some twenty-five miles to the west of St. Petersburg. It appeared detached. It was like a floating jewel in the Bay of Kronstadt, this easternmost branch of the Gulf of Finland, and people who came to this sanctuary from the city's madness were special people. He pondered that a moment, turning the word over in his mind. Yes, *special* people. The priests of Kronstadt offered asylum without obligation, hospitality without demands, without recompense of any sort, for to them all were brothers in Christ. And visitors came here by *salazki* (sleigh) over the ice as he had done and some stayed on and took their vows, and lived to be old in service to the faith and some returned to the capital with its false gaiety and unalloyed, festering depravity. But all were changed. He knew that absolutely. Kronstadt was a house with many doors. Those who entered even one of them were bound to catch a glimpse of the Infinite.

He leaned against the stone balustrade and gazed down on the vista below. Kronstadt. They said Tsar Pyotr had wanted it as a naval base for the protection of his new capital. And there was St. Petersburg, far away in the swirling sea mist, the sun causing the domes of its churches to glitter like so many gilded crowns rising out of gradually thinning haze. How long ago had he left that quagmire to come here? He remembered exactly. He had arrived on December 29, 1903, over two months ago now, and after mere days in the capital had come straight to the academy. He had done it because of one man, the desire to meet him, the *need* to meet him. Otyets Ivan Sergeiev, known as Ivan of Kronstadt, was probably the most revered holy man in Russia. He was very old now. He had become priest here in 1855, nearly half a century ago. In his youth he had seen the demise of Tsar Nikolai I, the beginning and end of the Crimean War, and in the fullness of years had been father confessor to Aleksandr III and closed his eyes at his death. Now, as he had been to the father so also to the son, for he served as the spiritual mentor of both Nikolai II and his wife, Tsaritsa Aleksandra Feodorovna.

Rasputin felt a surge of pride. He tried to stifle it, for it rose out of vanity, he knew, and that was dangerous. Yet he could not help it. In the basilica, out of the great multitude in the nondescript congregation that had offered up their prayers that day, Otyets Ivan had found him and singled him out, marked him intuitively. He was Archimandrite here, known from one end of Holy Russia to the other. Yet on that day of days, the service ended, he had descended from the altar and approached the soiled and still kneeling *starets* with the unerring certainty of the seer that he was noting the existence of a kindred spirit.

"My son, I could feel your presence in God's house. The divine spark is within you."

"I ask your blessing, Father."

"Take God's blessing, my son."[1]

And so it had begun. Through Otyets Ivan he had met the Archimandrite Theofan, one of the most influential of churchmen; then the renowned Hermogen, Bishop of Saratov. Was his destiny assuming shape and substance at last? Were its leaves unfolding like the petals of a rose as it turns its face to the sun? Theofan had the ear of no less a person than the Tsar himself. His high position as Inspector of St. Petersburg's Theological Academy alone would give him that. Even more important was the place he filled in the lives of the royal family. He was religious instructor to the *Tsarevnas*, at least to the two older princesses, and would be that to the younger pair as well when they had gained enough maturity to understand a little.

He heaved a speculative sigh. He had heard rumors. Ivan of Kronstadt had been deeply impressed by him. In theosophical discussion with the Siberian visitor, Theofan had been astonished and almost spellbound, as he had freely admitted to others. But it was not these whom God had chosen to fulfill his destiny. It was Hermogen. Even now, according to his admiring informants, the Bishop of Saratov, shrewd, affable, highly respected by the Tsar, was using his influence to induce Theofan to act, to take the new *starets* not only to St. Petersburg, but possibly to the very residence of the Emperor and Empress, their secluded sanctuary at the palace of Tsarskoe Selo. If this happened, who could say to what it would lead? Was it his fate to play a role in high politics? He knew nothing of the subject and was sure that this was not the case. Ah, but to succour the Tsar and Tsaritsa in their time of greatest need, indeed, to stand with them in dire peril. He seemed to have had a dream about them, a dark dream of intense foreboding, but today could not be certain whether he had been asleep or awake. They *needed* him. That much of it he remembered. Was it only wishful fantasy? He had met a young divinity student here, a tall, thin *muzhik* from Tsaritsyn on the great bend of the Volga, one Sergei Trufanov who looked at him with strange Oriental eyes and spoke to him with deep respect. Could he, Rasputin, command the *hearts* of men? Among all the gifts that God had granted him, had He given him this as well?

He turned and trembled uncontrollably. The wind gusts were chilling him through his clothes now, as sharp as knives. Maybe the Lord reminded him that he was only human after all, that willpower alone was not enough. Of course not. It never was, was it? On the long trek to St. Petersburg he had made many stops. One of them, he felt instinctively, might well decide his fate. It was in the last week of July, in the city of Sarov not far from the ancient and fabled Nizhni-Novgorod. There was a ceremony. Tsar Nikolai, father of four daughters, desperate for a son to carry on the royal line, had ordered the canonization of a monk called Seraphin, a petition for God's mercy in the matter of an heir. And he, Rasputin, had prayed. He had flung himself down before the altar of solid silver, beseeching the Lord's clemency on behalf of the Little Father, the Tsar of All the Russias who ruled by divine right. Nay, he had done more. Outside the cathedral he had spoken to the multitude, prophesying that in less than a year a male child would be born to the royal couple, a crown prince to inherit the throne of the Romanovs.

Would there be a *tsarevich*? Had God heard him? He was sure that reports of the incident had reached the capital, that the mysterious *strannik* had been identified as "the Starets of Pokrovskoye" and mentioned by name. If that were true, then much hung in the balance now. He had had his signs, his visions; experienced his persistent sense of augury. If Tsaritsa Aleksandra were delivered of a son not later than the end of summer of this year of 1904, all might yet be well, and the mission given him by the Virgin of Kazan, whatever it was, might still be accomplished. If not, he would be just another fool and quickly forgotten.

He took a final look at the world of universal snow, his gaze ranging to the distant, unseen reaches of the Baltic. What lay in a prophecy? Yet he was sure. To the unknown depths of his troubled soul, fearful for the destiny of the Motherland, he was *sure* the Tsarevich would come. He stepped away from the railing. With a prolonged shudder he suppressed the cold that was stealing over him, grappled with it, fought it down, defeated it. Then he descended the wrought iron spiral staircase into the building's lamplit interior and wondered what might lay beyond.

At the bottom he stopped and stood very still, pondering for a moment the imponderable. If it came to encounter, would St. Pe-

tersburg embrace him? If she did so, would it be a lover's embrace
or the chill enfolding of extinction? No one could say, he realized,
no sage or prophet, not even the Starets Makari at distant Verkhoture,
bound in his loneliness and chains. The question of life and death
was one of the great riddles of the universe, its solution dwelling in
depths unsoundable. Only the limitless stars held the answer. "*Tak i
bit*," said the quiet voice in his mind. *So be it*.

Of all the histories of all the countries in the world—and there
are very few without a plenitude of avarice, cruelty, and
viciousness—the history of Russia is outstanding for its violence and
savagery. Traditionally, when the dread hand of tyranny has clutched
the throats of the Anglo-Saxon peoples, they have risen against it,
broken it after great sacrifice, and replaced it with parliamentary forms
of government as truly democratic as that of ancient Athens where
democracy began. Even among the French, when their overthrow of
the hated class system in 1789–1794 resulted in the far worse excesses
of the bloody revolutionary tribunals, Fate decreed that following the
period of the Second Empire of Louis Napoleon,[2] the principle of rule
by the people would ultimately be reaffirmed.

Not so with Russia. Until the time of Ivan IV (Ivan the Terrible),
this vast, sprawling land was ruled by Tatar clans, Lithuanian dukes,
and numerous provincial warlords, the most durable of whom were
the *Velikie Knazi* or Grand Princes of Moscow. Then, as the German
sovereigns were to do later, the dreaded Ivan took the title of Tsar
(1547), which like that of Kaiser is derived from Caesar, and the claim
to universal absolutism by divine right was established by military
power. Ivan's wife, Tsaritsa Anastasia, was the first of the Romanovs
to come into prominence. Her namesake, the youngest of Tsar Nikolai
II's four daughters, the Grand Duchess Anastasia Nikolayevna, was
the last of them. During the nearly four centuries that passed between
the two, Russia saw almost continuous strife, perhaps more bloodshed
than any other region of the earth, a measure of glory (if that word
may be defined), and very little permanent progress toward the formation of anything that would benefit its seething conglomerate of
many disparate races.

The first profound social and political changes in Russia took place during the reign of Pyotr Veliki (Tsar Peter the Great, 1672–1725) and were sufficiently far-reaching to be accurately termed a *social revolution*. This dynamic young ruler, a giant of a man physically, saw very clearly that if Russia were to progress and join the modern world it must be forcibly detached from its Asiatic roots and propelled headlong toward the West, a wrenching dislocation that should, if doggedly pursued, result eventually in nothing less than a total cultural renaissance. Accordingly, he studied the societies and political institutions of the western European countries, particularly the maritime and military establishments, and awaited his chance to reduce the strength of rival monarchies, a reduction he planned to achieve through war.

Essentially his ambition was dualistic, aimed at two seas. His great design was to make Russia a mighty naval power based on a rocklike foundation of commercial supremacy in Eastern Europe. But the waters were not his. The Baltic was controlled by Sweden, a resurgent military nation, its renown firmly resting on the martial exploits of the dead Gustavus Adolphus, and its present ruler, the boy king Charles XII, was thought to have intractible advisors. In the east there lay the Black Sea, ruled by the Turkish Empire, Russia's only outlet to the ice-free waters of the Mediterranean and thence to the Atlantic. The Tsar warred against the Turks and was defeated (1695); then resumed the offensive the following year and wrested from the Muslim power the port of Azov, key to the Black Sea and still Russian today. He returned to Moscow. In 1697–1698 he made an incognito tour of Western Europe (his disguise deceived no one), even going so far as to ply the carpenter's trade himself in a Dutch shipyard. When revolt broke out in his capital, following an earlier one from the same source, he smashed it flat with great ferocity and cruelty. Then, having personally cut off the beards of his nobles to "end Russian medievalism" and distinguish nobility from peasantry, he attacked the Swedish behemoth to break its Baltic stranglehold.

There followed one of the most intense and dramatic duels in history. Charles XII, ten years the Tsar's junior, as ruthless, determined, and ambitious as he, was a military genius, perhaps the youngest in history. As France's Napoleon I was to do in a later era (and

indeed all Russian tsars by tradition), at his coronation he took the
crown of his country into his hands and placed it on his own head,
spurning the traditional oath, thus serving notice to all of his total
independence from political or clerical control. He was a seventeen-
year-old boy when the Great Northern War was upon him (1699),
and in addition to Russia he found himself facing the other members
of the coalition, Frederick IV of Denmark and Augustus II of Poland
and Saxony. In a campaign dazzling in its brilliance, Charles elimi-
nated Denmark (August 1700), defeated the Tsar at Narva (November), neutralized the Polish Duchy of Courland (1701), then broke the
defenses of Poland and replaced its king with a candidate of his own,
Stanislaus I (1704). In 1706 he invaded Saxony, crushed the German
levees, and stood supreme once again on the Baltic.

Pyotr Veliki and the boy king of Sweden had now become anathema to one another, and to each it was clear that Europe was not big
enough to hold the two of them. Unfortunately for the Swedish monarch, the Tsar's forces had not been annihilated at Narva and enough
training cadres remained on which to build a new army. Charles knew
this through his intelligence service. Securing an alliance with the
Cossack *Hetman* (Chief) Mazeppa,[3] who had been the Tsar's ally and
thus betrayed him, in 1708 Charles invaded Russia with 18,000 Swedish troops and was reinforced by about 3000 Poles and rebellious
Cossacks. As he passed through the lands of the Zaporozhe Kozaki,[4]
this wild tribe declared for him. According to the famous Voltaire,
"some thousands of Wallachians" from what is today southeastern
Romania joined him as well, a force provided by Russia's Turkish
enemy that increased his army to 30,000.[5] It was no good. There was
a ruinous lack of supplies, the army's leadership was fractious, and
its multinational elements made for division. A particularly vital short-
age was that of powder and ball. Unless Charles could supply them,
and soon, the final outcome could scarcely be in doubt. Still he was
full of the old confidence.

The key to the situation was the powder magazine in the city of
Poltava, once successively the stronghold of Tatar khans and Cossack
rebels. Both antagonists were aware of this. Here then, on the Vorskla
River some eighty-five miles west southwest of Kharkov in the
Ukraine, on July 8, 1709 the 5000 Russian defenders under Prince
Menshikov made their stand as the King began siege operations. He

lost the struggle. What a small but highly disciplined Swedish force had done at Narva could not be repeated. While making a reconnaissance Charles was seriously wounded in the heel. Thereafter he commanded from a stretcher. When the Tsar arrived on the field with an overwhelming host of 70,000 men the Swedish lines were cut to pieces. The King in agony from his injury, fled the battlefield. With Mazeppa, he made his way to Turkey where the Cossack chieftain died within the year. It was the end of an era.

Although Charles persuaded Sultan Ahmed III to open hostilities against Russia (1710), the Peace of the Pruth the following year cut the ground out from under him and his resounding defeat at the Battle of Poltava had left his position hopeless. With his failure and early death in combat in Norway, Sweden went into decline. Russia then rose to eminence as the newest great power in Europe, its shining sun the conqueror who wore its crown.

Pyotr Veliki. This monarch who married a peasant, Tsaritsa Ekaterina (Empress Catherine), who beheaded rebellious boyars by the score with his own hand, who nearly bankrupted Russia with his wars and vastly ambitious construction projects, and had his son Aleksei tortured to death for treason, was a man of stupendous drive and monumental contradictions. He was also the founder of St. Petersburg. The city which was destined to become one of the foremost metropolises in Europe was named after the Tsar and was to be his greatest monument. The site was on the Gulf of Finland, a branch of the Baltic Sea. It had strategic value. Pyotr was thinking of the needs of the Navy and a capital that would be defensible. The fact that the area was one vast quagmire dotted with low-lying islands no more deterred him than similar appalling conditions had deterred the builders of the Italian city of Venice centuries earlier. The cost did not deter him either, and in both lives and wealth it was enormous. Government buildings and palaces were built—parade grounds, parks, great scenic esplanades, boulevards, and Romanesque fountains. Ornate but solid bridges were constructed between the many islands of the estuary of the Neva River. The Peterhof Palace (German designations were much in vogue) was designed in the mode of the French monarchy's incomparable Versailles, which the Tsar had visited.

It is said that 200,000 men died during the years of the city's construction (1703–1713), most by disease (the swamps were pestilential) and by freezing to death in the wind-swept marshes. Even the Pyramids of Egypt cost less in human lives. If it is true, there is a sort of macabre irony in the statistic. For this "Venice of the North," as it was called, the locale of so many incredible scenes down through the sanguine generations, was also the site where Rasputin and the last of the Romanovs were to play out, like actors upon a stage, one of the most dramatic and bizarre episodes in the annals of human experience. Perhaps the place had been waiting for them all along.

The "Red Death" had long devastated the country. No pestilence had ever been so fatal, or so hideous. Blood was its Avatar and its seal —the redness and horror of blood. There were sharp pains, and sudden dizziness, and then profuse bleeding at the pores, with dissolution. The scarlet stains upon the body, and especially upon the face of the victim, were the pest ban which shut him out from the aid and from the sympathy of his fellowmen. And the whole seizure, progress, and termination of the disease were the incidents of half an hour.

But the Prince Prospero was happy and dauntless and sagacious. When his dominions were half depopulated, he summoned to his presence a thousand hale and light-hearted friends from among the knights and dames of his court, and with these retired to the deep seclusion of one of his castellated abbeys. This was an extensive and magnificent structure, the creation of the prince's own eccentric yet august taste. A strong and lofty wall girdled it in. This wall had gates of iron. The courtiers, having entered, brought furnaces and massy hammers and welded the bolts. They resolved to leave means neither of ingress nor egress to the sudden impulses of despair or of frenzy from within. The abbey was amply provisioned. With such precautions the courtiers might bid defiance to contagion. The external world could take care of itself. In the meantime it was folly to grieve, or to think. The prince had provided all the appliances of pleasure. There were buffoons, there were improvisatori, there were ballet-dancers, there were musicians, there was Beauty, there was wine. All these and security were within. Without was the "Red Death."[6]

In his famous short story, "The Masque of the Red Death," Edgar Allan Poe does not name his beleaguered sanctuary, for it existed only in his fecund imagination. Yet in certain of its more bizarre aspects it could almost have been a description of the great Russian metropolis of St. Petersburg at the opening of the twentieth century. Though it might not be apparent to the eye, it too was under siege. Everywhere, the political inheritors of the revolutionaries who had dismembered and all but eviscerated Tsar Aleksandr II in 1881 were in constant ferment. Everywhere they plotted, hid caches of arms and explosives, covertly preached sedition, and constantly recruited growing numbers of the disaffected to their ranks. When one political faction, the Bolsheviks (later called the Communists), would finally destroy or neutralize its rivals and assume leadership the flag it would adopt would be red, all red but for the austere device of a hammer and sickle, the color of blood. The hue was well chosen.

In the opinion of many a reactionary nobleman, Aleksandr II, "the Tsar Liberator," had fallen to a terrorist bomb not because he had failed to give enough freedom to the people of Russia when he had emancipated the serfs, but because he had given too much. Yet the seeds of chaos and the violent dissolution of the Monarchy had been planted well before his reign. In the broad sense, the social and political fermentations that were to result in murderous national upheaval, followed by the most dire worldwide peril, had their origin in that very system of royal absolutism whose structured rigidity made no allowance for change, no provision whatever for the slightest degree of popular representation.

Ivan the Terrible had set this inflexible mold by establishing the institution of tsardom and an ironlike autocracy. Peter the Great had solidified it in several characteristic ways: by formalizing autocratic rule through the Army Regulations of 1716 ("His Majesty is an absolute monarch who is not responsible to anyone in the world for his deeds"); by creating and codifying (through the *Table of Ranks*) a formidable bureaucracy from which the peasants were excluded, thus increasing the already wide polarization between the upper classes and the people; by persecuting the peasant-supported Old Believers and making the Orthodox Church subordinate to the Crown. When, having murdered his son Aleksei,[7] the Tsar announced that his successor would be chosen by his own imperial decree, thus negating the age-old custom of inheritance by primogeniture, it became clear to many that the unlimited power of the throne was almost godlike.

Yet, because the Russian people traditionally loved their tsar and were sincere in their affectionate accolade of the "Little Father," a sovereign who was able and willing to rule as well as to reign could normally expect to see the frustration and at least the temporary failure of revolutionary activity. Aleksandr III was such an emperor. This extraordinary man, balding in later life but with a thick, brown beard and grenadier mustache, was six feet four inches in height and when in top condition weighed not less than two hundred and fifty pounds, his physique heavily muscled. Possessing incredible strength and large, very powerful hands, he could and sometimes did bend iron pokers and other metal objects, and his destruction of silver plates by this method has been recorded.

As forceful of character as he was strong of body, Aleksandr III was the complete autocrat, never giving an inch in his belief in absolutist rule. Indelibly burned into his memory was the day when, as a young prince of thirty-six, he had stood at a window of the Winter Palace and choked back sobs for the dying man in the bed behind him, the horribly mutilated Tsar of Russia who had been his father. When the doctor quietly announced the merciful death of Aleksandr II, the huge Tsarevich, now suddenly Tsar only an hour after his sire's wounding, left the palace with his wife. With his face still wet with tears he came to rigid salute before troops of the Preobrajenskoye Regiment; then entered his carriage and left. Mounted lancers of the Donskiye Kozaki (Don Cossacks) in regimental strength went with him. To any who had seen his grim, impassioned face, there could have been small doubt that the new Emperor intended to rule.

Present in the death chamber that day were other members of the Imperial family, including the eldest son of the Crown Prince, thirteen-year-old Nikolai.[8] To all the children, the brutal assassination of their grandfather had been a frightful shock, but to this sensitive boy who might logically expect to be Tsar himself someday the traumatic effect went even deeper. There was no protection in the Imperial dignity. He saw that clearly. You could surround an emperor with loyal troops and still he was vulnerable. The highest prelates in the land could pray endlessly for his safety and still the heartless assassins could strike. And through this bloody tragedy, like the Neva flowing through St. Petersburg, ran the bitterest thread of irony. On the very day they killed the Tsar, only a few hours earlier he had approved the creation of a governmental group that might have been a beginning, a first step on the road to an eventual parliamentary legislature. All in vain. The revolutionaries never once relented. The assassination attempt that finally succeeded was their seventh. They were dogged, merciless, unbelievably fanatical, as the bomb-thrower who had killed the Tsar had proved when he died in his own blast. The boy Nikolai was to remember that, too.

During the late fall of 1894, the sudden sickening of Aleksandr III took everyone by surprise, including his doctors. Few men had seemed more healthy or vigorous. Moreover, the Tsar's lifelong regimen of almost Spartan self-denial, his wilderness treks and hunting trips, had convinced many that he would never succumb to city-bred diseases and would indeed grace this life for a long time. It was not to be. At the age of forty-nine, after a mere thirteen years on the throne, this bull-like man fell ill at Gatchina Palace near St. Petersburg. The royal physicians could not agree on the cause. Disregarding their advice when convalescent, he went to his Polish hunting lodge at Spala and there suffered a relapse. On November 1, 1894 he died at Livadia in the Crimea, having gone there to recuperate after a Viennese specialist made a diagnosis of nephritis.

Once again, a crown prince who was sure he would long remain one found himself thrust unexpectedly into the mainstream of history. Nikolai Aleksandrovich Romanov had not been trained for the succession, for in this one respect his father, dubious about the boy's abilities and confident of his own longevity, had been neglectful. Finance Minister Sergius Witte had warned Aleksandr about this. Now the son was frightened, indeed appalled by the responsibility thrust suddenly upon him at twenty-six. He had almost worshiped his father as a demigod. As far back as he could remember he had stood in awe of him. Had not the *indestructible* Tsar known the strength of ten? Nikolai remembered the fall of '88, the deadly derailment of the Imperial train outside the Ukrainian city of Kharkov. Always it reminded him of Dumas' novel *The Man in the Iron Mask*, how the giant Porthos, at the sacrifice of his own life, had held up the collapsing tunnel long enough for his comrades to escape. That had been fiction, but his father freeing his loved ones by supporting with his back the roof of the crushed railway coach had been fact.

Now the great man was gone. He had enacted labor and land reforms, launched the construction of the Trans-Siberian Railroad, even preserved the peace of Europe by the strategically sound entente with France. The whole world respected him. Yet something so small the eye could not detect it had entered his kidneys and killed him. Nikolai wept. Before the body of his father was cold he told his brother-in-law, Grand Duke Aleksandr, he was unfit to be Tsar and had never wanted it, that he knew "nothing of the business of ruling" and could not even converse knowledgeably with his own ministers. To a degree it was true. Yet he was well educated, much brighter than his words implied, of regal appearance despite his small stature of five feet seven inches, charming of manner and personally brave. And sovereignty could be learned.

In the years before he became Tsar, Nikolai had traveled considerably, had his share of romantic liaison, and even become something of a royal libertine, though rather less ardently than many another crown prince. Beginning in 1890, there had been a young dancer in the Imperial Ballet. Mathilde Kschessinska was only seventeen when he met her, a lovely thing with dark hair and eyes, full of gaiety and humor. Very quickly she fell in love with him. After their first intimacies, there is not much question that he was half in love with her. Then came the evening in 1889 when he paid one of his visits to the home of his uncle, Grand Duke Serge, and his very young wife, Grand Duchess Elizaveta (Elizabeth), known to the family as Ella. It was then that the seeds were planted that were not only to shape his destiny but to play a vital role in the destiny of Russia.

Fate took the form of a beautiful seventeen-year-old girl with blonde hair and blue-gray eyes that repeatedly but shyly sought the darker blue of his own. She was the younger sister of Ella, Princess Alix of the lesser German house of Hesse-Darmstadt, and a granddaughter of Queen Victoria.[9] From the beginning Nikolai was intensely attracted to her. Nonetheless, because she was not of sufficient rank he knew his parents would oppose such a match. After somewhat reluctantly taking a tour of Egypt, India, and Southeast Asia with two of his male cousins,[10] a trip during which he thought much of the Princess, he returned to the capital and the arms of Kschessinska, devoting more and more time to the young ballerina, assisting her in her career through the mere fact of their association. It could not last, of course. Knowing he could never marry his little dancer, aware of the injustice he did her, the Tsarevich eventually ended the relationship. Despite existing barriers, he then turned his mind and heart more than ever toward the Princess from Germany.

It was said that Princess Alix never got over the death of her mother. In 1878, when a diphtheria epidemic reached the grand ducal palace in the venerable city of Darmstadt, the six-year-old girl first lost her baby sister Mai to the disease, then her beloved parent the Grand Duchess Alicia, who succumbed at thirty-five. Alix, a child so known for her joyous temperament the family called her "Sunny," became morose and withdrawn, and the smile disappeared from her lips. Shyness and nervousness characterized her thereafter, so that when Nikolai encountered her in St. Petersburg he might have faced the problem of overcoming her introversion. He did not have to face it. She had fallen in love with him very early and apart from their tragic fate, indeed, partly because of it, their sojourn together on earth was to prove one of the great romances of history, an imperial idyll made beautiful by a rare devotion.

One of the biggest problems they had to overcome was that of their differing faiths. As might be expected of a German princess, Alix was Protestant, specifically Lutheran, the product of a strict, almost Calvinist upbringing (her English governess was of a puritanical bent) that was to prove very ill-suited to life at the Russian court. She took her religion seriously. Annually, she went with her family for a lengthy stay with Queen Victoria at Windsor Castle, and again she was exposed to Protestantism, specifically Anglican. Neither the ceremony nor the dogma of the Orthodox Church appealed to her at this stage (though it was to claim her fervent loyalty later), yet she was only too aware of the importance of religion in royal marriage arrangements.

In this regard, Aleksandr III had failed repeatedly in his efforts. Because she was the daughter of the French Pretender, the Comte de Paris, he had sought Princess Hélène for his son, hoping for a Bourbon

restoration and even closer ties with France. Hélène had declined on
grounds of religion. The Tsar had approached the Prussian court,
considering Princess Margaretha, whom Nikolai found unattractive,
but again religion was a barrier. As for Alix, in the same year (1889)
when at seventeen she had lost her heart to Nikolai, she had disappointed Victoria by gently rejecting the suit of Prince Albert Victor,
eldest son and heir of the Crown Prince who was to become England's
King Edward VII. Considering the dark cloud of insanity and suspicion that was later to hang over "Eddy," as the family called him,
it was surely just as well.[11]

And so it happened. It was the year 1894 and the cobbled streets
of Darmstadt, capital of Starkenburg Province and of Hesse since
1567, were garlanded with the flowers of June. A festive air prevailed.
Arriving to attend the wedding of Alix's older brother Ernst, now
Grand Duke since the death of her father Ludwig, were the elderly
Queen Victoria (she had been two years old when Napoleon died)
and her son the Prince of Wales; her grandson, Germany's Kaiser
Wilhelm II; and Russia's love-sick Crown Prince, on his mind a very
serious intent. All did not go well for Nikolai at first, even though
the pressing of a marriage suit on Alix had finally won the Tsar's
approval. He talked with the Princess for hours. She wept. She loved
him dearly. But how could God forgive her if she forsook the religion
that fate had made her own? The Tsarevich pleaded. Alix remained
adamant. To both of them it seemed a very sad and hopeless impasse
had been reached.

Then it all changed. Queen Victoria favored the marriage and said
so forcefully to Alix. She liked Nicky and saw much good in him,
she said, much to gladden a wife's heart. Did she remember Disraeli?
The British Prime Minister had never trusted Russia but the growing
power of Germany had concerned him as well. That growth continued
still, and Victoria's German grandson Willy was inordinately ambitious, vainglorious, and warlike. The Queen knew that Alix loved
England. An anglophile as Empress of Russia might give Berlin pause.
Even Wilhelm himself was in favor, it seemed. To the imperious
Kaiser von Deutchland, a German princess as future Tsaritsa could
only add to Prussian prestige.

In the end, it was Alix's sister Ella who saved the day. On her marriage to Grand Duke Serge *she* had become Orthodox, even though his ineligibility for the crown of Russia made it unnecessary. She had never regretted it. Love was all, she told Alix, and other considerations weighed little against it. [12]

The day after the Grand Duke's wedding the decorations came down in the streets of Darmstadt and disappeared, stored by the thrifty burghers until the next likely occasion. But in the hearts of Nikolai and Alix joy alone held sovereignty. She had agreed to marry him. Yet it was only April and, agonizingly, they must wait until the winter of the year. First Alix and then Nikolai went to England, both as guests of the Queen. As an engaged couple, their glorious six weeks of communion in a sylvan setting was something they were never to forget. But it ended in late July. Alix returned to Germany, Nikolai to Russia. As the Russian royal yacht, the *Polar Star*, entered the Baltic by way of the Skaggerak she was just off Jutland. German warships saluted her. In a few years, ships flying that same flag would fight a great battle in these waters against the British. [13]

Nikolai dreamed. In the diary he had kept so faithfully and long he read the words she had written there. "You are locked in my heart, the little key is lost and now you must stay there forever." They slipped past Elsinore Castle. Gazing at its grim battlements, did he think of the Prince of Denmark? One wonders if Hamlet's words to Horatio might have come to him at that hour, for he was conversant with Shakespeare. It was in the electric moments before the fight, the death duel with Laertes, and Horatio had tried to warn his friend. Hamlet's reply was cryptic: "We defy augury: there's a special providence in the fall of a sparrow. If it be now, 'tis not to come; if it be not to come, it will be now; if it be not now, yet it will come: the readiness is all: since no man has aught of what he leaves, what is't to leave betimes?"

But Nikolai was young and in love, and such fateful musings were probably spared him. Before the year was out, Aleksandr III would be dead, and he and Alix would solemnly walk together in his funeral cortege. One week later, on November 26, they would be married. After that there would lay before them a vast pool of darkness with here and there bright flickerings of molten fire. Holy Russia was seething with hatred. There were many to nourish it and spread it.

But first, as with a smoldering volcano that stirs and rumbles in its glowing, magmatic depths, there would be signs and portents, an outpouring of lava here and there; a bending and cracking; a remorseless, infinitely acidic effusion corrosive beyond description.

But Nikolai dreamed.

Amid the frivolity, the drinking that was still somewhat genteel but soon would become less so, the whispered confidences, the comings and goings of sober-faced liveried servants, Rasputin's mind recorded a whole series of impressions one after another. It was not his first visit to this mansion. It was maybe his fifth but he couldn't really remember. Tall colonnades, paneled mahogany, bronze sculpture, gold and silver filigree, elegantly brocaded tapestries, parqueted floors and marble balustrades, such were the trappings of an isolated world of wealth and splendor that had long ago separated the upper classes from the people. They were international, these nobility, with far closer ties to the nobles of other countries than to the people of Russia. Since coming to St. Petersburg, he had heard that Ilya Yefimovich Repin was the greatest Russian painter. He had seen his work reproduced in a catalog and sensed the artist's merit instinctively. A remarkable talent. There was one painting that had something to do with a letter from the Zaporozhi Kozaki (Zaporozhi Cossacks) to the Turkish Sultan. Realistic beyond belief. But he saw no Russian work *here*. The gorgeous carpets were from Isfahan in Persia, he was told, and from Marrákech in Morocco, and the paintings and statuary and all the rest of it was like them, international, as though the owners scorned the native product and flaunted their preference for all that was foreign.

Still, he asked himself, what did it matter? If it was preordained that the aristocracy should alienate the masses to an even greater degree in this century than any other, then it was God's will and not to be questioned. And Repin was a liberal, they said, so maybe the distaste the rich felt for him was political rather than artistic. Who spoke for the people? No one, it seemed. Not even the Little Father, for he lived in a world apart and knew them not, and the liberal leaders were bourgeois intellectuals, not peasants. Maybe he, Rasputin, could get to the Tsar and tell him certain things. It was not impossible. Nothing was impossible to God, and now he knew at last that this had been his life's mission all along, the task for which he had been born. It was for this that the Holy Virgin of Kazan had appeared to him that day, all aglow in her own miraculous light, just beyond the stalled plowshare and the horse's tossing head. This carnal St. Petersburg. This house of great riches. Maybe this very night.

Carnal. He drew a deep breath and exhaled slowly, appraising what he saw. It was all here. It was here as much as in any Khlisti "den of iniquity" if he wished to reach out and take it, and he had done so already and found it good. *Décolletage,* they called the cut of their gowns. These people loved to speak French. Indeed, they spoke it more often than Russian. But all it really meant was that women of this class exposed their breasts in a way that would get them horsewhipped, branded whore, and banished in any village in Russia. They were exposed now, dozens of them in this vast room, indeed every female who was not too old or made unattractive by ill health. They cast glances at him unceasingly, lowering their lashes, bringing their fans into play, as coquettish as so many mares *in season* with a stallion near. They had heard things about him. One of his recent paramours had told him so. He was the new *nonpareil* this season. Unequaled, for the moment. "Have you tried the *Starets*? But my dear, he is *incroyable!*" Incredible? He couldn't spell it. He couldn't even spell Russian, let alone French. But he could almost pronounce it.

Now his hostess was looking at him again, smiling. Her sister was with her and they made a lovely pair, all sparkling jewels and silk and satin, and their hair done in what he had heard was termed a high *coiffure.* "The Montenegrins" they called them. Apt enough, too, as the daughters of Prince Nikita of that country. But they were Russian grand duchesses as well. Their marriages had made them that. They were wives of two brothers, two of the Tsar's cousins. This evening's hostess, Grand Duchess Militsa Nikolayevna, was married to Grand Duke Pyotr Nikolayevich; her sister, Grand Duchess Anastasia Nikolayevna, to the tall general they said the Army loved, Grand Duke Nikolai Nikolayevich. And what a progression it had been, with the bearded *strannik* from unknown and mysterious Siberia passed from hand to hand, wearing the plain black kaftan and clumsy

boots that marked his peasant lineage. Ivan of Kronstadt, Archimandrite Theofan, Bishop Hermogen, Grand Duchess Militsa. He was
glad the Montenegrins' husbands were not here. They would talk of
the dreariness of the war with Japan, which had gone badly from the
beginning, and of the even more deadly subject of revolution. *Here*.

He returned his hostess's smile as his thoughts plunged on. Grand
Duke Nikolai's solutions were always military, it was said, Pyotr's
invariably political. But neither had the wit to see that all of it was
useless. The revolutionaries would continue to plot, their assassins to
slaughter, unless. . . . It seemed there were but two choices. Either
the Tsar must declare martial law, create a military dictatorship, and
strike with all his force and at once—or offer the people a constitution.
This was the year 1905. It was very late on the calendar of human
events. Moreover, the Japanese were going to win this war. He could
see that clearly. And who would defend royal absolutism then? Wasn't
it the British statesman William Pitt the Younger who had said it?
"Nations are never split by victory, only by defeat. Bonaparte will
unite France as never before." He couldn't remember who had told
him that. Perhaps the learned Theofan, but it did not matter. All that
mattered was the truth of it. Nations were split by *defeat*, torn asunder
by successful revolutions. And what force of evil might unite Russia
if the Tsar fell? But he would *not* fall. Not now. Not yet. He, Rasputin, would have felt such a thing, had visions, been warned in his
bones. But he had had no sign.

He shifted uneasily in his high-backed chair, feeling increasingly
nervous. He must meet the Tsar and talk to him. Enough time had
passed. Grand Duchess Militsa *must act as God's instrument*. That was
why he was here. That was why he was cultivating her. What did
he care for these highborn fools otherwise?

He saw the two sisters whispering to one another excitedly. Militsa
made a sign to the servants and several candles were snuffed. The big
room darkened. He knew what was coming. All of St. Petersburg
society was agog over what they called the "occult sciences" or "supernatural phenomena." Table rappings, disembodied voices, pianos
and organs that played with no one at the keyboard. Even levitation,
although no one seemed able to prove they had actually seen it. They
were going to have a séance. They would all sit in a circle and hold

hands, the men alternating with the women. There was a joke currently circulating about how many maidenheads had been sacrificed to this arrangement. He smiled at the thought of it. Unless they referred to girls under fifteen, he couldn't imagine who they meant.

And there was the medium for tonight, emerging impressively from behind a dark curtain. Oh yes, he had seen him once before. The hostess introduced him in French, so that his name got lost somewhere, but it didn't matter. Everyone stood up, shuffled about, sat down again in the chairs provided, and grasped the hands of those on either side. More candles were extinguished. The medium, nearly bald, with a stern and predatory face, sat in the center of the room, illuminated only by the flames still burning. His high forehead and aquiline nose were arresting points of light. He mumbled unintelligibly. Rasputin enfolded the hands of the ladies at his flanks and felt them grow moist within his, almost wet in seconds. They were little birds, he thought, doves that had found their nests. As for the medium, he was a charlatan. They all were. But the night was still young and so were his own interlinked partners.

He squeezed their hands and felt them squeeze back. He knew exactly what they were thinking there in the semidarkness. The one on his right was married. He could feel her finger ring. He held the wrong hand to judge of the other but his intuition told him she was single. It did not signify. They were both steering the same course. Intuition went a point further. The one who was married was here without her husband, a common thing in St. Petersburg nowadays, both in high society and in what people like these would call the *demimonde*. It was very simple. Affluent husbands with extramarital appetites went one way and their wives another. There was nothing religious about it, no urge to approach the godhead by the Khlisti teaching of redemption through sin. It was simply what these people called "sophisticated enlightenment," a sort of weak excuse for promiscuity. He could sympathize with it, too. For all their money, their balls and promenades, their gambling and drinking and horses, their lives were a crashing bore, always when humans had too much and could aspire to nothing. Who could blame them if they sought amorous diversion?

The entertainment was commonplace. He sat through it patiently, amused by the reactions of the onlookers, behavior running the gamut from fascination to amazement to superstitious dread. The wealthy audience was "educated" but knew so little. They lived like tsars and tsaritsas, yet crossed themselves in shuddering dismay when the knuckles "from beyond" rapped eerily on the table and the strings of the costly Beckstein piano sounded of themselves. He wondered that Militsa dared to contrive so obviously. Any Siberian *shaman* could practice deception with greater skill, and had done so countless times. Well before it was over, he predicted the remainder of the scenario. There would be sweetcakes and tea, Russian tea poured from at least three huge samovars of solid silver, and *that* he would enjoy very much. Then more conversation, the throng divided into tight little groups, some consisting only of older men who would talk war and politics. Then a Gypsy orchestra perhaps. He thought he had seen some of them about. And dancing, violins, couples drifting out of sight and into secluded corners, even leaving the premises when attempts to find privacy failed.

And himself? He could count upon it. At some time late in the evening, Militsa would introduce him to any he did not yet know, calling him their "most honored guest from Kronstadt Monastery, Otyets Grigori." She would ask him to bless the gathering. There would be a rustle of taffeta and silk as women moved closer to him, their eyes beseeching his attention like those of so many children, but with something else in their glances as well. He would raise his hand over them, his thumb and two fingers joined in the Sign of the Trinity. There would be audible feminine sighs. Yes, *audible*. From that point on, he could make any plans he wished and be certain of success.

When it was over, he detached himself from the women to his right and left and could almost *feel* their disappointment. He had changed his mind and chosen anew. It was Militsa who had invited him here. This was her sumptuous estate, shared with her husband, and these her noted guests. But it was not Militsa who felt the deepest fascination for him, not her whom he attracted like a powerful magnet. It was her sister, Grand Duchess Anastasia Nikolayevna, whose beautiful eyes were on him at this moment. They called her Stana, and he would call her that, too, at the first opportunity. She was important at Court, had equal access with her sister to the Tsar and Tsaritsa.

Moreover, he felt strongly that her soldier husband would soon grow to like him well, and as cousin to the Little Father he was highly placed.

Yes, it was Anastasia. It was Stana, and still her eyes had not left him. Rising from his chair, he moved toward her. "It is Russia who approaches thee," said a voice in his mind. "Holy Russia."

She smiled upon him with depthless, primeval beauty. She seemed to be waiting for him.

NOTES

1. Such was the verbal exchange as Maria Rasputin recalled her father had told it to her. See Maria Rasputin and Patte Barham, *Rasputin: The Man Behind the Myth*, Warner Books, New York, 1977. (Published by arrangement with Prentice-Hall, Inc.)

2. Napoleon III, Emperor of France, nephew to Napoleon Bonaparte.

3. Lord Byron's famous poem "Mazeppa's Ride" was based on an earlier incident.

4. From *za* ("over") *porozhe* ("the rapids"). Khortitsa Island in the Dnieper River (south Ukraine) was the stronghold of the Zaporozhe Cossacks from the sixteenth to the eighteenth centuries.

5. François Marie Arouet de Voltaire, *The History of Charles the Twelfth, King of Sweden*. Translated from the French by Smollett. Leavitt, Trow & Co., New York, 1848. (For an account of the fifteenth-century Turkish invasion of Romania, see the author's *Prince Dracula: Son of the Devil*, McGraw-Hill, New York, 1988.)

6. Edgar Allan Poe, "The Masque of the Red Death," *Tales of Mystery and Imagination*, Tudor Publications, New York, 1930.

7. Ivan the Terrible had likewise murdered his son Ivan (1580), but in a fit of rage, not through cold calculation. In the famous painting of the tragedy by Repin, the grieving Tsar's eyes are those of a hopeless psychopath.

8. He was not the Tsar's firstborn. A brother, Aleksandr, had died in the cradle.

9. This was their second encounter. The Tsarevich had first met Alix when she was twelve and had come to St. Petersburg to attend Ella's wedding.

10. In Japan he was attacked by a knife-wielding fanatic and never forgot it.

11. Consult Frank Spiering, *Prince Jack: The True Story of Jack the Ripper*, Jove Publications, New York, 1980.

12. Later, when the Grand Duke's brutality and incurable psychosis became manifest, his wife stuck with him and always excused his behavior to her friends. After his assassination she built her own convent and took the veil.

13. The First World War's Battle of Jutland (May 31, 1916) between the British Grand Fleet under Admiral Jellicoe and the German High Seas Fleet under Admiral Scheer.

"The Tsarevich
Will Live"

He was Nikolai Aleksandrovich Romanov, Tsar of All the Russias. But not today it seemed. Today, as he sat here alone in this holy place, the years melted into thin air as though they had never been, and he was once again a very small boy on his mother's knee. She was not yet Tsaritsa in that bygone day but the wife of the Tsarevich Aleksandr. Although long a subject of Russia and bearing the adopted Russian name of Maria Feodorovna, she was still in reality a Scandinavian, Princess Dagmar, daughter of King Christian IX of Denmark. And he? He was only Nicky. He wore no uniform today, no decorations, and his plain though rich civilian attire helped to heighten the illusion. If he prayed in a public place he would have to look like the Tsar. But here in this small private chapel he could be simply— a man. He sighed in penitent resignation. Who was he to flaunt political or national power in the face of God? Had high position protected his grandfather from the bomb they had made in hell? Was his father any the less dead of nephritis because he wore a crown? He knew he must humble himself utterly or the Lord would never hear his prayers. He must be again as he was as a boy. As a boy . . .

Suddenly, he shook off the torpor that was stealing over him and sat straight up. It was cold in this place. That was to be expected, of course, for the crypt was below ground level. Yet he must tell them to do something about it. This was his wife's chapel, the Fedorovski

Sobor, peculiarly her own, so much so that she seldom made her devotions in the palace now but came here to the Imperial Park, seeking what solace a merciful deity might give to her troubled soul. "Sunny" the family called her, and especially he, or "Sunshine." But she was no longer that, was she? His heart bled for what he saw in her now; for the pale and haggard look that seemed permanently to have blighted her beauty, aging her so rapidly; for her hopeless little smile that could not mask the growing tragedy of their lives. Oh God, he loved her so. He loved her so. Sunny . . .

He felt awkward sitting here in the semidarkness, and colder now, so cold he yearned to climb up and out of the crypt and seek the warming, life-giving support of his soldiers, his royal guard of the Semonovsky Regiment, six young men pledged to defend him with their lives, to protect their Little Father because they loved him. It was a sign of the times, he knew. Before the terrible events of 1905, not quite this amount of caution would have been necessary. Revolutionary activity had seemed to die down. His people had loved him. They loved him still, he was sure of that. But who *were* the people of Russia? Were they the professional classes, the bourgeois intelligentsia who forever plotted to overthrow tsardom and bring the Empire to its knees? Were they the nobility, purse-proud, full of vanity and insufferable arrogance, concerned only with themselves? The Church? He loved God and could and did venerate more than a few churchmen, but in a certain sense many of them were simply the other side of the aristocratic coin, venal and given to self-aggrandisement. Who then was Russia?

He shook his head as though in doing so he might clear his mind and think more rationally. Russia was the people of the land. The peasants. They had been here long before there was a nobility or even a religion, and they would be here still when all else had vanished. Was he truly Emperor? Yes, that by divine right, so it was said, yet always he had acknowledged one inescapable fact. He had been conceived under a dark star, born on the day of Job the Sufferer. Nothing could alter that. He believed his fatalistic acceptance of it was the only thing that prevented a lapse into madness.

He felt his palms grow moist with emotion. It seemed so strange to look back on it all, to remember. Once again it was May of 1896.

For a year the official mourning for the dead Aleksandr III had continued, but now it was the day of his son's coronation in Moscow. For twenty-four hours he and Aleksandra had been in seclusion in the Petrovsky Palace, acceding to tradition by fasting and prayer. Then the procession began, the passage of the Nikolsky Gate, the entrance into the Kremlin, the long walk through a worshipful crowd over red velvet and up the steps of the Ouspensky Cathedral, his wife and mother following just behind him into the glory of it all. The glory of it all. But in the most venerated Sanctuary, receiving the priestly sacrament as Defender of the Orthodox Faith, it had happened. The Order of St. Andrei, the very symbol of tsardom, had somehow become unfastened and fallen gold-encrusted chain and all to the floor. The heavy carpeting had smothered the sound, yet in his brain it had reverberated in a flash of dark premonitory fire.

Omen of disaster? Those who had seen it were told not to speak of it, even obliged to swear silence. But what an inauspicious opening for a reign. In due course, those dire events followed which some had predicted. January 1904. War with Japan. The agricultural Slavic giant against the newly industrialized Oriental midget. Ikons against guns. Outmoded warships against modern ones. Lost in eighteen months. July. Interior Minister Plehve and seven of his staff blown to pieces in Warsaw Station. January 1905. The march on the Winter Palace, "Bloody Sunday," and revolution. February. Only three weeks after the troops had attacked the demonstrators, his uncle, Grand Duke Serge Aleksandrovich, bombed into unrecognizable shreds of quivering flesh upon leaving his home, the remains found by his wife Ella. The fall of the year. The "October Manifesto" granted. A constitution and a *duma* (representative government), but that did not stop it. Always they demanded more and more. Always they killed to get it. 1906. The terrorist arm of the Social Revolutionary Party in action. Nearly 1600 people slaughtered throughout western Russia in the course of that fateful year, most of them with homemade bombs, nearly all of them government officials of every level, in an offensive intended to produce creeping paralysis through fear.

And now it was 1907, and with the coming of spring he and his family would go again to Livadia in the Crimea as they did every year. But the bombings would continue. Already they exceeded the carnage of the opening months of the year before. Last August they blew up Stolypin's house, the summer villa of the Premier of Russia, killing thirty-two people, injuring Stolypin's son and maiming his daughter for life, though the minister himself had escaped. And *this* year?

Nikolai closed his eyes. Born on the day of Job. It was all right. He could bear it. But what of his little boy, the infant Aleksei now nearing three? It was the baby's plight that was killing Sunshine, the curse of inbreeding they said, the curse of more than one of the royal families of Europe. Hemophilia.

For a long time he sat as though cast in bronze, seeming scarcely to breathe, seeing visions behind his closed lids. Maybe Sunshine's malaise over their child was like a reflection of the nation's increasing sickness. As the Little Mother she *was* Russia, wasn't she? Yes, as much as he. The peasants knew this. She very seldom appeared in public now, but in the days before Aleksei's birth on their trips to the Crimea the people doted on her, strewing her path with flowers, almost literally worshiping the ground on which she walked. She *felt* their love and was happy. It was the nobility she did not trust, and the ministers of state, so she turned to the Montenegrin sisters and other believers in the occult. Desperately she had turned to them, though no one in Russia was a more devout believer in Orthodoxy or a truer daughter of the Church.

By an effort of the will he momentarily arrested his thoughts, like a runner who slows in midstride to adjust his breathing. The clairvoyants, the *shamans* who stood aloof from the Church, perhaps even as secret sectarians, so many had come to the palace or were brought to it, wearing their reputations like cloaks that hid the emptiness beneath. But there was one man. What had he written about him? "We have met a man of God—Grigori Efimovich, from Tobolsk Province." He remembered the date recorded in his diary: November 1, 1905. Archimandrite Theofan had introduced him into society. The Starets had lived at Kronstadt Monastery in those days but had visited St. Petersburg, the guest of Grand Duke Pyotr Nikolayevich and his wife Militsa at their palace on the Angliskaya Nabereznaya (English Quay). And he and Sunny had gone there, and the holy man from Siberia had addressed them as equals, not as *Vyelichyestvo* and *Vyelichvestva*, but as *Batiushka* (Father) and *Matushka* (Mother) in the peasant idiom. He had embraced them, kissed each three times on the cheeks in the Russian manner, and even then, with the *strannik* still all unknown to them, the Tsar and Tsaritsa of Russia had sensed his power, spoken of it to each other later, marveled at the similarity of their strange, nearly otherwordly impressions.

Nikolai went to his knees and clasped his hands in mute supplication. It was cold in this chapel. Could he and Sunny nowhere find the warmth and mercy of God? That was two years ago, and where was Rasputin now? No longer at Kronstadt. No, he remembered. He was in the city, staying with Sasanov and his wife and children. Yes, Grigori Pyotrovich Sasanov, member of the Duma and the Holy Synod. And he, the Tsar, hating the Duma and all for which it stood, had taken the trouble to remember that, made a mental note of it as though Sasanov were of cabinet rank. Why? The reason was obvious. Rasputin's whereabouts were important to him. He recognized that instinctively. He and Sunny had seen him several times in the past two years, always as the guest of the Grand Duke or his brother the General. They liked him. They were fascinated by him as by no one else they had ever known. But now he loomed in the imagination as never before, as though God had chosen to speak through his lips. Was it only fantasy? The product of growing despair?

The Tsar closed his eyes. He had a sense that he was praying. His lips moved. Yet he seemed to lack any clear realization of the nature or meaning of his words. His eyes brimmed with tears. They overflowed and coursed down his cheeks, wetting his beard. It was a name that kept returning, weaving itself in and out of his subconscious like a slender thread of hope in a darkening world: "Otyets Grigori. Otyets Grigori."

He began to pray for his wife and the Tsarevich. Sweat broke out on his forehead. To find a more fervent pleading than his it might have been necessary to go back nineteen hundred years, to another man alone—on his knees in Gethsemane.

The "dark star" of the young Nikolai II had manifested itself very early in his reign. It was not only the incident of the Order of St.

Andrei slipping from his shoulders during his coronation. There was also the very real human tragedy of Khodynka Meadow on the day immediately following it. This large field on Moscow's outskirts, used by the garrison for military exercises, was crosshatched by a number of slit trenches dug to protect the troops under real or simulated fire. Traditionally, it was used for feasting on this occasion. Planks had been laid over many of the trenches. During the night following the crowning, many thousands of Muscovites came to this area with the idea of camping out, seeking positions of vantage from which to view the new sovereigns the following day. It is estimated that half a million people came to the field during the hours of darkness.

There are two versions of what happened. One deals with kegs of beer brought to the area in wagons, claiming a rumor that there was not enough of this beverage to go around started people running toward the source of supply in a precipitate movement that became a panic. The other version is similar. It states merely that the milling throng collapsed the planking in several places, the people falling into the trenches as those pressing on from behind lost their heads and started to run. Whichever was the case, it had the dire effect that panic so often produces where a multitude is involved. As with a herd of stampeded cattle, so it often is with humans. Panic breeds more of the same, very quickly; the ability to reason vanishes; fear and the instinct of flight are contagious. On that day men, women, and children were crushed under the feet of the churning mob. Many were suffocated. The death toll exceeded two thousand, with an undetermined number seriously injured.

Initially, the Tsar and Tsaritsa knew nothing about this frightful event. It had happened early in the morning, hours before the monarchs were scheduled to appear. When later in the day it was reported to them they were appalled. Their innate superstition was aroused. Suffering from genuine grief for their people, both regarded it as a black omen, and Nikolai spoke of going into seclusion in a monastery. Had he done so even for a short time, it probably would have suppressed the dangerous rumor of his "indifference." As it was, he listened to his uncles, as he often did in the early years of his reign, reluctantly accepting their advice that he and the Empress attend the ball being given that night by the French Ambassador rather than run the risk of offending their Gallic ally.[1]

The Imperial couple did attend. As might have been expected, it was not long before the rumor spread far and wide that neither of them were concerned for the suffering of the Russian masses, that they were callous, disdainful, uncaring. In all quarters, the ever-present revolutionaries were greatly encouraged. The subsequent efforts of the Emperor and Empress to alleviate the catastrophy (visits to hospitals, compensation payments to survivors, private burials for victims, all from the Tsar's personal treasury) had very little effect in counteracting antiroyalist propaganda. The Tsaritsa was German, people remembered. As she had walked in the funeral cortege of Aleksandr III just prior to her wedding, many said she had come to Russia "from behind a coffin." What good could result from such a marriage?

If the impressionable young Tsarevich Nikolai never forgot the unprovoked knife attack by a fanatical Japanese during his early Asian tour, the newly crowned Tsar received precisely the opposite impression during his subsequent visit to France in 1896. Never had he been so royally feted and lavishly entertained, and the enthusiasm of the common people exceeded anything he could have imagined. The already firm alliance between St. Petersburg and Paris was thus further strengthened. The Japanese remained "monkeys" to Nikolai, and thus he referred to them in his self-revealing diary. The French, on the other hand, though citizens of a republic under a representative government, he thought of as brothers. What more natural than to continue as their ally against the ever-increasing power of the German Empire.

In Berlin, Kaiser Wilhelm II and his ministers did not like it. Indeed, the seemingly unbreakable pact between Russia and France was a source of considerable German chagrin. In vain did Wilhelm plead with Nikolai that his "Gallic flirtation" was an unnatural one, that the only leader in Europe on whom the Tsar could count in a crisis was his cousin and fellow autocrat, the German Emperor. The appeal fell on deaf ears. Nikolai was civil to the vain and frequently irascible Wilhelm. On occasion, he even went out of his way to placate him. But the Tsar never forgot that his own revered father, Aleksandr III, had fashioned the tie with France. Germany was ambitious for expansion in any conceivable direction. With the exception of her colonial empire in Africa and Indochina, France was not, at least not openly. German statesmen still spoke of *"lebensraum,"* or "living space," and the old Teutonic battle cry of *"Drang nach Osten"*—"Drive to the East"—had never fully died on their lips. Berlin's very obvious desire to break the Franco-Russian alliance seemed highly significant. As for the ageless Saxon military dictum "Drive to the East," what had the words *ever* meant but Russia? They had meant that in the year 1242, when the Russian hero Aleksandr Nevsky had defeated the Livonian-Saxon alliance at Lake Peipus; and in 1410 when Ladislaus II had crushed the Teutonic Knights at Tannenberg. In the cautious mind of Nikolai they meant that still.

Blocked along one avenue of approach by Russian intransigence, German foreign policy came more and more to rely upon another. With the building of the Trans-Siberian Railway across the entire breadth of Asia, it was virtually certain that sooner or later St. Petersburg would cast covetous eyes on the strategically and economically important Far East. If Russia became involved in Asia her entanglement there might become inextricable, at the very least a costly drain on her treasure and manpower. At that point she would be ineffective in Europe. It therefore became a cardinal principle of Berlin's grand strategy to so involve her.[2]

Already militarily active against the Chinese in the Boxer Rebellion of 1900, the Kaiser subsequently wrote to the Tsar: "Clearly, it is the great task of the future for Russia to cultivate the Asian continent and to defend Europe from the inroads of the Great Yellow Race. In this you will always find me at your side, ready to help you as best I can. . . . I would let nobody try to interfere with you and attack from behind in Europe during the time you were fulfilling the great mission which Heaven has shaped for you."

For a long time Nikolai resisted these blandishments as Wilhelm continued to apply pressure. Yet somewhere in the Tsar's makeup, perhaps deep in the subconscious at first, was a desire to extend the frontiers of Mother Russia if such an aggrandisement could be accomplished through any means short of war. He knew that to make an overt move in Asia would mean to risk a war with Japan. Russia would win such a war. He and his generals were sure of that. Yet, to do him justice, he was fundamentally a man of peace. The human suffering he knew that any armed conflict would entail was more than enough to give him pause.

The question was resolved through a combination of circumstance, temptation, and a typically imperial sense of Russia's destiny. Historically, weakness, far from preserving peace, has invariably invited aggression. China was weak. As early as 1839, when Great Britain provoked the Opium War to obtain commercial concessions in that unhappy country, it was quickly discovered that the forces of the enfeebled Manchu Empire were no match for European weapons and tactics. England got what it wanted, including extraterritoriality in every major Chinese center of commerce, Hong Kong Island (ceded in 1841), and the right to establish a whole series of British *tai-pans* (commercial chiefs) to govern it. Before long, France, Germany, and Russia had all established enclaves on Chinese soil, maintained their flags inviolate there, and quartered troops around their legations. For a long time afterward nothing much changed. Empress Ts'u Hsi, last of the Manchu sovereigns, made that dynasty's final effort to expel "the foreign devils" during the Boxer Rebellion of 1900, doing all in her power to encourage Boxer belligerency. After that Chinese defeat, the country, moribund politically and economically, lay all but prostrate, waiting for what appeared to be its inevitable partition.

Actually, for all practical purposes that dismemberment had already begun with the victories over China that gave Japan a seemingly unbreakable grip on Manchuria (First Chino-Japanese War, 1894–1895). Yet with the completion of the Russian built and controlled Trans-Siberian Railroad all this changed rapidly. Fired with colonial ambition, the Russians founded Harbin, destined to become a vital junction of all the railroads in the Far East, established the naval base of Port Arthur on the Yellow Sea's Liaotung Peninsula, and laid the tracks for the Chinese Eastern Railroad. When a group of Russian paramilitary adventurers penetrated Korea, a Japanese sphere of influence, the government in Tokyo, every bit as expansionist as the one in St. Petersburg, had no choice but to take vigorous countermeasures and place its forces on a war footing.[3]

It is not part of the Oriental concept of conducting hostilities to first declare war on an enemy, thus giving him time to prepare a defense and ensuring a much higher casualty figure for the attacker.

On the night of February 6, 1904, Japan's "sneak attack" against Port Arthur was devastatingly successful, major units of the Russian squadron there being sunk or severely damaged by torpedoes, the surviving vessels blockaded by the Japanese Navy. Ashore, as one Russian redoubt after another was overwhelmed and taken by *banzai*-shouting soldiery, the difficulties of supplying an army across thousands of miles by a single-track railway became obvious to an astounded world. In January, 1905, Port Arthur itself surrendered. A major and decisive engagement loomed. With the Japanese Army in the very able hands of General Iwao Oyama, victor in the First Chino-Japanese War, Russia's defeat in the Battle of Mukden (February–March), while it may have shocked the chancellories of Europe, came as no surprise to the more astute students of war. Russia had lost the land phase of the struggle. Any chance it had to avoid a humiliating and probably ruinous defeat now lay with its navy.

Between the Russian and Japanese naval forces there were several vital differences. The Japanese Navy was more modern than its opponent, its ships faster and more heavily gunned, better armored in the crucial areas, its all-important optics (range-finding equipment) much superior. Its general training, tactics, gunnery, and discipline were all based on that of the British Navy. Its commander, Admiral Heihachiro Togo, had studied naval science in England, fought successfully in the Chinese war, and masterminded the attack on Port Arthur. Japanese morale was high with past victories. Far from rusting at its moorings, the fleet was constantly in training.

Moored at bases in the Baltic Sea, primarily Kronstadt, the Russian Navy was another matter. Not only were funds for essential gunnery practice often lacking, the money for the modernization of the ships and the improved training of their crews also was seldom available. One is reminded of the Napoleonic Wars, of the French and Spanish fleets bottled up in Spain's port of Cádiz by the British, with a greater naval genius than Togo waiting for them to come out and risk a battle.[4] The Russian commander was Admiral Zinovi Rozhdestvensky. When he finally sailed, there had been no time to careen his ships, their hulls being fouled by barnacles and long seagrass whose additional weight was certain to reduce their speed and maneuverability. The Admiral's dispatches indicate his awareness of this. Comparatively

inexperienced in war, his fleet inadequately trained and equipped, he
may have felt much like the French Admiral Villeneuve at Trafalgar,
an officer who knew beforehand that Napoleon's order to attack the
British fleet, even with superior numbers, was tantamount to suicide.

And suicide it proved to be. After an embarrassing encounter with
a group of British fishing boats at night off the North Sea's Dogger
Bank (the Russians mistook the small vessels for an advance squadron
of Japanese torpedo boats and fired on them[5]), Rozhdestvensky's ships,
after a three-month layover at the island of Madagascar off the southeast coast of Africa,[6] crossed the Indian Ocean, steamed north into
the South China Sea, and prepared to keep a sharp lookout for Togo's
expected screening force somewhere ahead. Entering the East China
Sea after sailing halfway round the world, they found the Japanese
Navy in the Tsushima Strait that divides Korea from Japan. It was
afternoon. The date was May 27, 1905.

It was on this occasion that Admiral Togo made the classic naval
maneuver of "crossing the T," a tactic where the defending fleet is
ranged broadside to the attacker, each of whose ships in turn as they
advance in order of battle must come under the concentrated fire of
the enemy. Given the Japanese superiority in speed, maneuver, and
gunnery, the predictable result was devastating. It was slaughter,
virtual annihilation, a nightmarish hell of shrieking shot, high explosive, and burning and sinking ships. Admiral Rozhdestvensky himself
was one of the few Russian survivors. As for the fleet he had commanded, in less than an hour after the opening salvos as a viable force
it no longer existed.

Tsarist Russia shuddered. The worst had happened, or so many
believed. But military defeats have a way of magnifying preexisting
evils and exacerbating the already fast-flowing currents of discontent.
In a squadron of the Russian Black Sea Fleet off Odessa the following
month, a bloody mutiny occurred aboard the battleship *Potëmkin* when
deplorable food and living conditions had made the crew desperate.
The captain and six of his officers were murdered, the remainder
spared by the mutineers only to work the vessel that was eventually
interned in the Romanian port of Constanza. Of itself, the incident
seemed relatively unimportant at the time, at least at the international
level. Yet it inspired by example. To the sailors who would be involved

in the Russian Revolution of 1917 the "saga of the *Potëmkin*" was to become a legend.[7]

Though the American-mediated Treaty of Portsmouth[8] in August went far toward robbing Japan of the fruits of a crushing victory, one emerging fact was clear. A new Pacific naval power had been born and from henceforth the Japanese, still worshiping their Emperor and believing in the *samurai* warrior's Code of *Bushido*, would be a people with whom to reckon. The obvious corollary to that was another factor in the equation. The tsarist regime had been drastically undermined by a lost war. Political unrest was spreading faster than ever in Russia. If the still largely covert revolutionary movement now struck with sufficient force and determination there was a better than even chance it would overthrow the government.

The attempt to do this was not long in coming. Revolution was already an established fact, sparked by the events of "Bloody Sunday" (January 22, 1905) when a priest named Father Georg Gapon led some thousands of his unarmed followers on a march to the Winter Palace in St. Petersburg.[9] Their stated intention had been peaceable though wholly unacceptable, a wish to read to the Tsar a petition not the least demands of which were those of universal suffrage and a fully representative government. Without the Tsar's knowledge (he was at Tsarskoe Selo), they were fired on by nervous troops, cut down by cavalry with sabers, and hundreds of them died in the snow.

That had been the beginning. In August, the month that saw the official ending of the Russo-Japanese War, the Russian Government made what it considered a major concession in first legalizing the establishment of a consultative assembly, the State Duma, then sanctioning elections to fill its offices. Neither the radical (leftist) nor moderate (centrist) opposition was remotely satisfied, and said so with ever more abusive invective. The government wavered. When it gave virtual autonomy to the universities, it made inevitable the open circulation of revolutionary propaganda on their campuses.

Agitation increased dramatically. In September, the bakers and printers of Moscow declared a general strike, to be joined only days later by the telephone and telegraph workers and other public services. A creeping paralysis ensued. It was like the repercussions of "Bloody Sunday" all over again. That tragic event had all but crippled St.

Petersburg industries with one major strike after another following hard upon it. Now, in October, the Petersburg Soviet of Workers' Deputies came into being as the proletariat became more organized and the stage was set for the rapid spreading of violence. For the first time, names later to be notorious were heard, that of the Jew Lev Bronstein, whose revolutionary alias was Leon Trotsky; that of the Eurasian Vladimir Ulyanov, called Nikolai Lenin.[10]

On October 17, the *Menshevik*[11] faction of the Petersburg Soviet published an inflammatory paper called *Izvestiya*. On the same day, Nikolai II signed with great reluctance a document that history would call the "October Manifesto." Transforming Holy Russia into a constitutional monarchy, it drastically altered the nature of the state. The revolutionaries ignored it. In an all-out effort to seize power, they declared it their unshakable aim to smash the monarchy utterly and establish a democratic republic. Had the government again given ground at that point there is little doubt it would have been crushed, but it held firm. Bloody events followed. As had happened in France in the eighteenth century during the dark days of "The Terror," revolution spread to the countryside, estates were rifled and gutted, and many a noble and government official was burned alive with his entire family.

At the eleventh hour the government acted. A state of emergency was proclaimed. Hard-pressed police were reinforced by troops. Army units were dispatched to threatened rural areas with orders to wage all-out war if necessary. The revolutionaries, unready for a carefully planned and coordinated military effort on the part of their intended victims, divided in their own leadership, began to lose cohesion and control. They had not prepared adequately. Their propaganda, though virulent in the extreme and often effective, had not been sufficiently widespread nor long enough applied. Attempting to flee the country, Trotsky was arrested and sentenced to life in Siberian exile. Lenin went into hiding, his role as an effective insurgent leader momentarily neutralized. Both were to be heard from again.

Though clandestine terrorist activity would continue for nearly two years, its sporadic and haphazard nature would render it largely ineffective. The revolution had been abortive. Count Sergius Witte, Premier of Russia since Phleve's assassination and author of the October Manifesto, wasted no time in rendering that document's provisions as meaningless as possible. His "Fundamental Laws" were promulgated. Even before the elections to the newly created Duma, they proclaimed the nature of the Russian state to be that of autocracy still, and the Tsar still the Tsar. Nikolai, who had never liked Witte personally but had always admired his abilities, waited just long enough for the minister to use his unparalleled prestige to obtain two billion francs on loan from Paris.[12] Then, having lost faith in the man's statecraft and his power to avert national catastrophy, he politely dismissed him from office, unfortunately replacing him with the colorless nonentity Goremykin.

The day of the locusts had not yet come. Weary from strife, Russia continued to be plagued by a horde of bureaucrats as venal, self-seeking, and stultifying as those to be found anywhere, the inheritors of the system established by Peter the Great. Taken all in all, the guidance of the Russian state at this particularly hazardous period of history would have been a monumental task even for Aleksandr III. For Nikolai II, the gentle family man who deplored force and violence, and was never really happy except when with his wife and children, the situation bore intrinsically the seeds of ultimate disaster. In a way, Aleksandr III is reminiscent of the prerevolutionary King Louis XV of France, who spoke prophetically of revolution, "*Après moi le déluge*" ("After me the flood.")—but with the difference that the powerful Russian ruler may not have been astute enough to see it coming. Unfortunately for himself, those he loved, and the many family members, courtiers, country gentry, and government employees who depended on him, it was an awareness that eluded his royal son as well—until it was too late.

The dreaded blood disease designated hemophilia is one of humanity's oldest curses. Called by many names, it was known to pre-Helenistic Greeks, to Etruscans before there was a Rome, in ancient Mesopotamia's Ur of the Chaldees, and in the Nilotic kingdoms of the Pharaohs in both Upper and Lower Egypt. In Iron Age Israel, talmudic scribes recorded its ravages. During China's Shang Dynasty (1523–1027 B.C.), it was also not unheard of. A mystery then, it has remained one down through the centuries. Although modern medical science has made some progress with seemingly related maladies such as hemolytic anemia, the cause of hemophilia has not yet been precisely pinpointed, nor is there any known cure.

On August 12, 1904, when Tsarevich Aleksei Nikolaievich was born, his ecstatic parents viewed his coming as nothing less than a divine miracle, for this very pretty child with his bright blue eyes and blonde hair appeared to the couple as God's response to their many prayers. Yet a month and a half had scarcely passed before the baby hemorrhaged from the navel, bleeding in an unquenchable flow which the Tsar, becoming alarmed, recorded in his diary as lasting all day, and this despite the best efforts of the finest court physicians. There was more blood on the second day. On the third it ceased, but over the ensuing months there developed an ominous group of symptoms which taken collectively were unmistakable. When, during the process of trying to walk, the baby fell repeatedly, his limbs quickly became swollen and discolored, the visible bruises being the result of subcutaneous hematoma. It was particularly evident about the joints. He was bleeding under the skin. As veins and capillaries ruptured sequentially, it became clear to the doctors that the infant's blood system lacked those coagulatory properties which in a healthy person would staunch the flow in minutes. Very reluctantly, with infinite regret, they announced their diagnosis to the Tsar and Tsaritsa. The Tsarevich Aleksei, heir to the imperial throne of the Romanovs and their only son, was a hemophiliac.

The disease is inherited. Although women are invariably the carriers, they are not affected by it themselves except in very rare instances, but they pass it to their male offspring (according to current medical thinking) in the form of a defective gene. Although referred to as a "disease," clearly it is not the result of bacterial or viral infection. Rather, it appears to occur when a gene harboring the defect penetrates the nucleus of a critical cell and alters the chromosomes within it.

All human cells, except those of sperm and ova at particular stages of development, contain forty-six chromosomes each. The latter carry cell information. They direct cell growth, reproduction by division, such chemical productivity as that of protein generation, and the body's entire metabolism, including the activation of its natural defenses. The disseminating units of information are the genes themselves, generally called DNA (deoxyribonucleic acid) because it is this chemical of which they are largely composed. A defective gene that has been chemically altered will give false information to the cell. White blood corpuscle defense against disease may break down drastically in what is called a *point mutation*. So may the chemical manufacture of coagulant to control blood flow, as in the case of victims of hemophilia. Admittedly, all this is still somewhat theoretical, although perhaps not far off the mark. In the opening years of the century, however, not even this information was available.

Of those female progenitors of Tsaritsa Aleksandra who collectively had made her a carrier of hemophilia, by far the best known was her grandmother, Queen Victoria, who with her German consort Prince Albert had produced four sons and five daughters.[13] It is characteristic of the malady's capriciousness that only the last born of those sons, Leopold, Duke of Albany, was a hemophiliac. However, subsequent births of royal males showed that two of the princesses, the afflicted babies' mothers Alice and Beatrice, carried the crucial gene. Alice was the mother of Aleksandra.

With the birth of her child and the ultimate identification of his dread illness, Tsaritsa Aleksandra Feodorovna became the bearer of several crosses at once. The most terrible of them to this stricken woman lay in the periodic intense suffering of her little son, a child all the more beloved of his parents because of his incurable infirmity. It was her helplessness to do anything about it that took the worst toll of her, as it would of any normal mother. But added to this was the inescapable guilt factor, for it had long been understood in medicine that those male offspring who contracted hemophilia received it through the female line. Though she may have given it little thought before her marriage, now that tragedy had befallen Aleksandra had no illusions about it. Her mother had borne eight children. Like herself, her sister Irene was a carrier. One of her brothers, Friedrich, had hemophilia and had died some years earlier from bleeding as the result of a fall. As one consequence of royal intermarriage in Western Europe, this curse, which may have spread to Great Britain through the German House of Hanover, was now prevalent among the royal families of England, Spain, and Russia. And she, Aleksandra, had carried it to St. Petersburg.

The other aspects of her misery, though less ruinously traumatic,

were magnified by the Tsaritsa because she felt herself driven into a
corner. This shy woman, sensitive and introverted, needed praise,
encouragement, and the support of those who really cared, but nearly
everywhere she looked she encountered only veiled ridicule and ill-
concealed hostility. She never knew how to cope with it. In a decade
of marriage to Nikolai she had produced four daughters, and in so
doing had incurred the contempt of nearly everyone at court, people
quite ignorant of the fact that the sex of a child is determined by the
father alone. Nikolai's mother, Dowager Empress Maria Feodorovna,
disliked her daughter-in-law and gossiped about her, and the clique
which had long surrounded the older woman was relentlessly antagonistic. It did not help that some said the Tsar's mother had incestuous
leanings towards him and would have had small sympathy for *any* life
partner he might have chosen. It was a game the Tsaritsa could never
win. The situation was aggravated by the fact that Russian court
protocol, with curious illogic, made a reigning empress second to a
dowager empress, a prestige factor bound to be resented by anyone
in Aleksandra's position.

When Alexei was born it seemed that she had vindicated herself,
having at last provided the heir for whose lack she had been condemned. But dark rumors were soon circulating about the child's
health. The parents became cautious, secretive, confiding only in a
select few. As they withdrew from public life more and more the
court shrank and its functions were drastically reduced. At first, the
courtiers—including the grand dukes and duchesses closely related
to the royal pair—were puzzled by this, and not a few considered it
a serious affront. Then, as it became obvious to them that their once-
active social lives (all for which most of them lived) were being rapidly
curtailed, the chagrin of many turned to outright hatred for the royal
couple they considered responsible.

In both intensity and scope the already long active salon life in
St. Petersburg redoubled, the direct result of a languishing court.
From having been more or less purely social affairs (albeit wildly
licentious in many cases), some salons acquired a political cast as
ministers of state no longer in the reclusive Tsar's confidence sought
other means of gathering information or other avenues to power.
Already by the year 1905, the new fad of parapsychology had invested

the capital and largely disreputable practitioners of the occult were spreading their practices like wildfire. There were mystics of every description, students of the Black Arts, prophets, clairvoyants, faith healers, alchemists, and more necromancers presiding at séances than any city of Eastern Europe had ever seen before.

It was a bizarre world. Caught in the midst of it yet desperately trying to remain aloof, the Tsar and Tsaritsa adopted outlandish measures. Because the Orthodox Church could not seem to help them, they turned to mysticism.[14] Because if Aleksei fell or bumped himself the doctors were helpless to control the awful result, they detailed Dyerevyenko, a brawny Ukrainian sailor from the Baltic fleet as the boy's guardian and constant companion, his primary duty to ensure the fact that the Tsarevich could *not* injure himself. This, of course, required intense and highly restrictive supervision. Having all the playful desires of a normal little boy, and considerable energy when not under hemophilic attack, Aleksei wanted to run, jump, play mischievous tricks on his sisters, and indeed indulge in all the more vigorous antics of childhood. Dyerevyenko, who loved him and feared for him, was diligent not to allow it. His assistant, a slender young sailor named Nagorny, was equally so.

All to no avail. It happened at the Aleksandr Palace at Tsarskoe Selo (the words mean "the Tsar's Village") when Aleksei was four. Accompanied by Dyerevyenko and his nurse, Maria Vishniakova, he had been playing in the park. He was not unusually active. Suddenly, as his companions for once failed in their duty, he lurched and fell. Within moments he was helpless and almost fainting, and had to be carried indoors and immediately to his bed. The Tsar and Tsaritsa were notified at once. So was Eugen Botkin, the Tsar's personal physician and chiefest of the doctors ministering to the Tsarevich. The boy was in dire straits. Already in internal hemorrhage, he was white as a sheet, mumbling incoherently between wailing groans, and twisted in fearful agony. Muscle spasms in one leg had bent it double and it could not be straightened. The distraught parents were in hell. It was the worst attack on their son they had yet seen.

At the end of three days a strange and fateful event occurred, an event which was to have worldwide consequences, which in the opinion of many historians was ultimately to affect the destiny of the human race. During all those many hours the Tsaritsa had not left her son's side, taken only the most meager nourishment, and prayed nearly incessantly. She had become weak from worry and grief. In vain did the tearful Nikolai, as sleepless as she, plead with her to give over and try to get some rest. She would not abandon her vigil. Seemingly, from somewhere in the depths of her terrible concern, she found the strength to maintain it even though her head nodded more and more frequently and her eyes closed as she sat in her chair.

It was in this pitiful condition that she was found by the Grand Duchess Anastasia Nikolayevna, called Stana, one of the Montenegrin sisters, wife to the tall general, Grand Duke Nikolai Nikolayevich. Stana has been accused of several unpleasant things, among them the vice of insincerity and of being politically unscrupulous concerning her husband's career. Be that as it may, she was able to comfort the Empress of Russia, to assuage to some extent the grief of a mother who only a short time ago had heard her child ask his father if he might be buried in the park. It was Stana who reminded the Tsaritsa of the great healing powers and holiness of the *starets* from Pokrovskoye, of the miracles he had worked on both sides of the Urals, of the certainty that he had been sent to them by God. When Aleksandra, exhausted and half faint, began to weep, Stana took her in her arms. But both knew it was time. Over and over, the name of the Siberian crossed their lips. Acceptance of God's will was in their eyes. Stana could think of no one else. Aleksandra longed for him desperately: Rasputin.

He was not sure of the time or even if it were night or day. He was Grigori Efimovich, and all that he now visually experienced was with the lens of his inner eye, a lantern of the soul unreliable as to outer impressions, a gleam from the living God that had come to him out of infinite vastnesses of space and endless eons of time. He could hear the pounding of the horses' hooves, vaguely feel the motion of the carriage, even sense, like a wraith on the dim periphery of consciousness, the huddled figure of the Grand Duchess beside him. Her servants had searched for him everywhere, she said. It was curious how he could understand her words, how her meaning penetrated his brain though they occupied different spheres of being on worlds that were far apart. He found himself responding rationally to the few anxious sentences she uttered, but all the time a most vital part of him was searching for the light on that rarified plain he occupied, praying with all that was in him for that miraculous, god-given power to heal the Tsarevich of Russia.

Fifteen miles to the south of St. Petersburg's outer environs it lay. This was the length of his journey to Tsarskoe Selo, he knew, an enchanted realm, a retreat of grandeur and solitude begun in the long ago by Pyotr Veliki's daughter Elizaveta and completed by Tsaritsa Ekaterina Velikaya (Empress Catherine the Great), whose many lovers gave her reason to yearn for a special privacy. They arrived almost before he realized it. Yes, there was the wrought iron fence he had heard about, so high and imposing, displaying the Imperial crest. There were the brightly uniformed guards, mounted Cossacks trotting in pairs, unmounted infantry stiffly at attention at the great gate. He looked beyond the railing through the tall trees. Yes, it was daylight. He saw it now. The Aleksandr Palace was before him, white, stately but comparatively plain as observers had said, yet graced by Their Majesties' presence. A quarter mile distant was the second one, the Ekaterina Palace, much larger and more ornate, unoccupied save for a host of servants and caretakers. He was like those servants, he thought, men and women who stood ever in readiness but served no one. But perhaps his time had come.

They passed through the main gate but did not approach the palace from the front. Instead, they took another way and arrived at a side entrance. Liveried footmen were waiting. Stana was helped to alight. Although the lackeys stared at him curiously and one of them made a slight bow, he, the bizarre wonderworker of questionable reputation, was allowed to fend for himself. Then he was in the palace. He had been in palaces before, for both Montenegrin sisters lived in them. But *here* was regal grandeur, here the soldiers of the Imperial Guard, armed, wordless, stiffly at attention, two of them escorting Stana and himself up what he believed was a rear staircase. Were they ashamed of him then? He felt no resentment. The Tsar and Tsaritsa could do no wrong, for they ruled by God's will. Everything was on their weary shoulders, the entire burden of state. They had woes and cares that people never dreamed of.

They made their way down a long corridor. More guards. Unsmiling, tight-lipped faces quarried from flint, silently expressionless. A man approached with a brace of beautiful *borzoi* (Russian wolfhounds) on gilded leashes, a breed he had first seen as a boy in Tyumen when Irina Danilova made such a fool of him. They stopped to scent him, then passed by. At the end, there were four huge Negroes uniformed and turbaned as what he supposed were Turks, and it was then he knew they stood at the door of the sickroom.

They were ushered in by guards. Those present, he was later to remember, were the Tsar and Tsaritsa; their daughters, the four grand duchesses; Archimandrite Theofan; Dr. Botkin with a nurse; and the Tsaritsa's favorite lady-in-waiting, Anna Aleksandrovna Vyrubova.[15] They all gazed at him intently. Stana seemed to fade from view. The Empress, dark rings under her bloodshot eyes, a figure of unimagined weariness, rose unsteadily from her chair to greet him. He lifted his hand and made the Sign of the Cross, blessing them all. He caught the Tsar in his arms and embraced him strongly, kissing the bearded cheeks three times in the Russian fashion, calling him *"Batiushka"* (Father) as he had done before. Then with infinite tenderness he embraced the Tsaritsa, calling her *"Matushka"* (Mother), kissing her in the same way, begging the Almighty to allow at least a portion of his vital energy and warmth to pass through his hands and lips into her chilled and weakened body. When she raised his rough hand with her own trembling ones and kissed it he wanted to weep, to go down on his knees before her and beg her blessing as the Little Mother of the Russians. He resisted the urge. It was *he* who had to be strong today, stronger than any of them; by God's will, stronger than death itself. With every fiber of his being he begged for this strength *now*.

As he moved toward the Tsarevich there was a perfect silence in the room, a stillness so profound he was never to forget it. He knelt by the bedside. The boy's eyes were closed, his gaunt face as pallid as wax, his breathing labored, shallow. "I am Grigori Efimovich, the carter of Pokrovskoye," he heard himself saying in his mind, "and by God's grace I cannot fail." Behind him, he knew without looking that the others, too, had gone to their knees, collectively offering up a single fervent prayer for the recovery of the child. Thus they all remained for many minutes. He took the little hand of the Tsarevich and held it. It was almost cold. Had it meant *anything* that day, the vision in the sun-dappled forest glade, the blindingly glorious light of the Virgin of Kazan? Or was he, Rasputin, mad? Everywhere he found more hate than love, a horde of enemies and few friends. Would they spit on his grave, call him liar and fake, dishonor his broken remains? It didn't matter. All that mattered was the child, the tiny dying prince who was the very *soul* of Russia. All that mattered . . .

Gradually he felt it. The vital energy that seemed to be his yet came from another world, the *cosmic force* that made him different from others yet would be the cause of his downfall, *this* force, like the ectoplasm of a phantom, the embodied spirituality of a Tungusic *shaman* a thousand years buried in the snows of Siberia, was entering the ravaged body of the boy. It was fulfillment. Redemption. If he never accomplished anything else as long as he lived—*this* he had done. This . . . he had done.

He stood up. He gazed at the pale and wasted face, the colorless lips which every doctor of the Court believed would never speak again. Something welled up inside him in a sort of effusion of inner joy as spontaneous as sunlight, and he smiled at the four-year-old, speaking to him quietly, tenderly.

"Open your eyes, my son. Open your eyes and look at me."[16]

All the watchers were on their feet now. No sound could be heard save his own voice, his own softness. He felt it flow from him, flowing and entering, flowing . . . and entering. The eyes of the Tsarevich opened. Blue eyes. Intensely blue. At first, he seemed not to see or know where he was, awakening as a dreamer awakens, not understanding. Then he looked at the man of the voice and smiled. It was a slow smile, developing in stages, but it brought a sigh of infinite joy from the Tsaritsa, made the Tsar's lip tremble, drew gasps of wonder and intense relief from the others. *Redemption.*

Rasputin heard them and his gesture brought quiet. Then he heard his own voice again, the words forming on his lips as though spoken by someone else.

"Your pain is going away; you will soon be well. You must thank God for healing you. And now, go to sleep."[17]

The tiny sufferer's eyes closed. Within moments he seemed to be sleeping peacefully, free of the feverishness and fitful squirming that had racked him before—free, above all, of pain. Both small legs were straight now. Rasputin turned about. All eyes were on him. In those of the Imperial couple was the sheer wonder of people who believed they had witnessed an act of God, and a boundless gratitude. Again he heard his own voice as though it was another who spoke.

"The Tsarevich will live."[18]

The Tsaritsa wept openly, believing, nearly overcome, awestruck to the depths of her soul, as only a woman could be who thought herself in the presence of a divine emissary. He walked to her and put his hand gently on her shoulder, knowing clairvoyantly her past agonies, his heart overflowing with sympathy. Then he spoke to her with his eyes.

"I love thee, Mother Russia. Thou art my life."

NOTES

1. The Tsar's uncles were Grand Duke Vladimir Aleksandrovich, Commandant of the Imperial Guard; Grand Duke Alexei Aleksandrovich, Grand Admiral of the Navy; Grand Duke Serge Aleksandrovich, Governor General of Moscow; and Grand Duke Pavel Aleksandrovich, without military or political distinction at the time. Only the latter did not attempt to influence Nikolai. In January of 1919, Pavel was executed by the Bolsheviks.

2. German Chancellor Otto von Bismarck's system of alliances had depended heavily on Russia. However, Wilhelm's support for Austria's Balkan policy would have made a Russo-German entente impossible in any case.

3. As it happened, the Japanese plenipotentiary, Marquis Ito, was given no chance to protest, for the Tsar and his ministers made themselves inacessible to him.

4. Vice-Admiral Lord Nelson.

5. The Dogger Bank "incident" nearly provoked a war with England. Especially galling to the British was the fact that even though they recognized their mistake almost as soon as it was made, in their haste to be off the nervous Russians failed to pick up survivors.

6. The delay was to allow the Tsar's government time to reinforce the fleet in the event that foreign warships could be bought. Despite the vigorous efforts of tsarist purchasing agents in various countries, they could not.

7. In 1925, the noted Russian film director Serge Eisenstein made the motion picture *The Battleship Potëmkin*. Though technically outstanding, it considerably distorted known fact, thus adding to the effectiveness of Soviet mythology.

8. The Russian and Japanese representatives went to New Hampshire at the invitation of President Theodore Roosevelt.

9. After the march, Gapon disappeared. Suspected by the revolutionaries of being a double agent working for the tsarist police, he was later tracked down by them and murdered in Finland.

10. Lenin's father, Ilya Ulyanov, was of mixed Great Russian and Tatar ancestry; his mother, Maria Blank, a Volga German.

11. From *menshiviki* ("minority"), as distinguished from *bolsheviki* ("majority"). Having been expelled from Brussels by the Belgian police in July of 1903, the leaders of the Russian Social Democratic Party, Nicolai Lenin and Georg Plekhanov, fled with their followers to London. There, splitting on the question of party organization, Lenin thereafter led the Bolsheviks (extremist wing) and Plekhanov the Mensheviks (moderates), much like the Jacobins (led by Robespierre) and the Girondins (led by Brissot de Warville and others) during the French Revolution.

12. Witte's reputation derived largely from his having been the "brain" behind the building of the Trans-Siberian Railroad, his improvement of Russian industry, and his successful negotiations at Portsmouth following the disastrous Russo-Japanese War.

13. Albert was the son of Ernst I, Duke of Saxe-Coburg and Gotha, and in Germany had been Prinz Albrecht.

14. One of the mystics they consulted was Shamzaran Badmaev (Russian name Pyotr Aleksandrovich), a Buriat Mongol miracle worker and magician who appears to have been born in Irkutsk, Siberia, and raised in mysterious Tibet. Although he developed a great reputation in St. Petersburg, with regard to treatment of the Tsarevich, his truly outstanding knowledge of Tibetan medicine was unavailing. Curiously enough, far from being jealous or envious of Rasputin, he was later to develop a close friendship with him.

15. Beginning with the eldest, the Tsar's daughters were Olga, Tatiana, Maria, and Anastasia. The latter's title and name, Grand Duchess Anastasia Nikolayevna, were identical to those of the younger of the Montenegrin royal sisters.

16. Her father's words as Maria Rasputin remembered them. See Maria Rasputin and Patte Barham, *Rasputin: The Man Behind the Myth*, Warner Books, New York, 1977. (Published by arrangement with Prentice-Hall, Inc.)

17. *Ibid.*

18. *Ibid.*

CHAPTER 7

Enter Iliodor

In the downstairs living room of the big two-story house he had built for his family Rasputin sat alone. Darkness had fallen and the evening was well advanced. Still, even though the turmoil within him was gradually growing as his anger deepened, he waited for the inevitable settling down of the household, for that profound silence that would tell him his wife Praskovia had at last dropped off to sleep. Beside him on the table a brace of candles burned, for this he had told Dunia Bekyeshova was all the light he needed. Into the flame of one of them he stared intently. It is like a miniature sun, he told himself, as though the blazing fires of that hot star had been reduced only to this, as though he sat in some far corner of the earth and would in time see it gutter and die.

He found that his mind that had been seized with rage was calmer now. Yet such was Dunia's fear of an emotional crisis that he had been here several days on this visit before she told him of the incident. His own Maria. His precious little girl. It was her ill luck that of all the girls in the village she had befriended the unfortunate child called Lili, worse luck still that with the ailing Praskovia absent at the time in a St. Petersburg hospital Dunia had given his daughter permission to accept the invitation of Lili's unhappy mother.

It should have been all right, shouldn't it? Such a simple thing, to stay overnight at Lili's tiny *isba* and sleep with her little friend. But Lili's mother had not counted on the child's stepfather, the drunken, bad-tempered *muzhik* with his eye on every female regardless of age. Apparently, she had not known what he would do or had not believed it. But the swine had shown his true nature soon enough. Rasputin winced at the memory of Dunia's words, of the things she had said to him only an hour before in this very room, repeating the tale his Maria had told her with trembling voice and tearful eyes. How rotten it all was. The man drinking cheap peasant wine until besotted, demanding and getting goodnight kisses first from Lili, then Maria, followed by his deeply sensuous mouth kiss of Rasputin's daughter and his attempt to seduce her on the spot.

The candles had grown dimmer, he noted. Outside, the murk had lightened somewhat as the moon had risen. His thoughts quickened. Maria in the drunken brute's arms, fondled intimately as Lili's mother pulled her away from him and turned to face his wrath. She had paid for her interference. He had ripped off her clothes, thrown her on the floor, and raped her in full view of the two very frightened girls. Then he had urinated in front of them. Then he and his bruised, exhausted wife had fallen asleep. Only afterward did Maria leave the place and return to her home, disheveled and burning with shame, to fall tearfully into Dunia's arms and speak of her experience.

Rasputin got up. If he examined his child he was sure he would find her hymen had been broken by the man's probing fingers. It was enough. Praskovia was asleep. He leaned over and blew out the candles.

Outside, there was a light breeze blowing as he stepped into the moonlit night. He knew the direction. Lili's *isba* was on the outskirts of the village and he would be there in minutes. He began to walk. Behind Pokrovskoye's shuttered windows the rustic settlement seemed almost empty. Here and there was a thin thread of light. Would Praskovia be all right now? Would she get well? He wanted to dwell on thoughts of his convalescent wife because he sensed that therein lay sanity, but his mind was like a kaleidoscope of conflicting emotions. Like the Hindu *yogis* so often the topic of conversation in St. Petersburg society, he tried to adjust his breathing. Could he do it? He feared his own rage, for he knew it could cause him to kill and thus imperil his soul. Moonlight. A quiet village. The bearded, hard-as-nails *starets* bent on a mission of vengeance.

He stopped in midstride and stood very still, a statue under the moon. What caused this nagging self-guilt? Ah, he knew. *He* was the real perpetrator. If he had not neglected his family by staying so long in the capital such things as this would not happen. And Dunia bothered him. Since his return this time she had troubled him continuously, for at last he had noted that look in her eyes, and at last he knew. She was in love with him. He realized now that she had *always* loved him, perhaps even from that day so long ago in Tyumen when she alone among her mistress's six maid servants would not join them in abusing him. How long she had suffered and yearned for him in silence, loyal to his wife in her own quiet way, loyal, also, to some self-imposed code deep within her conscience.

He started to walk again. Then he saw ahead the *isba* he sought, drew near it, and put all thoughts of her from his mind. In moments he was before the crudely fashioned dwelling. He stood very still. Was it time? Was it really time to put it to the test? He was aware of the ever-increasing potency of his psychic powers. Always he had used them for good, never once for evil. Now, for the first time he wondered if it were possible to kill with them, if by a greater and greater concentration of the will, by focusing the knife blade of his mind more and more intensely on the wrongdoer he could stop his heart and freeze his blood in his veins, strike him down like a felled ox. It was *unthinkable. Satanic.*

As the possibility expanded in his inner consciousness, growing there, the question of delivering death by psychically induced paralysis began to obsess him and he felt himself on the edge of summoning those occult forces into being, of conjuring the demon he had often believed was *within him.* He looked up at the trees. They seemed lined with shimmering flame. He looked at the sky. It glowed red—like a Siberian forest fire. He knew he must check this. He must stop it, force it back, smash it before it engulfed him and God knew who else. Fight the man, yes, kill him if necessary, but not with the forces of the supernatural, not with the Devil's wind that came from hell. Staring at the door of the hut, he called out the miscreant's name. There followed a long moment of silence. In a voice harsh with condemnation he shouted it a second time, demanding that he appear.

Seconds passed. From inside came the sounds of a commotion as though a chair might have been overturned. Then the door was flung open and the man came out, large and bearlike in the moonglow. Characteristically, he was drunk. He clearly staggered and the wine fumes were strong. Even in the poor light Rasputin thought he detected a sneer of scathing contempt on his face. He heard his own voice hot with rage and malice that was almost choking him.

"How dared you act as you did in front of my daughter? Maria is a young and innocent girl. . . ."[1]

He got no further. The hand the man had hidden behind his back appeared. It gripped an ax handle. Closing the distance with unexpected quickness he swung instantly, viciously. Rasputin was struck a glancing blow on the forehead. The light in his brain flickered out. Deprived of consciousness, he pitched headlong to the earth and lay still. From his torn-open scalp the blood flowed heavily.

Rasputin had the habit of parting his hair down the center. For the existence of the broad scar interrupting that part, hairless due to scar tissue, his biographers have given several explanations. Yet it seems obvious that his daughter Maria would know how the injury was incurred, having been close to the scene at the time, and it is from her that the above-stated cause was taken. Concerning the peasant who struck her father down (the blow produced a mild concussion but did not fracture the skull) there is little to add. Aware that angry villagers would punish him severely he fled Pokrovskoye, abandoning his wife and stepchild, and was never seen again.[2]

Rasputin's first return to his home after a little more than two years in St. Petersburg was not the visit during which he was attacked, for that came later. On this occasion, the existence of the Trans-Siberian Railroad spared him an arduous trek of hundreds of miles on foot. His wife Praskovia Feodorovna was not well. One night, Maria tells us, she heard the sound of her mother's agonized scream come from her parents' bedroom. She ran to the door and knocked. Her mother made light of the incident, and when the girl tried to question her about it the next morning her replies revealed nothing and she pointedly avoided the subject. Apparently, she deceived Rasputin as to the severity of her condition, for he returned to St. Petersburg shortly afterward.

Possibly the best-known photograph of Rasputin. The scar inflicted by the axe handle shows clearly. So does the incredible hypnotic power of his eyes. (*Culver Pictures*)

Rasputin as a young man on his Siberian farm with his children (*from left*) Maria, Varya, and Dmitri. (*Culver Pictures*)

Nikolai and Aleksandra in court ceremonial dress such as that worn by
the first Románov, Tsar Mikhail (1613–1645) and his wife, in an
engraving made from a photo by Levitsky, 1903. (*Culver Pictures*)

Nikolai II, Tsar of All the Russias. (*Culver Pictures*)

Nikolai and Aleksandra with Tsarevich Aleksei. (*Culver Pictures*)

Nikolai and Aleksandra with their children. *Seated, from left*: Olga, the Tsar, Anastasia, Aleksei, and Tatiana. *Standing*: Maria and the Tsaritsa. (*Culver Pictures*)

Rasputin in the midst of his court a few weeks before his murder. Identifiable are Anna Virubova (*standing, fifth from left*) and Akulina Nikichkina (*seated, on the floor at Rasputin's left*). A copy of this photo, mentioned in Chapter 7, is in the author's possession. (*Culver Pictures*)

Rasputin with two general officers, Loman (*left*) and Putjatin. The latter bears a strong resemblance to Premier Sergius Witte and may have been related to him. (*Culver Pictures*)

Prince Feliks Feliksovich Yussupov and his wife,
Princess Irina Aleksandrovna Yussupova, taken
shortly after their marriage. (*Culver Pictures*)

The deposed Tsar Nikolai and his three eldest daughters as prisoners of
the Communists (Bolsheviks) shortly after being taken to Tobolsk, Siberia,
in July 1917. They are shown on the glass roof of their temporary residence, a hothouse on the estate of the provincial governor. (*Culver Pictures*)

His second visit home was prompted by his wife's increasing illness. She had complained of recurring pain. She grew gradually
weaker. One day, almost without warning she went into vaginal hemorrhage, losing much blood before the flow could be staunched by
Dunia and the local midwife. Dunia urged her to go to the hospital
in Tyumen. Praskovia said she feared hospitals and refused; then
extracted a promise from her maid that Rasputin would not be told.
It could not last, of course. Less than a week later, while directing
field hands at work, she collapsed and had to be helped into the house
by Dunia, Maria, and the other maid Katya, and put to bed.

Under such pressing circumstances Dunia could not keep her
promise. She telegraphed Rasputin. He reacted at once. Now his
stricken wife did go to Tyumen, then to St. Petersburg where she
was examined by the best doctors of the Imperial Court. They found
a tumor of the reproductive organs. A renowned surgeon operated.
So highly was Rasputin valued by the royal family that Militsa's
husband, Grand Duke Pyotr Nikolayevich, not only paid all her bills
but hired a private nurse to remain in constant attendance on her as
long as might be necessary. Rasputin returned to Pokrovskoye with
her. It was then, while Praskovia was convalescing, that he confronted
Lili's stepfather and was injured.

It was this violent incident that was to change Maria's life. After
his own recovery, Rasputin, coming to the conclusion that life in
Pokrovskoye would never again be the same for their daughter, consulted with his wife and suggested that the girl return with him to
St. Petersburg. Praskovia was reluctant. Rasputin reminded her of
the advantages for Maria culturally and educationally, how she could
study music and art under famous masters if she chose, take courses
in Russian and foreign literature, attend the opera and ballet, even go
with him to Tsarskoye Selo to meet the Emperor and Empress as
their honored guest. When Praskovia questioned Maria about it she
found the child was eager to grasp this once-in-a-lifetime opportunity,
especially as occasional trips home could be arranged. At last the
mother relented. It was agreed that once a normal dwelling had been
established Dunia would join them as a housemaid. If Praskovia felt
any unease at this she did not reveal it.

It was the year 1907 and Maria Gregorievna Rasputina was ten years old. She had always idealized her father, a man who in her eyes was the most remarkable human on earth. Soon, in fabled St. Petersburg, she would have opportunities to see just how extraordinary he really was.

There is something in the Russian soul that yearns for pathos and tragedy, indeed at times seems actively to court a dark fate as though by so doing some fusion of as yet unresurrected humanity with the sublime majesty of the godhead might become real. England's Lesley Blanch has caught the essence of this philosophy in her book *The Sabres of Paradise*, heretofore mentioned, a study of the Murid Wars in the Caucasus. She writes

> The extravagant Slav temperament was to be traced in all classes of society and was never more marked than in the whole nation's positively abandoned attitude toward suffering. *Toska*, a sort of inner misery, a neuralgia of the soul, a compound of *cafard* and spleen, permeated the nineteenth-century Russian nature. . . . *Dousha*, the soul—ever a matter for introspective discussion among the classic Russians, as portrayed in their literature—was generally held to represent the *suffering* soul. This occupied a special place, becoming a national attribute, almost a matter of pride—like sex to the French.

From such an obsession with the deepest manifestations of the psyche it is only a step to the full embrace of every possible aspect of spiritualism and the occult. In the second half of the nineteenth century, in St. Petersburg in particular this tendency was reflected in the various aspects of Russian culture, especially in literature and music. Thus Tolstoi, in his great novel *Anna Karenina*, deals with the imponderable of predestination, with the fatalistic acceptance of that which cannot be avoided even unto death. Anna's end is as inevitable as her suffering over her lover Vronski. When she leaps under the all-obliterating wheels of the moving train, the reader is struck by the overwhelming conviction that for her no other consummation was possible.[3]

Tolstoi did not die until the winter of 1910, when he collapsed

at the railroad station at Astapovo. He was the last of the creative
titans whose names are associated with nineteenth-century Russia.
Pushkin had died in 1837, Lermontov in 1841, Gogol in 1852, Glinka
in 1857, Dostoevsky and Moussorgsky in 1881, Turgeniev in 1883,
Borodin in 1887, Tchaikovsky in 1893, and Chekhov in 1904. In 1907,
the year in which Rasputin took Maria to St. Petersburg, Rimsky-
Korsakov had but a year to live. His extraordinarily beautiful music
had strengthened the Russian fascination with mysticism. One saw
touches of it in his operas *The Snow Maiden*, *Sadko*, and *Le Coq d'Or*,
all of them highly fanciful and based on legend. With the production
of *The Invisible City of Kitezh* this trend had reached its fullest fruition.
Russians accepted the fabulous as normal. They earnestly embraced
the more outlandish aspects of parapsychology. They were, after all,
the only European inheritors of the age-old Asian tradition of shamanism.

Who was now left to carry forward this splendid creative legacy?
Almost from the soul of Tchaikovsky, as a phoenix rising from the
ashes, sprang the genius of his friend Rachmaninov; from Rimsky-
Korsakov, his pupils Ippolitov-Ivanov, Stravinsky, and Prokofiev.
There were other great strides in the arts, and with rare exceptions,
St. Petersburg was the scene of their development. In the rarefied
world of ballet, Mathilde Kschessinska (once the Tsar's love), Tamara
Karsavina, and Anna Pavlova were the unforgettable prima ballerinas,
rising to greatness under the famed choreographer Marius Petipa when
the still unknown Georg Balanchine was only a boy. In time, though
young Vaslav Nijinsky might sleep with his lover, the brilliant impresario Serge Diaghilev, his predilection for his own sex did not
prevent him from soaring to unprecedented heights in the art of the
dance.[4]

Added to the occultism and aesthetic creativity so prevalent in St.
Petersburg, and in a certain sense a comanifestation of both, was yet
a third ingredient which with the others collectively constituted the
warp and woof of life in this remarkable metropolis, that of highly
aberrant sex. No city in the world was more given to licentiousness;
not such flesh emporiums of the Far East as Shanghai, Bangkok, and
Saigon; or those of India such as Calcutta and Bombay; or those of
the Middle East such as Istanbul, Damascus, Beirut, Tyre, and Sidon.
As a market for child sex, for example, St. Petersburg was the peer

of Bombay and Bangkok, both notorious for this. As a center for lavishly staged scenes of sodomy, sadomasochism, and bestiality, the bordellos just off the Nevsky Prospekt were unequaled in their salacious ingenuity even by the notorious Reeperbahn in the German city of Hamburg. Girls of many nations and races were available. Some were West European, victims of kidnapping who had come to Russia via the distant slave markets in such forbidden Arabian cities as Mecca and Medina. Others had been transported to North Africa, had served for a time in the Muslim seraglios of Cairo, Tripoli, Algiers, or Casablanca, then been resold as used and marked-down merchandise already inured to the lower depths of depravity.

Why was the pace of life so frenzied, the endless search for diversion, sexual or otherwise, so intense? Remember Poe's short story, "The Masque of the Red Death"? When people are surrounded by a nameless threat and racked by fear, when some sixth sense rather than any conscious mental process fills them with dread of impending catastrophy, they invariably seek the wildest, most insensate pursuits of which humanity is capable.[5] St. Petersburg at the time was not only a city of endless harlotry, drinking, and gambling for high stakes, it also had what may well have been the world's highest suicide rate. Among noblemen, duels to the death were very common, much more so than in Berlin, Paris, or London, say, even though dueling was everywhere illegal and punishable by imprisonment. Life was short, planning for it useless, happiness fleeting. Therefore, why not game and carouse and drain life to its utmost dregs? Now, even more than at any previous time, the infamous game of Russian roulette was played by others as well as army officers. Take a revolver with six chambers, five empty and one loaded. Spin the cylinder, place muzzle to temple, pull the trigger. If no explosion occurs, raise the bets and spin again. Life in any case is merely an illusion. How many times can one spin and survive? Who knows? Play on, sons of the steppe. Just play on.

In eleventh-century Persia, the poet-philosopher Omar Khayyám wrote passionately of the insane inconsequence of life itself, life in *any* age.

> Yesterday this day's
> Madness did prepare;

> Tomorrow's silence,
>   Triumph or despair:
> Drink! For you know not
>   whence you came nor
>   why:
> Drink! For you know not
>   why you go nor where.[6]

Russians would have understood these lines then. Today, they would grasp their meaning more clearly than ever.[7]

Despite the diligent efforts of the Tsar, the Tsaritsa, and the officials of the Imperial Court to keep all knowledge concerning the Tsarevich from the public, rumors of the miracle of healing performed by the Siberian *starets* at Tsarskoye Selo were quick to reach the capital and circulate widely there. Once that occurred, it was not long before the revered holy man of Pokrovskoye and the trans-Ural region was linked with Rasputin as being one and the same, with predictable results. In the crowded but elegant St. Petersburg apartment which he and Maria shared with Grigori Pyotrovich Sasanov and his family he was almost literally besieged by people who daily came to seek favors of one kind or another. Most were poor and many were sick, and these came to him as in France the afflicted of that country, often enduring great privation, journeyed to the town of Lourdes at the foot of the Pyrenees, there to pray in the grotto where in 1858 Saint Bernadette was said to have seen the living Virgin.

Very quickly the fame of "the Starets" spread. As in the India of nearly 2500 years before the stricken and forsaken had sought the self-disinherited Siddhartha Gautama, the Lord Buddha, begging his divinely inspired intercession, so now they came to Rasputin. Many had traveled long distances for the laying on of his hands, others merely to hear his voice or catch a glimpse of him. Was he one of the Khlisti reincarnations of Christ? Not a few were absolutely convinced of it. People did not know precisely the nature of the Tsarevich's illness, only that it was thought to be grave. But here was the wonderworker who had saved the child's life. That much was evident. And who but one of God's "chosen few" could have done it?

There were others who came also. Although they were but a small minority of the total, among them were self-seekers with a wide variety of motives, the merely curious, and a motley array of females of all ages running from actresses and courtesans to highborn members of the nobility. From the more objective sources of information that still exist several things are clear. Although his main concern was for the poor, the ill, and the downtrodden, Rasputin turned no one away. He prayed for all. Many were the crippled and the sick who swore that he had cured them, though most of the written accounts corroborating this were later destroyed by the Bolsheviks. In money he had no interest whatever, taking not a *kopek* from the destitute. When some wealthy politician or aspirant for political preferment pressed a large sum on him (sometimes as much as several 100-ruble notes at a time), he took the cash without counting it, indeed with scarcely a glance. Some he sent home to Pokrovskoye. Far more, it was soon discerned, he gave away to the needy as fast as he had acquired it, and many were the aged widows whose tears he dried, whose hearts he filled with gratitude and hope.

During this period, there were two factors which tended increasingly to disrupt Rasputin's equanimity. The first had to do with Sasanov's fourteen-year-old daughter Marusa, whose room Maria shared. The girl was strikingly attractive. When to her beauty was added the circumstance that she was something of a coquette, it is not surprising that young men in their late teens sought her out with ever greater frequency. This fact was not lost on Rasputin. Fearing Marusa's possible influence he spoke to Maria frankly about it, voicing his misgivings, letting her know that a change of abode would soon be necessary.

The second factor to influence him in his decision to move was his sense of the fitness of things. Although his gracious host never complained and was hospitality personified, Rasputin became increasingly aware that his own hectic way of life was an imposition, something for which the Sasanovs had not bargained. With the growth of their guest's fame it could only get worse, for more and more supplicants and petitioners would surely come to him. As time passed, it became glaringly obvious that something must be done. But how should he go about it? He knew nothing of the vagaries of house hunting, St. Petersburg was overcrowded, and available space was at a premium. The person who came to his aid was one he could not have expected. She was none other than the Tsaritsa's close friend and the daughter of Aleksandr Taneev, Director of the Imperial Chancellory, Anna Aleksandrovna Virubova.

This plumply pretty young woman had first met Rasputin at the home of Grand Duchess Militsa Nikolaevna and had later seen him many times at Tsarskoe Selo. Initially, she was taken aback by his behavior at the grand ducal palace, describing herself much later to Maria (who became her close friend) as being "astounded" by his free and easy manner with the nobility, his audacity at embracing Militsa and giving her the triple kiss normally reserved for one's equals. Yet with the astonishment she felt there was much, much more, an entire gamut of emotions, chiefest of which appear to have been awe and what eventually became a profound reverence. Speaking of that first meeting, she said to his daughter: "I must admit I was quite shocked by his appearance. I saw an elderly *muzhik*, thin, pale of face, long hair, an unkempt beard, and the most extraordinary eyes, large and luminous. He was capable of looking into the very mind and soul of the person with whom he was conversing."[8]

At thirty-six, Rasputin was hardly elderly. His photos of the time reveal no gray in the hair or beard later to be flecked with it, nor were the lines in his face as yet deeply etched. However, even then he had a gauntness accentuated by high and broad cheekbones, a prominent nose, and a full though finely carved mouth, and that alone might have created the impression of greater age. Curiously enough, in some of the photos, especially those taken at close range, the extraordinary piercing quality of the eyes is readily apparent, so much so that to look at them is almost to experience vicariously that compellingly strange hypnotic effect described by his contemporaries. Anna Virubova was enormously impressed, of that there can be no doubt. Drawn very strongly to the Imperial couple, most especially to the Tsaritsa, her sense of wonder was magnified by her knowledge of the vital role Rasputin now played in the royal household.

As it happened, Anna was in something of a quandary. She was engaged to be married. At that time she was still Anna Taneyeva and her fiancé, one of the few Russian survivors of the Battle of Tsushima Strait, was a young naval lieutenant named Boris Virubov. He was highly nervous for one so young, as might be expected of a man who had experienced the tragedy of seeing his vessel go down with most of her ship's company still aboard. Anna was a virgin, well brought up. In Virubov she seemed to sense something that was not quite right. She approached Rasputin, on her lips a question of the utmost importance to her. Then she saw his eyes—"He was so overwhelming"—her courage failed her and she drew back. In the end, she induced the Grand Duchess to ask the question for her. Would her marriage be a good one?

Rasputin's reply was disquieting. The marriage would definitely occur, he told Militsa, glancing at Anna the while, but it would not be a success. And so it came to pass. Virubov, singularly inexperienced in sex for a man of his class, came to his wedding night as much a virgin as his bride. He had had too much to drink. His approach was both crude and direct, and Anna's shocked resistance led him into error, the most profound and ruinous mistake he could have made. He tried to get her to surrender by force. It was a total failure. Outraged and furious, she rejected him utterly. Afterwards, he apologized but to no avail, and before it had really begun the marriage was over. Although she retained her married name for the rest of her life, Anna Virubova wanted no further part of men in the sexual sense.

Yet there is a codicil to the story. Locked in self-imposed celibacy herself, she nonetheless became one of Rasputin's closest followers and a deeply devoted member of that circle of admirers, most of them female, who later came to be called his "court." As such, she could not have been unaware of the carnal nature of many of his relationships, especially in later years. How did she rationalize this? Historians have speculated. Some have said she had a blind spot where the *starets* was concerned, that though she may have deplored his actions she simply closed her eyes to them. The Bolsheviks, ever hostile to anyone close to royalty, later accused her of intimacy with him and of being his procuress, lies that were ultimately refuted.[9] The truth would appear very simple. To her, as to Tsaritsa Aleksandra, Rasputin, if not an actual reincarnation of Christ, was only one step removed. As such he was a prophet of God, an even greater man than the long dead Khlist Radaev, and his acts of whatever nature were sacrosanct and beyond criticism.

It was Anna Virubova who found another dwelling for him. It

was at 64 Gorokhovaya Ulitsa, a spacious third-floor apartment with
five rooms, accessible by front and rear stairways, and perfect for him
and Maria. Shortly after he occupied it, Dunia Bekyeshova came from
Pokrovskoye to serve those she loved. The new residence was to be
Rasputin's last.

    Down through the centuries, in most of the countries of the
world, religious fanatics have risen who have had the power to sway
multitudes, whose wild-eyed countenances, zealous speeches, and
aura of absolute conviction and godliness have made their awestruck
audiences as putty in their hands, believers eager to resign their individual fates to the will of their spiritual overlords. Among such
spellbinding dispensers of holy zeal were St. Augustine's mentor, St.
Ambrose; Jan Hus and Girolamo Savonarola, both burned alive;
John Wyclif, Jean Calvin, Martin Luther, and John Knox, to name
but a few. Such a man, also, was the Russian evangelical fire-eater
Iliodor, the monk-priest of Tsaritsyn (later Stalingrad and today Vol-
gograd), known to his devoted flock as "the Knight of the Heavenly
Kingdom."
    Rasputin had first encountered him at Kronstadt Monastery where,
as a young divinity student, Iliodor had used his real name of Sergei
Trufanov. The two did not meet formally until later. When they did,
Iliodor was already established in the growing town on the Volga,
quickly gaining fame and adherents there, and the men who introduced him to Rasputin were no other than Archimandrite Theofan
and Hermogen, Bishop of Saratov.
    That two such highly placed ecclesiastics should go to visit
Iliodor rather than summon him to come to them affords clear evidence of the respect, indeed the awe felt for the latter by his superiors. In a way, the monk had earned it. From the day of his
arrival at Tsaritsyn, no cleric had ever displayed more energy or
determination in bringing his parishioners into line, commanding
their loyalty, and rigidly and uncompromisingly advancing the cause
of Orthodoxy. When he preached hellfire and damnation, which he
did constantly, people shuddered before the dread mental imagery
his fiery oratory conjured for them. When he spoke of Paradise,

eloquently describing the pleasures reserved for the righteous, his enraptured congregation thrilled with unimagined ecstasy, visualizing the otherworldly scenes through the melodramatic impact and intensity of his words.

Not surprisingly, Iliodor was ambitious for fame. He wanted to build a monastery, the largest and most imposing the Volga had ever seen, and one by which his name would be remembered. He lacked the funds for this. Climbing to the top of a hill on the outskirts of Tsaritsyn, he gathered his flock about him, then spoke, as many said, "like Jesus in His Sermon on the Mount," asking that some contribute money, others materiel, still others their unremitting labor until the great structure should rise "as once did Solomon's Temple in Jerusalem." The local authorities said it couldn't be done and scoffed at the idea. But hundreds volunteered their time and labor, the weeks evolved into months, and at last a day came when the finished monastery, one of the grandest in Russia, stood on the spot where Iliodor had said it would stand, a monument to God wrung from human sweat and devotion.

The monk's relationship with Rasputin is one of the most curious and contradictory in modern history and began before the *starets* had made his first visit to Tsarskoe Selo. In his chapel at Tsaritsyn, Iliodor was on his knees in prayer when Theofan and Hermogen came to him with Rasputin. The distinguished prelates were loathe to interrupt the monk at his devotions and merely stood behind him, quietly waiting for him to finish. Not so Rasputin. Growing impatient after a few minutes, he addressed him pleasantly but forcefully. "You pray well, brother. Now cease persecuting God with your prayers; even He wants a rest sometimes. Come, those two there have something to discuss with you."[10]

It may well be imagined with what anger and consternation the proud and irascible Iliodor received this forthright approach. Rising in ill-suppressed fury, he caught sight of the *starets*, a torrent of invective ready to pour from his lips, and then their gazes were suddenly locked and the pale blue eyes seemed to penetrate the monk's soul. He stammered a greeting to the visitors. When Rasputin thrust out his hand Iliodor took it, behaving in a friendly manner in spite of himself, unable to understand (as he implied in his later writings) the nature of the spell cast upon him by the Siberian. He, Iliodor, firmly believed himself to be the greatest religious orator in all Russia, a man whose fame had already spread far and wide, a modern saint no less whose veneration would in time exceed even that of the much revered Ivan of Kronstadt. Yet this crude *muzhik* with his unkempt hair and beard, his calf-length peasant kaftan, and his earthy smell, this unlettered Siberian illiterate *dared* to address him as an equal. The monk was dumfounded. Not since the fifth century, when the Vandal king's emissaries accosted St. Augustine in the siege-strewn ruins of North Africa's Hippo Regius, had the world known such brazen effrontery.

Yet, for the moment at least, Iliodor was powerless against Rasputin and sensed it strongly, half-disbelieving the strange sensations that racked him. Wanting to avenge his outraged sensibilities, he was helpless. Wanting to attack with vigor and put the bold, smiling upstart in his place, it was almost as though he were paralyzed, his blood turned to water. Alluding to this curious emotional dichotomy felt by the monk for the *starets*, Rasputin's biographer Fülöp-Miller put it succinctly: "This divided state of mind, a blend of anger, disgust, impotence, fear, and admiration, Iliodor never lost."[11] Indeed, some time later, when Theofan and Hermogen, having nominated Rasputin for membership in the politically powerful organization called the Union of True Russian Men, had failed to win the day and saw their purpose all but defeated, it was Iliodor who leaped into the breach and carried the Central Commitee's vote with a stunningly forceful harangue. Literally browbeating his listeners first into acquiescence, then enthusiastic agreement, the Knight of the Heavenly Kingdom single-handedly swept all before him. Yet, oddly enough, in his memoirs he indicates he did it *against his will*. Rising to his feet to renounce Rasputin and render his candidacy void, he found himself *compelled* to do exactly the opposite, as though some force outside himself had taken control of his mind. It was unique in his experience. It filled him with superstitious dread. Unable to join Theofan and Hermogen in their jubilant celebration of victory, the monk abruptly left the room in silent and helpless anger, his mind in a state of unimaginable confusion.

Despite this ominous beginning, the two men did temporarily

become friends of a sort, sufficiently at least so that over a period of time they exchanged visits, Iliodor first going to Pokrovskoye,[12] then Rasputin once again to the monastery at Tsaritsyn. A subsequent visit of the *starets* to the ecclesiastical retreat on the Volga proved to be a momentous one. Although the two had discussed their religious differences before, as fate had decreed it was at this time, when each had much to lose by a feud, that they found themselves arguing the point which of all convictions Iliodor could not tolerate, that of Rasputin's belief in redemption through sin.

In essence the matter was a simple one. Iliodor contended that all sin was evil and must be shunned, that sins of the flesh in particular were intolerable in the eyes of God, a snare set by Satan to entrap humans and claim their souls. Rasputin denied this. Satan had not brought lust into the world, for he had no power of creation whatever. Moreover, there were many men who could not resist the temptations inherent in women. What of them? Must they suffer damnation because of the essentially libidinous nature God had given them?

Iliodor became excited. Clinging stubbornly to his beliefs, he insisted that lust derived from original sin, the sin of Adam and Eve in the Garden of Eden when they partook of the forbidden fruit and Satan in the guise of a serpent watched them do it. There was no salvation but in continence, and any falling off must be redeemed through endless prayer and contrition. Rasputin attempted logic. Iliodor's only concern was with the strictest possible interpretation of dogma. The *starets*, who had learned something of Hindu theology, introduced the Vedic Brahmanas and Upanishads, his words supporting the *bhakti* (the way to salvation) believed in by the millions of India. Deeply shocked, the monk said such heathen conceptions were blasphemous, un-Christian, and clearly barbaric.

The argument went on and on. It continued for hours, as Iliodor grew heated and Rasputin kept his head. Eventually, the night being well advanced and no inch of ground given on either side, Rasputin touched a particularly raw nerve, that of piety being often wedded to hypocrisy. He challenged Iliodor to make a private confession, strictly between the two of them, for the good of his soul. Had he not lusted after women? Most recently, when visiting Rasputin's

home at Pokrovskoye only the year before, had he not been seen
observing Dunia through her bedroom door, which was ajar, enjoying her in a state of undress? He, Rasputin, had noted this himself. Would the holy man of Tsaritsyn deny it? Why not confess the
truth? Why not admit that man was created weak, that no adult lived
who had not at some time fallen victim to temptation? What could
be more natural?

Now it was that Iliodor's growing resentment and frustration
turned to rage. Confronted with the truth about himself but unwilling
or unable to accept it, he called Rasputin a liar and a fornicator, a
false *starets* who seduced his female followers against their will, lusted
after more of the same, and was himself a hypocrite many times over.
He told him to get out, calling him charlatan and sinner, denouncing
him as unrepentant and therefore lost, and persisting vehemently in
his own innocence. Rasputin was left with no choice. As Iliodor
pointed to the door and with scathing disdain shouted "Go!", the
starets passed through it. The alienation was permanent; the monk's
hatred deep-laid and ineradicable. Stepping into the night and the
darkness, Rasputin knew intuitively he had created a deadly opposition. Iliodor would become one of the most dangerous enemies imaginable.

There is no question whatever that Rasputin retained his sexual
interest in women to the end of his life. There are times in her writings
when Maria, reacting defensively to the savage attacks of her father's
enemies, clearly overcompensates by stretching the truth, whether
knowingly or not. For example, in her final major work on the subject,
Rasputin, The Man Behind the Myth, she firmly denies the charge that
he was intimate with the women of his "court" in St. Petersburg,
claiming that she who lived in the same house with him would have
known if this were true. Had she restricted her observations to their
early days together at the Sasanov apartment, this would have held
up quite well, for there it seems the pressure of circumstances forced
Rasputin into an unwanted celibacy. However, to say that he maintained this status after their move to Gorokhovaya Street is plainly
to challenge credulity. He was still what he had long been, a product

of Khlisti doctrine and morality; he was living in one of the most blatantly lascivious cities in the world; he had what Maria herself describes as a "potent animal magnetism"; and finally, as the all-but-worshiped leader of a cult many of whose members regarded him as the living Christ, he had the same opportunities for sexual congress as once were enjoyed by the notoriously insatiable Radaev. Given these facts, it is simply not conceivable that he would deny his past and his own nature, and suppress the powerful urge that had characterized him since early manhood. On the contrary, reports on his activities kept on file by the ever-watchful Okhrana, the tsarist secret police, indicate precisely the opposite. In his attentions to women, most of whom were more than willing, Rasputin indulged himself more vigorously than ever before, sometimes with two or more partners at once. At this period of his life he appears to have been at the peak of his virility.

As destiny would have it, in the known lustful propensities of the *starets*,[13] Iliodor, now his sworn antagonist, instinctively sensed a weakness which if cleverly exploited could destroy him. Accordingly, the Tsaritsyn-based fanatic began to cast about for possible allies, enemies of Rasputin who would be ready and eager to join in an organized endeavor to bring him down. The Socialist revolutionaries would be one such foe, for Rasputin stood close to the royal couple. Therefore, the determined Iliodor, denying the sanctity of the cloth to which he had sworn allegiance, took his first step toward the Left, beginning the compilation of a dossier he ultimately intended for Leftist use.[14]

Other allies, more immediate and at the time more powerful, would be certain high-ranking dignitaries of the Church itself, specifically those close to Iliodor, Archimandrite Theofan and Hermogen, Bishop of Saratov. With Theofan, the monk seems to have failed in his pursuit. However, Hermogen had already been turned against the *starets* by an unfortunate circumstance, that of Rasputin's revelation that money was missing from the treasury of the Union of True Russian Men. When two of the Bishop's assistants were tried for the offense and sentenced as embezzlers, the bitterly embarrassed prelate quickly lost whatever sympathy he once felt for the Siberian and his regard turned to hatred.

Given Rasputin's background and increasing notoriety, it was not especially difficult for persistent and painstaking investigators to unearth damaging information. There was the affair of the demon-possessed nun, for example. Some years before, during the time of Rasputin's interminable treks as a *strannik*, he chanced one night to seek shelter at the Convent of Saint Tikhon (the Quiet One) near the tiny Ural community of Okhtoi. The nuns did their best for him. While he was seated at table and eating their humble fare, the quiet scene was suddenly interrupted by a piercing shriek coming from somewhere within the nunnery. It was repeated several times. There followed a loud wailing interspersed by cursing and other obscenities in what sounded like a deep masculine voice. Rasputin asked the abbess the cause of this. In the presence of her very frightened nuns she then told him all that was known of Sister Akulina Nikichkina, a young woman who had recently taken her vows. There wasn't much to relate. One day the novice had been normal, a well-liked girl of a sweet and gentle disposition; the next, while praying in her cell, she had been siezed by a frightful demoniacal rapture leading to convulsions, and had ultimately been confined for her own safety and that of others. Her face quickly became lacerated and blotched with bruises, her eyes opaque and unrecognizable. That she was possessed by a demon or even Satan himself was proven by the fact that she spoke in the voice of another, the voice of a man. The obscene words pouring from her mouth were not her own.

Rasputin knew little of exorcism. His knowledge of it was confined to the fact that the sacred rite was rarely performed nowadays, almost never by Orthodox priests and seldom by Catholics. Nonetheless, he asked for and was granted permission to enter Sister Akulina's cell and do what he could for her.[15] The details of exactly what he did will never be known. He was with the sufferer for quite some time. Judging from the methods he used with others his approach was direct and immediate, consisting of intense prayer, the laying on of hands in the ancient pre-Byzantine and Petrine tradition, and possibly something else—a secret way of combating satanic forces that this man of miracles took with him to his grave. In the end he won his battle. As he emerged from the cell he was pale and sweating but on his face was a look of triumph. He told the abbess and the others that God had heard his prayers, that the nun was free of the demon that had possessed her, and that it would never return. A short time later Akulina herself appeared. She was weak from her ordeal but completely restored to her former aspect, smiling and serene, and the livid marks on her face had vanished. In one way only was she changed. Now, when she looked at Rasputin, her expression was full of wonder and infinite gratitude, her countenance alight with the love she felt for the man she believed had saved her soul.[16]

Not long after this incredible happening, having asked that her vows be annulled, Sister Akulina reentered the lay world and became a private nurse, devoting her life to relieving suffering. Considering his growing fame, it is not surprising she learned that Rasputin was in St. Petersburg. She went to him and asked to become his disciple, a plea he granted at once. She was utterly devoted to him. Over the years, as a member of his following she served him with untiring zeal day and night, and whenever his adherents met she was usually to be found at his feet.[17] Maria Rasputin states that the former nun's love for the *starets* was "never consummated." Be that as it may, she holds an undying place in the life history of her beloved master and her story is the stuff of legends.[18]

In the group that surrounded Rasputin there was another woman whose relationship to him, though of somewhat lesser duration, was more evidently intimate. Olga Vladimirovna Lokhtina was youthful and attractive. Maria Rasputin says she was the wife of "a minor nobleman"; Fülöp-Miller that of "State Councillor Lokhtin"; Colin Wilson that of "a St. Petersburg officer." Indeed, it is possible that her husband may have been all three, but what is most obvious about her is the sexual attraction she felt for the *starets*. According to Sir Bernard Pares, she is the person who taught Rasputin to read and write.[19] If true, it would seem to refute the opinion of certain writers that her sojourn with him was brief, for even with very apt pupils learning of this sort requires time. Who else but one of his continuing cultists would have had the opportunity?

Unfortunately, this particular paramour was highly indiscreet. It was one thing to go to bed with Rasputin within the secretive confines of what has been called his "harem," quite another to reveal it to outsiders (apparently, she did not fear her husband's retaliation) and even attempt to flout it as a sort of celestial *cause célèbre*. The incautious woman appears to have been to a degree emotionally unstable. It is clear she became a fanatic, for there is evidence she referred to Rasputin as God and to herself as the Virgin Mother. The *starets* was embarrassed. He was also keenly aware of the danger to his reputation and his position with the Imperial family. He asked Olga Vladimirovna to desist, and when she found herself unable to do so he demanded it—but to no avail. Ultimately, he had no choice but to oust her from the group without possibility of return, a most upsetting expulsion for both and one that triggered an unexpected chain of events.

Somehow the lady in question had previously met Iliodor. Judging from her subsequent action, it is possible she knew of the bad blood existing between him and Rasputin. Was she seeking revenge? History does not say. Going to Tsaritsyn, she confessed to the monk her lust for the *starets* and apparently pleaded for absolution on her knees. Iliodor feigned sympathy. The irony of it was that some time before he himself had conceived a passion for her and he now saw in her distraught state a woman ripe for seduction. He made his move without warning. Caught by surprise, his would-be victim resisted him and struggled desperately, then screamed repeatedly for help. Within moments, Iliodor heard the commotion made by rapidly approaching monks and was forced to think fast. He could twist the truth, in fact distort it completely. As the clerics came through his door he thrust the woman from him with a look of withering scorn, accusing her, a married female, of attempted adultery.

It was a very serious charge, especially when it involved a man of the cloth. The accused hysterically denied it. None believed her. As was common in the villages of rural Russia, she was stripped naked by the monks, whipped without mercy, then lashed to the crupper of a horse and dragged into the surrounding wilderness. Eventually she was discovered by peasants who did what they could for her. She came under the care of a doctor. In time her injuries healed, but the shock of her fright and her suffering damaged her brain and she became somewhat deranged. Iliodor, never renowned for his charity, quickly forgot about her. As far as he was concerned the incident was closed.

It might have remained so had not Rasputin chanced to hear about it. His first reaction was an overwhelming sense of pity for the unhappy Olga Vladimirovna; his second, a blazing anger not only for the injustice that had been done to her but for the cruelty, cynicism, and deceit of her heartless accuser. It is almost certain the incident recalled to his mind an equally grim occurrence, the whipping and banishment of Natalya Petrovna in the early days of his youth. He decided to do something about it. He had some influence with the Holy Synod. His friend Sasanov was a member of it. But he failed to take two things into consideration. The first was that he had lost the friendship of Bishop Hermogen, that indeed this misguided prelate now despised him. The second was more pertinent to the case and involved a question of jurisdiction. It lay in the fact that Iliodor, as a cleric of Tsaritsyn, was subject to Hermogen and part of his bishopric. Any charge made against the monk must therefore be heard in Hermogen's own ecclesiastical see at Saratov.

Rasputin never had a chance. From the beginning the hearing was rigged against him. Far from being a normal defendant, during the odd course of the proceedings Iliodor became a veritable prosecutor, lying repeatedly with his customary eloquence and guile, working closely with Hermogen with whom he had obviously rehearsed. Rasputin asked to be heard and was put down with vicious denial. He demanded it, and was immediately attacked from all sides in a way which was a shabby mockery of a legal tribunal, religious or secular. If he needed any further proof of a planned entrapment there was the grotesquely birth-deformed dwarf, Mitya Koliava, gesticulating with the handless stumps of his arms, his twisted face full of hate. He was Iliodor's pawn. Said to have the gift of prophecy but actually insane and nearly speechless, he had for a time been acceptable at the Imperial Court when an ambitious sexton named Egorov interpreted his "visions" for him. Then Rasputin had come and the dwarf had been displaced. His presence alone was the clearest possible evidence of ruthless malice abetted by collusion.

The end was predictable. Nothing Rasputin said made any difference. Far from accepting his accusation that Iliodor was lying, it was *he* who was branded the liar. As he had done with his female victim, the forsworn monk again turned the tables, easily managed without the girl present to contradict him. Rasputin, he said, had hypnotized and seduced her, an experience so shocking it had unhinged her mind. Following that and still in a state of dementia, the wretched soul had traveled to Tsaritsyn, sought religious solace with Iliodor, then, being still crazed as the result of abuse, attempted to get him to break his priestly vows. Wild-eyed by now, Iliodor demanded the immediate arrest and punishment of Rasputin. Hermogen, in a tone of supreme clerical authority, rose from his chair and seconded this. The hearing was over.

Desperate, the *starets* saw two burly attendants approach to take him into custody. There would be no reprieve, no chance ever to be heard, and only God knew what deviltry they had planned to silence him forever. He picked up a heavy chair and made a threatening gesture. They still came on. He swung it like a club and they stopped, hesitant and fearful. He made for the door, kicking loose the dwarf who had scurried in behind him and caught him by the leg, taking the chair with him. Finding himself outside he slammed the door in their faces, then slipped the back of the chair beneath the door handle as a solid brace. He ran. He went through the gates of the monastery. He took the road leading west, empty now and full of dust. He ran and ran. Never in his life had he been in greater danger. Yet his unerring clairvoyance told him he would escape, for his time was not yet. He was Grigori Efimovich Rasputin—and his time was not yet.

Although there were many conversations in progress around them, seated at the long dining table in the vast, highly ornate banqueting hall of the palace Rasputin conversed silently with the Tsarevich by eye contact alone. He himself was seated at the Tsar's right hand, the place of honor on this or any other evening. At the opposite end of the table sat the Empress, seemingly far away. Across from him was Aleksei; next to the boy his sisters in order of age: Olga, Tatiana, Maria, and Anastasia. And where was his own Maria? She laughed and ate and amused herself close to the resplendent woman who loved her as her own daughter, Tsaritsa Aleksandra.

He knew that Aleksei understood him. The boy's blue eyes were full of joy as he gazed at the *starets*, reflecting a soul at peace and a mind tranquil with perfect confidence. Rasputin's thoughts repeatedly focused on him, narrowing, concentrating, excluding those around them.

"You are feeling fine, Alesha, and you are going to continue to feel fine. I will come to you as I always do and we'll talk about all the wonders of Siberia. They call them fairy tales but you and I know they are true, don't we? Just as we know that animals and trees and flowers all have souls and can talk. That's how I healed the horses when I was a boy, Alesha, by speaking to them in their own language. You will not have any more pain while I am with you. Your *novykh* promises you this."[20]

The Tsar leaned over to say something to Aleksei and the little one's attention was distracted. Rasputin looked beyond the child, beyond the dangling decorations on the Tsar's military tunic, beyond the attendants standing silently at intervals in the blue, white-trimmed livery of the Romanovs. So many advisors, sages, and miracle-workers had come and gone in the past; from the Frenchman Nizier-Vachot, called "Doctor Philippe," who had come from Paris and held séances in the drawing room of Grand Duke Nikolai; to such involuntary holy idiots—as Mitya Koliava and the simple-minded peasant girl, Darya Ossipova; to the *strannik* Antoni; the French master of illusion, Dr. Encaussé, called "Papus"; and Badmaev, dispenser of Tibetan magic and medicine, political advisor to the Tsar.

Rasputin reflected. Actually, Badmaev was still in St. Petersburg, though his influence had waned, and as godson to Aleksandr III he would always be welcomed at Court. But one thing must be admitted. He, Rasputin, had replaced Badmaev in the Imperial Family's favor, yet the Buriat Mongol, talented and intelligent, had sought and won his friendship. He had once asked him why. Badmaev had smiled, then stated simply that he believed in the prophecy of the clairvoyant Doctor Philippe, uttered on his deathbed in Paris and relayed to the Tsar by one of his followers. Philippe had spoken of "another" who would come after him, an advisor who would speak with God's voice. They should listen to this one, he said, love the newcomer as they had loved him, and follow him always.

He was toying with his wine glass now, gazing into the depths of

the claret. How fantastic it all was. Philippe's words could be compared to those of Ivan Krestityel (John the Baptist) prophesying the
coming of the Khristos in the third chapter of Saint Luke: "I indeed
baptize you with water; but one mightier than I cometh, the latchet
of whose shoes I am not worthy to unloose: he shall baptize you with
the Holy Ghost and with fire."

The comparison was blasphemous. Dared he even *think* such a
thing? The words of Jesus came to him unbidden: "This day is this
scripture fulfilled in your ears." No. Let the Khlisti teach what they
pleased, and those who thought they saw themselves in those teachings
believe what they chose to believe. He was not the newly risen Christ
of Pokrovskoye but only the ever-repentent fornicator and many times
fallen ex-carter.

In intense agitation he nearly dropped the silver fork he was holding. He must remind himself why he and Maria were here and seek
comfort in it. They were here because the Tsaritsa, told by Anna
Virubova of the insane "hearing" in Saratov, had urged the Tsar to
launch an inquiry of his own by summoning Hermogen and Iliodor
before him in the presence of the man they had accused. That inquiry
had taken place only yesterday here in the palace. The two had lied
as before, and the Little Father had seen through their lies—instantly.
He had branded them as men bearing false witness against their neighbor. Admitting their perfidy, they had pleaded for mercy. But the
Tsar was outraged. Shaking his head with quiet determination, he
had banished them to outlying provinces for life.

He looked again at the Tsarevich and winked, infinitely gratified
to see the lad wink back. It was the Tsaritsa who had suggested this
to her husband, a dinner for *Otyets* Grigori and his daughter by way
of celebration. *"This day is this scripture fulfilled in your ears."* The enemy
had been defeated, it seemed. Justice had prevailed. Dunia had prepared Maria's clothes, taught her how to curtsy, and kissed the large
crucifix round his neck when they departed for Tsarskoe Selo in the
royal coach provided for them. All so normal and good, so deeply
satisfying. He raised his head suddenly. Nikolai II, Tsar of All the
Russias, was looking at him with a wonderfully radiant smile on his
face, the smile of a loving friend. He returned it, wiped his mouth
with one of the brocaded napkins bearing the royal crest and grinned
broadly.

Then he stopped smiling. In place of the Tsar's dear countenance he saw another face, the stern, hate-distorted visage of Iliodor, monk-priest of Tsaritsyn. It turned his stomach sour and made him belch. Hermogen would live quietly and die the same way, a thoroughly discredited prelate eaten by his own guilt. But Iliodor? Here was one who would never rest until he had laid the *starets* in his grave. Was he seeing this clairvoyantly or only imagining it? He wasn't sure.

He laid his fork down and again took up the goblet as a lackey leaned forward to fill it. How clear was the wine. If he chose he could define figures within it, scenes and events from some day not yet lived. But he did not so choose, not yet. Raising it to his lips, he drained it at a single draught. To his mind came the words of Jesus from the sixth chapter of Matthew: "Take therefore no thought for the morrow: for the morrow shall take thought for the things of itself. Sufficient unto the day is the evil thereof."

It seemed to comfort him—if only a little. Were the scenes around them real? The gold and silver? The jewels glittering on the women? Or was all of it, all of life itself, merely illusion, a dream hidden forever within a dream? One thing had reality, he knew, the arms of his sweet Akulina waiting for him in the city. And something else. Another pleasure too long postponed. Too long. . . . He heaved a deep sigh. All casks should be breeched and their contents quaffed, for life was fleeting. He took the pendant cross he wore into his hand and held it. Was it getting warm from his flowing blood or was *he* growing warm from contact with it. *Djizn*—life. Ah how transitory. He knew of nothing else quite so brief. Nothing.

NOTES

1. Maria Rasputin and Patte Barham, *Rasputin: The Man Behind the Myth*, Warner Books, New York, 1977. (Published by arrangement with Prentice-Hall, Inc.)

2. According to the unwritten village code of the rural Russia of that day, such a crime could have been punishable by death.

3. Generations later, the cinematic restatement of this was very effectively made in the British motion picture *The Red Shoes*, when the ballerina, faced with an impossible choice, commits suicide in the same way.

4. Pavlova's artistry in such ballets as *Swan Lake* and Nijinsky's in *L'Après-midi d'un Faune* and *Petrushka* will ever be remembered. Even the latter's eventual madness cannot dim his very singular artistic renown.

5. Though in most quarters it had become unpopular to mention it, the threat was that of a bloody revolution which, unlike the abortive upheaval of 1905, would be successful. In 1917, like a rupturing thunderhead, it finally burst over Russia.

6. From the Rubaiyat of Omar Khayyám, translated by Edward FitzGerald

7. A recently released report by Moscow's Tass News Agency, quoted in the official Soviet Government papers *Pravda* and *Izvestiya*, states that uncontrolled drinking in the Soviet Union now threatens to reach *an unacceptable level of prevalence*.

8. Rasputin and Barham, *op. cit.*

9. In 1917, with revolution in full fury, Anna was arrested by the Communists and sent to the forbidding Fortress of Peter and Paul (the same that had held Dostoyevsky) in the St. Petersburg then renamed Petrograd. Accused once again of "crimes of immorality," she insisted on a physical examination by court-appointed doctors. This was done. At its conclusion she was pronounced to be still a virgin.

10. René Fülöp-Miller, *Rasputin: The Holy Devil*, Viking Press, New York, 1928.

11. *Ibid.*

12. Maria Rasputin relates that she disliked Iliodor intensely for his arrogance and pomposity and avoided him whenever possible.

13. During these early years, the members of the Imperial family were among the few who were not yet aware of this side of Rasputin's nature, primarily because those in a position to reveal it feared the Tsaritsa's angry disbelief were she informed.

14. Most of the Communist (Bolshevik) propaganda that later was to blacken Rasputin's name over many decades of time was concocted and supplied to them by Iliodor, a man who distorted facts with all the venomous unscrupulousness to be expected of such a zealot. Thus, before the defamer was done, Rasputin was impugned as having been intimate not only with the Tsaritsa but with her daughters as well, even including the youngest of them, Anastasia.

15. Although no investigator appears to have made the connection, he may have seen a good omen in the coincidence of names. Long ago, one of the Khlisti saints called Kondrati Selivanov had been proclaimed Christ by the venerable woman the sect thereafter designated the "Mother of God." Her name was Akulina Ivanovna.

16. Most biographers agree that the convent's written record of the exorcism was subsequently destroyed by the Bolsheviks with typical thoroughness.

17. A number of years ago, Elizaveta Dmitrievna Myles obtained from her mother, Olga, a faded and cracked photograph now in the author's possession. It shows Rasputin seated in the center of his coterie in his Gorokhovaya apartment, surrounded by fifteen women and five men. One of the women, and only one, is seated at his feet, her left hand on her right breast, her youthful face the picture of serenity. It is presumably Akulina Nikichkina. How the photo was acquired by its first owner, now deceased, is unknown.

18. Except for the discordant note of his polygamy, in certain aspects Akulina's relationship to Rasputin is reminiscent of twelfth-century France's Abélard and Héloïse and the romance made so famous by the poignancy of their correspondence. In recognition of her closeness to him, it was she who was chosen by the Tsaritsa to bathe and prepare his body for burial.

19. *The Fall of the Russian Monarchy*, Jonathan Cape, Ltd., London, 1939.

20. The word means "new man" and derives from the first name given to Rasputin by Aleksei. Subsequently, the Tsar conferred on the *starets* the name "*Novykh*" with a capital letter, like an official title.

CHAPTER 8

Enter Yussupov

He was Grigori Efimovich Rasputin. Riding in the plush back seat luxuriance of the carriage, which like its driver was on permanent loan from the Tsar, he wondered why he frequently repeated that thought. Was it because he had come to think of himself as so important? Was it that vanity of which the Bible warned, the certain downfall of any human fool enough to harbor it? Or was it his way of reminding himself of his own mortality, the stark vulnerability of the simple *muzhik* out of his element and in over his head? In the monotonous thudding of the horse's hooves he could find no answer.

His eyes were nearly closed. Now he opened them to observe the passing scene, this strangely benighted St. Petersburg caught like a netted ptarmigan in Mephisto's velvet noose. He supposed that very few cities on earth had more churches than this. Everywhere were to be seen their spires and Byzantine domes all consecrated to God. Yet everywhere it was vice that reigned, not virtue, and so it had been since the capital's tall founder, Pyotr Veliki, had lopped off the heads of the *Streltsy*[1] and launched his ruinous wars.

He smiled to himself. Emperors and princes. In this velvet-lined conveyance belonging to the Tsar he was riding in the eventful year 1909 to meet a prince of Russia, and all because one of his female disciples felt it was her destiny to bring the two of them together. The prince was Feliks Feliksovich Yussupov, the richest man in the country; the girl Maria Evgeniya Golovina, called Munia, who with her mother, Madame Golovina, was among his most devoted followers. Munia was a strange little thing but strange in a wonderful way. Even more than some of the others she was sure he was Christ. Together with the merest handful of the faithful she formed a feminine coterie at the very summit of his "court," one of those rare beings who would be with him to the end no matter how many others might come and go.

The smile he felt within himself deepened. Probably, the dear girl thought herself important for the first time in her life and he intended to do nothing to spoil it for her. She had suffered a recent tragedy. Engaged to be married to Nikolai, the older brother of Feliks, her world had come crashing down around her when that hothead had been killed in a duel over a woman with whom he had been having an affair. It had stunned the girl and turned her to religion in its more mystical aspects, yet with the Yussupov family she had remained close.

Like the inexorable ticking of some ethereal clock the minutes passed unrealized. His mind was returning to it now, the growing hatred of which he was the target: the nobility hating him because he was closer to the Imperial Family than they and would not keep his place; the ministers of the Third Duma because they saw in him one of the chief props of the autocracy they wished to undermine; Prime Minister Stolypin for a number of reasons, including a genuine belief that the *starets* would pull Russia down and destroy the Monarchy with her; the Army because they knew him to be a pacifist; the Church because they envied him his God-given power and were consumed with jealous rage at his saving the Tsarevich when their prayers failed; every doctor in St. Petersburg, particularly the frustrated Court physicians; the miracle workers he had replaced, only excepting Badmaev; Iliodor and his growing clique of malcontents, clerics of lower degrees, Leftist revolutionaries, the insane and the half-insane, all of them infused with the monk-priest's unreasoning wrath. It was quite a collection of enemies, becoming formidable, and daily they strove to increase their numbers. He knew that Stolypin or Iliodor alone, given half a chance, could break him.

He did not know exactly where they were now nor did he care.

From having wandered, his mind returned to Yussupov, pondering
on what little he knew about him. He was the richest man in Russia,
but was he happy? He had the reputation of being even more arrogant
and vain when the occasion suited him than the average noble spoiled
from birth, a typical ne'er-do-well scion of the idle rich capable of
haughty and very offensive petulance when crossed or unable to have
his own way. As such he was a challenge, was he not? Normally he,
Rasputin, could expect nothing from this man, not even simple courtesy despite what he was sure must be a glowing recommendation
from the Golovina women. But what lay deep inside the fellow? If
he was nothing but so much chaff on the threshing floor of a mill, a
creature without basic worth or substance, why had he agreed to this
meeting? Was it mere curiosity to meet the despised *muzhik* who
consorted with royalty? The idle diversion of a bored man-about-
town? Maybe, it was a peculiar form of dilettantism through the
cultivation of the art of snobbery. Who could say?

They were driving along the Winter Canal now, nearing the home
of the Golovins. Suddenly he felt his mind enter another plain, delving
as it often did into the hidden realm of the metaphysical. Though he
knew not why, of late he had become increasingly concerned with
the occult phenomenon of dematerialization, that total negation of
existence long deemed by science an impossibility. He was isolated,
in a separate world from the driver and the people in the streets.
Concentrating every ounce of his thaumaturgic power, feeling it double and treble and redouble again within him, his mind focused on
the problem like a ray of sunlight pinpointed on a piece of paper
through a prism. It was *not* impossible. He knew nothing of exorcism,
yet in Tsaritsyn, in the presence of the jealous Iliodor, he had done
for two possessed women what previously he had done for Sister
Akulina. If that were possible, why not this?

He closed his eyes. To dematerialize. To dissolve and disperse the
solid fibers of one's existence. To *disappear*. Into what? Others had
studied the thing, he knew. The French man of miracles, Nostradamus, was said to have investigated it; the Italian wizard Cagliostro
to have *solved* it, though he died in a Roman dungeon without ever
revealing its awesome secret. Had Cagliostro's powers failed at the
end, then? If he could dematerialize, how had they been able to hold

him? Why had the door and bars of a cell proved barriers to him? Could it be that like the *starets* himself Cagliostro's powers had been inconstant, changeable, sometimes nonexistent? This tendency to lose God's precious gift without warning was a heavy cross to bear. He knew that some day it could kill him.

He began to sweat profusely. He felt his body aglow with inner fires. Suddenly, it seemed to him that his right hand was only a faint outline and nearly invisible, as though the very atoms composing it had lost both substance and reality. Was it beginning? Was it *beginning*? Was he at last becoming incorporeal *by his own will*? The incredible phenomenon acted like a drug on his senses and he almost fainted. Then he saw the car had stopped. They had arrived. As though it had been mere imagination, his hand was whole again and he heard the driver opening the door for him. The vision, if vision it was, had vanished.

Often it has chanced in history that what are called "fortunate" or "advantageous" marriages have greatly increased the wealth, prestige, and power of royalty and nobility alike. In Europe, the Austrian Habsburgs are almost certainly the foremost example, so much so that their skillful marital maneuvering gave rise to the motto in Latin, *Bella gerant alii; tu, felix Austria, nube.* (Let others wage war; thou, happy Austria, marry.) Possibly at no other period of the dynasty were the Habsburg hereditary land holdings so extended as during the reigns of the Holy Roman Emperor Friedrich III (1414–1493) and his son Maximilian I (1459–1519). Friedrich may be said to have perfected the technique of territorial aggrandisement through marriage. Maximilian, for his part, furthered the process when by wedding Mary of Burgundy he brought most of the Austrian and Spanish Netherlands into the Empire.

In the Slavic world, perhaps no family in Russian history owed more to fortunate marriages than the Yussupovs. One ancestor was said to have been Yusup Mursa, aide to the Tatar conqueror Tamerlane (Timur-i-Leng or Timur the Lame). Others acquired minor prominence at the courts of Peter the Great and Catherine II. However, the enormous wealth that so distinguished Prince Feliks Yussupov had been largely acquired in just two generations. His paternal grandfather, a member of the lesser nobility and officer in a Don Cossack regiment, had borne the surname of Elston. Marrying the only daughter of Count Sumarokov, the last of her family, he subsequently acquired the title Count Sumarokov-Elston by Imperial decree, a distinction inherited by his eldest son, Feliks Elston. Then the process repeated itself. The heir married one of the fabulously rich Yussupovs, Princess Zenaidye, equally her line's last member, assuming her title and estates, and thus combining the titular dignities of Count Sumarokov-Elston and Prince Yussupov.

To all this, Prince Feliks Feliksovich Yussupov, as the surviving son, was heir apparent at the time he met Rasputin. However, he was not then at the summit of his fortunes. Still to come was the sheer good luck that would secure his tie to royalty, his marriage to Princess Irina Aleksandrovna, niece to Tsar Nikolai II and reputed to be one of the most beautiful women in Europe.

The Prince was many things. Heredity had made him handsome in a delicate sort of way, slender of frame and of medium height. A combination of chance and design in the lives of his forebears had made him incredibly rich. A curious admixture of circumstances dating from his boyhood had given him a decided bent toward effeminacy. There is a photo of him taken in his youth. In it he stands in the elegant fur cap and high-collared, large-cuffed fur coat of an early day *boyar*, his bearing regal, his closed left fist proudly on the hip from which is suspended the traditional dirk of Russia, the long-bladed *kinjal* of the fighting tribes of the Caucasus. Except for the richness of the costume he does not look natural. The pose is stylized, stilted, an uncomfortable assumption, the military air unreal. Judging from what is known of his character the martial role was clearly unsuited to him.

Not so with his father. The elder Yussupov was a soldier through and through, and hoped that his sons would follow in his footsteps. Had he not fallen in a duel, the firstborn brother Nikolai might have done so. As for Feliks, it was simply not in the cards. Even his birth seemed ill-starred. His mother, Princess Zenaidye, had hoped for a girl and ordered a pink blanket, sheets, and swaddling clothes. As though sensing a future alienation, his father neglected him. Only once did the senior intervene. In what was clearly an attempt to alter the course he saw his son was taking, the old campaigner had the boy's room refurnished with battlefield simplicity, even including a shower stall; then bade a servant douse him with cold water. Young Feliks hated it and complained bitterly, becoming nearly hysterical. The idea of trying to discipline him appeared to be more trouble than it was worth.

But if in his notion of soldierly austerity the father had to relinquish the thought of his son as Leonidas,[2] he had at least the right to hope he had not sired an Alcibiades.[3] Even so, in the sexual sense, to a considerable degree he had done exactly that. From early childhood Feliks liked to dress up in his mother's clothes, don her jewelry, and wear her makeup. His mother never discouraged him. His father either ignored him or pretended not to care. Feliks was very good at it. His cousin Vladimir, of the same age, was good at it, too, and the boys often played together as happy, excited transvestites. When they were twelve, borrowing wigs from his mother's hairdresser, Feliks pursuaded his cousin to go with him in feminine attire to a fashionable restaurant, where they were nearly seduced by guards officers and ended by being recognized. The punishment was a brief restriction to the estate grounds. The escapade would be repeated.

"As the twig is bent so grows the tree." Of the veracity of the old saying the subsequent adventures of the boy prince seemed proof enough. His first sexual contact was made at a spa in the south of France where he had gone with his mother, been picked up by a young man, and found himself in a *ménage à trois* with the older youth and a very willing girl. Feliks was twelve. Some time later, in Paris with his older brother Nikolai and the latter's mistress Polia, he amused both the couple and himself by accompanying them to the theater in women's clothes. On that occasion, one of his admirers in the audience was England's King Edward VII, always something of a rake, who made inquiry during the intermission as to the identity of Nikolai's charming young "female" companion.

Time passed and Feliks Feliksovich grew to adulthood. The 1905 revolution came and was broken. Russia lost its war with Japan. Eventually, the Prince met a kindred spirit with whom he was destined to share more than mere friendship, a youth considered as handsome and elegant as himself, Grand Duke Dmitri Pavlovich. This very sensitive boy, the only son of Grand Duke Pavel Aleksandrovich, held a lieutenant's commission in the Third Cavalry Regiment of the Imperial Life Guards. As his father was one of Nikolai II's four uncles, he himself was first cousin to the Tsar, but it was not this fact alone that made him such a social success in St. Petersburg. For a time at least, Dmitri Pavlovich was the celebrated toast of his regiment. As Fülöp-Miller says in reference to him, he was much loved by the officers of the Guards, "who could be rapturous admirers of beautiful youths." Very quickly, the Grand Duke Dmitri and Prince Yussupov became virtually inseparable, with the former more than content in the subservient role.

Of the first meeting between Feliks Feliksovich and Rasputin at the Golovin residence in 1909 there is more than one version. Reminiscing in the book he published in 1927, Yussupov has not a kind word to say for the man he shamelessly betrayed. When referring to Maria Golovina and her mother he uses only initials, apparently in an effort to protect their reputations, then writes of Rasputin as follows:

> My first glance at him filled me with dislike of his appearance; there was something repugnant about him. He was of medium height, thick-set yet rather thin, with long arms. His big head was covered with an untidy tangle of hair. Above his forehead there was a bald patch which, as I subsequently learnt, came from a blow administered to him when he was beaten for horse-stealing. He seemed to be about forty years old. He was wearing a long coat, wide trousers and long boots. His face was of the most ordinary peasant type—a coarse oval, with large, ugly features overgrown with a slovenly beard, and a long nose; his small grey eyes looked out from under bushy eyebrows with piercing yet shifty glances.[4]

After mentioning the exchange of greetings and describing Rasputin as walking about the room "muttering incoherently to himself" as the others drank tea and silently watched him, Yussupov continues:

> At last he came to the tea-table, settled down in an armchair by my side, and began to submit me to a searching scrutiny.
> A conversation about nothing in particular was started, Rasputin,

apparently wishing to maintain the tone of one inspired from above, held forth in a dictatorial manner. . . . As he talked I carefully watched his expression. . . . The longer I examined him, the more I was struck by his eyes, they were amazingly repulsive. Not only was there no trace of spiritual refinement in the face, but it called to mind that of a cunning and lascivious satyr. . . . His keen and penetrating gaze did, in fact, convey a feeling of some hidden, supernatural power.

His smile, too, was arresting, it was sickly yet cruel, cunning and sensual. Indeed, the whole of his being was redolent of something unspeakably revolting, hidden under the mask of hypocrisy and cant.[5]

It is not a pretty description. Yussupov ends his chapter with a brief observation. "A few days later, I heard from M____ that Rasputin had taken a great liking to me, and that he wanted to meet me again."

What Munia Golovina told Yussupov was correct. Rasputin had taken a liking to him, though when he bestowed on the Prince the invariable triple kiss on the cheeks he must have sensed the latter's revulsion. As concerns Yussupov's attitude toward the *starets*, when she later questioned Munia on the subject Maria Rasputin received another impression. She writes:

Papa was having a glass of Madeira when the resplendent Feliks arrived. He swept into the room with customary arrogance as if he were some sort of god paying a courtesy call to some minor prophet of his theology. But when he saw my father he deflated like the rupture of a hose under too much pressure. Overcome with some strange humility he did not understand, he approached Papa with head bowed as though he were the lowest menial in the land. No longer the pompous bon vivant with a thousand social graces and a wit as sharp as the Tsar's razor, he was not unlike a country bumpkin, or a schoolboy facing his headmaster.[6]

She then indicates that Rasputin did all he could to reestablish Yussupov's fallen self-esteem through kindness and flattery, and quotes Munia's words to her: "Oh, Maria, you should have been there. You should have seen Feliks. He was like some shy lad from a secluded life, blushing and tongue-tied. I'm sure your father will make him a convert, but it will take some doing."

At their apartment Maria questioned her father:

"What was he really like, Papa?" I asked during our short time together the following day. . . . "Oh," he replied indulgently, "a frightened boy, frightened by the world around him, his own desires, which I doubt even he understands, frightened by the future and torn between many demons."[7]

Those demons were about to have their way with Yussupov. The second meeting with Rasputin was canceled, and what the *starets* might have done to help him—or to change the course of history—will never be known. Within days, the Prince had departed for England, where he had enrolled as a student at Oxford. It was the worst possible influence on him. It was a time when male homosexuality was not only prevalent in this most distinguished institution of higher learning but fashionable as well. On Feliks Feliksovich it acted like a deadly drug. He had chosen the life of the wretched Dorian Gray and of his tragic, bedeviled creator Oscar Wilde, a choice which in this errant prince, dominant in at least one of his sexual liaisons, brought out his latent sadism. His marriage was still to come, but in the long run it would make little difference. Fate had struck its blow. The role he was to play in the often bloody annals of Russia was firmly established. The die was cast.

Although he was aware that it was happening to him and knew intuitively that its end would be disastrous, in the months following his meeting with Prince Yussupov, flinging caution to the winds, Rasputin was on a giddy escalade from whose toils he seemed unable to extricate himself. Sought after by high society, a frequenter of sumptuous palaces and glittering drawing rooms, his appearance altered markedly. Gone were the clumsy peasant boots, the crudely made linen shirts and coarse, overly wide trousers. In their place were boots of fine, soft leather, much as might have been worn by a plunder-enriched Cossack chief; shirts of costly silk in yellow, blue, and scarlet with contrasting waist cords and pearl and ivory buttons; trousers of ebony velvet. Only his calf-length black *kaftan* remained. The traditional male outer garment of peasant Russia, its retention was a matter of pride, even of defiantly flaunting his peasant origin. It was noticed by many that the pendant crucifix he wore was no longer of brass or pewter but of pure gold, large, ornate, and imposing. Some said the skillfully embroidered cornflowers on his shirts were the personal handiwork of the Tsaritsa, a token of the great esteem and affection in which she held him. They were right.

At the various social gatherings he attended among the nobility his approach now was sensational, at times even electrifying. He had only to enter a room to rivet general attention. Always he took both hands of people not yet introduced to him, holding them firmly, transfixing their owners with his unblinking, incredibly penetrating gaze. With the women in particular the hypnotic effect was overpowering, so much so that any in whom he was especially interested were normally stripped of their defenses and rendered helpless on the spot, certain conquests marked for later claiming. His face was weathered, showing signs of aging; his long hair and beard in need of grooming; he had not yet acquired the sophistication to properly clean his nails. It did not matter. Once firmly in the grip of those eyes, there were very few who had the strength or the will to break free until he released them.[8]

The years 1909 and 1910 saw the gradual consolidation of his position. By early 1911, however, the *starets* began to make his growing influence felt in matters other than those affecting the personal lives of the sovereigns, policymaking decisions which could ultimately affect the State. Logically enough, it began with the Church. In January, when the See of Tobolsk was left open by the death of the presiding prelate, Rasputin appealed to the Tsar to fill the position by appointing an old acquaintance, the semi-illiterate peasant monk Varnava. The appeal was granted. With the ignorant *muzhik* thus installed as Bishop of Tobolsk the reaction of the opposing forces could hardly come as a surprise. The powerful Holy Synod was outraged. From the first, they had counted on one of their own number being awarded the bishopric. Equally humiliated was the Union of True Russian Men, closely allied with the Synod, and to which Rasputin ostensibly belonged. He was of course immediately declared *persona non grata in absentia* by both organizations. It is probable, too, that the earlier findings of exiled Bishop Hermogen and the ecclesiastical tribunal at Saratov also were adjudged valid, though in secret, for an open declaration would have antagonized the Tsar.

Needless to say, whether overtly or covertly, the entire ruling

heirarchy of the Russian Orthodox Church was now ranged against
Rasputin. From this time, also, we find the Montenegrin princesses
in opposition, especially the younger sister Anastasia, who at first had
been so taken with the *starets*. The growing dislike of her soldier
husband dates from this period. Grand Duke Nikolai Nikolayevich,
a pillar of the Union and once so enthusiastically in favor of Rasputin,
was eventually to grow to hate him bitterly.

It is one thing to hate, quite another to have the power to imple-
ment that hatred. Of all the men in Russia, perhaps the one best
positioned to seriously injure the *starets* during these tumultuous years
was the country's brilliant senior statesman, Prime Minister Pyotr
Arkadyevich Stolypin. In 1905, as Governor of Saratov Province, he
had shown great personal courage in stemming peasant unrest, often
entering villages alone and unprotected, inducing the surrender of
insurgent forces by the sheer strength of his personality. His *sangfroid*
was legendary. Early in 1906, just as the ineffective Goremykin was
replacing Count Sergius Witte as Prime Minister, Stolypin came to
St. Petersburg to serve under the former and accept the portfolio of
Minister of the Interior. In this crucial office he was equally successful.
Although a large landowner himself and a staunch opponent of revolutionaries, the stubborn effectiveness with which he instituted agrar-
ian reforms so eased the harsh lot of the peasantry that both Lenin
and Trotsky feared he would further sap the impetus of the already
dying revolution.

These things were behind Stolypin now. Since July of 1906 he
had been Prime Minister, and no cabinet member in Russian history
had ever pursued his job with a greater determination to succeed. He
could be ruthless if that was what it took, and from 1905 until the
collapse of revolution in 1907 he answered terrorism with terror,
homemade bombs with the relentless use of firing squads. But great
sagacity was also his. Correctly pointing out that the slaughtered
Aleksandr II, "the Tsar Liberator," had liberated no one, least of all
the serfs, he worked unceasingly to eradicate communal holdings that
tied the peasant to the land and their villages as mercilessly exploited
labor, and to create a landholding peasant class. It was a resolve that
would cost him very dearly.

It was in 1911 that this dynamo of self-directed energy met Rasputin. The Tsaritsa had asked him to receive the *starets*, a visit that was to be followed by another to his destined successor, Vladimir Kokovtsov. Both politicians remembered these encounters. As quoted by Robert K. Massie,[9] Stolypin reminisced as follows to President of the Duma Rodzianko:

> He [Rasputin] ran his pale eyes over me, mumbled mysterious and in-articulate words from the Scriptures, made strange movements with his hands, and I began to feel an indescribable loathing for this vermin sitting opposite me. Still, I did realize that the man possessed great hypnotic power, which was beginning to produce a fairly strong moral impression on me, though certainly one of repulsion. I pulled myself together. . . .

Kokovtsov's recollection of the subsequent visit is remarkably similar, and he too was to become Rasputin's deadly enemy. He writes[9]:

> When Rasputin came into my study and sat down in an arm chair, I was struck by the repulsive expression of his eyes. Deep seated and close set, they glued on me and for a long time, Rasputin would not turn them away as though trying to exercise some hypnotic influence. When tea was served, Rasputin seized a handful of biscuits, threw them into his tea and again fixed his lynx eyes on me. I was getting tired of his attempts at hypnotism and told him in as many words that it was useless to stare at me so hard because his eyes had not the slightest effect on me.

Although Kokovtsov, holding at the time the lesser office of Minister of Finance and well aware of Rasputin's growing political influence, was wisely discreet during this interlude, Stolypin was not. On his own initiative he ordered the Okhrana to compile a special dossier on Rasputin's activities, omitting nothing, and the resulting report was given to the Tsar. If Nikolai was impressed one way or the other he gave no sign, neither did he return the document or offer anything but the most offhand comment. Momentarily frustrated, seemingly not fully aware of the extreme delicacy of the position in which he found himself, Stolypin was left with no choice but to bide his time and wait for Rasputin to make a serious mistake. It was not long in coming. This time, however, the offensive was taken by the Union of True Russian Men, who had hired a special agent.

Almost since he and Maria had first moved to 64 Gorokhovaya Ulitsa, a matter of nearly four years now, the *starets* had indulged his passion for dancing and revelry by leading an increasingly active night life, partially as a means of recovering from the effects of his very wearing schedule. Although an occasional prostitute was among the women who visited him at his apartment, he did not like brothels and was never known to go to one. Instead, he found delight in various restaurants where music was played, particularly one called the Villa Rodye, where Gypsy violinists, singers, and dancers entertained nightly. He was there frequently and all knew him. The Gypsy band actually lived there, and many an evening saw him rise smiling from his table to dance with its female members, even when tipsy from too much imbibance of his favorite Madeira.

Rasputin's frequenting of this place was well known to the Union, and indeed to all those organizations being supplied intelligence by Iliodor. In all probability, the plan to entrap and compromise him in or near there was hatched in Iliodor's place of exile but proof of this is lacking. Although she would have accomplices, it hinged on a single woman. Her name was Lisa Tansin. She was young, shapely, attractive, and scarcely noted for her chastity. In her native Finland, she had been a ballerina in Helsinki and now she taught ballet in St. Petersburg.

The plot had the merit of simplicity. All that was necessary was for Tansin to go to the restaurant when Rasputin was known to be there, to dance before him, to flirt with her eyes and swinging hips, to make obvious advances aided by practiced coquetry and a low décolletage. Nature and wine would do the rest. She did this with consummate artistry. Before long, Rasputin himself was dancing with the girl, fortifying himself with more Madeira between the dances, gradually losing his equilibrium and his sense of judgment. Clearly that was why, when the evening was well advanced, he accepted her calculated invitation to continue the party with her and a handful of companions at her home.

The scene is not difficult to imagine. Tansin was relatively successful professionally. Her house must therefore have been larger than the average and reasonably well furnished, hung with photos of dancers, an occasional impresario, even her lovers past and present. She taught ballet on the premises. Ergo, an exercise rail could have lined one wall. There might have been a buffet, a cabinet for drinks, even a bar for dispensing them. Whatever the décor, it is certain she encouraged Rasputin to take more wine, and still more, the others keeping pace, until the overheated guests surrendered to the urging of their libidos and began to strip. It was to be a Roman-style bacchanalia after all, but at no time did Union agent Tansin lose her head. Instead, she skillfully directed affairs as she or someone else took photos of a drunken and nude *starets* being kissed and carressed by several very shapely women, equally nude, "evidence of perfidy" tailormade for the Siberian's enemies.

Concerning the photographs, at the time Rasputin paid no attention to the popping flashbulbs, being too far gone in drink. Still inebriated, he returned to his flat. There, his daughter relates, Dunia found him in a helpless state and undressed him to put him to bed, an act that led to their first intimacies and marked the hour of her becoming his mistress at last. This may be so. However, as a man cannot usually function sexually when drunk, it seems more probable that this had happened earlier, that Dunia, when subsequently explaining things to Maria, had simply found that night's occurrences a convenient point of departure.

There is a consideration of note here. In those many Rasputin biographies where the writers bother to mention her at all, Dunia Bekyeshova is depicted simply as Rasputin's "housemaid," although usually with the implication that she was intimate with her employer. Fülöp-Miller, who refers to her as "a distant relative of the starets," even impugns her character. Referring to the squad of plainclothesmen who daily mounted watch on Rasputin's apartment, he writes: "Rasputin's servants, stimulated by copious bribes, gave the detectives the most exact information possible about what went on inside the flat. If conferences of some length or parties were taking place in Rasputin's room, the housemaid, Dunia, would slip softly out into the passage, where she was immediately surrounded and questioned." He then adds that the spies ". . . noted down the maid's reports of the shameless and disorderly scenes enacted in the flat."

It is not in character. Even though the detectives, unlike the handpicked Okhrana men under Stolypin's orders, were given this assignment by the Tsaritsa for Rasputin's protection, even considering he was on good terms with them and showed no resentment of them and their ever-present vigil, it is not Dunia. Maria records that her friend later spoke to her as follows: "I had loved your Papa for such a long time. It was because of that love that I left the Kubasovs to work for him. So I submitted, gladly."

Maria also writes: "From that night on until the end of his life, she was his mistress. I loved her as a mother and found the new liaison delightful."

If an idyll was thus begun it was soon overcast by menacing clouds. Only a short time passed. Then a day came when Rasputin sat conversing with his female followers and a little parcel was delivered into his hand by an unknown man, a man who waited for a response. Rasputin opened the package, saw its contents, then closed it without showing them to anyone. He was observed by Dunia. He took the messenger into his bedroom and conferred with him alone. When they came out together they were seen by Maria. Later, in a state of dejection such as she had never seen in him, he told his loving mistress (now, presumably, the foremost of several loves) the nature and possible consequence of the visit, and showed her the photographs. They intended to blackmail him. They wanted him out of St. Petersburg permanently or the evidence of his "lechery" would be handed over to the Tsar and Tsaritsa.

For once the *starets* was nonplussed, indecisive, almost in a state of despair. He could not fight this kind of war. He wasn't emotionally equipped for it. Had God indeed abandoned him to this? It was Dunia who kept her head and showed him the course he must take. There was only one thing to do. He had to steal a march on them, show the photos to the Tsar himself and explain how they came into existence. True, it might result in disaster but it was his only chance. Any other course would play into the hands of the blackmailers.

Dunia's sage advice brought to the fore Rasputin's peasant practicality. Of course she was right, but he must move quickly before his enemies were aware of it. Going immediately to Tsarskoe Selo, he asked for a private audience with the Tsar and was granted it at once. He told Nikolai everything, then handed him the photos and awaited the result. The monarch looked at them intently. Despite his experiences prior to his marriage, it may have been his only exposure to anything resembling pornography. He was surprised, possibly even shocked, but he did not show it. He took the pictures very seriously. He said they would use them to destroy him if they could, to crush the House of Romanov, end the Monarchy, and plunge Russia into turmoil and chaos. Rasputin had made a grave error but not an irreparable one. They must be on their guard, however, for these lice would not give up. Moreover, Stolypin, without knowing of the photos and on his own initiative, was again applying pressure for Rasputin's removal from St. Petersburg.

It ended with the Tsar mentioning the fact that the *starets* had spoken of a possible pilgrimage to Palestine and the holy places of Jerusalem. He said he thought it was time for it, that the Royal Treasury would pay for the trip in recognition of the work of Rasputin, the Crown's most valuable servant. It was without doubt the most propitious moment.

Humbly and gratefully Rasputin agreed.

It was a day such as the *starets* had never seen, a day not of this world, a day in which time seemed to hang suspended. As he sat alone on the uneven, sloping ground he could hear the wind rustling among the many cedars, the ancient olive trees and slender aspens, and see through their branches the rain-darkened clouds scudding across a sky of slate. Gazing into the shallow valley below, he saw a narrow road cutting his line of vision, beyond it an ancient crenellated stone wall with gates and watchtowers at intervals, beyond that a city that was old when Europe was young. Jerusalem.

He shivered as he gazed upon it. Seemingly out of the ether there came to his mind the bitter lament of Jesus from the twenty-third chapter of Matthew, and his lips formed the words silently: "O Jerusalem, Jerusalem, thou that killest the prophets, and stonest them which are sent unto thee, how often would I have gathered thy children together, even as a hen gathereth her chickens under her wings, and ye would not! Behold, your house is left unto you desolate. For I say unto you, ye shall not see me henceforth, til ye shall say, Blessed is he that cometh in the name of the Lord."

Yes, and the gates of The City of David were sealed with mortar, and the hearts of the people were sealed against God, and there was no health in them. He had tried to see it all, had he not? Many days he had been here. His feet had trod the stones of the Pool of Siloam where Christ had bade the blind man wash and receive sight; the street beneath which lay the Via Dolorosa, the path Jesus followed to Calvary; the Church of the Holy Sepulcher; the hill of Golgotha where the Cross had stood atop "the Place of a Skull"; the Garden Tomb from whence the resurrected Lord had emerged on the third day after His crucifixion.

And now he was here in another garden, that of Gethsemane; below him the Church of All Nations, on its cloister walls the Lord's Prayer in forty-two languages; above him the Orthodox church with its five blue Byzantine domes; and all around the lonely, withdrawn grandeur of the Mount of Olives.

"Jerusalem, the Golden Gate through which He passed is sealed. When will they open thy portal?" His voice sounded far away, detached. "If I forget thee, O Jerusalem. . . ."

He could not remember having been so dismally depressed. All during the trip he had felt it, suffered and fought against it, failed to conquer it. It was because of what his excesses had led to, because he had allowed the employers of Lisa Tansin to imperil the Imperial Family, to imperil Russia through *him*. And where were his precious gifts now? He felt nothing, not an ounce of strength, not a shred of his God-given power to heal or to prophesy. He was like an empty, wasted shell, a burned out candle on an altar that had crumbled to dust. Could it be *rekindled*? Could he find the flame again, *here* where the *Khristos* had asked the Father for mercy? The words uttered on this sacred ground hung upon his lips unspoken: "O my Father, if it be possible, let this cup pass from me: nevertheless, not as I will, but as thou wilt."

It was useless. There was no mercy for the transgressor, the repeated and never ending offender. Again and again the Bible spoke of it. When King Saul lost the favor of God he was forced to fight at Mount Gilboa, to meet the relentless Philistine host, to lose, to fall upon his sword in the manner of defeated kings, until at last he hung headless on the wall of Bethshan. Rasputin looked upward. The land had been plunged in heat but now the sky was dark and the air turned cold. Here, in the garden where Judas Iscariot had betrayed the Lord with a kiss, there was nothing of comfort, only a very tired Russian *strannik* who had sold his birthright on the altar of lust. Iliodor, the Union, the Holy Synod, all had won and he had lost. But with their victory what *other* victims would be claimed? Would it mean the slaughter of the innocents? He knew he must fight against that. If he could not fight on his knees, he would fight on his feet. Weak suddenly, struggling against his weakness, he rose and stood erect.

"O Jerusalem, Jerusalem, thou that killest the prophets. . . ."

Suddenly it happened. It was the phenomenon of the coach again, the miracle he had experienced on the day he went to the Golovina women to meet Yussupov. His right hand. He could not *see* it. Oh dear merciful Christ of the pains. What did it *mean*? What *could* it mean here in this place? Gethsemane to Jesus had been the forerunner of death and resurrection. But to the hopelessly sinning *starets*? What was it to him? What was it to *him*?

He was breathing very hard. He wanted to weep. Then it seemed he was lifted up, raised several feet above the earth, gazing on the body of a man below. It was *his* body. He was dead and looking at himself, and levitation was fakery, a trick of these charlatans he had always despised. No. No, he *was* suspended. Between himself and the cadaver that so resembled him was *several feet of air*. He was dead, the stuff of spirit, soul stuff, and that quiet clay below was all that was left of the weak and foolish man he had been. He would ride the glimmering either into Eternity. He would never come back. Earth would know him no more.

Then without warning he *was* back, one once again with the body that was his, just as he had known it to be. He tried to get up but fell in a half-faint, weak and helpless beyond imagining. He was burning with fever, shaking with chills, and then he knew that this at last was reality. He had never been so sick in his life. He had never been so close to death as at this moment.

The account of his experience Rasputin related to his daughter was very much like this, including the dematierialization of his hand

and his levitation. She records that "a small group of pilgrims" found him and took him to an inn in the Old City. He was put to bed there. For an undetermined length of time he hovered near the point of dissolution. As he had done on the Mount of Olives, again and again he slipped out of his body and observed himself, a phenomenon reminiscent of Abraham Lincoln who repeatedly saw himself dead and in a coffin in the White House, and walked as a disembodied spirit among the mourners. From his childhood to the present, Rasputin told Maria, the delirious and helpless figure he was at that time reviewed his whole life, even to the nightmares of the loss of his brother and mother, his humiliation at the hands of Irina Danilova, the blow of the ax handle that had laid him unconscious at Pokrovskoye. He had seen the Virgin of Kazan, he said, but only momentarily. He had cried out, imploring her not to abandon him, and at some time during his ordeal she had reappeared. He had longed to leave his body again and follow her into realms of celestial light, but her white hand had restrained him. Her message was clear. His task was not yet done. His fate was tied to St. Petersburg and the House of Romanov. As the biblical Mordecai returned to the king's gate, so must he.

After his illness he recovered his strength, and with it the deep and abiding sense that his powers had come back as well. He returned to Russia as he had come, partly by sea. Aboard the ship a woman was gravely ill. They told him about her. He went to her and ministered to her. Where was the first of the miracles of Jesus? In Cana, was it not? "This beginning of miracles did Jesus in Cana of Galilee, and manifested forth his glory." The Christ had turned the water into wine because He was the son of God. The *starets* was nothing. Like John the Baptist, he was not worthy to unloose the latchet of the shoes of the Anointed One, yet by God's grace he cured the afflicted woman. They said he had performed a miracle. He told them, as he always did, that the miracle was God's and God's alone.

Then he was back in the land of his birth, back in Holy Russia, and the Tsar and Tsaritsa welcomed him with open arms. Only on the childish face of his daughter Maria did he find joy and relief to equal that of his sovereigns.

*   *   *

During all the days of his pilgrimage, before his strange illness laid him low at Gethsemane, Rasputin had kept a descriptive written account. Laboriously, he had taken notes in his large, awkward, and semi-illiterate handwriting, and the resultant comments on his oddysey were made into a journal painstakingly and lovingly edited by the Tsaritsa herself.[10] While performing this task Aleksandra was radiant, a fact noted by the Tsar and others, for to her the words of their "Friend" were positive proof of his divine mission in life. In general, the health of the Empress was poor. She often complained of shortness of breath, and even palpitations from what she believed to be an enlarged heart. Yet while engaged in this work she seemed perfectly normal, indeed happier and more vivacious than she had been in years. She did not in the least mind the misspelled words or the uneven scrawl. She cared nothing for the fact that the scraps of paper were ink-blotched, even stained with grease from the food items that had lain with them in Rasputin's knapsack. Were saints necessarily *neat*? It was the words that counted, sometimes so beautifully expressed as to clearly reveal to her their heavenly origin. How, she asked herself, could a man not of God be even remotely capable of such thoughts?

To Fülöp-Miller we are indebted for the following partial exerpts:

At sea: What shall I say about the peace of the ocean? As I put forth from Odessa, a wonderful quietude at once surrounded me, my soul rejoiced in the sea and slumbered softly. I saw how the little waves glittered, and I desired to seek no further. When I rose in the morning, the waves spoke to me, and their movement refreshed my heart. And as the sun slowly rises from the sea, in its light the soul of man forgets all sorrow, and understands the book and the wisdom of life. . . .

In Constantinople: What can I, with my poor human understanding, say of the splendid and marvelous Cathedral of Saint Sophia? Like a cloud on the horizon is this Cathedral. Woe unto us that God's wrath at our pride was so great that He surrendered this shrine to the unbelieving Turk! May the Lord hear my prayer and restore to us this Church, so that it may be his Ark!

In this Cathedral is also to be seen the pulpit of St. John the Evangelist, and also the bones of St. Efim and the pillar to which the Savior was chained. We stand on the spot where St. John once preached, and it is as if we still hear his voice. . . .

On the journey through the Mediterranean: . . . The Greek bishops can all read and write, and can conduct divine service excellently; the services here are very ceremonious. But poverty in spirit is a higher thing. The bishop, who is not of the poor in spirit, weeps when he does not receive a cross; but who bears the cross in himself is fair even in his simple robe and enjoys the love of the people. . . .

In Jerusalem: I have reached the end of my journeying, and have arrived in the Holy City of Jerusalem. After passing from the great waves of the sea into the earthly paradise of peace, I first of all held a divine service. I cannot describe my joy, for ink is powerless in the face of so much happiness.

. . . What am I to say about the minutes as I approached the tomb of our Lord Jesus Christ? I felt that this tomb is a tomb of love; before it the heart is spiritualized, and we see before us all the people we love, and they too feel happy and at peace in that moment, no matter where they may be. . . .[11]

It is curious that when Rasputin wrote of Gethsemane he made no mention of his out-of-body experience or his subsequent serious illness, both of which he related to his daughter. He intended his notes for Aleksandra. Did he then think she would not believe him? As he used the pronoun *we* in this instance, he was apparently with a group of tourists or pilgrims when he went to the Mount of Olives. Just as apparently, when they left he remained behind. He wrote:

Next we went to the Garden of Gethsemane, in which the Savior groaned and prayed before His death. We unworthy ones greeted this place, and bowed in devotion at the thought that our Lord Jesus Christ here shed tears of blood. God save us, and have pity upon us in Thine heart! Then we saw the stones on which the disciples slept until Christ came to awaken them. But we sleep eternally in sin—awaken us, Lord God![12]

For a man whose enemies were already castigating him as "savage" and "Antichrist" he appended a very gentle reminder:

The greatest thing in the world is love, and only through love can we find the way to Heaven. A morsel of bread is often more important and precious to men than a great ship![13]

So it was that the prodigal returned home. But to what scenes of gloom and foreboding? One very important change had occurred. Vladimir Kokovtsov was now Prime Minister of Russia, a man whose hatred for Rasputin was equaled only by that of his predecessor, Stolypin. The new Premier's succession was not a pleasant thing to contemplate. Indeed, it resulted from a conspiracy so pregnant with treachery and sordidness that he had little reason to congratulate himself even though he had taken no part in it.

Pyotr Stolypin had endured a very difficult premiership. Although in some ways a political genius and possessed of excellent qualities of judgment and leadership, from the start he had been plagued by antagonistic forces both within and outside the government. Count Sergius Witte, the former Premier, so much resented his own ousting he had become an active intriguer whose goal was to bring Stolypin down. Because the latter upheld the Duma, nobility supporting rigid autocratic principles plotted against him. Most vital of all in the undermining of his position, his attempt to banish Rasputin from the capital had won him the undying enmity of the Tsaritsa. Who could be more vindictive than a mother fighting for her child's life?

Stolypin weathered it all, for a while. Though the Tsar's innate mysticism and fatalistic attitude in important matters of state frayed his nerves and were a factor in his declining health, although he had attempted to resign when bills he supported were defeated and suffered the humiliation of Nikolai's nonacceptance of this, as the fall of 1911 approached he had managed to maintain power by one means or another, to hold a very fractious Russia together, and in the purely pragmatic view of statecraft he had reason for calculated optimism.

Stolypin was not optimistic. By this time well aware of Aleksandra's antagonism, he was too astute not to realize that the days of his career were all but numbered. He was depressed and deeply resentful. It was in this mood that in September he joined the royal entourage on a trip to Kiev, where the Tsar intended to honor the memory of his late father. A statue of Aleksandr III was to be unveiled. There were to be the usual ceremonies. Once in the city and moving through the streets by carriage, Stolypin turned to his companion Kokovtsov and bitterly noted a callous distinction. Around the Tsar was a strong protective guard, both Cossacks and secret police. Around the Premier and Finance Minister was not one armed man, plainclothes or uniformed, a fact that in Stolypin's opinion spoke volumes. They would be easy targets for an assassin and he the primary one.

As fate willed, there *was* such a plot afoot. Revolutionaries were the presumed instigators. The instrument of liquidation was a Jewish zealot named Mordka Bogrov, a double agent who was simultaneously a Leftist underground insurgent and an informer for the tsarist police.[14] By the time the Tsar arrived in Kiev the scenario for political murder had already been written.

To this grim sequence of events there is a curious addendum. Fülöp-Miller relates that "just before Stolypin's assassination" Rasputin was in Nizhni-Novgorod (now Gorki), where the Tsar had sent him to examine the fitness of that city's governor, Aleksandr Khvostov, for the office of Minister of the Interior. The claim is creditable, for by this time the *starets* was wielding such power despite his unorthodox and offhand methods of examination.

However, another very reputable biographer, Robert K. Massie, makes no mention of this. Instead, at the time of the killing he places Rasputin in the city of Kiev itself, stimulating his readers' curiosity with only a few brief sentences:

> By a startling but purely coincidental meshing of fates, Rasputin was in Kiev that day, standing in the crowd, observing the procession. As Stolypin's carriage clattered past, Rasputin became agitated and began to mumble. Suddenly, he called out in a dramatic voice, "Death is after him! Death is driving behind him!" For the rest of the night, Rasputin continued muttering about Stolypin's death.[15]

British author Colin Wilson agrees with Massie. However, he adds one bit of information that gives more plausibility to Rasputin being in Kiev, for apparently he had not been invited. The *starets* was there, he says, as escort to Anna Virubova, who of course had carte blanche, and indeed he notes that she had earlier been with him twice in

Pokrovskoye, something Maria Rasputin neglected to mention. Vi-rubova then is the source for the strange instance of Rasputin's clair-voyance at the procession, and she is usually reliable. But how can one account for Fülöp-Miller?

Could it be that all three authors are right? Very few writers seem to precisely locate Rasputin at all at this time, yet a map reveals the logic of such an itinerary. From St. Petersburg, the *starets* may well have gone to Nizhni-Novgorod first, proceeding southeast by train and then southwest to Kiev, arriving there just in time to witness the prelude to tragedy. Would Vyrubova have been with him throughout? As one of his most devoted adherents, it is likely. Did he actually see this event clairvoyantly as his companion later reported? Massie does not cite witnesses to support Wilson's contention about Vyrubova. Nonetheless, from all that is known of Rasputin's life it is perfectly possible. He knew the Tsar would be in Kiev. He thought of himself as Nikolai's protector. If anyone in that vast throng saw this harbinger of destruction through the power of *déjà vu*, it was the Siberian.

Stolypin never had a chance. On the evening of the day after his arrival in the city, as a matter of course he was with the Emperor's following at the opera as one of several distinguished guests, the au-dience anticipating a gala performance of Rimsky-Korsakov's *Tsar Sultan*. He sat in the front row with other notables. The Tsar, with the two eldest grand duchesses Olga and Tatiana, was lodged in the Imperial box overlooking stage right. Using a ticket reserved for police to get in to the theater, Bogrov had no difficulty. He was well dressed and inconspicuous because of it. It was during intermission. Stolypin turned to face the aisle as Bogrov strode down it. Two shots were fired. Both hit the Premier in the chest. He crossed himself, looked up at the Tsar with what some say was an expression of reproach, and collapsed.

The victim survived five days. Bogrov was captured, tried, found guilty, and executed. The Tsar had been nearly as vulnerable. Why had not he too been shot? Historians have speculated. Some have posed the hypothesis that with the exception of the assassin himself the conspirators were not revolutionists but highly placed reactionaries of the far Right, nobles who hated Stolypin for his support of the Duma and used the Leftist Bogrov as their instrument. Because the murderer was a Jew, there were many who demanded universal vengeance by bloody and immediate pogroms. Kokovtsov, heir apparent to Stolypin's powerful office, prevented this. In the prevailing opinion of the time the killing of the Prime Minister had benefited no one.

Those who believed this were mistaken. Stolypin had been famous for his reforms and many of the nation's common people were beginning to rally to him. Had he lived, he might well and truly have launched Russia on a course of rapidly developing democracy. There was only one organization to profit from his death, the one whose leaders always talked of the people's "rights," but who in reality were concerned with their own acquisition of power and the armed establishment of ruthless dictatorship. Bogrov had been of their ranks; they stood on the remote Left; from the beginning, their banners had been the color of blood. The Bolsheviks.

Once in possession of the Government's top portfolio, Kokovtsov wasted no time in trying to remove Rasputin from the scene. Being formerly Finance Minister and with his finger still very much on the pulse of the Imperial Treasury, he began by secretly offering Rasputin a very heavy bribe, believed by some researchers to have been nearly a million rubles. The Tsar's internal security people may have informed him of this. In any event, his third daughter, Grand Duchess Maria, heard of it and told her best friend, Maria Rasputin, that the *starets* had laughed in Kokovtsov's face. Men had been killed in Russia for less provocation than that laugh, far less. If Rasputin was not reachable by the covert offering of a fortune, Kokovtsov knew he would have to make other plans.

One thing that was sure to aid the new Prime Minister in his relentless vendetta was the power of the inevitable spreading gossip once tales had been circulated in the city. Another was the strongly biased and unscrupulous press, which since Count Witte's Manifesto of October 17, 1905 had been free from official censorship. The press now attacked Rasputin with increasing vigor, printing unproved calumnies, knowing such "yellow journalism" to be a certain guarantee of greatly increased circulation. Their unrestrained vitriol knew scarcely any bounds. Old accusations were unearthed and brought forth anew with stronger venom. The "false starets" was corrupt to the bone marrow. He had long ago seduced the Empress and the four princesses were his playthings. So was Anna Vyrubova. Clearly implied but not usually stated in so many words was the charge that the Tsar was virtually a prisoner in his own palace, that Rasputin, a latter-day Boris Godunov,[16] controlled him utterly and had nothing less in mind than the ultimate seizure of the throne. Hot copy this. Sensational beyond living memory. In St. Petersburg and Moscow in particular, newspaper sales reached an all-time high as the honor of the Tsar and Tsaritsa of Russia was peddled for a few *kopeks* a sheet.

Needless to say, Nikolai was furious. As for Aleksandra, although all possible measures were taken to keep this scurrilous material from reaching her, some of it did in fact fall into her hands. Her feelings may well be imagined. Seldom in good health after the year 1908, her periodic shortness of breath, blueness of the lips, and what Dr. Botkin described as "progressive hysteria" all increased markedly. In a situation as grave and threatening as this, Aleksandr III would have counterattacked savagely and decisively, and heads would have rolled, but Nikolai abhorred violence. Exercising his royal prerogative, his feeble response was to forbid the press to mention Rasputin's name, fines being levied for violation of the order. It was ineffective. In the end, much to his wife's fearful chagrin, the Tsar surrendered.

Calmly, and with great gentleness and tact, Nikolai told Rasputin what the latter already knew, that the situation was extremely dangerous and rapidly deteriorating. Rasputin could no longer remain in St. Petersburg. His home in Pokrovskoye was recommended. The Emperor said this to the *starets* with his arm around his shoulder. Once again, as he had done during the previous crisis, *Otyets* Grigori acceded with grace, though in his eyes was a profound sadness. He said he would never do anything to hurt those he loved. Nikolai said he knew this. In moments of extreme poignancy Rasputin then blessed the Tsar, and minutes later, alone with her in another room, the stricken Tsaritsa. Tearfully, she told him she would bring him back. "I will talk to the Tsar. He will listen to me." Rasputin said he hoped so.

As he boarded the train at the station with Maria and Dunia a chill was in the air, a cold from the Siberian steppe that heralded the coming winter. In his mind's reflective mirror was the face of a small boy, his blue eyes wide with fear, his pale lips open in mute supplication. What would happen to this child now?

At last, what so many conspirators of varying degrees of influence had striven for had been accomplished. Rasputin was out of the capital. They believed he could not return this time. He had been damned as a liar and charlatan, a fornicator and false monk traitorous to Church and Tsar, a seducer of wives and young girls who was clearly a servant of Satan. Could he overcome charges like *these*? Perhaps, for Fate works in strange ways. Little did his accusers know that not a year would pass before their intended victim would perform one of the most amazing feats in all history. Before the ground whitened with the snows of another winter the unbelievable would happen.

NOTES

1. The *Streltsy*, or Archers, were a military caste allied with certain Cossacks who plotted to overthrow Peter the Great and replace him with his half-sister Sophie. In 1697, and again two years later, the Tsar's vengeance embraced the most frightful reign of terror seen in Russia since Ivan the Terrible.

2. The king who, at Thermopylae in 480 B.C., led his 300 Spartans and 700 Thespians against the Persian hordes of the invading King Xerxes.

3. Athenian statesman and general. As a child he was one of the lovers of the renowned philosopher Socrates, and others. Consult *Plutarch's Lives* in two volumes, the Sir Thomas North translation. Heritage Press, New York, 1941.

4. Prince Feliks Yussupov, *Rasputin*, Dial Press, New York, 1927.

5. *Ibid.*

6. Maria Rasputin and Patte Barham, *Rasputin: The Man Behind the Myth*, Warner Books, New York, 1977. (Published by arrangement with Prentice-Hall, Inc.)

7. *Ibid.*

8. Although Yussupov describes Rasputin's eyes as "grey," his daughter Maria says they were a "deep blue." According to Fülöp-Miller, there were others whose description of them conflicted, almost as though they had the power to change their hue with Rasputin's altering emotional pattern or a marked flux in his cerebral activity.

9. Robert K. Massie, *Nicholas and Alexandra*, Atheneum, New York, 1967.

10. In his calculated effort to denigrate Rasputin, Yussupov was careful to include in his book no fewer than three examples of the handwriting of the *starets*, apparently in the belief that its childish appearance would help establish a case for an ignorant

upstart who foisted himself on his superiors. Had he been given only the same amount of instruction and practice, one wonders how well Yussupov might have written.

11. René Fülöp-Miller, *Rasputin: The Holy Devil*, Viking Press, New York, 1928, Chap. VII, pp. 174–178.

12. *Ibid.*, pp. 177–178.

13. *Ibid.*, p. 179.

14. Bogrov's role appears to have been similar to that of the monk Father Gapon in the abortive revolution of 1905, and of the notorious Erno Azev, a leader of the Social Revolutionary Party's Central Terrorist Organization in the same uprising.

15. Massie, *op. cit.*

16. Godunov, Tatar favorite of Ivan the Terrible, became head of the Council of Regency during the reign of Ivan's feebleminded son, Feodor Ivanovich. So thoroughly did he make himself the power behind the throne that when the religiously crazed monarch died in 1598, Godunov assumed the crown with little opposition. Seizing on his strange saga as highly dramatic, the nineteenth-century Russian composer Modeste Moussorgsky wove Aleksandr Pushkin's dark tale into a compelling opera, *Boris Godunov*.

CHAPTER 9

The Miracle

In Pokrovskoye the increasingly chilly days drifted by pleasantly. All were placid in the Rasputin home. Although seemingly no word was ever spoken of it, the probability is that Praskovia knew of her husband's relationship with Dunia.[1] It did not matter to her. She still loved him and knew he returned her love, but it was in another way now. Her strict religious upbringing made her believe that the only real justification for sex was procreation. She could not bear more children. Years ago, her tumor and the resultant hysterectomy had ended that. As for Grigori, she knew that his need for women continued to be gratified, even believing he derived special strength from his concourse with them. He needed that strength, she thought, for his task in life was so arduous, so wearing. Concerning the giving of his sexual favors she once remarked "He has enough for all." Now she was his companion if not his lover, the companion of Dunia, also. The heart of Praskovia was big enough to embrace them both.

The winter came. Rasputin preached as he had done of yore and all were enraptured by his inspired words and simple, understandable logic. All save one. *Otyets* Pyotr had not changed. He was still the village priest of Pokrovskoye, still smitten with jealousy and bitterness at the mere mention of Rasputin's name. His anger did him no good. As had happened before, the people left his church nearly empty and went to listen to the *starets*. In vain did Pyotr rail against him from the pulpit, echoing the foul slanders that had appeared in the news-papers. No one believed the stories. Yes, Rasputin was probably a Khlist but *that* was not a crime here. Siberia was full of villages whose members sheltered The People of God and had done so since time immemorial. Who else made them feel that God was *within themselves*? Who else made them really believe it? Rasputin could be a Khlist. He could also be a Khlisti *vozhd*, a leader within the sect. They loved him all the more.

The year 1911 passed. When the following spring came, Rasputin spent much time on the Tura River fishing with his three children. Maria, Varya, and Dmitri were delighted to be with their father.[2] If the boy was retarded, he nonetheless knew very well he was loved. If Rasputin thought of how this same river had stolen the life of his brother Mischa in the long ago, he was careful not to let it dampen his spirits. Mischa was all right, he knew. He was with God and better off than any of them.

Summer came and was followed by a glorious beginning of au-tumn. Rasputin loved this time of year. The fall colors were magnif-icent, the woods and glades incomparably beautiful, and his soul rejoiced at the sheer splendor of it. St. Petersburg? Except for his fear for the safety of the Imperial Family and his compassion for the Tsarevich he was relieved to be away from it. What was it after all but a nest of vipers and den of iniquity, the unrepentant Sodom of modern Russia? What were its venal and jaded citizens but foxes? Solomon knew their nature well. "Take us the foxes, the little foxes that spoil the vines: for our vines have tender grapes." How great was the wisdom of Solomon.

Time drifted on. It grew later in the fall. Rasputin thought of the Romanovs and tried to see them in his mind. They would be in Poland now, first at the railhead of Skierniewice southwest of Warsaw, then at Bialowieza in the east where they went every year at this time, followed by the short drive to the royal hunting lodge of Spala. The Tsar hunted the nearly extinct European bison called the aurochs. Once the Little Father had mentioned that this bull-like creature had been a great favorite of the spectators in the Colosseum of ancient Rome, that trained gladiators had fought it single-handed and often were gored to death on its horns.[3] Yet it was only a dumb beast, only an unwilling victim after all. Had it *asked* to fight those men of iron? The Polish forests were its last retreat, its final hopeless refuge. He wondered at the contradiction. How strange that even the gentle Nikolai could kill.

Rasputin's belief was correct. In the deep, dark forests of eastern Poland the Tsar did hunt. Polish noblemen accompanied him. Recently he had been in Moscow, celebrating the centenary of the epic Battle of Borodino where the elusive General Mikhail Kutuzov had met the invading French in 1812, where Russians for the first time had fought Napoleon to a standstill, on their lips the age-old battle cry of "*Krov za krov!*"—"Blood for blood!" Now he was in Poland. Now he rode through sun-dappled verdure with his ever-active girls, the grand duchesses, and wrote to the Dowager Empress to tell her of their pleasure. Maria Feodorovna was happy for her son.

As usual, the Tsarevich did not go riding with them, for this was one of the many activities that was forbidden to him. Instead, he sought diversion by plying the oars of a rowboat on a small lake. All went well for a while. Repeatedly he rowed without mishap. But a day came when his natural exuberance was costly. About to take out the boat, he leaped into it and lost his balance, falling heavily against a metal oarlock. The injury was to his left upper thigh. On examination by Dr. Botkin, all that could be seen was a slight swelling near the groin and the discoloration characteristic of subcutaneous bleeding. The Crown Prince had to be immobilized at once. Botkin put him to bed and kept him there for the better part of a week, the Tsaritsa ministering to his wants meanwhile and trying to remain cheerful. Quite soon he seemed better. The doctor told the Tsar a crisis had been averted and all would be well. Yes, His Royal Highness would be up and about again shortly. Yes, the next leg of the planned itinerary could be safely undertaken.

For centuries, Spala had been to the Polish kings what ill-fated Mayerling was to the Austrian emperors, a hunting retreat intimately associated with the lives (sometimes the very private lives) of the crowned heads of state who annually took up brief residence there.[4] But Poland was not Poland now. It was Russian Poland and had been so since the final defeat of Napoleon at Waterloo and the deliberations of the Congress of Vienna had made the extinction of Polish freedom a certainty.[5] Under these changing conditions Spala became one of several royal hunting lodges of the tsars. It had its advantages. Although the villa itself was not structurally imposing and was dark and gloomy, the vast forest surrounding it was teeming with game of many species and virtually in its primeval state. Here Nikolai relaxed, sharpened his already expert marksmanship, and forgot the cares of sovereignty. Here also, Pierre Gilliard, Swiss tutor to the royal children, began at Aleksandra's request to give French lessons to the Tsarevich. The always stylishly dressed and punctilious scholar drew closer to the boy than ever before and began to indulge in a more careful scrutiny of him. He had always known of Aleksei's ill health but never its diagnosis. Now, as though for the first time, he noted the frequency with which lessons were interrupted, the child's ambulatory difficulties, even those occasions when he became unexpectedly bedridden. More than ever the tutor wondered about the identity of this strange malady.

The Tsaritsa fretted. Was there no way she could provide Aleksei with *safe* recreation? So full of cheer and hope he was. "I'll be all right, Mama," he would say. "I'll be all right." It was as though *he* tried to comfort *her*. Each time the Tsar and the princesses left to go riding, the mother could hardly bear the lost look on her son's face and it seemed that her heart would break.

It was October 12, 1912, a day a clairvoyant might have singled out as *fated*. Aleksandra discussed the problem with Anna Vyrubova. They agreed that a ride in a horse-drawn carriage would be the next best thing to a ride on a horse itself. Instantly Aleksei brightened at the suggestion. To an active boy of his age it seemed that the greatest enemy of all was that of sheer unremitting boredom. The real foe, however, the deadly and relentless foe that sought his life, got into the carriage when the lad entered it, lurking as always in his genes and his blood. He sat between his mother and her friend. This way the women believed they could protect him with their bodies, even grasp and hold him safely between them should anything unexpected occur. They didn't count on the condition of the road. It was of loose-packed sand, rutted in places by the passage of steel-rimmed cart-wheels, even crumbling here and there along its edges where eroded by flowing water. From the first rough jolt Aleksei exhibited signs of distress. Within a few minutes there was painful cramping in his abdomen and legs, and his face bore the characteristic pallor his mother so dreaded.

Realizing what was happening, Aleksandra ordered the carriage turned around, then clung to the Tsarevich in an effort to steady and support him for the return drive. It was of no avail. Although the horses instinctively followed a track offering the best footing, many of the ruts could not be avoided by the wheels, and for all three occupants the swaying, lurching carriage became a conveyance locked in the throes of a frightful dream. Eventually they got back to the villa. When they did so Aleksei was nearly in a fainting condition and unable to walk. Servants lifted him from the carriage and carried him into the house.

Now it was not as before. There was to be no reprieve this time, real or imagined. Dr. Botkin's examination revealed heavy internal bleeding in the groin and upper left thigh, positive proof that the injury sustained in the boat had not healed. He had never seen it so bad before. Although he told the royal parents there was every hope for eventual recovery, they sensed his deep concern and began once again that surrender to increasing trauma leading inevitably toward despair. Hastily sent telegrams to St. Petersburg summoned other doctors attached to the Court and they came quickly. Collectively, they represented some of the best medical brains in Russia, among them specialists in blood diseases with wide experience. They examined the groaning boy. They consulted together, engaging in spirited though discreetly hushed conversation. As it had been before, so it was now. They could find no solution.

Gradually, the bleeding increased until Aleksei was in agony and screams broke from his lips. As building venous pressure burst one blood vessel after another in his left leg his tortured body jackknifed as it had done before, leg doubling against chest, the unstoppable hemorrhage spreading until the entire region from sacrum to thigh to groin was one vast blood-filled hematoma. How large could this swelling become before the grotesquely stretched skin finally burst and the child's life literally gushed onto the bed? How long could the condition prevail before the victim lapsed into coma? The physicians could only guess. In nearly any patient but one suffering from hemophilia they might have drained some of it off, but to puncture Aleksei's flesh would almost certainly be fatal. None would take the responsibility for it. Once again the familiar and dreadful impasse had been reached. The doctors could offer no hope. Death within days, perhaps within hours, seemed certain.

So the ordeal began. As had happened five years before, Aleksandra mounted her ceaseless vigil by her son's side, exhausting herself emotionally and physically, sharing his agony in that filial unity with her offspring that only a mother can know. Not for her the softness and warmth of normal repose nor even a change of clothing. She slept sitting up. Occasionally she lay beside him. In the end, because his pain-racked moaning and his pleading for her help went on and on until she thought that her grief would drive her mad, there was nothing left but continuous prayer. The Tsar could not help her. Even more unstrung than she, he sometimes found it impossible to remain with them and left the room in tears. The Tsarevich pleaded for God to take him. He wanted to die. As the eyes of the Empress brimmed to overflowing, he asked for a small monument in the forest.

Day after day it went on like this. When word of Aleksei's grave illness spread in St. Petersburg, every cathedral and church in the city held special prayer services for the heir to the throne. Soon half of Russia knew of it. Everywhere the people went to their knees. As with the previous heavy attack years before, they did not know the nature of the malady that was killing him, only that it was deadly. Outside the villa the peasants of the nearby village gathered. They too prayed ceaselessly. They were Poles, not Russians; Catholics, not Orthodox. When he saw them the Tsar was deeply moved, for they had no reason to love him. They were human and possessed common humanity, and they understood pain and adversity.

Ultimately, a day came that was not like the others. Everyone close to the small sufferer sensed it. It was the eleventh day since the attack. Aleksandra knew that her son was dying. From the sickroom she sent a note to the Tsar to tell him so, conveying in her hasty scrawl a poignancy and torment indescribable. With Fedorov, one of the doctors, Nikolai, his face looking as pale and wasted as that of his wife, hastened to the Tsarevich. Yes, it was true. All could see it now. Falling to his knees, the Tsar begged for his son's life. Few scenes were ever more harrowing. As white as parchment, Aleksei lived through the day. Wailing piteously, he survived the night as well, but each hour of the following day that passed was like the tolling of a silent bell that could only betoken the child's certain death.

Time seemed to stop. An Orthodox priest administered the *Soborovaniyeh* (the Last Rites, or what the Catholics would call Extreme Unction). Arriving in St. Petersburg, the daily bulletin on the Heir's condition spoke guardedly of his imminent demise. It was the end. It *had* to be the end and everyone knew it. Aleksandra could bear it no longer. Haggard almost beyond recognition, her eyes bloodshot, her ravaged countenance as pallid as wax, it was shortly after sunset when she turned her tear-stained face to Anna Vyrubova. She would do it now. She would do it though all the demons of hell claw at her vulnerable flesh and rip her to pieces. They all hated him? What did it matter? What did it matter if the whole world was full of hate? Anna must send a telegram immediately. Only *his* prayers would be heeded by God, no one else's. Only *his*. The name on the lips of the Tsaritsa was one that had been there many times before. Aleksei had called him "*Novykh*," the New Man, but she had called him saint. She *still* called him that. *Otyets* Grigori.

The date was October 11, 1912.[6] Afternoon. With Maria, Rasputin walked at a leisurely pace on the north bank of the Tura. They talked. They listened to the flowing water and the sounds of wildlife, no longer a myriad chorus but already beginning to diminish with the coming of winter. They joked a little and watched their breath congeal in the crisp autumn air, each of them warmed by the close camaraderie. For the first time in years the *starets* felt almost at peace with himself. For a man so emotionally complex, he even knew some moments of happiness.

Then it all changed abruptly. The minutes passed with inexorable precision. Not one additional leaf seemed to fall. Maria's voice was far away. Like a measured beat coming from somewhere outside the universe he became acutely aware of the passage of time, of its flow in another dimension, an entity unto itself. *Was it happening again?* Oh the incredible worlds he must penetrate in order to enter other worlds. He felt his breath catch in his throat. Without warning, like the all-too-sudden revelation of a path soaked with human tears, a scene of indescribable pathos filled his mind and overwhelmed him. His hand went to his heart, and he cried out.

"Oh no!"

"What is it, Papa?" Maria asked fearfully. "What is it?"

"It is not I, little one," he said. "Do not fear for me. It is the Tsarevich. He has been stricken."[7]

He felt sick. They walked home together. So weak had he become suddenly that he placed his hand on Maria's shoulder for support. He did not know how bad it was with Aleksei and could not grasp the details. It was as though that part of the vision were blurred, as though an impenetrable veil had been lowered and his powers blighted, a gift that was not a gift because it was incomplete. That night he was restless, unable to sleep. It was serious. If it were less than that he would not have received the message. But then surely the Tsaritsa would contact him, would she not? Yes. Yes. Yes. He would wait. He would wait.

Within a few days, a bulletin on the Heir's condition reached Tobolsk and Tyumen and from those cities was dispersed to the outlying villages. The tidings spread rapidly. Pokrovskoye received them. The people said that by the grace of *Sudbina*, the Lady Fate whose hand was the hand of God, the Tsarevich lived. Rasputin knew they were tossing crumbs to the people, tiny, meaningless crumbs, and the absence of candor in those who knew the truth gnawed at his mind. His little prince, his golden-haired Alesha *needed* him, that much he knew. *Radi Bog* (for God's sake), if he were not called upon to act the child would die, *his* child in the spiritual sense, whose terrible accident he had foreseen clairvoyantly *the day before it happened*. Through the ether it seemed he could hear Alesha's voice. "Please, Mama! Please send for the Little Father! Please!" Would Aleksandra heed his cry? Would she send for him *now*? "Little Father" was what the nation called the Tsar, but for the Tsar's children it was he, *Otyets* Grigori.

The telegram from the Empress, Anna Virubova's telegram, was placed in Rasputin's hands at noon when the family was ready for the midday meal. As he read it, his features blanched. Yes, he had

been right. His prophetic soul had warned him truly. Now he went
to the household altar of Our Lady of Kazan. He fell to his knees.
While Praskovia and Dunia held the children in strictest silence, he
prayed with all the strength that was in him for the life of the Crown
Prince, imploring God Almighty, begging Him with a shuddering,
mind-enveloping intensity never equaled in the past, arms out-
stretched, hands clasped in abject supplication as his lips moved silently and the sweat poured down his face to soak his beard.

"Oh my God, hear me now. Oh my God, for the peace and
tranquility of Holy Russia, and the good of all, spare the life of the
Tsarevich. Do not let him die, O God! Succour him, O Lord of
Hosts, as thou didst succour the Children of Israel in the time of their
wandering and adversity!"

On and on he prayed; on and on until it seemed that time and
space and Eternity itself all rolled into one. His muscles cramped
agonizingly, but he ignored it. His knees became raw but he ignored
that, too, for pain was only of the mind and controllable. Then at
last, in a great blazing flash of divine luminescence he saw it again,
the blinding vision of the field in Pokrovskoye that had eluded him
so long, the Virgin of Kazan glittering and golden, her face radiant
beyond radiance, magnificent beyond splendor. She was smiling at
him. The Mother of God was *smiling* at him. Encompassed by a
wonderment such as he had never known, momentarily struck dumb
by the sheer power of the celestial miracle he knew was descending
upon him, he staggered to his feet and silently crossed himself. He
left the house without a word. He went to the telegraph office. With
his soul singing a paeon of praise to the Almighty he despatched that
telegram to the Tsaritsa which, as events were to transpire, must
surely have been the most remarkable ever sent. It read as follows:
"Have no fear. God has seen your tears and heard your prayers. Do
not grieve. The Little One will not die. Do not allow the doctors to
bother him too much."

At Spala, trembling visibly and with her eyes awash with tears,
the Tsaritsa read the telegram over and over. It was Father Grigori
who promised this, wasn't it? Aleksei's "*Novykh*" promised it. With
the scrap of paper clutched tightly in her shaking hand, she caressed
her son softly to make sure he was awake and showed him the message

from the Little Father. Fighting for control, suppressing as best she could the tears that came from happiness this time, she read it to him. Aleksei brightened. On the drawn little face, so wasted with countless hours of pain and fatigue, the pale ghost of a smile appeared, broadening very gradually on the colorless lips. Aleksandra could not bear it. She took him in her arms and wept with a joy and relief that all but overwhelmed and prostrated her. Nikolai joined them and he wept, too. They stayed the night with Aleksei. In the morning the Tsarevich was left with Anna Virubova. The parents descended the stairs to the drawing room of the villa, but it was Aleksandra who spoke for them both.

She was smiling. Her statement to the anxious members of the royal entourage and resident staff was short and simple. Although the doctors as yet saw no cause for optimism, she and the Tsar were no longer worried. A telegram had come from *Otyets* Grigori in the night. He had prayed for Aleksei's recovery and reassured them. It was now certain beyond all doubt that the Tsarevich was out of danger, for the crisis point had passed. The perfect serenity of the Empress seemed like the coming of a gloriously shining dawn after a savage storm.

Within hours, Aleksei's potentially fatal hemorrhage had ceased, his fever had gone, and his haggard face and emaciated frame had recovered some semblance of normality. He said he no longer felt any pain. Despite his startling pallor and the dark circles under his eyes he was smiling and asked for food. As they had done years before under similar circumstances all the doctors now examined him. They agreed he would survive and expressed their pleasure and satisfaction. Although they were not quite bold enough to confront the Tsaritsa with their denials and accusations, privately they voiced the opinion that Rasputin's prayers played no part in the child's incredible improvement, and more than one of them told this to Nikolai. Cessation of symptoms by so bizarre a method? Brought back from the brink of death by the nonexistent powers of a charlatan, a false monk little different from an African witch doctor? Ridiculous. Medieval. From Pokrovskoye to Spala was a distance of nearly *two thousand miles*. Had the abominable Siberian conquered *space*, then? Surely, His Imperial Majesty could see the utter fallacy of it. Various medications took time to take effect, that's all, *their* medications. It was even possible that certain unknown antibodies within the Heir's blood system had finally come into play and reversed the deadly process. The concept was not new. Long ago, Pasteur had proved its validity with his vaccine against anthrax. But Rasputin? Put quite simply, he was what he had always been, an unscrupulous but clever fake.

Though he appeared to have been nearly as convinced as his wife of the reality of Rasputin's powers, publicly Nikolai withheld judgment, nor did he confide to his diary a single word concerning the awesome telegram. Writing to his mother the Dowager Empress, he conveyed the joyous news, again without mentioning this aspect, for her constant hostility toward the *starets* made it clear that her reaction to it would have been highly negative. The case was carefully chronicled by the doctors. Needless to say, they too ignored the telegram as though it had never been, nor is it recorded in the memoirs of the discreet tutor Pierre Gilliard. Anna Vyrubova writes of it briefly. The telegram came. Aleksei recovered. She offers no explanation or analysis. It is possible the hand of the Empress is seen in this. Although it was she who made the initial announcement of the telegram's arrival, she feared for Rasputin's life and may have had second thoughts. Did not they accuse him of trying to poison Aleksei the last time? Did not they say he was in collusion with the Tibetan magician Badmaev who provided certain lethal powders, that between them they gave or withheld the doses to coincide with Rasputin's *pretended* prayers? People who would go to such extremes to make a spurious claim like that would do anything. Therefore, the less said about the telegram the better.

Recovery was not rapid. It was several weeks before the Imperial Family could leave Poland and return to Tsarskoye Selo, nearly a year before Aleksei could straighten his leg completely, its metal brace be removed, and his ability to walk be restored. None of this signified. From the moment the specter of death had been averted Aleksandra knew beyond all doubt that her judgment, her intuition, and her faith in the *starets* had been vindicated. His enemies would continue to plot against him, to hurl lying invective and slander, and that did not signify either. She made her position plain. For the safety of the Tsarevich the presence of the *starets* in St. Petersburg was vital. She would personally resist another attempt to banish him and God help those who risked her anger.

It was a signal turning point. From the moment the Tsaritsa made the decision to fight for and defend what was hers a new shadow rose over the land, a seemingly monolithic but actually many-faceted entity, a power eclipsing even the red sun of the ever-scheming Bolsheviks with their bloody, guilt-encrusted hands. Rasputin was in the ascendancy. In the conventional sense he was poorly educated and semi-illiterate, and seemed to have a talent for alienating people. Nonetheless, for the foreseeable future he could and would stand like a colossus poised over the Russian Empire.

With the return of the *starets* to his Gorokhovaya address in St. Petersburg (this time, in addition to Dunia and Maria he had his younger daughter Varya with him), his enemies became both more numerous and more determined. Although Hermogen, formerly Bishop of Saratov, remained silently in exile at the Zhirovetsky Monastery, Iliodor, similarly interned at the Monastery of Florishchevo, was entirely another matter. It is possible that personal defeat and professional eclipse may have unhinged his mind, for certainly the lengths to which he carried his hatred and his seeming indifference to the possible consequences are symptomatic of paranoia.

Added to everything else, the former "Knight of the Heavenly Kingdom" and monk-priest of Tsaritsyn was possibly a thief into the bargain. Although it is not known how he accomplished it, on one of his visits to Rasputin's home in Pokrovskoye (apparently in 1909 or 1910) he may have stolen some letters that Aleksandra and two of her daughters had written to Rasputin, and secreted them for future reproduction and widespread circulation. No one knows whether they are forgeries. If genuine, one from the Tsaritsa in particular is extraordinary. When the helplessness and desperation of the Empress are taken into account it also becomes a most moving document, albeit one that might easily be construed as the letter of a woman to her lover. It was precisely this interpretation that was put upon it, as

Iliodor knew would be the case. Apparently, in the late summer or early fall of 1912, *before* Rasputin's incredible telegram to Aleksandra, the vindictive monk managed to get the letters into the hands of Aleksandr Guchkov, Octobrist leader and future president of the Duma. Shortly afterward, they were published in the Muscovite newspaper *Golos Moskvy (Voice of Moscow)*. Purportedly, Aleksandra's letter read as follows:

> My beloved, unforgettable teacher, redeemer and mentor! How tiresome it is without you! My soul is quiet and I relax only when you, my teacher, are sitting beside me. I kiss your hands and lean my head on your blessed shoulder. Oh how light, how light do I feel then. I only wish one thing: to fall asleep, to fall asleep, forever on your shoulders and in your arms. What happiness to feel your presence near me. Where are you? Where have you gone? Oh, I am so sad and my heart is longing. . . . Will you soon be again close to me? Come quickly, I am waiting for you and I am tormenting myself for you. I am asking for your holy blessing and I am kissing your blessed hands. I love you forever.[8]

It is perhaps needless to add that the most pernicious use was made of this letter by the Bolsheviks both before and during the Revolution of 1917, though proof of its genuineness was lacking. In general, it is characteristic of the Tsaritsa's emotional style of writing. Given her undying devotion to Rasputin, it is also conceivable she may have regarded him as a lover if only in the spiritual sense, a sort of communicant with the innermost recesses of her soul. It is said that the deeply religious and ever-virtuous fifteenth-century heroine Joan of Arc loved one of her generals in this way, the subsequently notorious infanticide and sodomite Gilles de Rais (or de Retz), Marshal of France, a man remembered by history as "Bluebeard." In Aleksandra's mind, obsessed as she was with the divine mission of the *starets*, the distinction between godsent saint and earthbound sinner tended to blur.

Again, if the letters circulated by Iliodor are genuine, the eldest and youngest of the Tsar's four daughters also put their feelings for the *starets* into writing. There was a young officer named Nikolai to whom Grand Duchess Olga Nikolaevna, the Tsaritsa's firstborn child, was paying some attention. From Livadia Palace[9] in the Crimea where Aleksandr III had died, she penned the following lines to Rasputin:

My dear precious friend,

It is very sad that it is so long since I have seen you. I am longing for you and often think of you. Where are you going to spend the Christmas holidays? Please write to me. I am always so happy when I get a letter from you.

Do you remember what you said to me about that Nikolai? Ah, if you knew how difficult it is for me to follow your advice. Please forgive my weakness, my good friend. God grant that Mama will be better this winter, or I shall be very sad.

I am very glad to be able to see Father Feofan [Theofan] from time to time. Not long ago I met him in the new Cathedral at Yalta. Our little private chapel is very pretty. *Au revoir*, my dear, precious friend, it is time for me to go to tea. Pray for your true and loving

Olga[10]

Not even Rasputin's enemies could use a letter such as this to prove a sexual liaison between him and Olga. Indeed, it speaks rather clearly of a platonic relationship. The letter to the *starets* from the Tsar's youngest daughter, Grand Duchess Anastasia, though equally loving, would likewise seem free of any hint of physical intimacy. The young girl wrote:

My dear, precious, only friend,

How much I should like to see you again. You appeared to me today in a dream. I am always asking Mama when you will come, and I am happy even to be able to send you my greetings. I send you my warmest wishes for the New Year, and hope it will bring you health and happiness. I think of you always, my dear, because you are so good to me. I have not seen you for such a long time, but no evening passes without my thinking of you. I wish you the best of everything. Mama has promised that when you are here again, I shall see you at Ania's [Anna's]. This thought already brings happiness to

Your Anastasia[11]

But the enemies gathered, and they gathered. Virtually assured of ultimate publication as well as sensational sales, Iliodor began work on a book apparently intended as the exposé of the ages. Branding the Empress of Russia as Rasputin's mistress was only one of its virulent charges. Unfortunately for him he made the error, insensate in the circumstances, of boasting of its contents to some of his cronies, thus precluding any possibility of prolonged secrecy. The result was predictable. Regardless of how bitterly they opposed Rasputin, the authorities of the Orthodox Church were forced to take action against the hate-filled monk. Quickly they unfrocked him. With excommunication and arrest staring him in the face, he donned feminine clothes and slipped across the Norwegian border. From this country he pursued his labors. Ultimately, he tried to blackmail Aleksandra. When her refusal to pay took the form of ignoring him, he simply bided his time. In the end, with World War I raging and the Imperial Family prisoners in Ekaterinburg (renamed Tobolsk by the revolutionaries), an American magazine publisher bought his material without attempting to verify its accuracy. The legend of Rasputin's viciousness and betrayal of his country (Iliodor accused both him and the Tsaritsa of working secretly for the German Government) was born in the mind of a half-crazed fanatic.

It was this pivotal year of 1912 that saw extraordinary changes in Rasputin. For one thing, he began to drink and carouse far more than ever before, and his favorite Madeira was rapidly becoming an incurable wine addiction that promised ultimate ruin. For another, his influence over the Royal Family was giving greater and greater political power to a man who originally had never sought it. For a third, his fascination with women and sex, now allowed unlimited scope, had become an obsession that was beginning to exceed all bounds, albeit a kind of safety valve for his truly phenomenal energy.

But these were all *symptoms* of a disturbed state of mind, not *causes*. The question recurs: Why, when he knew that a return to the seat of power meant virtually certain death by assassination, did he go back to St. Petersburg? Why, when his incredible clairvoyance presented the grimness of his fate as a deadly inevitability, did he deliberately choose to reenter the struggle and embrace this awful destiny? A careful study of the situation in which he found himself, buttressed by a psychoanalytical delving into the extraordinary mind of this man, may provide the answer.

Initially then, Rasputin returned to St. Petersburg and its melancholy promise of early extinction because, given his character and beliefs, he had no other choice. Inherently brave, of peasant origin and Russian to the core, he genuinely believed in monarchy and autocracy, and loved the Imperial Family perhaps even more than he knew. His precognition told him their peril was both grave and gradually increasing. His visions, all of them, pointed in the same direction and to the same task. In his mind, it was his irreversible destiny to succor these royal ones in their time of dire need, especially his beloved Aleksei, who without his "*Novykh*" must surely perish. God had appointed him their guardian. The Blessed Virgin had made the signs and portents clear. The path he must trod was laid out for him long before, perhaps in another life.

Still, even a firm belief in predestination does not armor the body or soul against the rigors of incessant attack. In 1912 Rasputin was under more intense fire than ever before. The hatred against him had doubled and trebled and redoubled again; he felt it acutely, and man of iron though he was, he reacted to it with defense mechanisms that were very human indeed. Excessive drinking was one of them, for he was surprisingly sensitive and drink numbed the senses. A stroll down the corridors of power? He could use political strength to fight off his foes. If he could acquire enough of it he could break some of them, thus gaining back a little of his own, momentary satisfaction against the day of his ultimate demise. And women? To some men sex is a drug more vital, gratifying, and life-renewing than all other stimulants combined, no matter how pleasurable. Sex is a foretaste of Paradise to some men. He was one of them.

In ancient times, when Moses, foremost lawgiver of Israel, climbed Mount Sinai to receive from God the clay tablet bearing the Ten Commandments, the "Word of Jehovah" thus inscribed was placed in a wheeled protective casket which with its contents was called by the Jews the "Arc of the Covenant." Ultimately, in the days of Solomon, when that great Judean king built his temple at Jerusalem, the sacred Arc was placed in the innermost chamber of that colossal tabernacle and the name given to this most venerated sanctuary was the "Holy of Holies."

As concerns the activities of Rasputin and his disciples at his Gorokhovaya flat, no one seems to know exactly how this title came to be applied or by whom. It may first have been used by one of his followers and approved by Rasputin. However, the probability is that he was the author of it. From having been at first a location, specifically the dining room, the "Holy of Holies" evolved to include those members of Father Grigori's coterie who associated with him on terms of physical and spiritual intimacy, for with this fanatically devoted group the two states of being were indivisible. Ironically, it was perhaps no accident that the name of a chamber in an edifice built by Solomon was selected, for the son of David and Bathsheba had a harem of over 700 women. Rasputin had far fewer than that. The hard core of his circle in the early years was perhaps fifteen. New initiates were frequently tested. Some tried the life only briefly and their contacts with the *starets* soon faded. Others remained indefinitely, and there is little doubt that those who did were intensely happy and voluptuously fulfilled.

Completely democratic in its membership, the group was composed of women of every class, not even excluding princesses and other titled personages. An occasional prostitute made her appearance among them. In those days they were frequently referred to as "actresses." But there were more ordinary types as well. Katya Ivanovna, Rasputin's maid servant from Pokrovskoye, was with him now, joining Dunia to share her labors and, quite obviously, her master's bed. Fülöp-Miller mentions a second Katya as well, a seamstress who also granted the *starets* her favors at his need and discretion; as did Yuravleva, described as the wife of a man known only as "the concierge"; Utilya, an attractive masseuse working in the same building; the wife of a resident porter whose name has not survived; and so on.

Lest it be thought that Rasputin was at any time stricken with conscience over his liaisons with married women, it should be remembered that among the Khlisti no marriage performed by an Orthodox priest not of the sect was ever considered valid. To the *starets*, therefore, all the females who came within his ken were *single* and fair game. The married ones flocked to him like all the others. His redemptive doctrine of salvation through sin made it much easier for them to rationalize their carnality. Indeed, they gloried in it, for sex with the "Holy Father" was not only a thrilling act of devotion but a joyous privilege that might readily be construed as a sign of God's favor.

As time passed, Rasputin's methods of seducing new prospects became more and more direct until he dispensed with all manner of delay and pretense, and the finesse that might be expected of so experienced a man gave way, in some instances at least, to an undisguised animalistic crudity. Often he would begin an acquaintance by fondling a woman intimately, especially her breasts, and if he was met with feeble or no resistance, he would unceremoniously conduct her into the small and very private room adjacent to the "Holy of Holies." Observing this, his female disciples merely smiled knowingly or nodded their heads with complacent and often radiant-eyed sympathy, happy to think of their master's pleasure as well as the forthcoming ecstasy of the new and often quite shy candidate. They even made a sort of salacious guessing game of it. How long would it take him to disrobe his partner, one minute or two? How would the lady emerge from the room? What would be her state of mind, and to what degree would the emotional intensity of her experience show on her face?

Occasionally, a woman freshly taken would show anger or deep resentment, even mild emotional shock in some cases, coming from the scene of her seduction disheveled and obviously distraught. To Rasputin's followers she would simply be a person to be pitied, a very unenlightened creature with no understanding whatever of the rare privilege that had been granted her. Her type was the exception, however. In the great majority of instances, though shame and embarrassment might seem to predominate on the visage of the female in question, the very experienced disciples also could discern something else. The newcomer was thrilled and in a state of divinely inspired rapture, and her early return was a virtual certainty. They who had served the *starets* so well and so long, and remained at his beck and call, knew well the sensations that throbbed in her bosom. She had glimpsed the true Earthly Paradise, this planet as it must have been before the sin of Adam and Eve, the Original Sin, brought evil into being. Never before in her life had she been made to feel the depths of her womanhood so intensely. There was more than one reason for this. In addition to his incredible sensuality and very broad experience, his amazing virility, and the undeniable power and intensity of his mesmeric faculties, Rasputin had still another romantic advantage granted to very few men, that of extraordinary sexual endowment. Speaking of his former Khlisti orgies over which her father presided as *vozhd*, or leader, Maria Rasputin writes:

> Mention has been made of the Shiva lingam and other phallic symbols, and the way they were worshiped as the representations of the creative principle. When his [Rasputin's] female devotees danced their dervishlike dances around his nude figure, they, too, were drawn to the worship of his phallus, endowing it with mystical qualities as well as sexual ones, for it was an extraordinary member indeed, measuring a good thirteen inches when fully erect. Theirs was by no means a wholly lustful approach at the start of the rite, but a worship of God in His Priapean form; and whichever of the female disciples was the first to perform fellatio upon him did so in a sense of religious practice. Of course, as their passions were aroused, there was a tendency to forget the ritualistic aspect of the ceremony, and the participants would fall into a general orgy, seeking whatever outlet for their lusts was available.[12]

As to the size of her father's generative organ, Maria does not mention the source of her information at first, arousing some speculation, until at the close of her book she explains it. Because it was a revelation attendant upon darkness and death, upon the dénouement of a great and extraordinary life, the answer to the riddle will be withheld here, too, to be revealed at the proper time, for thus the creative muse would have it.

NOTES

1. All things considered, it is not conceivable that Rasputin and Dunia indulged themselves secretly while staying there. More credible is the probability that they either temporarily abstained from sex or had by this time worked out an arrangement similar to those found among the Mormons in nineteenth-century America, i.e., a mutual acceptance among wives and concubines that precluded jealousy and rivalry.

2. By this time, Maria's true given name of Matriona had been all but abandoned and she had assumed the one by which she would be known for the rest of her life.

3. An example of this is found in Henryk Sienkiewicz's great classic novel, *Quo Vadis?*, in the scene where the giant Ursus breaks the neck of an aurochs in the Roman arena with his bare hands.

4. In 1889, at Mayerling, fifteen miles southwest of Vienna, Archduke Rudolf von Habsburg, Crown Prince of the Austro-Hungarian Empire and only son of Kaiser

Franz Joseph and Kaiserin Elizabeth, carried out a double suicide with his beautiful mistress, Baroness Maria Vetsera. Their romance and tragedy have been the subject of endless historical speculation.

5. It was to stir Polish patriotism and inspire his countrymen to throw off the Russian yoke that Frédéric Chopin composed his magnificent *Twelfth Etude* for piano, the "Revolutionary Etude."

6. Maria Rasputin is very certain about this date.

7. This brief exchange is as Maria remembers it.

8. From Robert K. Massie, *Nicholas and Alexandra*, Atheneum, New York, 1967.

9. Although an Imperial residence, Livadia was a suburb of the resort city of Yalta.

10. From René Fülöp-Miller, *Rasputin: The Holy Devil*, Viking Press, New York, 1928.

11. *Ibid.*

12. Maria Rasputin and Patte Barham, *Rasputin: The Man Behind the Myth*, Warner Books, New York, 1977. (Published by arrangement with Prentice-Hall, Inc.)

CHAPTER 10

Prelude to Holocaust

The Russia that saw the end of the year 1912 was a land to which internal peace and its blessings had become an utter stranger. As always, the various revolutionary groups, though forced to operate clandestinely, were extremely active, their members as athirst for the power that had so far eluded them as they were for the ruin of their intended victims. With the closing of the Third Duma in the winter, the Fourth took its place, and the violently anti-Rasputin Michael Rodzianko was elected as its president. The year 1913 arrived. As had happened before, a wave of strikes carefully organized by the radical Left all but paralyzed the cities of St. Petersburg and Moscow, idling almost three-quarters of a million laborers, and unrest spread across the country generating more strikes.

One of these strikes, at a gold mine near the Lena River in east central Siberia, resulted in needless violence when well-armed police units under an unstable officer fired on the miners. Blood flowed as two hundred died. As usual, the revolutionaries were delighted, for on all such incidents, whether accidental or intentionally provoked, their skilled propagandists instantly capitalized. Among labor officials investigating the incident was a young man named Aleksandr Kerensky, of whom much was to be heard later.

In Geneva, Switzerland, another man resided in bitter, self-imposed exile. Having failed to win in 1905, Vladimir Ulyanov, called

Lenin after his Lena River detention, had pledged himself to endless war.[1] He retained great influence. Though far from the scene of insurgent activity, he continued to direct much of it through secret dispatches and couriers. He was ruthless and extremely efficient, and well understood that money was the key to his movement's survival. Desperately in need of funds, the revolutionaries organized increasingly professional crime rings, robbing banks, trains, and business establishments, and once again carried out widespread assassinations of government officials, acts of arson and sabotage, and other terrorist activities. They were much loathed and feared. Even the peasants, who ostensibly they favored, despised them and in large measure would not aid them.[2] Never able to claim a significant degree of public support, they nonetheless persisted. They grew larger, more powerful, more ferociously intimidating. The spirit of tyranny flourished in their ranks and sparked their vaunted idealism. Their principal leader in Georgia was a particularly ruthless and savage individual named Iosef Vissarionovich Dzhugashvili, later to startle the world as Joseph Stalin, a man who had committed his first bank robbery in Tiflis in 1906. The word *stalin* is Russian for "made of steel." The revolutionary alias once adopted, this man spent his entire career living up to his name, and many tens of thousands of Russians were to pay for his ambition with their lives.

Faced with these dire developments, Nikolai II was rendered more or less helpless by reason of his character, for at a time when firm and unrelenting action was desperately needed his most crippling failure was not a lack of courage but an ultimately fatal indecisiveness. All that was required was that he take a definite stand, let everyone know his intentions beyond any shadow of doubt, then stick to his guns like grim death. Many would have rallied to him then. Even among those who opposed him, such a firm posture on the part of the Tsar would inevitably have resulted in much side-switching to his advantage. But unyielding firmness was not in the nature of the last of the Romanov emperors.[3]

Though he tried his best to love them, the Tsar never really understood the people he ruled. He could have made a choice. He could, for example, have buttressed the liberals and other moderates on the Left, thus eroding proletarian support of the Bolshevik extremists and almost certainly strengthening his regime. Taking a leaf from his father's book, he could have done the opposite, too. Aided by an adroit propaganda campaign (the Government controlled more facilities for this than its enemies), he could have attacked the Far Left with everything he had, proving their leaders cared nothing for the laboring class in reality, thus gaining even more worker support and the inevitable backing of the Extreme Right: the Army, the nobility, the Church, and the industrial and landowning wealthy. Nikolai did neither. It was his vacillation that cost him whatever chance he may have had to gain adherents, undercut the respect due his rank and, in the end, left him virtually besieged and without reliable allies.

The international situation, meanwhile, was becoming highly volatile, and the key to its explosiveness lay largely in that tumultuous corner of southeastern Europe known as the Balkans. This area included what is today Yugoslavia (Serbia, Croatia, Bosnia, Herzogovina, Slovenia, Macedonia, and Montenegro), Romania, Bulgaria, Albania, Greece, and all of European Turkey, the latter being that portion of the Ottoman territories to the immediate north and west of the Sea of Marmara and its interconnecting straits. Not without reason it was called the "Powderkeg of Europe," for here, as in the Middle East of today, were found the focal points of fiercely contested racial and nationalistic ambitions.

One of these influences lay in the long-nursed and ever-smoldering Serbian discontent. Until the year 1905, the Serbs, a warlike people and full of pride, had looked to Russia, "Big Brother of the Slavs," not only for protection in crisis but for support in their plans for Serbian territorial expansion at the expense of the Austro-Hungarian Empire. Russia's startling defeat by Japan changed that. As the Serbs looked about them, they found a very powerful Germany economically entrenched in the Near East by virtue of the Baghdad Railway, begun in 1902, that the Germans built and controlled; the Habsburg power enhanced by increasing cooperation between Berlin and Vienna; Turkey in continued decline; England and France undecided as how best to blunt a new German *Drang nach Osten* (drive to the East), this time toward Constantinople and the Strait of the Dardanelles.

Concerning German expansion, still as relentless as when Bismarck had been in power, originally Britain's answer had been to strengthen her already formidable fleet. The early years of the century had seen impressive strides. Eventually, British naval engineers developed the dreadnaught, a battleship more heavily armed and armored than anything else afloat, and the first *HMS Dreadnaught*, prototype of a new breed, slid down the ways in 1905, just a century after Nelson's great victory over the French and Spanish fleets at Trafalgar. Unfortunately for Whitehall's plans, this revolutionary concept in design had a tendency to boomerang. A superb fighting machine the new craft surely was, and if the only shipyards in the world capable of building it had been those on the Clyde River in Scotland there is no question that Britain would have retained her mastery of the oceans without serious challenge. But the dreadnaught battleship made every other obsolete, including those already in the British Navy. German Intelligence got hold of the plans. It meant the Germans could build these vessels, too, which they promptly undertook, thus in quality if not quantity starting at an unheard-of parity with the British in capital ships.

As Europe drifted more and more rapidly toward a major conflict another development may be noted. Although the once mighty Turkish Empire was in what appeared to be a fatal decline, it did not necessarily follow that the youth of that nation were willing to stand by idly and see the Ottoman power slide inevitably toward extinction. The Sultan of Turkey, Abdul Hamid II, called "Abdul the Damned" because of his fiendish cruelty, was as mad as most sadists, and far more concerned with the activities of his harem and his torture chamber than with any efforts to restore Turkish strength and prestige. He had earned other sobriquets in the past, "the Great Assassin," for example, arising from the Armenian massacres of 1894–1896, and "Abdul the Bloody." In 1908, his regime was overthrown by a revolt of the Young Turks led by Mustapha Kemal, called "Ataturk" (Father of the Turks), and a constitution based on Western political concepts was promulgated. The upheaval and resultant confusion in Constantinople gave a clear signal to Vienna. Austria now annexed the nominally Turkish provinces of Bosnia and Herzegovina, administered by the Habsburgs since 1878 (according to the Treaty of Berlin), but long the target of Serbian nationalists as prime candidates for Slavic absorption.

The cherished plans for "a greater Serbia" were apparently des-

tined for ignominious eclipse. Serbs fumed in frustrated impotence.
At the clandestine meetings of their more fanatical secret societies,
among them the Black Hand and *Narodno Obrana*, there was talk of
political assassination. The blow had to be telling, however, the target
as highly placed as possible, of vital political importance, and a Habsburg. It did not take them long to agree on a potential victim. The
heir to the Austro-Hungarian throne was the middle-aged nephew of
the octogenarian Emperor Franz Joseph, Archduke Franz Ferdinand.
If they could somehow lure him out of Vienna his liquidation would
be comparatively easy. If not, well, assassins had penetrated well-
guarded strongholds before. Why not the royal palace of Schönbrunn?
Would Austria be driven into war by this? Serbian zealots hoped so.
What they did not take sufficiently into account was the intricate
system of alliances which by this time bound much of Europe in a
deadly entanglement, needing but a spark to ignite the most terrible
conflict the world had ever seen. On the one hand, Russia was sure
to support Serbia against Austria-Hungary; France and Russia were
entente powers, with Paris sympathetic to St. Petersburg; Great Britain's pledged support of Belgium would mean her automatic backing
of France. On the other, the certainty of Germany going to Austria's
aid was well known, with Turkey and Italy expected to join them.
What was the key to German strategy? It embraced a plan to attack
France through Belgium in the very shrewdly conceived "Schlieffen
Envelopment," the brainchild of an elderly but brilliant German general, the Graf von Schlieffen.[4] Britain could not allow it. "Belgium
in German hands," said Whitehall, "is a pistol aimed at our head."

So the lines were drawn. It merely remained for a young Bosnian
student, a tuberculosis victim named Gavrilo Princip, to carry out
the rashly fatal act that would precipitate the vast explosion.

It was a brilliant February morning in this year of 1913. Down
the broad course of the Nevsky Prospeckt through which he had come,
Rasputin had been cheered to see the vastness of the multitude that
lined it. They were not nobility or high clergy, landowners or ministers of state. They were the common people of the nation, merchants,
artisans, petty shopkeepers of scores of trades, even peasants like

himself who had come here in their thousands to witness a regal ceremony, to honor the persons of the Tsar and Tsaritsa, indeed to share with their sovereigns in a very real sense the historic significance of the occasion. The Romanov Dynasty had reigned in the land for three centuries to this very day, and this was the capital's celebration of that very distinguished tercentenary the like of which could be found now in every city in Russia. Witnessing the jubilant spirit of the crowds, the *starets* rejoiced. What more proof than this was needed to give the lie to the revolutionaries? A thousand times over they had shouted stridently that the rulers of Muscovy were tyrants and hated by the people. Yet, observing this enthusiastically acclaimed pageantry, a ten-year-old child would know they were loved.

Now the crescent-shaped colonnade of the Cathedral of the Virgin of Kazan loomed over him, partially blotting out the sun. He stopped and stood looking up. He even prided himself on his knowledge that the architect, Voronikhin, born a peasant like himself, had studied the columns of Bernini at St. Peter's great church in Rome. Then he caught himself. Pride was a grievous sin of which he was frequently guilty lately. Even his clothes proclaimed it. The pectoral cross he wore was of intricately fashioned gold; his boots of the finest patent leather; his silk tunic of a nearly imperial purple, crimson they called it, its flowers embroidered by the Tsaritsa's own hand. He was freshly washed, too, and manicured. Only his long black kaftan revealed the peasant. Ah yes, he must guard against vanity.

He proceeded on. As he passed through the great doors he was struck by the irony of his position. Outside their own children, he was closer to the Tsar and Tsaritsa than anyone in the world, yet they could not acknowledge this publicly. They would be along soon, gorgeous carriages bearing the Romanov coat-of-arms amid masses of household and Cossack cavalry; gilded pennons, splendid horses, lance points glittering in the sun. Yet he, Rasputin, could not stand in attendance upon them. He was alone. He would enter this lofty sanctuary alone. Unescorted and largely unnoticed, he would find a seat somewhere and occupy it—alone.

But what did it matter, he asked himself? He was staring upward at the grand interior now, as ornate as that of any cathedral he had ever seen. The magnificent dome covered on the outside with gold leaf was vast, unbelievably high, enclosed by many tall, narrow windows that admitted the rays of the sun in pale, illusory fingers of light. They were not really there, he knew, and this ethereal edifice itself was only illusion, the product of a dream of some itinerant shaman in the long ago. Built by the mad Tsar Paul, son of Catherine the Great? Perhaps. But then Paul himself was illusion, was he not? What was it the Little Father had said of him? Something about being more insane than they knew, about recalling Suvorov when that great strategist was about to break the military back of a young unknown general named Bonaparte. Yes, Paul was mad, and he, Rasputin, was perhaps even madder. Why had he come here? Was he *seeking* assassination? Suddenly, his stark vulnerability made him shudder. *Any* hand could strike him down this day. It wouldn't take much. Just as it had taken so little to kill Stolypin.

He made his way down through the nave, stopping once to allow the passage of a priest wielding an incense-burning silver censer swung on silver chains. He was a little late, he thought. The enormous structure was literally jammed with hundreds of people awaiting the arrival of the sovereigns. Only in the front were vacant seats. He knew they were reserved, but he was merely one man and would not occupy much space, and there were always people who failed to show up. He reached one of the seats and sat down in it. From here he could see the members of the huge choir filing into their places high up in the chancel, so soon to begin the ageless chant and thrilling strains of the *Te Deum*. From here, too, he could see Tsar Paul's miraculous ikon raised aloft in a corner, the relic to which the cathedral had been dedicated, surrounded by golden seraphim and winged cherubs.

Paul the insane. The ikon. He tried to concentrate on its strangely shimmering luminescence but failed. He was thinking of something else, of the Winter Palace on the Neva River, how the Tsar and Tsaritsa had gone there to be close to the center of celebration, how Aleksandra hated the place that always reminded her of her lost youth and her carefree life in those days. She wanted to stay at Tsarskoe Selo, almost literally to wall it up and entomb herself there. She was afraid, deathly afraid of her own people. They called her "the German woman" and she knew it. They said she plotted secretly with the Reichstag and she knew that, too, she who had loved England and

Victoria, never militant Germany. And this was twentieth-century Russia, and the poet Pushkin had been the grandson of a black Abyssinian prince, and the sea was green, and the air was full of starlings, and of all the astral bodies in the universe planet Earth was the maddest. My God, my God, what did *any* of it matter? All that mattered was to go to the Villa Rodye and get drunk.

He found himself sweating. He was losing utterly his grip on reality, just floundering. Best if he had expired on the Mount of Olives. He had been stricken there, stricken unto death. What had been God's purpose in sparing him? To save the Romanovs? But with *what*? Their destiny was preordained, was it not? Could a wandering unlettered holy man, a *strannik* from the Siberian wilderness make any difference? Suddenly he became aware of a commotion to his rear, harshly spoken words by a stentorian-voiced man who seemed to be directing them pointedly and viciously. He half-turned to view the one who accosted him. The cathedral seemed to hang adrift in a slowly swirling haze and through it a giant came toward him; a face whose craggy features were twisted in terrible anger; loud, accusative accents that seemed literally to spit at him. It was the Duma president, Rodzianko, 300 pounds of enraged Ukrainian who appeared to be making no sense. He heard himself reply to him. He wasn't really aware of the meaning of his own words. Rodzianko's harsh phrases were likewise incomprehensible.

"If you address me as 'thou' I'll drag you from the cathedral by your beard! You are a notorious swindler!"

Rasputin half rose, sat down again, then slipped slowly to his knees. The big man's face was flushed and growing livid, and he didn't look sane. He gesticulated wildly. It seemed that one of the guards was trying to calm him but without success. It was the seat the *starets* had occupied. *That* was it. All reserved for members of the Duma? The whole section? Rodzianko was acting like a raving lunatic, almost frothing at the mouth, hate-filled eyes starting out of his head. The *starets* showed him his signed invitation from the Tsar. The huge man waved it aside.

Suddenly Rasputin felt sick. It was not a physical thing but a sort of sickness of the soul far more enervating than anything of the body. Did the destiny of the Russian people then depend to any great degree upon men like *this*? He found himself trying desperately to concentrate, his lips moving silently in prayer that this might not be so. Then he felt a blow. It was directly to his ribs and knocked the breath out of him. With a leg the size of a tree trunk the man was kicking him, showering curses on him. Should he resist? He did not fear Rodzianko. He knew exactly where and how to hit him to stop him. Again came the smashing impact and he felt himself reeling. What had he ever done to the man to deserve this? What evil had he inflicted on him? The vicious assault was wrong. It was unjust and he *hated* injustice. About to rise up in righteous wrath and smite the foe, he held himself in check as yet another blow struck home and all but made him collapse. There was a voice here in this hallowed place, a male voice, but its beauty far transcended the voices of men. He could hear it clearly: "*Ye have heard that it hath been said, Thou shalt love thy neighbor, and hate thine enemy. But I say unto you, Love your enemies, bless them that curse you, do good to them that hate you, and pray for them which despitefully use you, and persecute you.*"

He groaned. The spittle dripped from his mouth. He warded off yet another kick with his arm. It was some sort of miracle that found him on his feet again and still able to walk. He did not look at Rodzianko. He did not trust himself to look at him for fear the violent urgings of his manhood would prevail over his faith.

"Lord, forgive him his sin," he said quietly, aware that several people had gathered to watch but that none offered him help.

He stepped out of reach of the Duma president. It was not difficult with so clumsy a man. He looked neither right nor left. With his eyes on the shaft of brilliant sunlight shining through the far off open doors, he silently left the cathedral.

Russia's leaders during this period were not men to willingly share political power. This was particularly true of the typically bourgeois members of the Duma. Lifted into unexpected prominence from the relative nothingness of middle-class existence, they were somewhat comparable to the *nouveau riche* of various class-structured societies, clawing and ripping their way to the top unashamedly, ever ready to crush with hob-nailed boots anyone they considered of a lesser breed.

Peasants were generally held to be in that category. Until their so-called emancipation by Tsar Aleksandr II in 1861 they had been called "serfs," were in a state of what amounted to slavery, and were considered little better than animals. Now an "animal" stood close to the crowned head of state. In his novel *Cid Bozhji* (*Ordeal*), the writer Aleksei Tolstoy (1882–1945), though he became with Maxim Gorki (1868–1936) one of the foremost literary lions in a Soviet Union ostensibly fashioned for the common people, could not resist a turn of phrase redolent of class distinction when referring to Rasputin.[5] Speaking of Tsarskoe Selo, its royal occupants, and the *starets*, and unfortunately echoing the unfounded claims of the most scrofulous and unregenerate newspaper accounts, he wrote in the approved Bolshevik idiom: "And to the Palace, up the very steps of the Imperial throne, came an illiterate peasant with insane eyes and tremendous male vigor; jeering and scoffing, he began to play his infamous tricks, with all Russia as his plaything. . . ."

As has been noted, this hatred of the increasingly powerful Siberian was echoed by many in the Government. One such man, Duma president and one-time war hero Aleksandr Guchkov, had gone so far as to introduce a motion to the members of that body proposing that the subject of the *starets* as a threat to the safety of the State be debated. The proposal was discreetly rejected but it did not endear him to the Tsar and Tsaritsa. It was this man who was followed into office by Michael Rodzianko, and a more dangerous, determined, and fanatical successor Rasputin was not likely to find.

According to Rodzianko's own account, it was on March 10, 1912 that Nikolai II granted him an audience for a special purpose, though the Emperor was unaware of his intention. Rodzianko was taking chances. In their own efforts to discredit and vilify the *starets* Stolypin had been stopped dead in his tracks, Bishop Hermogen put down and neutralized, Iliodor driven into hiding in a foreign country. Even Anthony, Metropolitan of St. Petersburg and Ladoga, had importuned the Tsar on the subject of Rasputin and met with decisive defeat. Rodzianko was defeated, too. When, ostensibly with the Emperor's permission, he managed to get his hands on the Lukianov report on Rasputin's sectarian activities, he only got himself into serious trouble with the Empress.[6] She ordered the report to be replaced in the files and forgotten. Half prepared to defy her, Rodzianko desisted. He might have spared himself the trouble. Rasputin's membership in the Khlisti was not of the slightest interest to the Imperial couple, not anymore. Their uppermost and constant thought lay in the survival of Aleksei.

Like the fugitive monk Iliodor, Rodzianko bided his time. Related to the Yussupovs, he knew their enormous wealth had given them power out of all proportion to their actual political stature. He frequently contacted Princess Zenaidye Nikolayevna, the mother of Prince Yussupov, and was delighted to discover two things about her. First, along with the Tsaritsa's sister, Grand Duchess Elizaveta Feodorovna, she was leader of one of two covertly functioning salons with the same purpose, their aim being nothing less than to have Aleksandra deposed and institutionalized on grounds of insanity.[7] Second, she hated Rasputin bitterly. Rodzianko felt he could use a woman like this. He began to form a sort of embryonic plan. At the time of the Duma president's first pondering of it Yussupov was still at Oxford, but his mother said he was soon to return. Rodzianko knew the youth was impressionable, that in some measure at least his haughtiness and devil-may-care *joie de vivre* was a mask to conceal his basic lack of inner strength and self-esteem. Out of this might not something be made? The prince was rash and unstable. That, too, was obvious. His mind set on deviltry, Rodzianko determined to put to the test the psychological power of suggestion.

Prince Feliks Feliksovich Yussupov returned to Russia from England in the autumn of 1912, and soon thereafter he gravitated toward Rasputin's enemies in St. Petersburg. There is some evidence of conflict in him, his religious leanings at war with his innate perversities of cruelty and sadomasochistic lust. Two influences began working on him almost at once, the Tsaritsa's estranged sister and Rodzianko. The latter appears to have been the first to speak candidly to Yussupov of assassination as the only possible solution for the "Siberian upstart," calling it the patriotic duty of any Russian in a position to accomplish it. Yussupov listened but did not commit himself. Each man knew he was dealing with a trustworthy sympathizer. At no time, however, did Rodzianko offer *himself* as a likely candidate for the role of assassin.

It is not difficult to imagine Yussupov riding about town at night in one of his chauffeur-driven limousines, his restless and sensuous spirit seeking exciting diversion. Far more difficult would it be to think of him rejecting for long his favorite homosexual pursuits. This he did not do, of course. Within a week of his return he had resumed his intimate relationship with his former love, Grand Duke Dmitri Pavlovich, the pair being seen together from time to time in some of the capital's more discreet places of entertainment. This could have proved a serious mistake for Yussupov. From childhood Dmitri had been close to the Emperor and Empress. He'd had the run of the palace and had lived with them there, and his mild and gentle manner had made him a rather special Court favorite. It did not take long for reports of his aberrant sexual behavior to reach the Imperial couple. The Tsar called him to account. He told the youth he must break with Yussupov immediately, that Okhrana operatives would place him under observation to see to it that he did so. Opposition bore its usual fruit. After a short separation, the highborn lovers simply went to live together in an unpretentious house in the city. If they were especially worried about the Tsar's restrictive mandate they did not show it, for no arrest threat had been made.

For a while, despite occasional lovers' quarrels, the two coexisted peacefully enough. Then a day came when Yussupov took a step that was to have fateful consequences. Since his early adolescence, Grand Duchess Elizaveta Feodorovna had assumed a nearly maternal protectiveness over him. He needed this desperately now. She was none other than that same "Ella," as the family called her, widow of the Tsar's half-insane and much-hated uncle, Grand Duke Serge. She had remained in Moscow all these years, becoming the Abbess of the convent she had founded there. If hearing the frightful bomb blast long ago had not traumatized her, if rushing out of the grand ducal mansion to find her husband only scraps of flesh had not unhinged her mind, neither had it done anything to improve her understanding of people or sharpen her judgment. Without a shred of evidence to support the primary contentions of Rasputin's enemies, she had sided with them. In simple fact, no small part of her belief in the insanity of her sister the Tsaritsa was based on Aleksandra's love of the *starets*.

It was this woman Yussupov now visited, leaving his male paramour behind in St. Petersburg. Feliks had been having one of his periodic attacks of guilt and remorse over his life of uselessness and dissipation. The religious side of his nature momentarily held sway over him. Tearfully he told the Abbess that his consciousness of his own grievous sins was gradually destroying him. Then, in a state bordering on despair, he confessed to her what she doubtless already knew, the simple fact of his affair with Dmitri. Ella was all sympathy and understanding. She told him, however, that God's forgiveness would be based entirely on his willingness to abandon his unnatural life and pursue henceforth only heterosexual liaisons. In fact, she made pointed reference to a proper and early marriage being the best of all possible solutions. Yussupov agreed. He left Moscow feeling deeply cleansed and almost rejuvenated, and still in this mood when back in St. Petersburg, he managed a reluctant goodbye to a tearful and emotionally stricken Dmitri.

At this point the life of the rakehell Prince took a sharp turn. Forgiven by the Imperial couple, who quickly found out about his "reform," he became once again a courtier in their good graces, most welcome at royal balls and other increasingly infrequent palace functions, even more than an occasional visitor to Tsarskoe Selo. Despite his questionable past, he was again a quite eligible bachelor. His great wealth alone would have ensured that. But the lovely young woman who now made his acquaintance was not interested in his money, for she was rich in her own right.

In Yussupov's biography of Rasputin, facing page 100, there is a photograph of Princess Irina Aleksandrovna.[8] By present-day standards her features are rather severe, almost masculine, but by those of her own day she was a beauty indeed. From the beginning she was charmed by the Prince and deeply attracted to him. When he voluntarily made confession of his dissolute life to her, she saw only his handsome face. When he spoke of "l'affair Dmitri," she said it didn't matter, even displaying a certain fascinated sympathy with male homosexuality. She fell in love with him quickly, and he, after his fashion, with her. Yes, her parents *would* object to her marrying him, for to them the Yussupovs were descended from commoners and ineligible for their daughter's hand. Yes, the Tsar and Tsaritsa also might be against it on the same grounds. What did it matter so long as they loved each other? Irina was positive that love and persistence would win out in the end.

As events transpired she was right. In a short time they gained the necessary approval all around and became engaged. Irina's grandmother, Dowager Empress Maria Feodorovna, even showed a certain eagerness that the wedding be held in the most beautiful chapel of her own stately domicile, the Anichkov Palace. Not unexpectedly, it was a sumptuous affair, so lavish indeed that at least some of St. Petersburg's high society began to think the old days of Court grandeur and noble opulence were returning. Feliks was at his most fatally charming. However, when later the wedding party went to the station to see the newlyweds depart on their honeymoon on the Yussupov private train, he was perhaps less so.

On the platform, nearly deserted save for the wedding guests, Feliks saw Dmitri. There was no one with the distraught youth and he did not look much like a grand duke. He stood at a distance, dejected, forlorn, utter and hopeless despair in every line of him. In his diary, Yussupov described his former lover on this occasion as "a lonely figure." The newly made bridegroom was not much moved. If he felt any genuine compassion for the other—who had once attempted suicide because of him—it was not an emotion on which he wasted much ink. After all, his own enviable social position was on an equal plain now even with Dmitri's. He had married a Romanov.

If the First Balkan War of 1912 very glaringly revealed the weakness of the Ottomans, reducing the Turkish Empire's European holdings to the ancient city of Constantinople and its environs, the one that followed it in 1913 made another fact equally evident. Between those allies who had fought the Turks, Christians all, there was no unity whatever nor an ounce of goodwill. The Second Balkan War, essentially a fight over the spoils of the first, saw land-hungry Serbia demand of Bulgaria a larger share of Macedonia, whereupon Bulgaria attacked Serbia. The conflict quickly spread. Romania and Greece went to Serbia's aid. Then, hoping to retrieve at least a part of her lost territories, even Turkey joined them. The predictable result was Bulgarian defeat. Equally predictably, she then lost territory (Treaty of Bucharest, 1913) to all those powers that had jointly attacked her.

Throughout this struggle, Tsar Nikolai II had been repeatedly tempted to intervene. There would have been several advantages.

Russia was badly disunited and war unites a nation. Russia was besieged internally by determined revolutionaries but a successful war
would cut the ground from under them. There was the matter of
Imperial prestige. Since the defeat by Japan in 1905 it had been at an
all-time low. This could be restored by victory. And dabbling in
Balkan affairs might even bring to the Empire that prize so long sought
by Romanov tsars, an ice-free outlet for Russian shipping through the
Bosporus, the Sea of Marmara, and the Dardanelles to the Mediterranean.

As usual, the Tsar was of two minds. He feared the many strikes
and their increasing influence on other workers throughout the nation,
and he knew that for a time at least war would solve unemployment.
He was also aware, however, that Russian intervention in the Balkans
might invite entry by other great powers, leading to a general and
spreading conflict of unpredictable scope and unknown outcome. He
did not believe Russia could risk that. Rasputin warned him against
it with utmost vigor and very deep conviction, reminding him that
war was calamitous for a people and a sin against God. Standing in
the wings as an advisor on both domestic and foreign affairs was the
long since deposed premier, Count Witte, whose opinion Nikolai still
valued and respected. He, too, strongly advised against military involvement, forming an unlikely but effective alliance with the *starets*.

The "war party" in St. Petersburg, however, was entirely another
matter. Composed of men both inside and outside the Government
who favored a sudden and unexpected *coup de maître*, this group never
ceased its efforts to stimulate the Tsar to aggression and provoke him
to immediate action. In terms both of militant fanaticism and power
their natural leader was Grand Duke Nikolai Nikolayevich, the tallest
general in Russia, a man who envisaged himself, not without cause,
as the Army's inevitable Commander-in-Chief. His wife, Anastasia,
youngest of the two sisters called "the Montenegrins," was of a family
having a very personal ax to grind in the Balkans. However, as it
happened, the couple at this time had taken their never-ending occult
activities a step further. At their frequently held séances they claimed
to be in contact with none other than France's sainted Joan of Arc,
whose spirit advised something that the tragic Maid of Orléans had
always deplored in life. She urged the superstitious General, or so he
said, to do all in his power to bring Russia to war.

Under the circumstances it is not surprising that "the giant," as some called him behind his back, met Rasputin in head-on assault, all past friendship effaced by Nikolai's hatred. It happened after a particularly animated conference between the *starets* and the Tsar, one in which Father Grigori's pleadings for peace were apparently reported to the soldier. Nikolai went personally to the Gorokhovaya flat. There, according to Maria, he attacked her father viciously in her presence and that of her sister Varya, accusing him of ungratefulness and betrayal, calling him *svinya* (swine), and reminding him of the vital role that he and his Grand Duchess had played in introducing Rasputin to St. Petersburg society. During this harangue, in which Rasputin did much more listening than talking, the General entirely forgot himself. Maria remembered his words concerning the Tsar as follows: "What's more, Nikolai Aleksandrovich should be forced to abdicate. It would not be difficult to replace that spineless weakling."

The manner was insulting, the words treasonable, the implication abundantly clear. The inference was that the Grand Duke himself could replace the Tsar and indeed was planning to do so. Yet the lesson was not lost on Rasputin. This general officer was stupidly rash. To talk treason to a man and make an enemy of him at the same time? What kind of a chess player was that? After several failed attempts to reach an understanding the *starets* made no further rejoinder, but all the time the other, red-faced, was working himself into a rage, his listener took mental notes. The *starets* by this time was not without a certain military knowledge, the result primarily of keeping his eyes and ears open. The Grand Duke as a strategist? Most of the men on the German General Staff could outthink this fellow. Hindenburg in all likelihood; Ludendorff, Mackensen, and Falkenhayn for a certainty. As Commander-in-Chief of the Russian Army, Grand Duke Nikolai Nikolayevich would, in the event of war with the Kaiser's powerful forces, be an unmitigated disaster. He, Rasputin, must prevent war if he could. Failing that, he must do everything possible to see that Russia had a fighting chance. If he had any influence with the Tsar at all, and he thought he had a good deal, he would have this traitor set aside.

As events transpired, Rasputin was not immediately able to accomplish this, though who can say what would have happened had he reported the incredible conversation to the Emperor? What pre-

vented him? Perhaps it was some remaining gratitude for favors done
him by the Grand Duke before they had reached this sorry state of
affairs. There was another target, however, a figure even more highly
placed than the General and equally a supporter of the war party,
Premier Vladimir Kokovtsov. Through direct solicitation of the Tsar
and Tsaritsa by the *starets*, this man, as much a personal enemy as
Stolypin or Rodzianko had ever been, was politely but firmly dismissed from office by Nikolai in February of the following year, 1914,
and succeeded by Ivan Longinovich Goremykin. This politician had
held the office before. In 1906 he had succeeded Count Witte, was a
known quantity, and as blindly reactionary as Pobedonostsev had
been. None of this mattered, for he was something else as well, as
Rasputin plainly saw, a mild and unthinking figurehead completely
controllable by Tsar and *starets*.[9] In the exalted office of Premier of
Russia, Goremykin might not prove much of an asset, but properly
supported and guided, neither would he prove a liability. Rasputin
knew he would have to settle for that.

There now stepped onto the sanguinary stage of history one of
the most deadly gnomes ever to issue from the fiery mouth of hell.
He was the invisible Satan-spawned demon who whispered here and
whispered there into the ears of mere unwary mortals, suggesting
havoc, and because the Devil generally has his way with long-suffering
mankind, tempting humans to slaughter, most of an entire generation
of Europe's young males were to die.

To the central theme of universal death by bayonet, bullet, high-
explosive shell, and poison gas there were very curious side issues,
one of the strangest dealing with the sinister reentrance into world
affairs of the utterly ruthless monk-priest Iliodor. Never for one moment had his bitterness subsided nor his hatred lessened. Indeed, a
mercilessly driven man and scarcely sane, he now hated for the sake
of hatred itself, obsessively, and every ounce of his bitter-as-gall vin-
dictiveness was directed against Rasputin and the ill-starred family
he served.

Maria Rasputin relates that at about this time (the fall of 1913)
Iliodor slipped quietly back into Russia, where he masterminded a

plot to carry out a wave of assassinations, "sixty high government officials and forty bishops," most to be slaughtered by "one hundred and twenty high-explosive bombs" in the hands of trained fanatics. She states that the plan was betrayed, Iliodor arrested and imprisoned, and that none other than Grand Duke Nikolai Nikolayevich himself visited him secretly in his cell, offering to arrange his escape in return for the murder of Rasputin.

While it is not at all impossible that such a plot was actually formed, nor that the Grand Duke would have recklessly joined in it, the evidence to support a contention that Iliodor reentered Russia at this time is lacking, and Okhrana files for the period do not record such an arrest. For the other part of Maria's account, however, there is ample proof in substantiation. It deals with a deranged peasant woman, lame and facially deformed, named Chionya Guseva. One of the most zealous followers of Iliodor, she apparently visited him in Norway at this time (after which he may or may not have left that country), was stirred to hatred and violence by him, then returned to Russia determined to kill Rasputin at all costs.

The early months of 1914 were palmy days for Maria. With a memory scarcely dimmed by the passage of the decades, she records most charmingly how she and her beautiful former roommate, Marusa Sasanova, frequented St. Petersburg's Nevski Prospekt in the hope of meeting boys; how they flirted outrageously with any likely prospect; and even mentions how skillful they became at using shop-front windows as reflecting mirrors admirably suited to keep the prospective swains in more or less constant view. Maria was fifteen at the time, romantically eager but inexperienced, and could hardly be expected to see anything odd in the fact that one of these young men began to telephone her at the Gorokhovaya apartment. He would not give his name. He said he'd been following her and was very attracted to her. On one occasion, he told her, he even followed her home and was deeply impressed when he learned her father's identity. He asked if he might call upon her. Very reluctantly, for she says she was "already half in love with him," she was forced to decline on the ground that in only a matter of days she would be leaving with Rasputin for Siberia. The man expressed regret. The calls stopped.

The reason usually given for Rasputin deciding to visit Pokrovskoye at this time is his fear of being assassinated if he stayed in the capital. This seems likely enough. The Okhrana had warned him of Iliodor's continued plotting, Rodzianko's hatred was abundantly clear, and he knew that Grand Duke Nikolai, now that the bone was in his teeth, would literally stop at nothing to have him butchered without mercy. Moreover, he could not protect the Imperial Family now, for in a few days they would be boarding the royal yacht *Standart* for a two-week cruise in the Gulf of Finland.[10] It was the British who had augmented the nautical tone. Only recently, in a show of naval strength, their First Battle Cruiser Squadron had entered the Baltic and dropped anchor at Kronstadt. Its commander, Beatty, and some of his officers had even visited Tsarskoye Selo, where everyone had found them charming.[11] Few foreign diplomats, however, failed to get the point. British sea power allied with Russia's "unnumbered hordes" and the redoubtable *poilus* (infantrymen) of France would make a formidable fighting coalition.

Accordingly, with his children, Dunia, and Katya the maid, Rasputin left St. Petersburg in late June, boarding the eastbound train for the city of Tobolsk, thereafter to take the river steamer by way of the Tobol and the Tura to Pokrovskoye. We can readily imagine how pleasant this latter part of the journey must have been, for June in western Siberia is a beautiful month. Maria relates that it was while enjoying the pleasures of the boat trip that a youth of dark complexion introduced himself to her, giving his name as Davidsohn and his trade as that of newspaperman. It did not take her long to identify the voice of her unknown caller on the phone. While indicating that his Jewish features did not especially attract her, she adds that she was flattered by the attention, making it clear that his willingness to follow her so persistently rekindled her visions of romance.

Alas, poor Maria. Far from having any interest in her, Davidsohn's mission was concerned primarily with the spilling of her father's blood. A reporter for a St. Petersburg paper he may well have been, in which case he would not have been averse to returning to his desk and filing a spectacular frontpage story. But, beyond that and far more vital, his subsequent action makes it obvious he was an agent of Iliodor, indeed the contact man at the point of assault for the preselected assassin. Disembarking at Pokrovskoye, knowing exactly the lodging where Chionya Guseva was staying, he went to her immediately, told her the unsuspecting victim had arrived, and proceeded to coordinate plans to carry out the murder.

In the light of what happened afterward, it seems clear that he intended to let the half-crazed woman be taken by vengeful townspeople while he escaped, and may well have advised her to resist them in hopes of her being killed. Iliodor would have wanted it that way, knowing that a dead assassin could name neither him nor his confederates. Things were proceeding according to plan. The boat's arrival at Pokrovskoye was on a Saturday, June 27, 1914.

The following day, nearly 3000 miles to the southwest as the crow flies, the Bosnian capital city of Sarajevo basked in the morning sun. There were crowds in the streets. There was shouting and frivolity. A certain gaiety seemed to be in the air, but to what degree it was mere superficial sham would have been hard to say. Certain it was that Austrian Archduke Franz Ferdinand did not trust its nature. An intelligent realist who saw hard fact more clearly than perhaps any statesman in Vienna, he had come here to do that which even he felt was probably impossible, to win the trust of the Slavic people by extending the hand of peace and friendship and offering them a share in government, and to do it before the storm he envisioned burst in all its fury. They had a right to it, he knew. They comprised three-fifths of this sprawling, polyglot nation. Yet, as though he foresaw his mission would fail and his life be forfeit, out of the hearing of his archduchess he had said to the tutor of his children: "The bullet that will kill me is already on its way."

His words were indeed prophetic. Guided by a general directive of the Black Hand, the secret society to which he belonged, the nineteen-year-old Bosnian student, Gavrilo Princip, moved through the throng of people. He had a concealed bomb. He also had a Browning revolver whose cylinder held six rounds. As forty-nine years before, John Wilkes Booth had murdered Lincoln, the only man in the United States who could and would have spared the assassin's own South from its postwar nightmare, so now, by one of the bitter ironies of history, Princip's bullet was to strike a terrible blow at the country he was trying to save, dashing its people's hopes, then bringing to much of the world an unimaginable horror.

Inconspicuous in the multitude, Princip positioned himself. The Archduke's motorcade came on slowly. With Archduchess Sophie he sat in the rear of an open touring sedan, the second car from the front, unguarded but for police engaged in crowd control, his gesture of good will having emptied the streets of the troops that would normally have been there. The friendly overture was fatal. One bomb was thrown, two officers wounded, the would-be assassin arrested. The route was changed. The Archduke's chauffeur became confused and took a wrong turn. Princip was waiting.

Coming suddenly out of the crowd, closing to a range where a miss was nearly impossible, the youth with the gun pumped two bullets into the target vehicle's distinguished occupants. Hit in the abdomen, Sophie died immediately. The other slug struck Franz Ferdinand in the neck, claiming his life in a quarter of an hour. Princip was captured. He said he had acted on behalf of his people. But no one, no one in all the world, was to benefit from this.

In Pokrovskoye, Chionya Guseva had finally finished studying the photograph of Rasputin with which Iliodor had supplied her. She was sure she could recognize him. She went out into the village street, concealed in her clothes the long knife the one-time monk-priest of Tsaritsyn had also given her. It was two o'clock in the afternoon. At a quarter past the hour, Rasputin received a telegram from the Tsaritsa sent from the wireless room of the *Standart* at sea. It had been reported that Archduke Franz Ferdinand had been assassinated by a Serbian nationalist, and the Tsar feared war. The *starets* was asked to return to St. Petersburg immediately. Writing a message in compliance, he left the house and took it to the telegraph office, his mind completely preoccupied with this sudden turn of events. Perhaps it was that which made him careless. Normally, he would have identified Guseva, divining her intention as once he had done with the woman who bore a concealed pistol. Now, however, it was as though his power of divination had been shut off.

He walked toward his home. When the strange-looking peasant woman approached him he reached in his pocket to give her a coin. She was very quick. Instantly her blade glittered in the sun like a harbinger of Fate. She thrust. Before he could ward it off with his hand, he found several inches of it buried in his abdomen as his assailant jerked the knife upward to disembowel him. She almost succeeded. The razor-edged weapon had torn his intestines.[12] But even then, before he collapsed, Rasputin's agonized command was enough to keep the enraged villagers from beating her to death. "I've killed the Antichrist!" she screamed hysterically again and again. Incarcerated in the one-room village jail, she whined like a beaten animal, still uttering this sentence repeatedly.

His head swimming and close to unconsciousness, Rasputin was supported by a man on either side who helped him get back to his home. Bleeding profusely, he cupped his belly with his hands, the only thing now that kept his bowels from dropping out. They lifted him into the house. There, Praskovia and Dunia, both as white as death but amazingly in command of themselves, had their loved one placed on a table, stripped him of his clothes, and examined his wound. They recognized its gravity immediately. No ordinary human could long survive it. Even this man of steel, wide open to peritonital infection, would surely die if medical treatment were long delayed. Now, while the nearest doctor in the city of Tyumen was sent for, while the afternoon waned and nightfall ensued, there began an hours' long struggle first to staunch the bleeding, then to prevent its recurrence to any dangerous degree. Aided by Rasputin's phenomenal inner strength and his tremendous will to live, this effort was successful. He was eventually taken to the hospital. There, as week followed week he fought as valiant a battle against death as could be imagined—and he won.

But Europe lost. From the day of the assassination in Sarajevo, some time passed before Vienna made its move. Then, on July 23, Austria-Hungary followed the advice of its chancellor, Count Berchtold, and sent to Serbia an ultimatum so arrogant and insulting its authors knew it would be rejected. The plot to kill Archduke Franz Ferdinand, it was stated, had been hatched in Belgrade by members of the Serbian Government, who themselves had provided the murder weapon. In violation of Serbian sovereignty, Austria now demanded the right to send a team of its own investigators into the country; all Serbian nationalist organizations were to be disbanded and their propaganda suppressed; all army officers known to support independence dismissed from the service. The time limit for a reply was set at forty-eight hours.

As might have been expected, in this shocking crisis Serbia looked to Russia. The Russian foreign minister, Sazonov, gave assurances of St. Petersburg's support. Serbia, uncertain as to how much that support could be counted on, chose a course of moderation. Belgrade would satisfy all of Vienna's demands gladly, all save one. If the Emperor's government would withdraw the provision allowing Austro-Hungarian officials on Serbian soil a rapprochement might be reached. To this Vienna made no reply. An appeal by the British foreign minister, Lord Grey of Fallodon, to mediate the dispute was likewise ignored. On July 28, Austria-Hungary declared war on Serbia. The most terrible, costly, and brutal conflict that history had witnessed up to that time was about to begin.

Referring to the coming holocaust, the British historian Colin Wilson makes an interesting observation. He writes: "There are fifty degrees of longitude between Sarajevo and Pokrovskoye, which means that eleven o'clock in Sarajevo is about two-fifteen in Pokrovskoye. It is a strange coincidence that two assassins struck at almost exactly the same moment—a coincidence that makes one inclined to doubt the 'blindness of history'. Ferdinand's death made war probable; Rasputin's injury made it certain, for he was the only man in Russia capable of averting it."[13]

Near the close of July, writing to the Tsar from his hospital bed in Tyumen, an enfeebled Rasputin made his final passionate effort to prevent his country from joining in the hostilities:

> My friend: Once again I repeat; a terrible storm menaces Russia. Woe . . . suffering without end. It is night. There is not one star . . . a sea of tears. And how much blood!
> . . . Do not let fools triumph, do not let them throw themselves and us into the abyss. Do not let them do this thing. . . . Perhaps we will conquer Germany, but what will become of Russia? When I think of that, I understand that never has there been so atrocious a martyrdom. . . .[14]

When the doctors pronounced Rasputin to be out of danger, Praskovia and Dunia went back to Pokrovskoye, leaving Maria alone with her father to help look after his needs. It was then that Dunia experienced something she was later to describe to Maria, an event which for sheer transcendant spirituality closely resembled the phenomenon known in the Roman Catholic world as the stigmata. Maria relates that Dunia was "not a particularly religious woman." Yet this mistress of Rasputin loved him very deeply, so much in fact that once back at the Pokrovskoye house she spent part of each day on her knees before the image of the Virgin of Kazan, giving thanks for the sparing of his life.

It was on a day like any other that it happened, with Dunia on her knees before the Virgin. Looking up, she saw what appeared to be a tear below the eye of the Madonna. She wiped it away. It instantly reappeared. Spellbound by the wondrous sight, she dried the holy cheek repeatedly, but as often as she did so the wetness returned. Excitedly she summoned Praskovia and the other family members, and all witnessed what she had seen. All kneeled. All prayed together, awestruck. When an account of this was sent to Maria in Tyumen and she read it to Rasputin as he lay in his sickbed, she recalled that his haggard face turned noticeably pale. In the last work she ever penned about her father's life she recorded his reaction, a thing to which she and she alone bore witness. "The Holy Mother weeps for Russia," he said somberly. "It is a sign that a great misfortune is about to strike us."[15]

The event was to prove the *starets* right, *dead* right in every particular. The war that would be fought "to make the world safe for democracy" in the American phrase, would destroy three empires and their ruling dynasties,[16] paralyze Europe economically and bleed her white, and sow the seeds for the rise of some of the most hideous and barbaric totalitarian dictatorships the world had ever seen.

NOTES

1. In May of 1887, Aleksandr Ulyanov, Lenin's older brother and conspirator in a plot to assassinate Tsar Aleksandr III, was hung for this offense, a fact to which some historians have attributed Lenin's hatred of tsarism. Others have pointed out, however, that the brothers detested each other, Aleksandr's feelings deriving from Vladimir's shabby treatment of their mother. The view persists that a cold-blooded drive for power chiefly sparked Lenin's single-minded animosity.

2. As in the France of 1789, the coming revolution in Russia was not engineered

by its peasantry, but by bourgeois (middle class) intellectuals with considerable education. This that had been true in the time of Michael Bakunin (1818–1872), founder with Karl Marx of the First Communist International, was still true when such men as Lenin and Trotsky came to the forefront.

3. Part of Nikolai's problem was the long-lasting childhood influence of Constantine Pobedonostsev (1827–1907), an inflexible reactionary who had been advisor to his father and then to himself. This man, Procurator of the Holy Synod and an astute jurist, had fought the idea of representative government all his life, inculcating in the young ruler a posture of rigid autocracy to which a fatalistic and essentially do-nothing approach was intrinsic.

4. Alfred von Schlieffen died in 1913 at the age of eighty. Even on his deathbed he was thinking of the defeat of France. Referring to his plan already adopted for future battle contingency by the German General Staff, his last words were a potent reminder: "Remember to keep the right wing strong."

5. This writer, a later and lesser artist, should not be confused with the great Leo Tolstoy (1828–1910), author of such famous classics as *War and Peace* and *Anna Karenina*.

6. Lukianov was Procurator of the Holy Synod, a position requiring investigative functions of an often unsavory nature, indeed, not unlike those of the Okhrana.

7. Grand Duke Nikolai Nikolayevich, army general and husband to Montenegrin Princess Anastasia, was secretly in strong support of this.

8. The edition published by Dial Press, New York, 1927. She was the daughter of Grand Duke Aleksandr Mikhailovich and Grand Duchess Xenia Aleksandrovna.

9. As with many another unfortunate prisoner, Goremykin was executed by the Bolsheviks in 1917.

10. The overage *Polar Star* had been sold and replaced by the *Standart*.

11. In the coming Battle of Jutland, the very audacious Rear Admiral Sir David Beatty would fight in a manner reminiscent of Nelson at the Battle of Cape St. Vincent. In the latter struggle, Nelson had hauled his own single ship out of the British line and plunged it into a gap in the enemy fleet, a maneuver that completely disorganized the Spaniards. At Jutland, Beatty would use his battle cruiser squadron as bait to lure the German High Seas Fleet into position for destruction by the British Grand Fleet, and Admiral Scheer's ships would narrowly escape annihilation.

12. Maria Rasputin, who saw her father afterward, said the terrible slash reached to the sternum.

13. Colin Wilson, *Rasputin and the Fall of the Romanovs*, The Citadel Press, Secaucus, New Jersey, 1964.

14. Maria Rasputin and Patte Barham, *Rasputin: The Man Behind the Myth*, Warner Books, New York, 1977. (Published by arrangement with Prentice-Hall, Inc.)

15. *Ibid.*

16. The German Empire of the Hohenzollerns, the Austro-Hungarian Empire of the Habsburgs, and the Russian Empire of the Romanovs.

CHAPTER 11

"Would You Be Tsar?"

In 1918, at the age of thirty-eight, the German philosopher-historian Oswald Spengler published his masterwork *The Decline of the West*. In it he posed the hypothesis that all civilizations follow a cyclic pattern, passing from youth through maturity to old age and death. Having witnessed the seething holocaust of the First World War he was convinced that Europe would never recover from it. The economic devastation was ruinous in its scope, the social and political dislocation profound, the staggering losses in human life and property utterly indescribable. Western culture would collapse irretrievably, he predicted. It was in the nature of things, and an inescapable part of the cycle, that the former importance of this culture in the international fabric would be replaced by the soon to rise "yellow race."

Only four short years earlier, very little of this sort of thinking could be found in the chancellories of Europe. On the contrary, if there was any trepidation on the part of war's participants it was well masked by propaganda, by rampant nationalism and its concomitant bravado, and by what the heavily engaged commanders on both sides were convinced was strategy so adroit as to ultimately spell certain doom for the enemy. The movements of large bodies of troops was one thing, but for France in the opening days of the war the shrewd diplomacy of her ambassador in St. Petersburg was more vital to her cause than anything that could be accomplished by a single French

general. This man was Maurice Paléologue, plenipotentiary extraor-
dinaire. His task had been clearly defined. It was nothing less than
to convince the Tsar's government that it was in the interest of Russia
to attack the German armies on the Eastern Front immediately war
should be declared, thus buying desperately needed time for France.
What did the French expect? They contemplated an all-out German
drive to take Paris. In this prediction their intelligence organization
was highly accurate.

Due to the nature of the interwoven alliances the march to destruction followed a pattern of terrible inevitability. Austria-Hungary's
declaration of war against Serbia on July 28, 1914 was followed by partial, then general Russian mobilization all within forty-eight hours.
Predictably, the German reaction was immediate, a fact sorting well
with the Kaiser's swaggering militancy. On July 31, Berlin's ultimatum to Russia demanding cessation of military preparations along
Germany's frontier received no response, resulting the following day
in a German declaration of war on Russia. France came next. Sure
that Paris would support St. Petersburg, Germany declared war on
France on August 3, then proceeded to invade Luxembourg and Belgium in the first phase of the Schlieffen Envelopment. Unaware of
London's guarantee to Brussels, the Germans had hoped for British
neutrality. Of this notion they were disabused on August 4 when
England declared war on Germany. Within a short time Montenegro
and Japan declared for the Allies, consisting of Britain, France, Russia,
Belgium, and Serbia, and Turkey entered on the side of the Central
Powers, Germany and Austria-Hungary.[1] Localization of the conflict
was now impossible.

Logically, it might be supposed that the political leaders of all
nations would be students of history or, if not actual scholars, at least
have enough acumen to benefit from the more obvious mistakes of
the past. However, in reality this is seldom true. As military power
in modern times is largely based on technology and mass production,
it is axiomatic in war that a primarily agricultural country, such as
Russia was in 1914, cannot successfully engage a highly industrialized
power like Germany. St. Petersburg should have known this. Before
them, had they cared to examine it, was the example of the American
Civil War, wherein the valor and élan of the Confederacy (which had

no navy and only two cannon factories in 1861) could not long prevail over the industrialized might of the Union. Much more recently, also, and certainly more pertinent, there was the disastrous Russo-Japanese War, a struggle in which the ill-armed, ill-fed, and all but immobile Russian troops proved no match for a Japan recently awakened to industrialism. But to the self-evident facts of the overall military equation the Tsar and most of the members of his government were blind.

Initially at least, of the factors influencing Nikolai II toward an increasingly enthusiastic acceptance of the war, one of the more significant was the sudden upsurge in his own popularity. Although he had reigned for a quarter of a century he had never enjoyed the unalloyed approval of his subjects, let alone basked in their affection, and he knew it. Now, caught up in the spirit of patriotism, for the first time the masses fully identified the sovereign with the nation itself and took the figurehead that was the Tsar to their hearts. Never had Russian nationalism been more to the fore. Flags bravely flew; soldiers marched off to the waiting trains that would take them to the battlefront; military bands played their hearts out while the crowds cheered and waved the troops on. There is something very exhilarating about war. Everyone was full of the spirit of self-sacrifice, full of thoughts of God, too. For as much as Saxon and Norman, fighting at Hastings nearly nine centuries before, had each thought that God was with him, so now the same belief was held by all belligerents (people change very little), nor did it occur to any that someone had to be in error. In Russia the strikes, most of which were being fomented by the Bolsheviks, ceased outright. Even vodka, traditional drink of the people, was banned by the Tsar's edict on the ground that overindulgence in it hurt the nation's war-making capability. No one complained.

When in the late summer of 1914 Rasputin returned to St. Petersburg, he was still a very sick man, so ill indeed he became exhausted very easily and could scarcely walk erect for the pain it caused him. The inference is that within the area of visceral damage there were unhealed lesions, possibly even internal bleeding. He tried to ignore this. At first he tried also to ignore the profound changes that war had brought to the capital, in some of which he saw the omens of disaster. Even the name of the city was altered, also by royal proclamation. Peter the Great had been pro-German and the name St. Petersburg was Teutonic. Now the teeming metropolis bore the Slavic designation of Petrograd, being still the City of Peter.[2]

The *starets* quickly discovered the opposite polarities that once had existed—bitter hatred for him at the one extreme and popularity, even adulation, at the other—were now heavily weighted in favor of the former. At the Gorokhovaya flat, which he again occupied, gone were the crowds of petitioners. It was known that he opposed hostilities and that was very close to treason. The rumors spread by the Bolsheviks to the effect that he and the Tsaritsa were working for the enemy had not been believed by many. Now, however, with the nation at war, the mere absence of a published denial was in itself a potent poison tending to substantiate those charges in the public mind. Rasputin felt old, worn out and half-decrepit before his time. To the few who came to see him he gave his best, and both he and they found it inadequate. To the ladies of his "court" he appeared lethargic, with a much reduced sex drive. They sympathized deeply, but even the most optimistic and loving among them could not help but fear for his survival.

When, taking Maria in company, he went to Tsarskoye Selo, it must have been with an omniscient sadness in his heart. It would be the final meeting in the loving spirit of the past. Never again would he and the Tsar exchange thoughts in quiet conclave, nor drink Madeira together, nor rub shoulders not as sovereign and *muzhik* but simply as two Russians standing in the sight of God. The *starets* knew intuitively that the antiwar telegram he had sent from the hospital in Tyumen had angered Nikolai. Now he was to discover the extent of the royal opposition. Maria, the all-important surviving eyewitness, relates that for the first time the Emperor's manner was cool and distant toward her father. After the affair of the compromising photos and threatened blackmail, the affair of Lisa Tansin, Nikolai had been apprehensive and admonitory, but this was more than that. To do the Tsar justice, his feelings went far deeper than anything based on mere self-aggrandisement. He feared for the security of his son's future crown, indeed for Aleksei's very life for political as well as medical reasons, and was certain that victory in the military conflict would ensure the continuance of the dynasty.

Rasputin, on the other hand, feared for the nation itself, the dread of what he foresaw cutting more deeply than the knife that had wounded him. Casting caution to the winds, knowing what he risked but making the effort regardless, he immediately brought up the same subject, doggedly attacking Russia's entry into the war while Maria, as she recalls, sat at the Tsaritsa's feet. No one could win the thing, he told the Tsar, for in the end the Four Horsemen of the Apocalypse would conquer all.[3] Stern-faced, the Emperor listened as the *starets* poured his heart out. It was no good. Except for emphasizing the religious aspect, Count Witte had employed the same argument. Nikolai would not heed it. In his own mind he could not *afford* to do so. From the chair he sat in the Tsar toyed with wine, silently. Aleksandra was silent, too, though Maria remembers the face of the Tsaritsa was "pained." As the *starets* became more impassioned his eyes brimmed with tears that overflowed. He wept for Russia. Nikolai knew this. Yet when, like a fountain gone suddenly dry, the outpouring of words had ceased, the ruler of the Russian Empire had but small comfort for the weary peasant who had given his all.

Rasputin was still seated. He said nothing further. The Tsar got up, paced twice across the room, then approached him closely and stood gazing down on him.

"Little Father," the Emperor said quietly, "there is a time to listen and a time to do something. This is our grand opportunity to save the realm and the good name of Romanov. You have served us well, and we know that. But what more can you want of us? Would you be Tsar?"[4]

The effect these words had on Rasputin is not easily described. Maria writes: "His spirit was broken with one question from the one man he most respected and loved in the world." When, moments later with his hand on the shoulder of his crestfallen guest, the Tsar said plainly that times had changed, that "the old ways must give ground to the new," he unintentionally struck at Rasputin's principal reason for existence, at the very core of the divine mission he believed the Holy Virgin had assigned to him, that of saving Mother Russia by keeping her Christian and autocratic as opposed to revolutionary atheism. The scene was not new in human history. In the dim dust of another age, Arthur and Merlin had enacted it when the mystical

Wizard of Camelot had bade the great Celtic chieftain farewell and left him to his fate.[5] Now, however, the roles were reversed. It was the Tsar who abandoned the *starets*. Never in his life had Grigori Efimovich felt so forsaken, never before so alone. He went home defeated and disconsolate. He began to drink more than ever. Nothing would comfort him. As he drank, during his increasingly less frequent moments of lucidity he prayed more than ever for the celestial restoration of his lost powers. Yet the more he drank the more totally those powers withdrew from him. Very deeply he began to feel he was lost. The world now made little sense to him, his own blasted existence none at all.

During this period it is probable that the one vital factor preventing the *starets* from descending into madness was Dunia Bekyeshova. Almost miraculously she was able to exert what little stabilizing influence still remained in his life. She catered to his every need, and when, at increasingly rare intervals, he wanted her physically, she provided that, too. Long were the hours she would sit with him day and night attempting to soothe him, doing her utmost to distract that still amazing mind from the troubled dreams that beset it, yet sensing all along that in the end she would fail. So desperate to save him did she become she urged even his return to Pokrovskoye, something which as his mistress she must have done with great reluctance, for she knew that as long as he remained in Petrograd his constant lot would be the misery of unending frustration. She feared something else as well, a threat against which she felt utterly helpless—her love's almost inevitable assassination. How often she must have tried to pursuade him to leave the city permanently will never be known. She endured all. Even to his carousing, from which she was excluded, she turned a blind eye, always welcoming her drunken lover at whatever hour he returned and tenderly putting him to bed. Viewed in retrospect, she was probably the best thing that ever happened to him. Yet at this juncture, when his great need for her transcended all else, fate intervened to leave him suddenly without her.

From Siberia word came by telegraph. Dunia's mother had taken to her bed and would never rise from it. Her daughter had no choice and knew she must go, even if only to attend a funeral. What could she do for her sick man now? She did the only thing that occurred to her. The maid Katya Ivanova had been with him here before. She could be sent for and be with him again. This was done. With a sadness and sense of misgiving that well may be imagined, Dunia left. She was scarcely on the train before Rasputin took to the wine and debauchery more strongly than ever, fighting it less and with less ability to fight, a man seemingly resigned to a bitter destiny. The Villa Rode saw him more often than ever. So did less savory dens. Though no longer with the same vigor, he danced with the Gypsies, sang, drank, and even found the strength for occasional uninhibited lechery. He felt his occult powers had vanished never to return. He was stricken to the very soul with the nearly unbearable knowledge of it. Sobriety scarcely remembered him.

While the *starets* was undergoing this heavy trial, the dire predictions he had made for his countrymen, and particularly for his own peasant class, whose numbers made up the rank and file of the Army, were coming true. When the nation had fought the Japanese in 1905, Russian infantrymen were said to have remarked acidly, "The enemy has rifles. We have ikons." Things had changed little since then. Incredible as it may seem, it frequently happened that only the first wave of Russian assault troops were armed. The second and all subsequent waves were commanded to attack without weapons, the standing orders being to equip themselves from their own fallen who had advanced to their deaths before them. The effect on morale may readily be imagined.

Still, the blazing courage that had confronted Napoleon at Austerlitz in 1805, Friedland in 1807, and Borodino in 1812 had not deserted the common Russian soldier. As these "sons of the steppe" had done before, and were to do again in World War II, they showed a singular disregard for life, their own as well as the foe's. Attacking in great hordes over the bodies of their own dead, often against withering machine-gun fire from invisible barrels in defilade position, they overran enemy emplacements by sheer weight of numbers and inflicted great slaughter on the invaders. In this fated year of 1914 this occurred at the Battle of Lemberg (Lvov in Russian), fought between August 26 and September 1, with the result that the badly mauled Austrian Army abandoned eastern Galicia and largely ceased to be an effective fighting force on this front. Almost before word of the victory was digested by the people, however, it was drastically over-shadowed by news of a crushing defeat.

Is it believed that the memory of nations and peoples is short? Five centuries earlier in 1410, near the Polish village of Tannenberg (*Stebark* in Polish) that by now was in East Prussia, Slav and German had met before. A great battle was fought on that long gone day. When it was over, the German Order of the Teutonic Knights had been almost annihilated by the Poles and Lithuanians. Now, as Russians and Germans converged, the same small settlement was near them. And what was the German battle cry? "Remember Tannenberg!"

Ludendorff has sometimes been called "the brain behind Hindenburg," and so it proved on this occasion. The fighting was ferocious and desperate. Badly outnumbered by the Russian armies under Rennenkampff and Samsonov, the Germans had no choice but to retreat to prevent their forces from being flanked. They had but one chance to turn almost certain defeat into victory. It lay in the fact that the two Russian armies had not yet been able to unite, that the closely spaced Masurian Lakes lay between them. Ludendorff's plan was followed, the tactic of all great generals of engaging the enemy in detail, i.e., one unit of his forces at a time. It is not always possible. On this occasion, it involved leaving only two cavalry brigades against Rennenkampff as a screening force while almost the totality of the German strength was hurled against Samsonov. The outcome for the Russians was unparalleled disaster. Samsonov was enveloped. Heavily outgunned, his army was shot to pieces by extraordinarily accurate artillery. Ninety-two thousand men were taken prisoner, among them 13 generals and 350 guns. In the harsh tradition of defeated Roman and Japanese generals, Samsonov committed suicide, in his case with a revolver. Shortly afterward, Rennenkampff, the man who had moved too tardily to reinforce him, paid for his error in the Battle of the Masurian Lakes, thus completing the Russian rout in East Prussia and enabling Germany to increase its forces on the Western Front in France. The result was to bolster the gray legions at the First Battle of the Marne.

While it is true that victory tends to unite a nation behind its leaders, it is equally a fact that defeat breeds a ruinous disunity.

Tannenberg was devastating in Russia. As one hospital train after another discharged thousands of wounded in Russian cities, it rapidly became clear that what the nation had fought in the war with Japan was scarcely more than a series of skirmishes compared with this. Russia would continue to fight because she was so deeply committed she had little choice, and in any case surrender was unthinkable. But the means continued to be sadly lacking. To serve her gun batteries she had only a few artillery spotter planes, all of them foreign made. The slow production of guns could not replace soon enough those which were captured or destroyed. The supply of shells of every caliber was dangerously inadequate and promised to become disastrously so. Before the end of the year, almost a million uniformed men were lacking rifles. By the beginning of 1915, the toll of Russian dead had reached a sobering and deeply shocking four million. Still, engaged now in a massive holding action in the East and locked toe to toe with the French and British in the West, Germany fought on, and no one knew how long it would continue.

The Germans were making serious mistakes, too. Giving free rein to brilliant generals such as Ludendorff and Mackensen on the Eastern Front paid off handsomely for Chief of the General Staff Helmuth von Moltke,[6] but letting himself be influenced by lesser talents was very costly in France and led directly to his replacement by the Prussian War Minister, General Erich von Falkenhayn.[7] That influence took the form of a change in the Schlieffen Plan. From the right wing, its preponderant strength so vital to the plan's success, two army corps and a cavalry division were withdrawn to reinforce the left in Alsace-Lorraine. Had this not been done the German Army might well have flanked the French, or at least driven a wedge between them and the British Expeditionary Force with disastrous results for the Allies. As it was, the shifting of forces slowed the German drive and threw it out of balance, thus enabling a formidable Franco-British defense to be formed on the line of the Marne, September 6 to 9, 1914.[8] This development altered every aspect of the struggle and condemned millions of soldiers on both sides to an unutterable hell. Replacing the "war of maneuver" envisaged by von Schlieffen there now ensued a "war of position," the thing he had feared most, with the hideous stalemated immobility of a years' long death struggle in the trenches.

The men fought in conditions so shocking and gruesome that a British general visiting the front at a later date burst into tears of anguish at the magnitude of their sacrifice. Diseases such as typhus fever, "trench foot," and "trench mouth" were the soldiers' lot. The incessant shelling induced abnormal weather conditions of endless rain. They fought in a welter of mud and water indescribably fouled with the stench and putrifaction of unburied corpses minced by artillery fire. Gains were measured in yards. Direct frontal assaults (the only tactics possible against entrenchments extending from the mountains to the sea) produced enormous losses of life. It was hellish. Nightmarish. As the months dragged on in a downpouring of endless blood the only victor was the ubiquitous, ever-ravenous creature with "the obscenely naked tail," the plague-carrying trench rat.

Although the stupefying casualty reports bore out his most dire predictions and vindicated all that he had said, Rasputin's only reaction to them was one of horror and infinite sadness. In his mind's eye, so different from that of most of his fellow humans, he could actually *see* the battlefields with their cluttered corpses, could hear the screams of the newly wounded and the moaning delirium of the pitiful stretcher cases. He tried to drown it all in wine, to seek merciful oblivion by numbing the brain. It was of little use. He still saw things only too clearly.

On a day when he was unaccustomedly sober an old peasant woman came to see him. She was full of pain, disfigured and twisted with arthritis, her gnarled and vein-wreathed hands like the claws of birds. With piteous inarticulation she mumbled to him about her wretched condition and implored his help. *"Oh Otyets Grigori, khranit vas Bog!"*—"God preserve you!" He was deeply moved. For the love of God he did his best to aid her but quickly sensed that his healing powers had vanished utterly. At this confirmation of what he already knew he felt despair. He could give her no comfort nor the slightest ease of her suffering. He could do nothing. He ended with a few words of kindness and hope, and a scrawled note of introduction. Pyotr Aleksandrovich might have the answer, the famed Tibetan healer, Dr. Badmaev. She could try.

When he closed the door behind her, bowed by the great weight of his failure, he felt that from this forgotten limbo of the godforsaken and outcast he would never find his way back. Maria was there. She saw his face, a strange and wasted visage nearly unknown to her. She heard his words, those uttered by the Christ from the cross on Golgotha: " '*Eli, Eli, lama sabachthani?*' "[9] Few martyred saints in their pain could have been more agonized. He returned to the taverns, the insensate wassail that led to nothing and solved nothing. If the Virgin of Kazan were substituted for the lost and ever-unattainable Cynara in the famed English poem, its lines might well have been appropriate to this failed Galahad who had sought his own Holy Grail in vain. "I cried for madder music and for stronger wine. But when the feast was finished and the lamps expired, then fell thy shadow, Cynara, the night was thine. And I was desolate and sick of an old passion."[10] It mattered not that the one love was sacred, the other profane. The Mother of God and the Goddess of Love were alike beyond reach.

About this time, another determined enemy of the *starets* reared his head, the ambitious and foolhardy General Dzhunkovsky, director of the metropolitan police in the capital. Heedless of the Tsaritsa's known sentiments, he prepared a report that detailed some of Rasputin's more flagrantly salacious activities at places like the Villa Rode and submitted it to the Tsar. Nothing came of it. Nonetheless, as had happened before, Aleksandra discovered it. She did not forget such things. The rash Dzhunkovsky had made himself a marked man.

It was shortly before Christmas 1914 that Dunia returned to Petrograd. If her mother's funeral had made her melancholy, what she found at 64 Gorokhovaya Ulitsa must have made her infinitely more so. But this enamorata of Rasputin was very brave. To the task of repairing his physical and mental health she brought every ounce of love and dedication of which a woman of her deep feelings and sensitivity was capable. She was quite firm with him. While her adored one was convalescing there was to be no more Villa Rode; no more indulgence in wine, women, and song; nor in any other activity that would sap his strength and delay his recovery. She would prove now that the great respect, indeed the profound awe felt for her by the other ladies of the "court" was deserved. She was Dunia Bekyeshova, and not one of them was quite like her. With the possible exception of the very devoted ex-nun, Akulina Nikichkina, she was closer to her *starets* than anyone in the world. She had always loved him. With the sure intuition which is woman's most startling and inexplicable attribute, she knew without doubt that he would gladly die for her, just as she knew that her life was his—to the very end.

In one of the coaches of the moving passenger train Anna Aleksandrovna Virubova sat muffled in fur, feeling chilled despite the fact that the car was supposed to be heated. She was looking out the window. Once she made a fist and rubbed the glass pane with her gloved hand; then realized that most of the frost was on the outside and unremovable. Still, she caught glimpses of the passing landscape. It had been snowing all day. It fell a little less heavily now it seemed, yet everything was a dreary, glistening white, and when they had moved out from Tsarskoye Selo the steam-driven wheels had spun and shrieked on the ice-encrusted steel of the tracks.

She lay back in the seat and stared straight ahead, a plump but attractive woman who led a life as strange as any in Russia. Why was she going to Petrograd? She was going to see *him*, of course, as she so often did, taking a train because she distrusted cars on the icy roads. The neighbors would see her enter his flat. There would be the usual gossip, many a wagging tongue to continue the dreary years' long process of repeating tales of their "intimacy." Yet her hymen remained intact. How would they explain that? They could not explain it any more than the fact that she, a commoner, was the closest friend the Tsaritsa had in the world. Friend and confidant, bosom companion—to the Empress of Russia. And to Rasputin? No one would ever know how much she loved him or in what way. Let them drive themselves crazy with guessing. This was the year 1915, the fifteenth day of January. The Holy Father was sick. He had never recovered from the knife wound. She had been lucky to get this train, she knew, since most of them were shunted aside to make room for troop trains. And she went, and she would see him, and that was all that mattered.

Actually, it wasn't this particular gossip that worried her. It was the talk about him and the Tsaritsa, how she, Anna, had turned her small house near the palace into a trysting place, a romantic sanctuary for the two of them. That was the talk. And what choice had this wonderful but oddly assorted pair? They met secretly because the

Tsar had turned against Rasputin, he wasn't welcome at the palace, and there was nowhere else they could go. Intimate? The Tsaritsa and the *starets*? The Tsar gave his time to the war now, precious little of it to his wife. Who could really blame her if she *were* to break her marital vows? Intimate? A question of definition. No matter what it was she knew that she, Anna, would not see it as that. Self-delusion? Maybe. They had only to see Rasputin's poor, sick body. But people were seldom concerned with the obvious.

She laid her head back on the worn cushioned seat. In moments the monotonous hum of wheels on rails and the dull chugging of the engine had nearly put her to sleep. She heard the whistle blow, was aware of the porter passing down the aisle. Dimly she wondered how train engineers could see each other in weather like this. Could they always rely on switching devices, the alertness of snow-blinded switchmen to see trains approaching each other? The minutes passed. Then she heard the whistle again. It seemed much louder this time, more long sustained, then frantically insistent. Suddenly, without warning there was a terrific lurch as the brakes were applied with full force. There was a roaring, the ear-splitting impact of a titanic crash, and she felt herself hurtling through space. A sickening crunch was followed by a breathtaking falling away into nothingness. Her last fleeting impression before the darkness closed in was one of excruciating pain, an agony like the blades of knives ripping through her skull and her legs, and a high-pitched whirring sound like the flight of a million arrows. It was pressurized steam escaping from torn-open boilers.

Like a snake whose body had been repeatedly severed by the blows of a shovel the great train lay on its side and back, broken into many parts, its spine shattered, most of its coaches derailed and some of them telescoped into others. On the same track was the other train that should have been switched and wasn't. The two engines that had collided head-on were unrecognizable masses of smoking, twisted steel. The dead and the dying were everywhere, both within and without. No one knew how many of those still possible to save might be aboard the wreck. The scene was frightful. Unreal. From dozens of isolated sources came moans of dire torment punctuated by muffled screams. It seemed to go on and on.

Already there were several teams of doctors and nurses on the site, with more rapidly arriving. Police made their appearance, and even some off-duty soldiers hastily assembled by a noncommissioned officer. In their search for victims who might still be alive they literally crawled over the riven steel like insects. Eventually they found Anna Virubova, freeing her from the chaotic entanglement as carefully as they could. That her condition was critical, even hopeless was obvious. Propelled through the air like a missile, a steam radiator had smashed both her legs causing compound fractures. Across her head lay a heavy metal girder. A hasty examination showed a severely fractured skull with virtually certain brain concussion and quite possibly a broken back.

Rising from their stooped position, a doctor and his assistant looked at each other, and the doctor shook his head. He did not know her identity. He muttered something about her injuries being terminal, words making it clear that their efforts must be concentrated on those who had a chance. They applied gauze compresses to staunch her bleeding but little else was done. Two male bystanders were recruited. Using a ripped off door, they placed her on it and carried her away to the nearest public shelter, one of many who were being lifted clear of the wreck. Then they laid her down quietly to die.

For hours she drifted in and out of unconsciousness. In the course of time, identification was made from her effects and someone telephoned the royal palace at Tsarskoe Selo. She was taken to the hospital. When the grief-stricken Tsar and Tsaritsa dropped everything to come to her in haste, they were told the truth. The royal favorite had been fighting a valiant battle for her life, almost as though she refused to die until she could see her beloved sovereigns once more. But now it was a priest that was needed. Her severely damaged spine had not been broken but her head injuries were fatal. The end could not be far off.

It was late on the following afternoon before Rasputin heard of the accident, being told by a badly upset Maria who had been with Marusa Sasanova at the latter's home when the young girl's father got word of it. The *starets* was in bed, Maria remembers, a usual enough thing with him in his days of slow convalescence. Shakily he rose, ignoring Dunia's attempts to restrain him as he dressed with all possible speed. His Anyushka dying? Impossible. They had taken her to Tsarskoe Selo? Yes, the Tsar and Tsaritsa loved her, too. They would want her there with them at the last. He tried to think. Dunia's phone call could fetch a car but he would need help getting in and out of it. He would take Maria. She was very strong. In a world of the sick and injured, she was like an oak. Indestructible. In a comparatively short time the two of them were in the back seat together and on their way.

At the palace Rasputin went straight in, his daughter beside him, watching him carefully for fear he would fall. No ceremony today. He barely greeted the Tsar. The doctors had given up hope? A priest had administered the last rites? But they had done that with Aleksei, too, had they not? In the room where Anna lay he found the Tsaritsa and smiled at her wanly; then kneeled at the bedside of his beloved one and took her pale hand in his. With every shred of spirituality he could muster he prayed for her survival. It was the old way, the way felt deep in the intestines, as though he were at the bottom of the sea and fought his way upward, ever upward through decades and centuries and eons of time, upward to the Light no matter what the odds. Unbowed. Unbeaten. Upward to the Light . . .

"Anyushka. Anyushka. Look at me."

The girl lay as though dead, her eyes closed. As though no breath of life stirred within her, the lineaments of her face beneath her bandaged head were like those of a graven image, masklike.

"Anyushka, look at me. I am here."

She moved. She too struggled up from the depths. She too sought the Light. He saw her eyelids open. Her eyes could not focus and they closed. Then they opened again. They were like the fluttering of birds' wings. Her lips trembled. They would not take her away. They *would* not . . .

"Otyets Grigori," she murmured feebly. "Thanks be to God."

Maria began to weep. She later told her father she was sure that Anna was at the point of dissolution. He spoke to her softly. "Hush, child."

When he got to his feet he could hardly stand. He was very pale. With trembling hand he made the Sign of the Cross over Anna, who now seemed to be sleeping peacefully. Then he turned his haggard face to Nikolai and Aleksandra, his features like those of an old man.

"She will live," he said with a voice that cracked with pathos, "but she will always be a cripple." He glanced at Maria. "Come."

Together they left the royal presence. They went through the magnificently ornate doors. Two servants closed them. Rasputin tried to walk but could not. He was shaking in every limb. Was *this* what it had taken out of him? Anna's life force replenished at the cost of what little energy he had left? But it did not matter. He had triumphed. He had triumphed in God's name and once again the power of healing, nay, of *rekindling life* when life was all but lost, had been restored to him. His knees gave way. He fell like a great tree cut through by the woodsman's axe—but even as he fell he was smiling. He heard Maria scream in her fear.

"Get a doctor!"

"No. No," he muttered. "Take me home."

When she did so, Dunia was waiting. Rasputin was as cold as ice and his lips had turned blue. He could not stand. Dunia undressed him and put him to bed; then held him close to her body, desperately trying to suffuse him with her own inner warmth. It was a long night for her. With the coming of dawn a touch of color appeared in his cheeks. Still, she had told Maria with her face streaked with tears, "I think he has not long to live."[11]

The coming days would show whether or not she was prophetic. As for the sad prophecy of the *starets*, Anna Virubova did survive—but never regained the full use of her legs.

It was only a few months later, in April of 1915, that Petrograd's police chief, General Dzhunkovsky, finally got the chance he had been seeking.[12] This time it was more than a routine "disturbance." Rasputin had gone to Moscow. In the Ouspensky Cathedral within the walls of the Kremlin he had kneeled to offer his devotions before the crypts containing the remains of the Orthodox saints, his mood clearly one of contrition and humility. Unfortunately, his evening was free and his wine addiction had by this time a strong hold. He gravitated toward the Yar, a rather shady bistro where he had been before. As often happens with inebriates, when he got drunk he became argumentative, when sufficiently opposed combative. According to witnesses, he was closeted with women in one of the private rooms. A commotion ensued, doors were slammed, and glass was broken. When police appeared on the scene, one observer claimed the *starets* had exposed himself, arrogantly boasting he could do the same thing in the Royal Palace with impunity and even have his way with the Tsaritsa.

While the occurrence of the fracas is likely enough, it is not really credible that Rasputin, drunk or sober, would have said such a thing about Aleksandra, for it would have been entirely out of character. Nonetheless, he was arrested and detained briefly before release, and the official report of the Moscow police was sent to Petrograd. Dzhunkovsky seized on it immediately. Discretion was not his strong point. Apparently, he did not fear the Empress. Enlivening the account with what we may be sure were suitable "embellishments," he took it directly to the Tsar. For some obscure reason, a copy of it also got into the hands of Yussupov's erstwhile love, Grand Duke Dmitri Pavlovich, after which its contents became known to the infuriated Tsaritsa. She was not slow to express her opinion of it to her husband. "My enemy Dzhunkovsky has shown that vile, filthy paper to Dmitri. . . . If we let our Friend be persecuted, we and our country will suffer for it."[13]

Considering he had so thoroughly earned Aleksandra's ire, Dzhunkovsky showed unusual longevity. He had attacked the *starets* in April. It was not until September that the Tsar deprived him of his office.

Rasputin's telegraphed warning to the Tsar from Siberia at war's beginning, a prediction of total disaster, was based on more than a prescient knowledge of future military defeat. Although hardly a student of what has been called "the science of revolution," he had the astuteness to realize that the overthrow of Russian armies in the field would quickly be turned to revolutionary purposes at home. Indeed, after Tannenberg, the Bolsheviks, the Mensheviks, the Social Revolutionaries, and other insurgent organizations had wasted no time in reasserting themselves. Like moles brought out of their holes by a spring freshet, they were now everywhere fostering sedition, printing thousands of clandestine pamphlets all over Russia, and had even initiated the inevitable "peace movement" designed then (and in later struggles elsewhere) to undermine a nation's morale and do everything possible to weaken its war effort.

In this, as the *starets* also knew, the Leftist elements were greatly aided by some of the most incompetent and pernicious ministers of state ever to plague a country fighting for its life. The Minister of War was General Vladimir Sukhomlinov, a small, soft, and heavyset individual approaching seventy, a man preoccupied with pleasure rather than work, and with catering to the expensive tastes and lavish mode of living of his young Jewish wife. He was perhaps the nation's foremost example of outmoded military thinking, the sort of officer invariably prone to fight the latest war with the strategy and tactics of the last. Sukhomlinov believed in dashing cavalry charges with leveled lances and drawn sabers and advances by masses of infantry armed with the bayonet. He was perfectly willing to ignore the lesson the German artillery had taught at Tannenberg, willing, too, to overlook the reports of British Intelligence, secret memoranda stating that for every two machine guns the British and French were manufacturing German industry was producing three. None of this concerned the War Minister. Russia, after all, had *unlimited* numbers of men.

Sukhomlinov's primary enemy was the man who should have been his close collaborator and colleague, Grand Duke Nikolai Nikolayevich, now Commander-in-Chief of the Tsar's field forces. They detested each other intensely. To Sukhomlinov, the aristocratic grandson of Tsar Nikolai I was an arrogant, bullying blunderer whose power was based solely on the advantage of birth. Nikolai's opinion of him was even lower. Quite simply, the man was a minister of state who failed in his duty. To the austere and rigidly militaristic nobleman, trained in an inflexible tradition, this was the greatest crime of all.

Despite their mutual hostility, in the end it was not Sukhomlinov who would overthrow the Grand Duke. Rather, it was that officer's increasingly obvious hatred for Rasputin. When this became known to Aleksandra she could no longer find anything good in the General. She had heard of his response to Rasputin's offer to go to the front and pray for the hard-pressed, intensely suffering troops. "Yes, do come. I'll hang you." From that moment on, her resolve inexorable, she did not cease her efforts to influence her husband to decide on his cousin's dismissal. By the summer of 1915, continuing Russian military reversals had made this feasible. On August 5, with the fall of the city of Warsaw to the enemy, the Tsar had become desperate. Three weeks later, in a letter that was characteristically kind and full of praise for the Grand Duke's abilities, the Tsar dismissed him and announced he was taking over the position of Commander-in-Chief himself. Nikolai Nikolayevich, the giant who conferred spiritually with Joan of Arc, would assume command in the Caucasus.

As concerns the Grand Duke's martial talent, Rasputin and others had judged hastily. While perhaps lacking the genius of a Suvorov or a Kutuzov, the tall General had an extensive fund of military knowledge, was extremely daring and resourceful on the attack, and had a palpable "aura of command" that never failed to inspire his men. The Germans were much relieved at his departure. Robert K. Massie quotes from the subsequently published memoirs of Erich von Ludendorff: "The Grand Duke was really a great soldier and strategist."[14] Substantiating this opinion was the transferred commander's campaign record on the Caucasian front, where his later victories over the Turks all but paralyzed their efforts in that area. It was a woman he could not defeat, not an army.[15]

It was against this ominous background of thundering violence from without and creeping revolutionary terror from within that Rasputin continued to function as best he could. Physically and spiritually he was still far from well, but since God had allowed him to save the life of Anna Virubova he had emerged once again from what he called "the dark night of the soul" and had partially regained his interest in living. The dismissal of Nikolaska (the name by which the Grand Duke was known within the Imperial Family) did not affect his mood one way or the other, for he considered that general's whereabouts and influence extraneous to his earthly mission. That he seemed once again to be in God's grace, if only to a small degree, was a thought that made him rejoice. Nonetheless, he began to have an increasingly strong presentiment that he would not survive the war. In another man this augury might have produced a cynic, embittered and disillusioned. Rasputin rejected these sentiments as he did all self-pity. His chief emotion was one of regret heightened by a sense of waste. There was so much to do and so little time, and he was but one man.

It was during this period that he began to earn his later reputation as a deliverer of the Jews, later because his intense efforts on their behalf were not known to them at that date. The fighting in Poland had caused the destruction of thousands of Jewish homes and the owners lacked the means to rebuild them. Hostile Germany lay to the west. To the east lay a Russia that may have been hostile, too, but to masses of Jewish refugees, on the edge of starvation and facing the coming winter in the open, emigrating there could hardly be any worse and it might save their lives. The trouble was that many Russians believed the Jews to be pro-German and hostile to their interests, the acts of a few having condemned the many. They entered Russia. They were persecuted, reviled, and spat upon by peasants and city dwellers alike. Not only were they denied sanctuary, but in many cases they were simply seized and lynched wholesale. When Rasputin heard of it, to redress the grievances of these wretched displaced persons became one of his chief aims. Indeed, he plunged into it recklessly, making more enemies as he did so, as though he were trying to prove to himself that he still had some value in the eyes of God.

To this task he brought every ounce of influence he had. With the Duma he had none at all and was well aware of it. On the contrary, to a man their members detested him. But through the Tsaritsa, and in some cases directly, he was able to reach important ministers of state, and through them the necessary pressure was brought. Eventually, much to the annoyance and chagrin of that very venal body of politicians, a bill was introduced and passed that guaranteed the Jews' civil rights, for as Poles they were technically Russian citizens and subjects of the Tsar. No such legislation had ever been heard of in Muscovy before. Now, thanks to the man who was the nation's primary target for assassination, some tens of thousands of helpless unfortunates were given their chance in life. Jewish children could be taught in the state-run schools. A Jew could not be brought to trial without due process of law. There was even the possibility that Jewish males might eventually become eligible to occupy seats in the Duma, a thought particularly galling to its gentile membership. That Rasputin should champion "the people who murdered Jesus" was one more "proof" that he was indeed that perfidious being identified by Chionya Guseva and others, the very incarnation of the Antichrist.

Gradually, the *starets* began to recover some measure of his once vigorous health. He would never again be the man he had been, and of this he was well aware. Nonetheless, as the months passed, despite his continued imbibance of wine his incredible vitality began to re-assert itself. He was going to need it. He was a man virtually alone. Although since the incident with Virubova he stood once again in the Tsar's good graces, Nikolai as Commander-in-Chief was geographi-cally displaced, seldom in Petrograd, and fear had made the Tsaritsa more neurotic. She was a woman who wrote endless letters to her husband. Some people said she ruled in Petrograd in his stead, but Rasputin knew the truth. Though she still loved her *starets*, "our Friend" as she always called him in her letters, Aleksandra Feodorovna could not even save herself, let alone anyone else. More than ever, she could be found these days surrounded by her favorite mauve—that meant her bedroom with its predominant color—and an empress so withdrawn and isolated was not ruling anything, least of all Russia. To a marked degree she had been politically neutralized. The revo-lutionaries branded her "whore" and "traitor." And now, since the death of Witte in March of this mad year 1915, he, Rasputin, was the single most hated man in the realm.

He did not let this worry him unduly, though he knew the knives they were sharpening for him were long and their edges keen. He would do his best to serve Almighty God and pray for the forgiveness of his weaknesses. When his time came he would hope to die like a man. What mortal could do more?

NOTES

1. Belatedly reversing its policy, Italy later came in on the side of the Allies.

2. Other names were similarly changed. The notorious site of Ekaterinburg, for example, was renamed Sverdlovsk in 1924 after a Communist leader, presumably to commemorate the mass regicide that took place there.

3. The Four Horsemen were war, famine, pestilence, and death. From the apoc-alyptic vision in The Book of Revelation 6: 2–8.

4. Maria Rasputin and Patte Barham, *Rasputin: The Man Behind the Myth*, Warner Books, New York, 1977. (Published by arrangement with Prentice-Hall, Inc.)

5. Far from considering Arthur and Camelot as myth, the consensus of modern scholarship is that the legend concerning them had its basis in historical fact. Consult Geoffrey Ashe, *In Quest of Arthur's Britain*, Praeger, New York, 1968.

6. Called "von Moltke the Younger," he was the son of the famous Helmuth Graf von Moltke, the field marshal chiefly responsible for the defeat of France in the

Franco-Prussian War of 1870–1871, resulting in the abdication and exile to England of Emperor Napoleon III.

7. After the extremely heavy German losses at Verdun (February to June 1916), Falkenhayn himself was succeeded by Hindenburg.

8. Curiously enough, the conceptual brilliance and continuing validity of the Schlieffen Plan was finally proved by the German Army during World War II. In the battles in Flanders and France of May-June 1940, the Nazi "blitzkrieg" adhered to it precisely, split the French from the British, isolated the British Expeditionary Force at Dunkerque, and achieved the collapse of France in five weeks.

9. The translation from the Aramaic is "My God, my God, why hast thou forsaken me?" Matthew 27: 46.

10. William Ernest Dowson, "Non Sum Qualis Eram Bonae Sub Regno Cynarae." Most of the titles of Dowson's poems were in Latin.

11. The spoken exchanges at Tsarskoe Selo are as Maria remembers them. Recalled by her, also, were Dunia's pathetic words.

12. Colin Wilson refers to him as Petrograd's "head of the police department." Robert K. Massie identifies him as "commander of all the police in the empire." Feliks Yussupov says he was "Vice-Minister of the Interior." Maria Rasputin, René Fülöp-Miller, and Heinz Liepman fail to mention him.

13. Robert K. Massie, *Nicholas and Alexandra*, Atheneum, New York, 1967.

14. *Ibid.*, p. 321.

15. Deprived of his final command by the Revolution of 1917, the Grand Duke remained in hiding in the Crimea until he was able to escape from Russia in 1919 and emigrate to France. He died at the Mediterranean winter resort of Antibes in 1929, convinced to the very end that his role in life should have been that of Tsar.

CHAPTER 12

The Lethal Conspiracy

By the summer of 1915 it had become obvious to even the most diehard optimist among the Allies that something had gone dreadfully wrong with the war. Although the Battle of the Marne had temporarily saved Paris,[1] although the British, fighting with their backs to the sea at the First Battle of Ypres (October–November 1914), had prevented the Germans from seizing the Channel ports and now stood rocklike with the embattled French on the ghastly Western Front, it was generally realized among Allied councils that an isolated Russia which could not be supplied was doomed to early defeat.[2] Emulating as they so often had the Napoleonic credo "*L'audace, toujours l'audace!*"—"Boldness, always boldness!"—the British sought to remedy this. The strategy, conceived in the very fertile brain of First Lord of the Admiralty Winston Churchill, was to reestablish contact with Russia by gaining control of the Strait of the Dardanelles and capturing the Turkish capital of Constantinople. After landings by English, Australian, and New Zealand troops at Gallipoli in April and again at Suvla in August of 1915, the attempts against stubborn Turkish defenders proved a costly failure, nor had the entry of Italy on the side of the Allies in May appreciably affected the balance.

In Russia, the picture was one of gradually growing disorder leading to chaos. Everything was in short supply. There was insufficient fuel to heat the homes and the common people in their millions were in danger of freezing in the bitter winter. The military draft had taken too many peasants off the farms and landed estates, with the inevitable result of increasingly severe food shortages. The nation's morale, so high at the war's beginning, had been eroded by repeated defeats. One predictable result of this was army desertions, first by the hundred, then by the thousand. The penalty if taken was death, but to men who daily saw their comrades slaughtered in droves the threat of extinction by firing squad was meaningless.[3] Nor had the people of Russia individual heroes who, when discovered by the press, could be spotlighted by publicity to invigorate national pride. The air forces of the West were an example. While the names of such aces as Richthofen, Guynemer, and Mannock were to dominate the headlines on both sides of the struggle, in Russia this potent stimulus was absent. Although they produced airmen such as Kazakov and de Seversky, each with a handful of victories, the planes they were forced to fly were inferior in quality and very few in number, obsolete machines provided by their allies. Russian industry had failed to meet the challenge. No viable air force existed.

Other than Lenin, who continued indefatigably to mastermind revolutionary activity from Switzerland, the most ruinous influences on the tsarist military effort were undoubtedly War Minister Sukhomlinov, who had done next to nothing to arm the Russian troops, and Minister of the Interior Maklakov, who had failed miserably to organize the grossly deficient transportation system, thus greatly aggravating the problem of resupply. Concerning these two, Duma President Rodzianko, whose efforts to undermine Rasputin had proved abortive, was able to influence the Tsar in this matter at least, and at the beginning of June they were cashiered. General Polivanov replaced Sukhomlinov, an intelligent move. However, when Rodzianko, having put Russian industry on a sounder footing through prodigious efforts, convened the Duma on August 1, he was unable to maintain that body in unbroken session. The reason lay with the Tsar. Nikolai had always distrusted the Duma, seeing in it an instrument existing solely for the ultimate establishment of representative government, and he listened to the Tsaritsa when she repeatedly said it would mean the death of autocracy. Both were right. In mid-September he declared the assembly in dismissal for two months, thereby enraging every liberal in the nation. It was another palpable slip for tsarism. The revolutionaries took immediate advantage of it. Lenin's agents spread the word that a country without popular representation could never win against a determined enemy and must face the inevitability of defeat.[4] Many people were listening.

Perhaps one of the most unfortunate psychological maladjustments is that of the would-be heterosexual male who finds himself repeatedly the victim of a powerful and ever-compelling homosexual component, a deep-seated urge toward members of his own sex that he finds irresistible. One thinks of the great Russian composer Peter Tchaikovsky with his weakness for boys, his lifelong fight against it, the sad admission of defeat inherent in his knowingly drinking unboiled water during a cholera epidemic.[5] Readily coming to mind also is the British author and poet Oscar Wilde, a married man who nonetheless could not resist homosexual experimentation and paid a heavy price for it. In the case of Prince Feliks Yussupov this trait was present in abundance. Yet, giving in to it repeatedly, he was determined that if a cost were to be exacted he would not be the one to pay it.

Initially, after marrying Princess Irina Aleksandrovna, he had made something of an effort to govern his behavior. In March of 1915, when his wife was delivered of a girl, he appeared exuberant, even proud of his newly achieved fatherhood. It did not, however, prevent the renewal of his intimate relationship with Grand Duke Dmitri Pavlovich, nor of other similar liaisons within the confines of the Petrograd demimonde. Yussupov had not changed much over the years. Possessing everything that untold wealth could offer, he had ceased to find life a challenge. There was little he had not done and nothing he could not have. Look where he would, the sense of anticipation had been removed from his life, adventure of the more bizarre mode seemed to have lost much of its relish, and the extraordinary had been reduced to the commonplace. In a word, he was bored.

Just when he conceived the idea of approaching Rasputin sexually and seducing him is unknown, nor is his motivation entirely clear. Was it because he found a man of such powerful and sinister reputation fascinating? Or was there something in the *starets* himself, his personal

magnetism and aura of mystery, which appealed to the jaded tastes
of the Prince and was infinitely compelling to him? Whatever it was,
Yussupov, who had adroitly managed to stay out of the military service
and whose time was therefore largely his own, decided at long last to
do something about it.[6] People were his playthings, were they not?
What did he care for anything except the unlimited exercise of his
own hedonism? After all, he was a Romanov now, at least by marriage.
The Tsar was godfather to his child, the aging Dowager Empress
Maria Feodorovna her godmother. And he? He was Prince Feliks
Feliksovich Yussupov who could do as he pleased.

With regard to Rasputin the young profligate, now twenty-nine,
appears to have reached his decision in the summer of 1916. Over the
years, his family had remained friendly to the Golovins. Now, even
though he deeply resented Munia Golovina's slavish attachment to
Rasputin, he was reminded of the fact that she had once been his
dead older brother's fianceé, that she admired the survivor, that
through her he could more surely reach the *starets* than by any other
course. He went to her house and talked to her about it, claiming he
had an "emotional problem" that only Rasputin could successfully
treat. He even indicated it was sexual in nature. He did not elaborate,
nor would Munia necessarily have understood him if he had.

She was all eagerness to help. She may have been excessively so.
Being well aware of the reduced prestige from which she believed her
adored Master suffered, seeing him largely unpatronized by the masses
despite his continuing political influence, she not surprisingly welcomed this sign of interest and attention from the man whose father
had recently been appointed Governor General of Moscow. Yet what
a singular irony is here. By a peculiar twist of fate Munia Golovina,
who had always loved the *starets* dearly, thus became the unwitting
instrument for bringing him once again into contact with his ultimate
nemesis.

The meeting took place at her home as planned. The no longer
young Madame Golovina was there, also Rasputin's follower, and
mother and daughter did all they could to make their two illustrious
male guests more than welcome. However, what Yussupov had in
mind could not be accomplished at their house and he regarded the
meeting only as a necessary preliminary, a first step toward more con-

venient arrangements. He and the *starets* talked amicably. The Prince revealed nothing of his lascivious aspirations. It was agreed they would meet again very soon at Rasputin's Gorokhovaya apartment.

With regard to what went on at the flat which by now the *starets* had made so famous, how stark is the contrast between the two accounts, that of Yussupov himself and the subsequent writing of Maria Rasputin. The Prince makes no mention of a sexual motivation on his part but indicates that he suffered from a sort of general malaise, possibly a nervous affliction from whose ravages he hoped Rasputin might cure him. His description of their second meeting during this period is surely one of the most dramatic in historical literature.

My second visit to the *starets* proved still more interesting than the first.

We were alone together almost the whole time.

He was particularly well-disposed towards me, and I reminded him of his promise to give me advice on the score of my health.

"I'll cure you in a few days. You just wait and see. Come into my study; nobody will interfere with us there. Let's have some tea first, and then with God's help we'll begin. I'll pray, and drive your illness out of you. You just listen to what I say, my dear, and all will be well."

After tea he took me to his study. It was the first time I had seen it. It was a small room furnished with a couch and armchairs upholstered in leather, and an enormous writing-table littered with papers.

The *starets* told me to lie down on the couch. He stood in front of me, looked me intently in the eyes and began to stroke my chest, neck and head. He then suddenly knelt down and—so it seemed to me—began to pray, placing his hands on my forehead. He bent his head so low that I could no longer see his face.

He remained in this position for a considerable time. Then he suddenly jumped to his feet and began to make passes. He was evidently familiar with certain of the processes employed by hypnotists.

His hypnotic power was immense. I felt it subduing me and diffusing warmth throughout the whole of my being. I grew numb; my body seemed paralyzed. I tried to speak, but my tongue would not obey me, and I seemed to be falling to sleep, as if under the influence of a strong narcotic. Yet Rasputin's eyes shone before me with a kind of phosphorescent light. From them came two rays which flowed into each other and merged into one glowing circle. This circle now moved away from me, now came nearer and nearer. When it approached me it seemed as if I began to distinguish his eyes; but at that very moment they would again vanish into the circle, which then moved further and further away.

I was conscious that the *starets* was speaking, but I could not make out his words; I could only hear a vague murmur.

Such was my condition as I lay motionless, unable to call out or stir. Yet my mind was still free, and I realized that I was gradually falling into the power of this mysterious and sinister man.

But soon I felt that my own inner force was awakening and was of its own accord resisting the hypnosis.

This force grew stronger within me, enveloping my whole being in an invisible armour. Into my consciousness floated a vague idea that an intense struggle was taking place between Rasputin and myself, and that my own personality in battling with his made it impossible for him to dominate me completely.

I tried to move my hand; and it obeyed me. But I did not alter my position; I waited until Rasputin himself should tell me to do so.

By now I could clearly distinguish his figure, face and eyes. That terrible circle had completely disappeared. . . .

"Well, my dear, that'll be enough for the first time," he said.

He kept watching me closely, but evidently he was able to note only one aspect of my sensations; my resistance to the hypnosis had escaped him.

There was a self-satisfied smile on his face, and he spoke to me in the assured tone of a person conscious of his entire mastery over another. He was obviously convinced that I had been completely subjugated by him, and that he could henceforth count me among his submissive followers.

With a brusque movement he pulled my arm. I sat up, feeling dizzy and weak. With an effort, I rose from the couch and took a few steps about the room; but my legs seemed half-paralyzed, and would not fully obey me.

Rasputin continued to observe every movement I made. "This is God's grace," he said. "Now you'll see how soon it will heal you, and drive all your illness away."

We parted, and he made me promise to visit him again very soon.[7]

How curious Yussupov should claim Rasputin addressed him repeatedly as "my dear," an expression which when used by one male to another becomes effeminate. What is the Prince's purpose here? That the *starets* was not only exclusively heterosexual but had a satyrlike obsession with women is repeatedly proved by everything that is known about him. Yet, seemingly, Yussupov would have his readers believe that such was not the case. Which one is the seeker? Yussupov writes that his host extracted a promise from him for an early subsequent visit. Yet it was he and not the *starets* who arranged for the meetings initially, Yussupov who went to Rasputin, not the reverse.

Maria writes: "When Papa and Feliks had their first meeting at our flat he came straight to the point: 'You must know, of course, that I have homosexual desires as well as heterosexual, and the former is interfering with my marriage.' "[8]

She explains that it was doing more than that, the marriage being in serious danger of failure, but informs her readers that despite his deviant behavior the Prince had enough love for his wife to remain with her to the end of his days.[9] She states that her father's motive in attempting to eradicate his homosexuality was primarily patriotic. The Prince's mother and the Tsaritsa's sister were plotting against the regime. Both were very concerned about Feliks. Since in their minds Rasputin was closely linked with the Imperial Family, the theory was that if he cured Yussupov and saved his marriage he would win the gratitude of this scheming pair and cause them to desist. On reflection the argument seems untenable, for we must assume the *starets* knew these women better than that. The more credible assumption is also the simpler one. It is that there was something about Yussupov that fascinated Rasputin and presented him with a challenge. Indeed, when Maria asked her father the reason for the other's visits, she remembered his answer as follows: "He has a problem, and he needs me."

She records that there were a number of meetings at the Gorokhovaya address, indicating she was not privy to most of them but that Dunia was. Apparently, Yussupov, who seems never to have been aware of the latter's special status as Rasputin's mistress, regarded her as nothing more than a servant and as such considered her beneath contempt, a mere menial in whose presence discretion was unnecessary. It was from Dunia that Maria later obtained the details. The older woman sensed the true nature of Yussupov, feared him at first, and ultimately detested him. Maria and her younger sister Varya distrusted him and were repelled, nor did his handsome face and elegant attire do anything to dispel their feelings.[10] After long ignoring Dunia as though she were a piece of furniture, a day came when the

Prince finally deigned to address her. Maria committed his words to memory. "How strange it is, Dunia, that you never married. A crude sort of man, perhaps some *muzhik*, could find you quite attractive."

Few words could be more character revealing. Cruelty is there and arrogance, a monstrously inflated self-esteem, a monumental callousness and indifference to the feelings of others. The culmination of the meetings was startling, so gauche indeed that apparently Yussupov had intended to win a devastating psychological victory as well as a libidinous one. He had timed it to a nicety. It happened when Varya was attending classes at school and Maria was with her French tutor. Both the *starets* and Dunia had momentarily left the room and the Prince was alone.

Maria writes: "And when Papa entered the study a few moments later, he found Feliks lying stark naked on the couch. There was no doubt what he had in mind, and Papa was dismayed to see that all his efforts had been in vain."[11]

She relates that when the nude Yussupov got up and approached her father he was firmly rebuffed. We can almost hear the outraged Dunia telling her about it. The *starets* even went so far as to lay his hands on the princely chest and push Yussupov away, causing him to fall on his back on the sofa. Stern words of reproof followed, much like those of a father reprimanding a wayward son. Taken together with the revulsion on Rasputin's face they perhaps indicated more than the speaker intended to convey, the hurt of unexpected provocation. It is said that "hell hath no fury like a woman scorned," and there was much of the woman in Yussupov. Controlling himself by a great effort, he dressed in silence and left without a word, nor did he cast a backward glance.

A point of departure had been reached, a crossroads, a decisive and irreparable rupturing of relations. Rasputin would see Yussupov again, but when he did so the latter's purpose would have changed —drastically. The difference would be as that between day and night, burgeoning lust and burning hate, life and death. A spectre was bestriding history's stage. It had been there before. It had stood on the Mount of Olives in storied Jerusalem and tried to kill the *starets*. It had guided Guseva's shining knife at Pokrovskoye. It had failed and failed. But would it fail again? This time its instrument was a man who was not a man, a prince without enough courage to serve his country in its hour of need, a wastrel who lived for nothing so much as the gratification of his appetites. But he was something else as well, a rejected suitor made dangerous by intense bitterness. History had seen lesser weapons strike fatally.[12]

The year 1916 has been called "the most terrible in the history of warfare," and even the diabolically brutal struggle of the Second World War saw none to exceed it for sheer horror. In the preceding year, the bloody stalemate on the Western Front had not been broken by the Second Battle of Ypres, though the Germans introduced to the world the latest refinement in the science of the frightful—poison gas. The French offensive in Artois did not break it either, although the cost to France was on the order of 400,000 men. The French General Joffre attacked in Champagne and was repulsed. The British advanced toward Lens and Loos, and were likewise halted. Now, determined to break the deadlock in 1916, in February the Germans under Crown Prince Friedrich Wilhelm launched 1 million men against Verdun, a fortress which ironically was no longer the key to the French defenses in that sector, and were met by a similar number of equally determined *poilus*. The result was fearful slaughter on an unprecedented scale. The Germans lost 282,000 men, the French an only slightly more staggering 317,000.[13] Never before had such devastating bombardments been seen. Yet, fighting under Pétain and Nivelle as they had not done since Napoleon's day, the beleagured French rallied to the battlecry *"Ils ne passeront pas!"*—"They shall not pass!"—and held on. The German assault, the most massive history had ever seen, bogged down in its own blood.

It was in order to relieve the pressure on the French at Verdun that the British now attacked, inaugurating "the blackest day in the history of the British Army" in the unbelievably costly First Battle of the Somme.[14] By sunset of that opening day (July 1), British casualties were nearly 60,000 men or, as one historian so graphically put it, "two for every yard of their front."[15] True, the offensive did accomplish its main objective, giving the French that vital breathing spell which allowed them to recover by December most of the ground lost at Verdun. But the British were never to forget this hurricane of blood. At Jutland on May 31, their fleet had fought through "the day the sea bottom was paved with admirals" and had neutralized the battered German Navy for the rest of the war.[16] At Passchendaele the following year, Field Marshal Sir Douglas Haig was to repeat his monumental mistake and live to see "Flanders fields where poppies blow" turned into one vast grave for a million British. Still, in the public mind of the English nation, the First Battle of the Somme remained the struggle which forever after would signify the tragic end of an era. For many, all glory was past or plunged into indefinite limbo. War had lost its ageless romance. Talk of "the Nelson touch" at Trafalgar, "the thin red line" at Waterloo, and "the last eleven at Maiwand" in Afghanistan, while it still might conjure feelings of national pride, had become for all practical purposes meaningless. The more horrifying aspects of evolving science had made themselves manifest. Henceforth, wars could not be won in any realistic sense. They were simply holocausts spawned of hell that had to be endured.

The Russians were beginning to think so, too. In the more halcyon days of 1915, General Aleksei Alekseyevich Brusilov had turned back the Teutonic tide in Galicia, gaining victories over the enemy at Lutsk, Czernowitz, and Ternopol. Not so in this fateful year. In the spring of 1916, the great "Brusilov offensive" met with disaster when the German forces operating on the Eastern Front were unexpectedly reinforced by fifteen divisions with resultant Russian losses of an additional million men. In Petrograd it at last became obvious to most members of the government that visions of decisive victory were purely illusory, that any additional casualties would simply be lives laid down in vain, and for the first time there was guarded talk at high levels of a possible separate peace with the Central Powers.

It was now that Rasputin's dire prophecy began to be realized with a vengeance. Desertions from the Army increased and there was greater unrest in the Navy. Transport was breaking down. While the hard-pressed troops suffered hunger on half-rations, thousands of cattle carcasses were putrefying on railroad sidings without refrigeration, the locomotives that were to haul them sidelined also for lack of coal. The bread lines grew longer. In every city and town the people stood in lengthening queues in all weather only to find in the end there was no bread. There was very little fuel as well. Bakeshops not only lacked the necessary wheat but could not find sufficient wood to stoke the ovens. Every scrap of it in sight was being scavenged, including furniture in many cases, and almost all of it was being burned for warmth. The Russian fleet lacked fuel. The cordite in its powder magazines was low. If it were forced to fight a battle it would run out of ammunition after the first salvos.

All this depressed the *starets* beyond description. Despite the fact that his fame drew far fewer petitioners he was still a power in the land. Indeed, from the time of the Tsar's assumption of the role of Commander-in-Chief and his prolonged absenses from Petrograd it was the *starets* who ruled if anyone did. Not only had he been instrumental in the dismissal of the elderly and incompetent Goremykin on February 2, but the appointment of Boris Vladimirovich Stürmer as his successor in the premiership was equally Rasputin's work. Stürmer had not proved a success. His elevation to high office had only further alienated the Cabinet, meanwhile enraging the Duma, whose hatred for "the perfidious Siberian" was by now an obsession. Only in the role he had played in the appointment of Protopopov could Rasputin take any satisfaction. From September 10, when this small man, a landowner and something of a mystic, had become Minister of the Interior, that highly important department had been run for the most part with vigor and intelligence. There was nothing that could alter the disastrous course of the war, for it was too late for that and Rasputin knew it well. Nonetheless, Protopopov, a longtime reactionary on the side of autocracy, was a man of courage and conviction, and this was something his political benefactor had always admired.[17]

The winter of 1916 was extraordinarily rigorous, bringing a biting cold from the high tundra of Siberia scarcely equaled in living memory. The troops froze in their trenches. The oil in the recoil cylinders of the cannon turned so viscous artillery batteries on both sides became inactive and more vulnerable to infantry assault. The German air squadrons were grounded, as were the very few planes available to the Russians. Generally, military action on the Eastern Front was temporarily reduced to the sending out of largely ineffective reconnaissance patrols.

For Rasputin it was a period of blackest depression. No longer were his spirits buoyed by the assurance of being needed by his sovereign. Though he knew the Tsaritsa and the Tsarevich still loved him dearly, the profound uplift he had felt by his saving of Anna Virubova had by this time largely worn off, and he fell prey to an ever-persistent fear that his healing powers were once again sadly diminished. And there was Russia, the sacred Motherland. The future he foresaw for it was the bitterest dram of any he had drunk, for try as he would he could see no legacy for the people but one of utter misery under a ruthless revolutionary tyranny, a Satan-spawned dictatorship that would make the worst of the tsars pale into insignificance by comparison. The aspect infused him with a grim foreboding he could not dispel.

For a while, wine could numb his sense of impending doom, but he was intelligent enough to know that in such a refuge lay ultimate madness and death. For the time being, he involved himself in not always savory business transactions, more as a diversion than with any serious desire to profit. The Jewish manipulator and spy Manasevich-Manuilov became an associate and confidant, but he knew he could never trust him and his friendliness toward the man was assumed rather than genuine. They were wasted days, he felt. He seemed to be marking time with no point whatever to his life, no reason for existence. There were continuing plots to murder him, and the Okhrana and Petrograd police had warned him of some of them. One originated with his own appointee, Interior Minister Khvostov, and his assistant, a particularly wily and unscrupulous animal named Beletski. The ever-present threat of assassination heightened his sense of the futility of it all.

Then there came a day that proved to be a pleasurable if brief distraction. His son Dmitri had been relieved of his duties on the hospital train, probably because of his mental retardation, and had gone home. No work was done on the farm in winter. Consequently, Praskovia allowed both the young man and Katya Ivanova to go to Petrograd for a visit, and the mere sight of them brought cheer to the heart of the *starets*. Would they remain for a bit? Of course they would. It was understood, wasn't it? But it did not work out that way. As the Christmas season approached, Rasputin asked his continuously smiling Mitya to stay with him over the holiday. Indeed, out of Dunia's hearing he even told the lad what he was certain was the truth. It would be the last *Pozdyestvo Krislovo* (Christmas) they would share. Mitya perhaps did not understand. He seldom did, poor fellow. Grinning as always, he told his father Praskovia's wish that he return to the village before the New Year. Then he told him something else: She wanted Dunia with her as well.

Why Rasputin agreed to the departure of his precious love will never be known for certain. His daughter does not explain it. It is obvious he could have prevented it, for no wish was dearer to Dunia's heart than to remain with him to the end. Perhaps he made his decision protectively, out of fear for her life since he knew his own was forfeit. We can imagine the heartrending melancholy of that parting; the scene at the bleak, windswept Warsaw Station; the crisp crunching of boots in the snow; the slow, dreamlike curling of smoke above the engines; voices full of tenderness and longing scarcely heard above escaping steam. A wisp of the Arctic chill stirs the beard of the *starets*. His gnarled hand lifts in farewell. The eyes in whose azure depths the fortunes of an empire have hung in balance slowly fill with tears as the train begins to move. It increases speed. Vanishes in the whiteness. The hand falls.

He was never to see Dunia again.

It is now more than ever that the last remaining days of this extraordinary man take on the semblance of Greek tragedy. He could not stay indefinitely cooped in the apartment, ignoring the ladies of his "court," seeing the deep hurt in their eyes and suffering even more than they because of it. He could not go on neglecting his devoted followers, knowing what it did to them. The walls of the place seemed to be gradually closing in on him, encompassing him like a stifling hand that would not let him breathe. Dunia. Where was Dunia? Was he worth anything since she had left? She was the air he breathed, the blood that flowed through his veins. What good was the adoration of all the others without her? He had to get out. Despite the winter chill he began to take long walks on the frozen bank of the Neva, muffled to the eyes in fur, doing his best to disregard the evident signs of Okhrana and police surveillance. He knew he should be glad of it. At least the Tsaritsa still cared enough to continue trying to guard him. But her efforts were all in vain, he was sure. In the end, the Lady Sudbina (Fate personalized as a woman) would have her way.

On a still winter day whose chill crispness reminded him of Siberia, he came home from one of these walks and threw himself into a chair. The mood that was upon him was morose in the extreme. He did not speak. He did not even turn to wine. Not one of his female entourage dared approach him, and even she who was now closest of them all, the devoted Akulina, remained silent. At last, Katya Ivanova found the courage to ask him the reason for his profound depression. He seemed to hesitate before answering, his eyes far off, as though he gazed on vistas of a world infinitely distant. Then he spoke simply. He told the maid he had seen a vision of the future, the waters of the Neva stained scarlet with the blood of grand dukes.

He did not say more. Getting wearily to his feet he went into his study, a rumpled looking man in a stained silk tunic that had once been embroidered by the Empress of Russia. He sat down at his desk. Taking pen and paper he wrote a letter to his daughter Maria, then sealed it, entered her bedroom, and put it in a drawer of her bureau as she stood watching him. To her unspoken question he made brief reply, very softly and gently: "Don't open it until after I am dead."

For what seemed a long time he gazed upon her now troubled face silently. Then he left her presence, went into his own room and closed the door, leaving the girl to wonder at the meaning of it all. Dead? Maria may well have been startled. Her father was immortal, wasn't he? Like the wind. Like the Siberian sun whose rays glistened on the frozen tundra or the mystic *shamans* of Tungu legend who never died. She couldn't remember a time when he had not been there. Why did he now speak in riddles? Dead? The Tsaritsa still telephoned every morning at ten o'clock but she could tell the Little Mother nothing about this. Nothing. Whatever it meant, the girl was instinctively aware she must face it alone.

Rasputin's nocturnal carousals, though less frequent than in former years, took considerably more out of him now because of his generally weakened condition. Many were the times when he returned to the flat in the early morning hours so drunk he could not climb the stairs.

He was noisy in his helplessness, frequently stumbling and falling. It was then that Maria and Katya, roused from their sleep, would go down to help him, putting his arms over their shoulders and almost literally hauling him upward by sheer determination buoyed by love. Not surprisingly, the progressive worsening of his health was inevitable. His once great physical power seemed to have all but dissipated. The iron constitution was dissolving.

It was on a night like this, with the dawn already encroaching on the dark, that the *starets* had returned still again from the Villa Rodye. Once in his bed, the unhealthy, fitful stirring that passed for sleep with him these days had begun. Maria and Katya had retired to their rooms. The telephone rang. As Maria picked up the receiver and spoke, it was the Tsaritsa who answered. She was terribly upset. With a voice on the verge of breaking she told the girl the Tsarevich was sick, that he was bleeding at the nose and no one could stop it. Her words poured out in a torrent. The Tsar and Aleksei had left by train for the front. The boy had begged to go. Believing it would raise the spirits of the soldiers to see him, the Tsar had relented against his own better judgment. They had just returned. And now? Now . . . Oh God, where was Otyets Grigori? Maria must tell him to go to the Palace immediately.

In a state almost of panic, Maria ran to her father but found him strangely changed. He was lying on his bed. She recalls that his eyes were open but he seemed to be staring at nothing, nor did he appear to hear her or be aware of her presence. She had never seen him like this and at once became alarmed. She writes: "Because of the urgency of the occasion, I persisted in trying to rouse him, and finally I broke through his near-catatonic state, but he would only raise a blue-tinged hand in a weak gesture of refusal, and whisper, 'Not yet. Not yet.' "[18]

The scene that followed was incredible. Katya joined her. Together they attempted to dispel Rasputin's lethargy, doing all in their power, talking to him, trying to tell him of the call from Tsarskoe Selo, gradually realizing with growing despair that his mind was inexplicably closed to them. Eventually, the *starets* found his voice and brokenly lapsed into prayer. It did not last long. Like a once-powerful dynamo that has run down and become inert he began to weep. Shocked and dismayed, Maria could hardly believe what she was seeing. The great man reduced to this? Her tower of strength shattered? As his tears wetted the now partly grizzled beard, the feeling that overwhelmed her was one of infinite sympathy and sorrow for this man she loved so much. Then she heard the phone ring again and went to answer it.

It was the Empress. This time Aleksandra was frantic, close to hysteria. She told Maria her son was dying, the attack was the worst since Spala, that unless her father came at once it would be too late. Never did a mother plead more fervently for the life of her child. The Tsar came on the line, his voice very tense. Nearly overwhelmed with her own sense of urgency Maria begged him to wait.

Recalling the event many years later, she writes of how Rasputin despite his great weariness and depression of soul had agreed to go, how the Imperial limousine came to the flat, how she and Katya helped her very unsteady father down the three flights of stairs. Tiny details cling to her memory. Inadequate clothing. She offered to run back and get a warmer coat for him. But all was haste with the man of God who was sick. As the car pulled away she saw that his eyes were closed and remarked that she knew he was praying. Did he perhaps think of that day in the field so long ago, of the blinding vision of the Virgin of Kazan? If so, it must have seemed to him like something from another age.

At the Palace, in the presence of Nikolai and Aleksandra, the *starets* did what he had done more than once before. He prayed, begging and pleading for the life of Aleksei with what he felt were the last vestiges of his spiritual strength. And again God heard him. Again the Tsarevich rallied. Again the miracle occurred. The Tsaritsa wept. Choking back his own tears of infinite gratitude and relief, the Tsar tried in vain to put their feelings into words; then approached the *starets* with almost awed respect and humbly asked for his blessing. It was a strange moment. Emperor and peasant faced each other, and in the bloodshot eyes of Rasputin was an even greater humility. Then he spoke words to the monarch never previously uttered: "This time, Little Father, it is I who need your blessing."

The embrace with both Tsar and Tsaritsa. A hand touching Aleksei's. Otyets Grigori with his palm raised and turned outward in benediction. The Sign of the Cross. The Tsarevich would have no more attacks, he told them. Did they perhaps see him in another light than ever before? A look. A faint smile. He was gone. He left Tsarskoe Selo with the prescient knowledge which so often now was proving a curse. Royal blood in the Neva? If only that were all he foresaw. He had loved this family with all his heart and soul, and had never forsaken them. He would not forsake them now, yet what would be would be. Descending the Palace steps had been like the closing of a door. Never more would his eyes behold them.[19]

It is a known fact that rats can sense when a ship is about to go down, that at such times they begin to swarm, endeavoring to escape the stricken vessel by passing through the hawseholes in its bow and leaping from the anchor cables into the sea. In the dark winter of 1916, the excitable Duma politicians were reminiscent of this phenomenon. Faced with the fact that the Army could not win, many of them were ready to desert the nation's cause, to abandon their duty and people, indeed to seek any sanctuary by any route as long as it offered protection for their own precious skins.

First, however, they sought scapegoats, this in the interest of self-exoneration. Rasputin and the Empress were the obvious choices. Was she not "the German woman"? Was it not a known fact that she and "the Holy Devil," as Iliodor had called him, had long been plotting with the Reichstag in Berlin to bring the country to its knees? Since the Tsar had declared the august body in session again in November, day after day certain of its members had railed more or less openly against the *starets* while making insinuations and casting aspersions against the Tsaritsa herself. It was infamous, but in attacking "traitors," whether overtly or covertly they felt themselves justified. Men such as General Gurko, the President of the Zemstvo Union, were active in this. Guchkov, Chairman of the Commission of National Defense, made his melodramatic appeals, as did Maklakov, the former Interior Minister ousted through Rodzianko's efforts. But of them all, one member, an impassioned orator and well-known demagogue, spoke before the assembly with particular vehemence. For two electrifying hours he harangued his captivated audience with a scathing denunciation of the Satanic influences, the "dark powers" as he called them, that he said were certain to destroy the monarchy and lay Russia low. Chief among these demonic forces was the foresworn *starets* who was so damnably false to his vows, the perfidious monk Rasputin.[20]

The speaker, a small, nearly totally bald man whose nose seemed too short for his face, was Vladimir Mitrofanovich Purichkevich, an embittered office seeker. On several occasions he had gone to Rasputin's apartment. On each, using the argument that no one stood further to the Right than he, that none, therefore, was a more staunch protector of monarchy, he had pleaded with the *starets* to make him Minister of the Interior. But Rasputin, withholding trust and respect for the man, had denied him this. Now Purichkevich showed his venomous gall. Repeatedly grasping the pince-nez he wore, snatching it from his nose and gesticulating with it, even sweating in the poorly heated immensity of the chamber, he pounded home his points in a savage display of pique and vitriol, impressing everyone with his courage in daring to attack the Tsaritsa's favorite. He seemed to go on and on, inexhaustible, as one who is very ambitious and feels he is making history. His listeners were almost literally spellbound. Never before in living memory had this venerated hall of the Tauride Palace rung to such glittering oratory.

At the end of the long speech, the rousing finale now punctuated with the most dramatic expletive, the members were on their feet applauding and cheering wildly, most of them wide-eyed with boundless enthusiasm. Purichkevich had called for nothing less than Rasputin's overthrow. "Be off to Headquarters and throw yourselves at the feet of the Tsar. Have the courage to tell him that the multitude is threatening in its wrath. Revolution threatens and an obscure *moujik* [peasant] shall govern Russia no longer."[21]

How splendid he was in their estimation. He had attacked Andronikov[22] and Protopopov, too. Many now remembered his ardent patriotism, his labors on behalf of the Russian Red Cross, how he personally directed one of its hospital trains standing at Warsaw Station, working day and night, maintaining an office in one of its cars.[23] Rumor had it that even the Tsar had mentioned him most favorably in one of his letters from the front. Was it any wonder that both Petrograd and Moscow were electrified by his published political satires, his bold and nearly unique verse? At this point, few doubted that Vladimir Mitrofanovich was a coming man, someone to watch.

There was a special box set aside for visitors. At the moment of the deputy's oratorical victory it was occupied by only one person of note. Prince Yussupov sat there. He did not join in the cheering. He spoke no word to anyone. Wrapped in princely aloofness, he could afford to look down his nose at these perfectly plebian souls at the moment so obsessed with their own importance. Nonetheless, the gross and noisy commoner who called himself Purichkevich had very distinct possibilities and might just be reachable. He would have to test him. He knew which car he occupied at the train station. He would pay him a visit and feel him out. If he hated Rasputin half as much as he claimed . . . Yussupov was sweating. He was not at all surprised to find himself so emotional about it. On his pale, delicate features was the faintest tracery of a smile.

A few days after the Purichkevich speech had been reported to him, Rasputin, reacting to his ever-strengthening premonition of imminent death, wrote what must surely be one of the most incredible and prophetic valedictories of all time. Scrawled in his childlike hand, the curious document primarily elicited the Tsar's attention and bore the heading: "The Spirit of Grigori Efimovich Rasputin—Novyhk of the village of Pokrovskoye." It read as follows:

I write and leave behind me this letter at St. Petersburg. I feel that I shall leave life before January 1. I wish to make known to the Russian people, to Papa, to the Russian Mother and to the Children, to the land of Russia, what they must understand. If I am killed by common assassins, and especially by my brothers the Russian peasants, you, Tsar of Russia, will have nothing to fear for your children, they will reign for hundreds of years in Russia. But if I am murdered by *boyars*, nobles, and if they shed my blood, their hands will remain soiled with my blood, for twenty-five years they will not wash their hands from my blood. They will leave Russia. Brothers will kill brothers, and they will kill each other and hate each other, and for twenty-five years there will be no nobles in the country. Tsar of the land of Russia, if you hear the sound of the bell which will tell you that Grigori has been killed, you must know this: if it was your relations who have wrought my death, then no one of your family, that is to say, none of your children or relations, will remain alive for more than two years. They will be killed by the Russian people. I go, and I feel in me the divine command to tell the Russian Tsar how he must live if I have disappeared. You must reflect and act prudently. Think of your safety, and tell your relations that I have paid for them with my blood. I shall be killed. I am no longer among the living. Pray, pray, be strong, think of your blessed family.

Grigori[24]

Although it was by now a thing of the past, during the period of his greatest popularity Rasputin had employed four male secretaries to handle his voluminous correspondence ("I hate writing. Oh, how I hate writing!") and other business matters. The second among them, Dobrovolsky, was made Minister of Justice soon after his death. The favorite, a Jew named Aaron Simanovich, was born in a ghetto in a small town in the Ukraine and became progressively a diamond cutter in Kazan (where Rasputin met him in 1900) and the owner of a small jewelry store in Kiev. It was Simanovich who personally delivered the letter to Aleksandra with Rasputin's request for secrecy, the secretary subsequently claiming he recovered it merely for the asking after the Tsaritsa's death. It is probably true. As noted by Colin Wilson, the British historian Sir Bernard Pares relates that Simanovich had a facsimile of the letter at a later date, as well as the Tsaritsa's prayer book embossed with her favorite swastika emblem.[25]

The way was now open to Yussupov. It did not require genius to see that Rasputin was all but deserted, ringed in by enemies on every side, his erstwhile collaborator Count Witte dead, the Tsar outpositioned to offer any real protection. With monumental lack of conspiratorial discretion the Prince went to Maklakov first, visiting him at his flat, openly eliciting the as yet untried ex-minister's aid in the commission of murder. Maklakov appeared highly nervous, suspicious of Yussupov's motives in approaching him, clearly reluctant to become involved. As the battle-shy aristocrat grown suddenly bold put it, "I realized he was too cautious to venture on decisive action."[26]

He next conferred with Purichkevich at the railroad station. As they sat in the latter's private car, they could not be overheard. Having recognized the very cream of fellow fanatics Yussupov was relatively sure of the Duma deputy. Yet should the man reject and then seek

to betray him it would be the word of a prince against his. Purichkevich accepted enthusiastically at once. Yussupov said he had two
others in mind as well, both intimates of his. Grand Duke Dmitri
Pavlovich would do anything he wished, agree to any enterprise as
long as it sprang from the mind of his "friend." There was also a most
reliable young captain of cavalry, Ivan Sukhotin. His motive was that
of a soldier, a man of action but not of thought. Rasputin's hatred of
war, so the twisted theory went, made him the natural enemy of those
whose job it was to fight it, nor could his claim of wishing to spare
the lives of peasants carry weight with anyone of officer's rank. To
the devil with the peasantry. Nearly as an afterthought Yussupov
included his valet Nefedov, whose proximity to the killing would in
any case make him privy to it.

Purichkevich nodded his understanding. We can almost see him
with his pince-nez in his hand, tapping with it lightly as he made his
points in subdued tones. He reminded the Prince that Rasputin was
guarded by police and Okhrana agents. Yussupov replied, "All that
has already been arranged," explaining how a recent phone call he
had made to the *starets* had healed the former breech so completely
that their current meetings were very frequent. Rasputin seemed more
than willing to continue them. Barring the unforeseen, all should go
as smoothly as glass.

At 5 P.M. the following evening, Yussupov, Purichkevich, the
Grand Duke, and Sukhotin met together at the Prince's great mansion
on the Moika Canal, one of four palaces he owned in Petrograd alone.
The conspirators talked animatedly. Purichkevich recommended that
they get still another to join them. Dr. Stanislas Lazovert, the Polish
physician who assisted him with the military wounded, had a knowledge of poisons. Like most doctors, he detested Rasputin as a charlatan. They could trust him. His skill was virtually guaranteed to
make assurance doubly sure. Yussupov agreed to this readily enough.

And so it was all decided as simply and pitilessly as slaughterers
in an abattoir might prepare to kill an ox. With Maklakov the sole
exception, Yussupov had been confidant of each of his chosen confederates. Dmitri Pavlovich had assented without demur. Indeed, he
seemed to accept his involvement in a murder plot with the heady
exhilaration of a young virgin about to experience love, eagerly and

sensually anticipating it. Sukhotin and Lazovert proved no problem. Nefedov would do as he was told, a task mainly involving staying well in the background. The Prince, perfectly aware of Rasputin's fundamental affection for him and his unwillingness to bear a grudge, had been more or less sure of his intended victim. Was he troubled by conscience? What he planned to do was the most heinous violation of hospitality imaginable, one which among the proud mountain tribesmen of the Caucasus, for example, would have earned him instant death. Urged by Purichkevich, he went to see Maklakov one more time. The latter appeared to sympathize profoundly but would not join. At Yussupov's departure he gave his guest a wicked looking truncheon loaded with lead, expressing the thought that he might need it.

Concerning the lethal conspiracy Yussupov wrote:

> This decision caused me much heart-searching. The prospect of inviting a man to my house with the intention of killing him horrified me. Whoever the man might be—even Rasputin, the incarnation of crime and vice— I could not contemplate without a shudder the part which I should be called upon to play—that of a host encompassing the death of his guest.[27]

Did he so thoroughly deceive himself as to his real motive even then? As though he had sublimated it entirely, driving the truth deep into the subconscious, he wrote years later (whether with awareness or not) behind an unconvincing mask of patriotism: "My meetings with Rasputin, and all that I had seen and heard, had firmly convinced me that he was at the root of all the evil, and the primary cause of all the misfortunes which had befallen Russia." Thus might Brutus and Cassius, with consummate self-delusion, have rationalized their treacherous dagger strokes against Caesar.

The decision taken, only a few things remained to be done. The conspirators set the date for the homicide, December 16 by the old Julian calendar then in use, a schedule involving some delay.[28] This was due primarily to the room alterations in progress at the Moika Palace, the intended locale of the murder, and the continuing presence of workmen there. The newly renovated site was an underground room whose two narrow windows overlooked the Moika Canal. At first an adjunct to the wine cellar, the larger and broader part of it had been converted into a dining room. Once it had been as austere and uninviting as a monk's cell but not now. Yussupov had been thorough. The granite floor was laid with a large, deep-piled Persian carpet from Tabriz. The gray stone walls were handsomely papered. Heavy dark red curtains gave a feeling of warmth and security.

No detail had been spared. The cellar had never been used for social gatherings but no one would know it now. To give it a lived-in appearance expensive furnishings had been taken out of storage. There were hand-carved, leather-upholstered chairs, high-backed chairs of oak, and several small cloth-covered tables, perhaps reminiscent of Yussupov's visits to Paris, Monmartre, and the West Bank bistros along the Seine. Italian fine art lent much grace and charm. So did ornately wrought drinking goblets of solid ivory. One of several cabinets, a most spectacular *objet d'art*, had small vertical supports of bronze in its construction, their beauty endlessly multiplied and enhanced by inlaid reflecting mirrors. Set on top of this, also imported from Italy, was a two-hundred-year-old crucifix of cut crystal and silver rising nearly to the low-vaulted ceiling, as though the princely host invoked the approval of God in his bloody enterprise. An ironic touch was added. On the floor before the cabinet was all that remained of another denizen of Siberia: huge, staring endlessly at nothing with eyes of glass, its life taken with equal injustice, a great white bear of which only the fur-covered skin remained.

All in all, Yussupov believed the setting was perfect, precisely the atmosphere to lull the *starets* into a sense of well-being. Places would be laid for an intimate *tête-à-tête* of only six, just as Irina Aleksandrovna might have ordered. Rare imported teas, mouth watering cakes with chocolate and almond icing, and the finest wine would be provided. Once the servants had done their work and departed they were to return to their quarters and remain there until morning, in effect to be sealed in their apartments.

The cakes with the almond icing were left as they were. However, the wine and the chocolate-covered cakes would be a bit *different*. Dr. Lazovert, the newly recruited practitioner in the art of sudden death, would very liberally lace both of them with finely powdered crystals of potassium cyanide, the most deadly poison known and one that would kill within seconds. It was generally agreed the body must disappear, never to be found until it was unrecognizable. Better yet, it should disintegrate utterly, fuse with the elements, vanish as though it had never been, a nightmare creature out of hideous shamanist legend destroyed by his own iniquity, dissolving over time, fading away—lodged somewhere in the clutching, all-obliterating bottom mud of the Neva.

NOTES

1. With admirable expediency, the French commandeered hundreds of Paris taxicabs and buses to hurriedly transport troops to the front, a move without which defeat would have been inevitable.

2. Russia's surrender to Germany would have freed several hundred thousand German troops for use on the Western Front, a catastrophe for the French and British that actually occurred after the Treaty of Brest-Litovsk, signed March 3, 1918, took Russia out of the war.

3. Many of the deserters, without means of sustenance, organized themselves into criminal bands and roamed the hungry land in search of food and booty. One is reminded of the *Écorcheurs*, the marauding soldiers who terrorized the French countryside in the Hundred Years War (1337–1453), or the ruthless "jayhawkers" from both armies in the American Civil War (1861–1865) who ravaged the Southern Confederacy.

4. One seeks in vain for even the remotest semblance of representative government in the repressive regime later established by the Bolsheviks.

5. Tchaikovsky quickly died of the disease, one of the strangest suicides on record.

6. The training academy for future Army officers in Petrograd was the Corps des Pages. By attending it, Yussupov avoided active service and also found a fertile field for additional homosexual contacts. He had no fear of being called up. By failing repeatedly in his examinations he became what might be called a professional cadet.

7. From Prince Feliks Yussupov, *Rasputin*, Dial Press, New York, 1927.

8. Maria Rasputin and Patte Barham, *Rasputin: The Man Behind the Myth*, Warner Books, New York, 1977, p. 239. (Published by arrangement with Prentice-Hall, Inc.)

9. He died in 1967 in the Auteuil District of Paris at the age of eighty. His home there, at one time a barn, is reported to have been small but comfortable.

10. At this time, Rasputin's retarded son Mitya (Dmitri) was working as an orderly on a hospital train, a position his father had gotten him to keep him from being drafted as a combat infantryman.

11. Rasputin and Barham, *op. cit.*

12. Anyone doubting the basic homosexuality of Yussupov need view only

the painting done of him by the society portraitist Serov when the Prince was in his late teens. In it, he has his arm around a pug dog and is holding one of its paws. He appears nonchalant, a large, flowing cravat at his throat. The delicate features are heavily made up, including the use of a dark lipstick, hardly *de rigueur* attire even for the Russian nobility.

13. The figures are from Walter Goerlitz, *History of the German General Staff*, Praeger, New York, 1953.

14. It was now that the decided German advantage in the number of machine guns per unit was to pay its most deadly dividend yet.

15. Martin Middlebrook, *First Day on the Somme*, W. W. Norton & Company, New York, 1972.

16. Although the British ship losses at Jutland were greater than the German losses (fourteen ships to eleven), the High Seas Fleet remained bottled up in its harbors thereafter, coming out only at war's end to surrender and be interned at the British naval base at Scapa Flow. In 1919, the German crews scuttled it there. No new naval construction was begun until Hitler's violation of the military clauses of the Versailles Treaty shortly after his assumption of power in 1933.

17. Aleksandr Dmitreyevich Protopopov, a firm believer in tsarism, was one of the most faithful supporters Rasputin ever had. In February of 1917, he secretly provoked armed insurrection in Petrograd to afford a pretext to use force against the revolutionaries. As with so many others who had served the Tsar, he was later executed by the Bolsheviks.

18. Rasputin and Barham, *op. cit.*, p. 263.

19. Rasputin's prophecy concerning Aleksei was accurate. Although remaining a hemophiliac, he was not again laid low by it. He continued relatively well until murdered by the Communists at Ekaterinburg on July 16, 1918.

20. Rasputin had never been a monk nor sworn any vows.

21. Robert K. Massie, *Nicholas and Alexandra*, p. 369.

22. Prince Nikolai Petrovich Andronikov. This man, described by Colin Wilson as "a dubious homosexual," for a time ran one of the most profitable political salons in the capital. His business was selling information to interested parties about what went on at secluded Tsarskoe Selo. His primary source was the royal Groom of the Chamber.

23. On behalf of the wounded soldiers, the Tsaritsa's efforts far exceeded those of any individual in Russia, including Purichkevich. The Catherine Palace at Tsarskoe Selo became a military hospital where the Tsaritsa and her two oldest daughters, Olga and Tatiana, worked devotedly as nurses. Moreover, the Tsaritsa saw to the funding and staffing of eighty-four other hospitals in Petrograd. All this the Duma members and her other enemies chose to ignore.

24. Colin Wilson, *Rasputin and the Fall of the Romanovs*, The Citadel Press, Secaucus, New Jersey, 1964, p. 189.

25. Pares is author of *The Fall of the Russian Monarchy*, Jonathan Cape, Ltd., 1939.

Although associated in more recent times with the German Nazi Party, the device of the swastika is of considerable antiquity.

26. Yussupov, *op. cit.*, p. 119.

27. *Ibid.*, p. 121.

28. According to the Gregorian calendar, favored by the nations of the West but not adopted by the Soviet Government until 1923, the date would have been December 29.

CHAPTER 13

And Farewell

As Rasputin stepped from the limousine into the snow he looked upward. The Moika Palace of the Yussupovs was immense beyond belief, and on this chill winter night it seemed to float on air. The simile it brought to his mind was the great ark of Noah. That had been a seaborne menagery which, lightened of its burden of many animals after the Flood, had come to rest somewhere on Mount Ararat. But what was this lofty structure of gray granite? What secrets did it house? What hidden purposes?

He saw a servant open the door to the side entrance, felt rather than observed Prince Yussupov step to one side to usher him in. For a fleeting moment he felt ridiculous. He was dressed in his best: blouse of white silk, the Tsaritsa's cornflowers embroidered on it; large-tasseled waist cord the color of raspberries; black velvet *pantaloni* (trousers) cut to the mode of the *Zaporozhe Kozaki*[1]; his long black boots of the finest leather. Was he really stupid enough to think he would impress these people? Their land holdings alone were incredible. Four palaces in St. Petersburg, two outside Moscow, an estate at Rakitnoye in the district of Kursk, God knew how many in the Crimea, Baku on the Caspian Sea. . . . The list was endless. And they were going to find his *appearance* memorable? These people richer than the tsars themselves? In the days when God had favored him, they might have been putty in his hands. He could have been in *rags* then and held sway over them. But now? He stepped through the open door.

Immediately, the music which before he could barely hear became louder. It was something popular, the sort of thing often heard in the homes of Russian nobility nowadays. American. It seemed to be coming from a gramophone upstairs. He arrested his stride and stood still, listening. If they had arranged it for his benefit they had failed. He didn't like it. It wasn't Russian. Gypsy airs whether sad or gay were infinitely more beautiful. Violins and *balalaikas* (Russian triangular guitars) were what he loved, not brass. If it must be foreign, let it be the Spaniard Pablo de Sarasate and his *Zigeunerweisen*—but never this. He heard Yussupov's voice but could not understand him. There was another voice superimposed over his. His own Maria. "Don't go, Papa." Louder now. "Don't *go*, Papa!" But the heavy door had closed.

They went down some steps. He doffed his fur coat. He could see that most of the room was underground. It was really two rooms and he stood in the smaller one, before him a spiral staircase. How plush it all was, like the setting for a play. *"Ochen krasivaya komnata"*—"Very beautiful room." His eyes began to take in the details. There were two wall niches. In each stood a gorgeous red porcelain vase, Chinese, he supposed. Then he was in the larger area, a dining room with place settings already laid on an inviting table, a large red granite fireplace, ebony and ivory carvings. The whole thing was both lavish and charming, reflecting what he now knew to be exquisite taste. Rasputin felt himself flattered and intrigued. Yet of course it was not for him especially, hardly that. What a way to live. He knew this was only a small adjunct to the truly splendid quarters that must exist above.

He walked over to a cabinet before which lay a bearskin, a white bear from Siberia. The doors were open. Inside was a labyrinthine affair of some kind, very intricate and elegant, a maze that relied for its effect of endless depth on numerous mirrors. It pleased him immensely, filling him almost with a sense of awe at the wondrous workmanship. Knowing Yussupov was watching him he nonetheless began to look it over, opening and closing the little portals, gazing at it from different angles to see the play of infinitely reflected light. The fire on the open hearth was having its effect. To the splendors of the cupboard's interior the dancing flames seemed to have given life.

Yussupov made a polite gesture and they sat down at the large table. They talked, the subject changing from the Golovina women, to crippled Anna Virubova, to Tsarskoye Selo and the Tsaritsa's largely sequestered life there. Yussupov offered tea. Rasputin declined it. His host then offered wine and he declined that, too, wondering what made him suddenly so uneasy. Ultimately, the conversation turned to the here and now, to this very evening. The Prince seemed to be choosing his words carefully: "Grigori Efimovich, why did Protopopov come to see you? Is he in constant fear of a plot against you?"

Rasputin hesitated before replying. He, too, was phrasing his sentences selectively. "Yes. I'm a stumbling-block to a good many people because I'm always telling the truth. Your aristocrats don't like the idea of a common *muzhik* wandering about the palaces. It's all sheer envy and malice. But why should I be afraid of them? They can't do any harm to me. I'm proof against evil designs. They've had more than one try, but the Lord laid their plans bare. Take Khvostov. He tried it on, but he was punished and dismissed. They daren't even touch me. They'd only get into trouble."[2]

As he spoke, he was wondering if he believed all this himself, or if it were mere bravado to bolster his own courage. There was something wrong with Yussupov's face, something in the eyes. Or perhaps it was that soft mouth that seemed somehow crooked, invested with a faint tinge of mockery. They talked about nothing important, indulging in what the debonair Prince might call chitchat, polite repartee. Rasputin's mouth grew dry and he requested tea. Yussupov poured. He then offered the *starets* biscuits with an insipid smile. Rasputin took one. The conversation became slightly more animated but remained perfectly inane. From upstairs there drifted down the sounds of laughter and conversation, albeit somewhat forced it seemed. Irina Aleksandrovna's guests, of course. By now they were probably getting ready to leave.

Finally, Yussupov passed a plate of chocolate cakes to him, small individual ones that seemed to share the same touch of elegance with everything else in the room. The *starets* shook his head: "Don't want 'em. They're too sweet."

A few minutes later, however, he changed his mind and tried one. The pastry was delicious and he took another. Now *that* was a rare confection. As they continued to talk, he noticed the Prince was failing to hold up his end of the conversation. Yussupov's eyes were troubled now, deeply so. Then they seemed to hold an expression almost of fear. He offered wine, remarking that it came from grapes grown in the Crimea. Rasputin declined. Eventually, Yussupov simply poured two glasses and slid one toward his guest, meanwhile sipping his own delicately. Rasputin picked it up and drank. Delicious. Yussupov told him there was a lot more of it. Rasputin nodded.

"Now give me some Madeira."

Yussupov rose to fetch a dry glass.

"Pour it into this one," said Rasputin.

"But that's impossible, Grigori Efimovich. You can't mix red wine with Madeira."

The *starets* insisted. With a hand that appeared to tremble slightly, Yussupov poured. Then he seemed suddenly to shake violently. The glass fell on the floor and burst into fragments. Rasputin was watching his face intently. The Prince poured again. Rasputin drank. He was taking his time and drinking very slowly. There was something the matter. He did not feel right. He felt suddenly very hot, in fact, and his breathing seemed shallow and labored. His hand went to his throat. He rose and began to walk about the room unsteadily.

"Anything wrong, Grigori Efimovich?"

"Oh nothing much. Just an irritation in the throat." Rasputin stopped and looked at Yussupov, extending his hand with the empty glass. "That's very good Madeira. Give me some more."

Yussupov poured again. His face was noticeably pale even for him. Quite abruptly, as though some inexplicable inner change had devastated him, he appeared far older than his twenty-nine years, and sick, the owner of a visage as gaunt and sallow as a dead man's. Rasputin continued to pace. From time to time he stopped and sipped. Then he sat down opposite his host and just stared at him, seeing the Prince almost literally wither before his steady gaze. "Don't *go*, Papa!" How his child's voice haunted him now. Had she known then? Been sure of it? Even three short years ago he would have known as well. No one could have deceived him then, in the days before Guseva's knife. It seemed she had cut the gift out of him. With elbows resting on the table he lowered his head into his hands. Maybe it was time to go after all. He had told Mitya it would be the last Christmas. Why should he fight it? What good would it do if God had deserted him? Above the roaring and buzzing in his head he could hear Yussupov offering him tea, and he needed it. His throat was burning . . . burning. . . . In a cracked voice so unlike his own he heard himself accept. But acceptance was followed by other words of his, words he had spoken before, yet sounding now only in his mind: "No, not yet. Not yet."

He got up. Slowly, knowing his strength was fast failing, he walked about the room. Then he saw Yussupov's guitar.

"Play something. Play something cheerful. I love the way you sing."

Yussupov appeared unwilling to comply. Then, thinking better of it, he picked up the instrument and began to pluck the strings, launching somewhat tremulously on a familiar Gypsy air. It took the *starets* back. Once again he was in the Holy of Holies in the days of better fortune. Once again he could hear Akulina's sweet soprano voice as she sang the beautiful song "Strannik" and he sang with her. Those had been the times. Princesses had been in his bed then. Dolgorukaya. Shakhovskaya. Tenisheva. Nastiya Polakova had sung for him, the greatest Gypsy enchantress of them all. Yes, at the Villa Rodye in Novaya Derevna. And there was the colonel's wife, the opera singer. She used to sing to him over the telephone sometimes, but not arias. She would sing "Barinaya," such a lovely thing. Or "Troika," gay beyond compare and pure Gypsy. . . . And he had saved the Tsarevich. Let them take *that* away from him.

He felt his head fall. He could not hold it up. Nonetheless, when the song ended he asked for another, and then another. Very vaguely as in a dream he was conscious of the passing of time. He had come here more than two hours ago. The visitors upstairs had not left. He could hear them. With a great effort he asked Yussupov about the noise. The Prince seemed hardly able to speak. In a voice hoarse with some deep emotion he said he thought the guests were leaving, then suggested Rasputin wait as he went to see. Without another word he vanished up the staircase.

Time appeared to become meaningless, even nonexistent. Rasputin felt his head was bursting. It seemed to be wobbling on his neck, spinning in circles. He breathed with increasing difficulty, gasping periodically. After an unknown interval he became aware that Yussupov had returned and was sitting close to him. He raised his head and looked at the pallid face of the Prince, who now asked if he were unwell. He heard himself answer. He told his host his head was heavy and his stomach burning, then asked for more wine.

"Don't *go*, Papa!"

He drank it down at once. Where was she now, the Virgin of Kazan? Did she really want it to end like this? Silently he called on her again and again and again. Doctored wine? But that was only a human device and she could overcome it. This was her Grigori who was naked and alone, stripped of arms and armor, helpless, Grigori between the pillars as Samson had stood so long ago at Gaza. "O Lord God, remember me, I pray thee, and strengthen me, I pray thee, only this once, O God, that I may be at once avenged of the Philistines for my two eyes."[3]

Blind. Yes, O God of Hosts, he was *blind*.

Was there not one to listen? Not even *she*? Then—a miracle. As though it raced through his veins like quicksilver he felt the return of his energy, his strength, his life. He sat up straight. Irina Aleksandrovna was not here. He knew that now. She was probably not even in St. Petersburg but what did it matter? To her husband, whose face was now overcast with a corpselike pallor, he made a suggestion. They could go and listen to the Gypsies. He saw Yussupov's ashen lips move. Something about it being too late. Yes, it was nearly three in the morning and he knew that. He brushed the objection aside.

Suddenly, Yussupov got up. He would not go to the Villa Rodye. His impatient gesture made it obvious. Instead, he walked to the mirrored cabinet and stood before it looking up, his eyes apparently fixed on the crucifix above it. He stood for some time. Rasputin asked him what he was doing. The Prince replied that the cross was very beautiful, a favorite piece of his. Rasputin concurred, remarking on the obvious cost. He was all right now. He could get up and walk. He did so and approached the other, going once more to the fabulous cabinet and commenting on its marvels. All his life he had seen crucifixes. It was the labyrinth that fascinated him. As he again examined it Yussupov seemed eclipsed. He was behind him now, and the *starets* heard his voice. High-pitched. . . . Trembling. . . . "Grigori Efimovich, you had better look at the crucifix, and say a prayer before it."

Rasputin turned. So this was the moment, was it? He approached Yussupov and stood within arm's reach of him. What were those final words of the dying *Khristos*? "Father, forgive them, for they know not what they do." He looked the Prince in the face. Too girlish. He was too girlish for a man. He felt no hatred, only pity. He saw Yussupov's hand come from behind his back holding a revolver. Mossin-Nagant. Caliber 7.65 millimeter. It was time. Now he must be The *Starets* of Pokrovskoye, the worthy one. He averted his face and beheld the crucifix, concentrating on its gleaming surfaces, binding it to his soul. The roar of the explosion was like the bursting of a thousand suns.

The pain in the chest was beyond the conception of pain, beyond the conception of life and death. The *starets* lay on his back. Around him a world of mist revolved slowly, nebulous, light-enshrouded, advancing and receding like the waves of a silent sea. Gradually it evanesced. Fading. . . . Fading . . . as the blessing of the Eucharist faded when one had betrayed one's God. There was darkness followed by sudden light. He could see it through his eyelids. Then voices, rough and outrageous handling, the harshness of expressed hatred. Something went on in the region of his groin but he was too far gone to identify it, too numb to feel or to care. Even the knife in the hand of one of them was meaningless. They had come down to view their work, to torment him, too, for that was the fate of martyrs. They talked. Nothing was comprehensible. They gloated, he was sure. Then they left him in this room as in a shroud. A key turned in a lock. He could almost hear the sound of his own dripping blood. Time. Time passing. He knew the bullet had pierced his heart and he could not be alive. Yet one of them had returned and he knew that, too. The figure was alone. Bending over him. Yussupov.

Abruptly, he felt a change in himself. The sudden concentration of energy was dynamic, God-given, miraculous. She *had* heard him. The light from her face was as he remembered it, a glowing radiance. She might not sustain him long, perhaps only for moments, but she would get him to his feet. He felt his left eyelid flutter. Then it opened. His cheek was twitching. The gasp of horror he heard was Yussupov's. His right eyelid fluttered and opened as well. He could see his murderer if only faintly. Like the skiff of Charon breasting the black waters of the River Styx, he heaved himself up and caught the accursed one by the shoulder. Forgive him? He *hated* him. The whole peasant world had hated his kind for centuries. The vermin in silks and satins who drove the poor into the ground. The vicious exploiters who kept them down, degraded and abused them, turning them into slaves and cannon fodder.

"Yussupov!" As he clutched the felon dog he heard his own croaking whisper. "Yussupov!"

Aghast, the killer struggled to break away, whining like the coward he was, groaning and kicking, gouging with his fingernails. Desperation and horror gave Yussupov strength and he jerked free, his epaulet coming loose in Rasputin's hand. Rasputin fell back, giving himself to death. But not yet. . . . Not yet. . . . Once more he hauled himself to his feet. With a cry of unspeakable dread Yussupov made for the staircase weaving like a drunken man and climbed it, shouting to Purichkevich as he neared the top.

"Quick! Quick! The revolver! He is alive!"

Rasputin went up those steps. He knew he *could not* climb them but he did, struggling on all fours like an animal, seeing the murderer's terror-racked face just before he went through the door. There was more shouting from above, several male voices, the frenzied sounds of panic-stricken commotion. The *starets* climbed. Finding himself in a long corridor, he groped in his semiblindness for a door, any door that might lead to freedom. He was dead but he wanted that—to lay himself down in God's clean air under God's sky. He found the door he sought but it was locked. And now *she* must do it for him. His strength was gone. He was poisoned and shot and had withstood it but there was nothing left. Nothing.

He looked at his hand. It was stained with his own blood. Twice that hand had vanished in recent times, dematerialized before his eyes. No dream. It had *happened*. Could it happen now? Had Cagliostro told the truth? Could all the atoms of being be separated from reality? Transmogrified? There was another dimension. He *knew* there was another. He seemed to be bleeding into himself, but his lips moved in prayer.

"Once more, O God. Once more . . . more . . . for the *starets*."

Purichkevich was looking for him. Revolver in hand he desperately searched, spurred on by the expression of near madness he had seen in Yussupov's eyes. The foul creature was nowhere to be found. Not on the staircase or the landing above it. Not in any of the corridors. Dear God, it was *impossible*. Was he truly Satan's own spawn then? Coming at last to the same wicket door Rasputin had approached he discovered it was open. He could *not* have gone through it. The door had been locked. Only Yussupov had the key. But where in the name of God was the Prince now?

To shoot Rasputin, Yussupov had used the Grand Duke's revolver and afterward had returned it to him. Then, finding himself unarmed, he had remembered the shot-loaded rubber truncheon Maklakov had given him, and had gone to his study and snatched it off his writing desk. Now he pursued Rasputin feverishly. He heard two shots. He thought they came from the snow-filled open courtyard. Purichkevich.

Leaving the house by the main entrance, the Prince reached the canal embankment and ran along it as fast as his trembling legs would carry him, hoping to get to the unlocked central gates of the courtyard and prevent their victim's escape. He could see Rasputin through the railing. The fantastic being was staggering but still moving, making for precisely this exit. There was a loud report and then another. In the brightness of each of the glaring muzzle flashes Purichkevich appeared. Garish. Unreal. Even without their fleeting light the *starets* remained visible. The last two shots had felled him. He was down in a pile of snow. Yussupov, whose vision seemed to be faltering, saw Purichkevich standing over the body looking down on it. The Duma deputy walked away. Yussupov entered the courtyard and examined the man they had killed.

He saw at once that the corpse was in bad condition. Blood was everywhere. There were severe facial injuries. On the left temple a vicious looking wound had been inflicted and the genital area was a darkly glistening swath. Emasculation? Had they lost control to that degree? There was no sign of breathing, no apparent pulse nor any other evidence of life. He was later to learn that Purichkevich had kicked the victim in the head and ground his heel into his face.

It was then that others came upon the scene. Two of them were Yussupov's servants. The third was a policeman who by merest ac-

cident made directly toward the murdered man. Though trembling
with extreme nervous tension Yussupov still had enough presence of
mind to head him off, confronting him as though to answer his questions honestly. The man had heard the shots and was inquiring about
them, using the polite "Your Highness." The Prince dismissed it all
lightly. A tipsy guest had had too much to drink and had fired a pistol
in sheer exuberance. "Nothing serious. A stupid business. . . . If
anybody asks you what's been going on, just say that everything is
all right."

During the brief conversation Yussupov gradually edged toward
the gates, taking the law's unprotesting minion with him to ultimately
dismiss him offhandedly. He then returned to the dead man. To his
horror he saw that the body was no longer in the same position, that
it had moved of its own will in the last few minutes. Yussupov was
sickened. When Purichkevich arrived with the servants and told them
to remove the remains to the house, the Prince hurried ahead of them,
sure he was going to be ill. Moments later, having gone to his dressing
room for drinking water, he encountered an excited Purichkevich.
The same policeman was back, the deputy said, and wanted to talk
some more. The sound of the reports had been heard at the police
station. This man had explained them to his superiors but they appeared skeptical. Now they wanted a detailed account. Everything.
It did not require keen perception to see that Yussupov was in no
condition to be interrogated by experts. Purichkevich was desperate.
Not knowing what else to do he resorted to desperate measures. Taking Yussupov with him, he accosted the policeman boldly.

"You have heard of Rasputin?—the man who has been betraying
our country, our Emperor, and our soldiers at the front? He's been
selling us to the Germans—do you hear?"[4]

The approach was palpably insane and it appalled Yussupov.
Purichkevich must have felt trapped and hopeless or he never would
have resorted to this. To confess? To give it all away and plead
patriotism as an excuse? He heard the Duma deputy announce his
rank, then enjoin the policeman to silence. "If you love your country
and your Tsar—."

The policeman agreed on principle not to speak of it, but reminded
them of his duty to speak if sworn as a witness. He left. A servant

informed Yussupov that the body of Rasputin had been taken to the house and now lay in the wine cellar. This was where the Prince found it, sprawled at the foot of that very staircase the dying *starets* had so recently climbed. Again Yussupov saw the scene in his mind. The loaded truncheon was in his hand. As he gazed at the blood-smeared corpse he was suddenly seized with a wild, uncontrollable urge and flung himself on it, smashing at it repeatedly with the club. It was the returning Purichkevich who stopped him. Moments later, Yussupov collapsed and fell into a dead faint.

The rest was comparatively simple. The closed touring sedan that was to transport the body to the river had been kept at the Grand Duke's palace. Taking a cab, he, Sukhotin, and Lazovert now brought it back. There was no question of taking the prostrate Yussupov with them. Purichkevich decided to stay with him. Rolling the corpse in a length of canvas, the other three put it in the back of the car and started driving toward the Neva a little after dawn. Their destination was Petrovski Island. There was a bridge there. Having reconnoitered, the Grand Duke said he knew of a spot where the ice was probably thin enough so the impact of a falling body would break through it. There was also a hole at that point, the perfect depository if the drop were accurate.

The bridge was not difficult to find. Concealed under its mass of ice the Neva flowed beneath it. They even found the Grand Duke's hole and were relieved to see dark lines around it indicating the ice was fractured at depth. They tied the victim's arms and legs to the body. Then they carried it to the rail and flung it over, watching as it glanced soddenly off the ice edge and slowly became submerged.

And so the deed was done.

As the chill of the frigid water embraced him, the tiny, flickering spark which was all that was left of life in Rasputin flickered yet, delivering along thousands of nerve ganglia a primitive survival command to the battered brain. *Breathe.* The mouth opened. The lungs filled with the river's flow. The grim finality of it all was instantaneous.

The Neva flowed on. The simple peasant from Pokrovskoye slept at last amid the perfect peace that had always been denied him. There, under the great winding sheet of glittering ice, he had become one with time and the river.

NOTES

1. The Zaporozhe Cossacks were previously mentioned in a note in Chapter 5. This is the clan made famous by Taras Bulba, the *hetman* (Cossack chieftain) whose adventurous life was immortalized in the novel by Nikolai Gogol that bore his name.

2. All conversation is as Yussupov remembered it. See Prince Feliks Yussupov, *Rasputin*, Dial Press, New York, 1927, p. 144.

3. Judges 16:28.

4. Yussupov, *op. cit.*, p. 161.

Epilogue

There is nothing unusual about the slaughtering of prophets, for humans often cannot tolerate what they cannot understand. In A.D. 33, they failed to understand a man from Nazareth named Yeshua ben David, and in Jerusalem they tortured him to death on a cross.[1] On the day he died there was a great storm, and in Solomon's Temple the sacred cloth covering the Holy of Holies was torn asunder. Immediately on the murder of Rasputin there was no such supernatural event, for he was merely a mortal and only too thoroughly human. Yet, as he had predicted, his death was followed rapidly by the destruction of tsarism and the collapse of the Russian Empire as then constituted. As he had predicted, also, after his assassination by nobles of the Russian state the Imperial Family did not long survive.

The story of what occurred after the disappearance of the *starets* is in itself remarkable and will be dealt with briefly. Readily recalled is the extreme concern of Maria on the night of Rasputin's departure for the Moika Palace, her distrust and dislike for Yussupov, the finality of her prophetic utterance of a word she had never before used with her father: "*Proshchaitye*, Papa"—"Farewell."

She records that after seeing him go she slept fitfully and was much disturbed by nightmares. The ever-loyal Protopopov telephoned early. When a sleep-starved, bedraggled Maria asked him the time he said it was seven in the morning; then asked if her father had come home. Maria went to see. When she told him the *starets'* bed had not been used he thanked her and hung up without comment. By now the girl was thoroughly alarmed.

She did what she could. Her first effort was to call Munia Golovina and ask if she had seen or heard anything of Rasputin. The gentle reply was negative. Maria then said Rasputin had left with Yussupov around midnight and asked her father's devoted follower to telephone the Prince and inquire about him. All sympathy and understanding, Munia agreed. However, she did not call back within the hour, and after waiting as long as her badly strained patience would allow Maria called Anna Virubova. The Tsaritsa's lame favorite did her best to reassure her. Nothing could happen to the *starets*. It was simply unthinkable. She would let Maria know what she discovered at the earliest possible moment.

Events now took an even stranger turn. News of Rasputin's disappearance arrived at the Palace with a breathless Anna Virubova. The Tsaritsa was visibly stricken. She recalled her conversation with her lady-in-waiting on the previous day, when Virubova had returned from Rasputin's flat after taking a message to him from the Empress. He had told Virubova he was going to visit Yussupov at midnight. She had advised him against it, saying the peculiar lateness of the hour gave her a feeling of uneasiness. The *starets* had dismissed her fears. The Prince knew his parents despised Rasputin and simply did not want them to find out about it. He was going to introduce the *starets* to his lovely wife Irina Aleksandrovna. The odd timing was merely a discreet precaution. "There must be some mistake," the Tsaritsa had said. "Irina is in the Crimea." This she repeated several times in increasing agitation. "There must be some mistake."

Rapidly things were coming to a head. To Tsarskoe Selo came one phone call after another. Protopopov had consulted with the police. He related what was known but the available facts were sparse indeed. Grand Duke Dmitri Pavlovich came on the line. Curiously, he wanted to pay a visit to the Empress but she was far too upset to talk with this known intimate of Yussupov. Then it was the latter himself, asking for Virubova, requesting to see her. Virubova told him it would have to be at a later time. Then he must speak with the Tsaritsa, said Yussupov, ". . . to give her an account of what has taken place."

Virubova's reaction was disturbing to the caller. Without mincing words she asked him what he meant; then immediately tried to question him about the *starets*. In a testy flurry of obvious nervousness Yussupov denied all knowledge of Rasputin's disappearance and rang off, saying he would call again. There followed an instance of a man caught in the toils of his own falsified account and forced to stick to it. It will be recalled the policeman who originally investigated the shots received what amounted to a confession of murder from the panicky Purichkevich, that this same officer, though apparently sympathetic, then warned the killers he would have to tell the truth if sworn as a witness. Yussupov understood this. Yet when interrogated that day by General Grigoryev, whom he describes as "Chief of Police of the Kazan district," he adhered unswervingly to his original claim.[2] He writes that he addressed Grigoryev as follows: "Your visit is probably connected with shots which were heard in the courtyard of our house?"[3]

" 'Yes, I have come to learn from you first-hand full details of what occurred. Was not Rasputin a guest here yesterday evening?' "

"Rasputin? He never visits me."

" 'The shots heard from your courtyard are nevertheless associated with his disappearance, and the Prefect of Police has ordered me to make immediate inquiry into what happened at your house last night.' "

Yussupov then asked him the source of his information, whereupon Grigoryev gave him a fairly detailed account of the policeman's report as the latter had told it to an inspector. Yussupov feigned amazement. "What an incredible story! How tiresome that just because this policeman did not understand what was said to him, so much unpleasantness may arise."[4]

The Prince proceeded to concoct a tale of a drunken guest who accidentally shot and killed one of his yard dogs when "excited by wine." A policeman arrived, he told Grigoryev. Purichkevich spoke to him. He, Yussupov, noted the officer "became confused." Purichkevich told the policeman of the dead dog and compared it to Rasputin, that was all. He "regretted that it had not been the *starets* instead."

What Grigoryev may have thought privately is unknown. To Yussupov's face, however, he was all politeness and understanding. " 'I am very grateful, Prince, for your information. I shall drive straight to the Prefect and report to him all you have told me. Your explanation clears up the incident, and completely guarantees you from unpleasant consequences of any kind.' "[5]

As might have been expected, the Prince was not even required to produce the body of the dog. Had he been so he believed he was ready. In his chapter entitled "Why a Dog Was Killed," he relates that he had his servant (probably Nefedov) shoot one of the dogs, then drag its bleeding body over the tracks Rasputin had left in the courtyard and leave it on the mound of snow where the *starets* had collapsed.

So much for the relative invulnerability of rank and wealth. Yussupov then states that no sooner had Grigoryev departed than he received a phone call from Munia Golovina, whose identity he still attempts to conceal as M_____. He writes that she was extremely upset about Rasputin having vanished. " 'I am in a terrible state of mind.' "[6] Of course, the Prince knew nothing. He agreed, however, to go to her house at once and discuss the situation, and this he did within the hour. The young woman he found there was close to hysteria. " 'Tell me, for God's sake, where is Grigori Efimovich? What have you done with him? They say he was killed in your house, and that you are his murderer. . . . Oh how terrible it all is! Both the Empress and Anya[7] are sure that he was killed during the night, and that it was done in your house, and by you.' "[8]

Yussupov appeared to be appalled, as indeed he must have been due to the precariousness of his position. He asked Munia to telephone the Tsaritsa at once, saying he would explain all if she would receive him. Munia did so, then told him Aleksandra agreed to this. As he was about to leave she begged him not to go, expressing her genuinely deep concern for his safety. She crossed herself before him and made the sacred sign over him. He relates he was deeply touched, so much so that he restrained himself from making a full confession to her only by "a supreme effort." About to leave, he was stopped by a phone call at that moment. Anna Virubova was on the line. The Empress was unwell and would not be able to see him after all. However, she wanted a detailed report in writing immediately.

The noose began to tighten around Yussupov. While still with General Grigoryev he had asked for an interview with General Balk,

Prefect of Police. On returning to the Moika Palace he got his written answer. General Balk would see him at once. Yussupov was surprisingly cool. At Balk's office he reiterated his statement to Grigoryev. It was all a question of the policeman misinterpreting the words of Purichkevich. Couldn't the thing be cleared up? He, Yussupov, was on leave from the Corps des Pages and intended that very evening to depart for his Crimean estate where his family expected him.

General Balk appeared to be in sympathy. Of course, Yussupov's explanation of the gunshots was perfectly acceptable and he was free to leave at will. He should be told, however, that the Tsaritsa was not entirely satisfied and had ordered that the mansion on the Moika be searched. Yussupov protested. He was married to the Tsar's niece and as a member of the Imperial Family was immune to such procedures except by His Majesty's express command. Balk conceded the point. Picking up the phone, he immediately canceled the search order.

Yussupov had gained a bit of time if little else. He was now perfectly aware that his only possible escape from retribution lay in removing himself from the scene and the Crimea was definitely indicated. Still, he wanted to test ministerial reaction. It must not look like flight. He went to see Minister of Justice Makarov, who had been replaced through Rasputin's influence and then reinstated. Would there be repercussions? Did he specifically have the minister's *permission* to leave Petrograd? Makarov acquiesced. Not only was the wind of public opinion blowing in favor of anyone who might have harmed Rasputin, but the reaction of the nobility and most government officials was remarkably similar to that of the city-bred masses. The Tsaritsa's wishes in the matter were not mentioned. In the absence of specific orders from the Tsar, Makarov saw no impediment. Furthermore, he was unsure of himself, uncertain he had the authority to detain a man of Yussupov's rank.

It was on this day, the day after Rasputin's disappearance, that a police inspector showed a bloodstained galosh to Maria and her younger sister Varya, footgear easily identified as belonging to their father. It ended all doubt for the girls, who now realized the *starets* had been murdered. Deeply shocked by their loss and in a state of profound depression, they sent a telegram to Pokrovskoye. Despite their torn emotions it was carefully phrased. It did not speak of death, saying only that Rasputin was unwell and urging Praskovia to join them in the capital. Maria relates she then remembered the letter in her bureau drawer, the one Rasputin had asked be left sealed until he was dead. Varya and Katya listened as she read it to them in a trembling, pain-racked voice.

My Darlings,

A disaster threatens us. Great misfortune is approaching. The face of Our Lady has become dark and the spirit is troubled in the calm of the night. This calm will not last. Terrible will be the anger. And where shall we flee?

It is written: Beware as you know neither the day nor the hour. The day has come for our country. There will be tears and blood. In the shadows of the suffering I can distinguish nothing. My hour will toll soon. I am not afraid but I know the break will be bitter. God knows the path your suffering will take. Innumerable men will perish. Numerous will be the martyrs. The earth will tremble. Famine and disease will strike men down. Some signs will appear to them. Pray for your salvation. By the grace of Our Lord and the grace of those who intercede for us, you will be consoled.

Grigori[9]

Even as the two young sisters and the housemaid wept over the letter's contents, Yussupov was discovering he had made his move to leave Petrograd just a bit too late. Fearing that if the Tsar came back from General Headquarters Grigoryev's recent desist order would be countermanded and the mansion on the Moika searched, he had gone to the palace of the only one of the murderers more frightened and indecisive than himself, Dmitri Pavlovich. There they were taken by police sent by the Empress and both were put under house arrest. It was all the Tsaritsa could do for the moment. Earlier, she had told Protopopov she wanted the assassins executed by firing squad at once but the minister had said it was impossible. There was no *corpus dilecti*, and until a body had been found there was not even proof that Rasputin was dead.

That proof came soon enough. On that same afternoon, divers searching near the Petrovski Bridge where the galosh had been found discovered Rasputin's remains. He had been wedged in the ice. When the body was examined in a small hut near the Neva there was incontrovertible evidence he was still alive when he entered the water. In his efforts to escape the cord with which they had tied him his wrists had been rubbed raw. His right hand was on his breast. When they saw that hand those who were present were awestruck. The middle finger was bent at a right angle. If taken together with the forefinger it formed the earliest stylized symbol of Christ's suffering on Calvary. Even in death the *starets* had made the Sign of the Cross.

Informed of the grisly discovery, Protopopov telephoned Maria. Explaining that he hated to put her through it, he said that a positive identification was necessary and asked her if she might do it. Getting the best grip on herself she could, she agreed to come. Varya and Katya went with her. Once in the hut with the covering removed from the body the sight of the horribly mangled corpse made her nauseous, yet she knew it was he. The injuries were frightful. She records that one eye was "dangling against his cheek, held there by a slender thread of flesh." It was not until later that Sister Akulina, whom the Tsaritsa had chosen to prepare the body for burial, told her of the ultimate outrage. Rasputin had been sexually mutilated and his penis was missing.

Five days passed before Praskovia and Dunia arrived in the capital, with Rasputin's son Dmitri accompanying them. At this point they believed only that the *starets* was ill, yet the tone of Maria's hastily sent wire had been serious. Then they saw the black mourning clothes. Apparently, Dunia had wrapped herself in a cloak of rigid self-control and she held on, but for Praskovia the shock was too great. She screamed in her anguish, then wept brokenly and was driven with the others to the Gorokhovaya address.

Few tasks were more unpleasant than Maria's. When they asked her how Rasputin had died she told them, omitting the more harrowing details, saying nothing of the fiendish emasculation or other disfigurements. As to the funeral itself she could not bear witness. Fearing for the safety of the daughters of the deceased if made vulnerable to lurking assassins, the Tsar had kept her and Varya away. It was at Tsarskoe Selo, Maria knew. The casket provided by the Tsaritsa was incomparably beautiful. The interment was at a plot Anna Virubova owned, one that she asked with solemn pride should be used for the purpose. The Tsaritsa had prayed fervently that night. Maria knew that much from her loving namesake, Aleksandra's third daughter, Maria Nikolaevna. Her mother had spent many hours in her private chapel, the Grand Duchess had said. She had prayed on her knees beside the coffin. When at last she emerged her eyes were red and swollen from endless weeping.

A royal limousine having been provided for them, it was on the following day that Praskovia and her three children went to Tsarskoe Selo, where the Imperial Family and Anna Virubova received them with open arms. The Tsaritsa, very pale and worn looking herself, was loving sympathy personified. The Tsarevich, a handsome but fragile boy of twelve now, tried manfully to control himself but broke down and wept. The Tsar approached Praskovia and tried to reassure her. She could leave her daughters in Petrograd to further their education. They would be provided for and loved. Nikolai would guarantee it. Although the bereaved widow had no way of knowing it, the promise had little to support it. There was a man in Switzerland. He spent much time in the library at Geneva. It would not be very long before the situation in Russia would invite his return like an opening door, and Vladimir Ilyich Ulyanov, called Lenin, would step out from behind the bookshelves.[10]

Maria found everything changed. While she and the rest of the family had been at Tsarskoe Selo someone stole the money her father had left her, a matter of three thousand rubles, and other funds deposited with the banking firm of Rubinstein were inexplicably missing. Some days passed. Then, realizing the farm could not long be neglected, Praskovia took Dmitri and Katya and boarded the train for Siberia, leaving her two daughters in Petrograd.

Like the ripples made by a flung stone in a pond, all was passing outward and away. Seemingly, the Tsar, although physically brave, could not find the moral courage to do what his wife so strongly urged. Amazingly, Purichkevich, Lazovert, Sukhotin, and Nefedov were never officially connected with the murder and went without punishment. Nor did the Grand Duke and the Prince pay the price of it. Still on active duty with the Army, Dmitri Pavlovich was posted to Persia, a noncombat area. Yussupov, the ringleader without whose baneful influence the tragedy would not have occurred, was exiled to his Rakitnoye estate in the Kursk district, after which he moved to Koryeiz in the Crimea. This final retreat was a shrewd one. In the event of revolution it assured his escape by way of the Black Sea, and a day was to come when he took ready advantage of it.

It was during these weeks, when the two teenage sisters and Dunia Bekyeshova lived together at the Gorokhovaya flat, that Maria and the devoted mistress of her late father drew closer than ever before, and much that Dunia was to relate was noted by Maria in her diary. In later years she referred to it often. Wednesdays were the days for the girls to visit the Palace. There, in spite of the increasing signs of approaching nationwide catastrophy an artificial composure was maintained, for Tsarskoe Selo was an island of peace in an ever more turbulent sea.

The year 1917 arrived. Desertions in the Army increased. Indeed, they became so prevalent that officers of the General Staff all but despaired of ever being able to launch another offensive.[11] It was at February's close that Dunia returned to Siberia. Her father, old and ailing, could not manage things himself and she had no choice. Maria and Varya were left to themselves in the apartment. With Varya at school much of the time Maria was especially lonely, and the weekly sojourns at the Palace became the only thing in life that gave her any pleasure.

Her diary speaks of the increasingly overt signs of the renewal of revolution: barricades in the streets of Petrograd, Army deserters and an unruly civilian rabble manning them, the Bolshevik clenched fist seen everywhere, looting and ever-increasing violence, a progressive and widespread breakdown of law and order. A day came when she could not reach Anna Virubova by phone because the wire had been cut or disconnected. She took Varya out of school. Days later, when the sporadic rioting appeared to have subsided, she let her return there only to discover that communications with the Palace were cut. At this point Maria displayed a dauntless courage reminiscent of her father's. Told by Varya of the rumors at the school, contrary tales of the Tsar's abdication and flight, his arrest and incarceration, knowing the streets were unsafe and totally ignorant of the conditions at Tsarskoe Selo, she nonetheless called a cab and had herself driven to the Palace.

The Tsar was at the front. Ironically, except for the Tsaritsa herself, the entire Imperial Family had come down with the measles and all were in bed with it. As always, Aleksandra showered affection on the girl she loved as her own. This time, however, she told her she would have to leave to avoid possible harm. The Empress would let her know when it was safe to return. They said a tearful goodbye. With a sinking heart Maria realized that her world had now shrunk to the Gorokhovaya apartment and the hazardous uncertainties of what might lie in the streets below it.

Although the progress of the Revolution of 1917 is beyond the scope of this account, a few things might be said where pertinent. By the beginning of the year it was becoming obvious that no major segment of the Russian population would any longer support the Tsar's government. In Petrograd and Moscow strikes were once again spreading. Confronted by a desperate situation, Nikolai II ignored the Duma's demand to form a new cabinet and instead declared that body dissolved on March 11. If he had control of the armed forces he might have won out at this juncture, at least for a while. As it was, his decision forced the Duma to a test of strength, and with many units of the Army already on the verge of mutiny they could hardly lose. They simply ignored the sovereign's order. A provisional government was formed under Prince Lvov and including Miliukov and Kerensky. The royal family was put under house arrest and the Palace temporarily became their prison. The Tsar was forced to sign an instrument of abdication. It was the end of Romanov rule.

Perhaps nothing more clearly demonstrated the chaotic state of affairs than the atrocity that now occurred. No longer were there royal guards around the Palace grounds, only revolutionary ones. They made no attempt to do their duty. Confronted the next night by a gang of drunken soldiers, they admitted them to the area. Then they stood idly by as Rasputin's body was disinterred, carried into the forest, and made the object of a gruesome sport as ghouls in soiled and dishonored uniforms pitched it back and forth on the points of their bayonets. How pitiful they were in their efforts to degrade that lifeless clay. How the spirit of the *starets*, soaring free, would have laughed at their useless desecration. In the end they burned the corpse in an open fire. Then, joined by a group of women from an outlying village, they indulged themselves sexually to the point of exhaustion.

The story of the murder of the Romanovs by the Communists in a cellar in Ekaterinburg (on July 16, 1918) is well known.[12] Much less so is the fact that Maria Rasputin, through a particularly ironic twist of fate, became intimately associated with the one individual who made that tragic outcome inevitable. It was odd how the various threads drew together. In July 1917, Kerensky succeeded Lvov as Provisional Premier. The Tsar and Tsaritsa with their children and retainers were still at Tsarskoe Selo. Kerensky, a thorough moderate who had no special animosity for the Imperial family, felt himself responsible for their safety. Yet what was he to do? Lenin was back in Russia, Trotsky his chief lieutenant. In the same month Kerensky had come to power they had jointly launched "the July uprising" in a bid to unseat him. It had been put down, Trotsky arrested, Lenin driven into hiding in Finland. Yet the Bolsheviks were well organized and would try again. Kerensky believed the Romanovs must be removed from Petrograd for their own safety. He thought, too, that it must be to a remote area where the people had not already been successfully propagandized by the Radical Left.

The town that eventually suggested itself was Tobolsk in western Siberia, the old Cossack fishing and fur trading center that Rasputin had known so well. On August 14, the Tsar and his family were transported there by train. Almost at once, the place became the focal point for a number of royalist plots to rescue the Romanovs while it might still be possible. Most of these groups, though well intentioned, were inefficient. A few were crackbrained. All competed with each other and their total lack of cooperation made their schemes self-defeating. The obvious primary need was for an organizer who would coordinate their efforts, cull out the nonessentials, and formulate a workable plan of action. Could anyone be found? After many fruitless secret meetings, a young man emerged who seemed to possess the necessary qualities. His name was Boris Solovyov.[13]

Maria Rasputin knew this man. As an Army officer stationed in Petrograd he had occasionally found himself with time on his hands.

He had studied psychic phenomena and hypnotism. As a member of a group of amateur mystics in 1915 he had met Anna Virubova and through her had made the acquaintance first of the *starets* and then his elder daughter.

Time passed. There is evidence to show that Solovyov was romantically interested in Maria but at first it was not returned. Then Rasputin was killed. Almost overnight the notorious, bearded Siberian became a cult figure in Petrograd. People gathered and held séances, intent on contacting the spirit of the *starets*. Maria was among them. Ultimately, she found herself drawn to this soldier with an interest in the occult and the two came closer together. Surprisingly for a man who was a known supporter of the Duma, Solovyov joined a group dedicated to freeing the Romanovs. Maria's interest in him redoubled.

Not long after the Tsar and his family arrived in Tobolsk, Solovyov went there to reconnoiter. He was by now engaged to Maria. In early October of 1917 they married in Petrograd, then journeyed to Pokrovskoye and lived for some weeks with Praskovia and Dunia. Solovyov was by this time discharged from the Army, reason unknown. When, having left his bride behind in her native village, he reemerged later at Tobolsk it was in the role of a clandestine monarchist leader plotting to save the Romanovs.

Where others engaged in the same pursuit had been haphazard and amateurish, it soon became obvious that Solovyov was working to a plan. Very early he contacted the Tsaritsa. It was done through one Romanova, a royal maid. Notes were secretly exchanged. Because the daughter of the *starets* happened to be his wife, Aleksandra had every confidence in the man and soon came to believe that help was almost at hand. Rescue was certain, she told the Tsar. In Tobolsk alone there were some 300 staunch sympathizers awaiting their orders to act. Solovyov was the key. Then a message of hope was whispered to the Tsar while in church: "Put your faith in us, Your Majesty."

Months passed. Actually, for anyone astute enough to detect it a pattern had been established, a strange *modus operandi*, and that pattern had little to do with the escape of the Romanovs. Solovyov did not stay in Tobolsk. Instead, with sound strategic instinct, he lay athwart the only railroad leading in or out of it and interdicted this line as surely as a military force might have done by physically cutting it.

He did this by quartering himself in Tyumen. For any group or individual involved in a plot to save the Imperial family, he became *the* essential contact. Royalist agents went to him first. Funds for the purpose came into his hands. Rescue groups not under his immediate control were forcefully discouraged.

In November of this fateful year 1917, achieving at last what Lenin and Trotsky had been striving to achieve since well before 1905, the Bolsheviks came into their own. The November Revolution swept all before it. The Provisional Government was overthrown. Kerensky and those of his cabinet ministers who were able to escape arrest were forced to flee. True, the Communists, as the Bolsheviks would soon be called, would yet be forced to fight a very hazardous civil war against the Whites or counterrevolutionary forces. Nonetheless, their control over most of the major centers of population was total, and to keep it that way they enlisted such skilled butchers of humanity as Feliks Dzerzhinsky, head of the Cheka.[14]

Curiously, through all this monumental upheaval Solovyov remained solidly in place, displaying something of the survival qualities of a modern-day Talleyrand. Unlike his wife, the Tsar had never entirely trusted him nor believed in the "Brotherhood" of Tobolsk based rescuers supposedly preparing to come to their aid. Unfortunately for him and his loved ones his instincts in the matter were the more sound. About the foremost "tsarist agent" operating in Tyumen, British historians Summers and Mangold have written the following:

> History has branded Solovyov as a dangerous triple agent, paid by the Germans to supply information, in league with the Bolsheviks, while posing all the time as a monarchist hero. Loyal officers travelling to Tobolsk were briefed to contact Solovyov en route, and walked right into a trap. At least three were captured and shot by the Bolshevik secret police—just after they had met Solovyov and voiced suspicion of his motives. Until now efforts to help the imperial family had been bogged down in indecision and bungling, and now they were obstructed by a traitor.[15]

Perhaps there is no greater evidence of Solovyov's shrewdness than the fact he was able to deceive his own wife for years. Maria did not discover his duplicity. So far as his function in Tyumen was concerned, his eventual downfall was triggered by a French secret agent operating under the cover name of Bronard. It was mid-April, 1918. Momentarily implanted in Solovyov's zone of activity by *Le Douzième Bureau*[16] based on Paris, this daring spy managed to make the leaders of the local soviet (council) distrust Solovyov as a possible counter-revolutionary working for the royalists. Needless to say, this past master of treachery and intrigue faced arrest. When he escaped from Russia, his dutiful wife Maria Grigorievna Solovyova (née Rasputina) went with him.

For a number of years thereafter Maria's life was colorful and adventurous but, considering the character of her spouse, perhaps not especially satisfying or happy. She was still with him in the 1930s. Becoming a cabaret dancer, she toured the capital cities of Western Europe, occasionally adding to her memoirs of her father, even getting things published from time to time. The year 1935 found her in London, her unlikely profession that of a trainer of wild animals in an English circus.[17] The Tsaritsa would not have believed it. Still less would she have credited Maria's eventual move to the United States and her quiet settling down in Los Angeles, California, a woman who had been part of history virtually unnoticed by all.

It is to Maria's literary collaborator, Patte Barham, American author and newspaperwoman, that one must turn for a fittingly incredible addendum to the wondrous tale of Rasputin. Although his biography that she wrote with Maria was not published until 1977, the two co-authors began their research for it a decade earlier. In 1968 Miss Barham went to London. In her possession was a list of names provided by Maria, Russian expatriots they thought might be helpful. From them she obtained other names. The second group were all in Paris. Maria was already there, visiting her daughter Tatiana. The plan was that Miss Barham would interview the Parisian émigrés before joining Maria and returning to the United States, and this she did.

She elaborates on only one of these meetings, and this with a man she did not know and had never heard of before. He telephoned her at her hotel. He was familiar with some of the names on her list and said he could put her in contact with someone of interest. He gave no surname, referring to himself only as Georges. He also spoke excellent English. They talked a short time and arranged to meet that evening.

With Georges she took a long drive, so long in fact that she writes of him following "a deliberate circuitous route" to make sure she would not be able to find their destination again. From the first he had been mysteriously uncommunicative. When he asked if she were writing a book on Rasputin she acknowledged it, and he then said there was someone who wished to meet her. In the car she tried to get more information. He told her he was taking her to meet his grandmother. She asked if it had a connection with Rasputin. He replied that the lady in question had once been in love with him. Suddenly, the thing took on a new and intriguing allure. The romance, the possible historical significance were most inviting. The chance of having stumbled onto something important filled Miss Barham with hope.

She was not disappointed. Arriving in an area she recognized as St. Denis, they came eventually to an uninviting old house enveloped by trees, a setting perhaps reminiscent of Miss Faversham's abode in Dickens' somber tale, *Great Expectations*. She describes the dark and cluttered living room as "like a faded Tsarist museum." On a table was a very large samovar of sterling. Above the fireplace hung an imposing oil of Tsar Nikolai and Tsaritsa Aleksandra, and numerous additional relics of another place and time were in evidence, all Russian.[18] Georges had excused himself. When he came back he told his guest that his grandmother would see her now.

Miss Barham describes a bizarre experience that could be out of Dostoevsky. Led by her host to the rear of the dwelling, she passed with him through a thick wooden door and found herself in a gloomy, unpretentious bedroom. Immediately her gaze riveted on a wall-mounted photograph of Rasputin, one obviously much enlarged from the original, the candles burning beneath it giving the impression of sanctification. Then she saw the occupant of the bed. The woman was very old, the skin of her face like parchment enhaloed by thin white hair. The impression she gave was one of being barely alive, a transient evanescence of life hovering between two worlds. Her grandson spoke to her in Russian. Miss Barham asked to be told what she had to communicate. Georges translated into English.

" 'She wants you to know that Father Grigori was a great man, a reincarnation of the Christ.' "[19]

Miss Barham asked the extent of the old lady's acquaintance with the *starets*, then listened with increasing fascination as the tale that unfolded wove a kind of enchantment. In St. Petersburg, the young girl that Georges's grandmother was then had worked as a maid at the Hotel Europe. Rasputin used to frequent the place, giving dinner parties, bringing women there. She had become one of them and an ardent disciple. When the Revolution struck she had fled, fearing for her life because of her connection with the *starets*. In the end, she found herself in Paris but had not come empty-handed. There were certain relics still in her possession. One in particular . . .

Miss Barham expressed immediate intense interest. From the bureau under the photo of Rasputin, Georges took a gleaming wooden box surmounted by a medallion of inlaid silver. Old but still elegant, in appearance it was not unlike the small caskets seen in collections of Egyptology, the funerary recepticles of mummified cats and small crocodiles. He brought it to the visitor and opened it. "I saw what looked like a blackened, overripe banana, about a foot long, and resting on velvet cloth."[20] Miss Barham asked what it was. Georges voiced his mother's claim that it was Rasputin's generative organ. When he closed the lid and returned the box to its place the woman in the bed crossed herself feebly.[21]

Miss Barham writes of her amazement. To her question as to how the elderly owner came by the curious memento her host explained simply. His grandmother's sister had been married to one of Yussupov's servants, who had found it after the killing. There followed more questions. From the woman who had been Rasputin's love, now so close to expiration, came an account of the murder taken from the only person in the Moika Palace that night who had not been one of the assassins. Heretofore, the part about sexual mutilation had been mere unsubstantiated rumor. Now it seemed confirmed. Miss Barham felt grateful. For a few moments, as she stood there, a person who would soon bid farewell to life had made her feel the pulse of history. The experience had been gruesome and distasteful, yet she felt rarely privileged. It was as though one more cord in the Gordian Knot of the unsolvable had been cut through.

There are many still today who claim that Rasputin was a fake and his occult gifts more mythical than real. They cannot explain away his remarkable clairvoyance, yet they try very hard to do so, as though all that is wondrous in life is somehow offensive to them. Being unable to account for his incredible healing powers, these individuals say they did not really exist. Some say he did not save the Tsarevich at all and insist the boy would have recovered without him. Others speculate that, at the most, this "false *starets*" had a knowledge of hypnotism, that through its employment he slowed Aleksei's heartbeat, thus reducing the rate of blood flow and permitting coagulation. But what of the telegram from Pokrovskoye? Did he then hypnotize the sufferer at a distance of *two thousand miles*? What of Anna Virubova, abandoned to that death the doctors admitted they were utterly powerless to prevent? What of his subsequently confirmed predictions? And how, above all, do they account for Rasputin's incredible end: the cyanide, the mortal gunshot wounds, the mutilation and clubbing, the final icy immersion and proof of continuing life? To the author's knowledge, only one man in history displayed an animal vitality anywhere near as remarkable as this, the English pirate Edward Teach, known as Blackbeard. But *he did not survive cyanide*, and nothing about him is suggestive of the miraculous.

Are such powers as these truly alien to human beings? Must it really be assumed that all we do not understand is mere charlatanism and lies? Let those who believe this read the life of the American seer and faith healer Edgar Cayce, a man without medical knowledge who correctly diagnosed illnesses, who prescribed successful treatments without a day of study, who repeatedly and accurately described people he had not seen.[22] Let them investigate the remarkable work on extrasensory perception of Sir Hubert Wilkins and Harold Sherman, an account of repeatedly successful thought transference between the two over 3400 miles (from the Arctic tundra to New York City) three nights a week for six months.[23] Let them, if they will, review the works of Sheila Ostrander and Lynn Schroeder on recent Soviet experiments with ESP; or that of David St. Clair on the remarkable feats achieved by Brazilian voodoo and spiritism.[24] Even many scientists now acknowledge that the natural world, a world detectable through the five senses, may not be the only one that exists. There is still the supernatural, thus far almost entirely unexplored. There is even, as Einstein pointed out, another dimension than those long recognized and held to be absolute, that of time.

When my grandmother was a little girl she was one of nine children, and her oldest sister, fragile and ultimately consumptive, was called Eliza. Although she did not know it herself, this frail maiden was a remarkable girl. She used to go into involuntary trances, remembering nothing later. During one of them, she raised off the floor with only her fingertips touching the surface a round oak table with my grandmother (a child of five at the time) standing on top of it—apparently through some unknown and little understood transference of electrical energy. This she did repeatedly before witnesses. On another occasion, in a state of trance she spoke with the voice of a recently deceased four-year-old girl, badly frightening the grieving parents but inducing the father of the child to permanently end his drinking.

This sickly young woman with gifts as inexplicable as Rasputin's died of tuberculosis at twenty-one. I think of her often. As I sit here writing, there is before me a small and very lovely silver creamer, ornate, exquisitely delicate, fashioned well over a century ago in England. I take it up and hold it in my hand. Does it possess the miraculous properies of the lamp of Ali-ud-Din?[25] Will I perchance detect a hidden and secret warmth, an internal glow? I gaze at its softly rounded contours. Etched in beautiful Victorian script on the front is a name to remember—Eliza.

So let them scoff if they wish. There are other worlds than this, other treasure houses of knowledge whose vastness no human can begin to comprehend. How was it that Hamlet put it to his friend? "Horatio, there are more things in heaven and earth than are dreamt of in your philosophy."

NOTES

1. In his native Aramaic the name of Jesus was Yeshua, the word *Jesus* being derived from the Greek *Iësous*. In Hebrew his name was Joshua. During his lifetime it is unlikely he was familiar with the name of Jesus and was certainly never so addressed.

2. Yussupov does not explain why a police official whose headquarters was so far from Petrograd would be involved in the case.

3. Prince Feliks Yussupov, *Rasputin*, Dial Press, New York, 1927, p. 166.

4. *Ibid.*, p. 168.

5. *Ibid.*, p. 169.

6. *Ibid.*, p. 170.

7. Virubova. In transliterating from Russian into English, Anya is a variant of Anna.

8. Yussupov, *op. cit.*, pp. 170–171.

9. Maria Rasputin and Patte Barham, *Rasputin: The Man Behind the Myth*, Warner Books, New York, 1977. (Published by arrangement with Prentice-Hall, Inc.)

10. Lenin's reentry into Russia was financed by German gold, and the Kaiser's government supplied a sealed and heavily guarded train to transport him. The agreement was that if his revolution were successful he would take Russia out of the war. This he did, but at the heavy cost of signing the humiliating Treaty of Brest-Litovsk.

11. Nonetheless, Brusilov as Generalissimo made another maximum effort in July, only to see the Russian lines broken and the Army forced to make a general retreat. Unlike most high-ranking Russian officers, he later joined the Bolsheviks.

12. There is considerable evidence that the youngest of the Tsar's four daughters, Grand Duchess Anastasia, may have escaped. Consult Anastasia Nikolaevna Romanovna, *I Am Anastasia*, Harcourt, Brace & Company, New York, 1959.

13. The spelling is a variant of Soloviev.

14. The Bolshevik secret police. The initials stood for "Extraordinary Commission for the Suppression of Counter-Revolution." The organization later became increasingly infamous under a succession of names, *viz.*, the Ogpu, the NKVD, the MVD, and the KGB, the latter designation still unchanged at this writing.

15. Anthony Summers and Tom Mangold, *The File on the Tsar*, Harper & Row, New York, 1976, p. 262.

16. The Twelfth Bureau—French military intelligence.

17. In her final book on the subject of her father, *Rasputin: The Man Behind the Myth*, there is an old photograph of her in circus costume working in a cage with a leopard.

18. The author of this book experienced something similar many years ago. In a tiny flat in an impoverished Mexican district of Los Angeles lived my late father-in-law, Dmitri Vladimirovich Gussakovsky, already elderly in the 1960s. As a loyal artillery officer of the long dead Nikolai II, it is not surprising he surrounded himself with cherished memorabilia. In one corner was an ikon with photographs of the

Imperial Family. Even the big sailor Derevenko was there with his small charge Aleksei. And candles burned at Russian Easter and on the fallen Tsar's name day; and vodka was bought from Mitya's modest purse, and he and I and my wife Elizaveta drank to a day that was gone.

19. Rasputin and Barham, *op. cit.*, p. 308.

20. *Ibid.*, p. 309.

21. From this it would seem logical to infer that Maria's knowledge of her father's genital size came from Patte Barham's description of the organ she saw in St. Denis, somewhat shrunken due to desiccation. Mummified remains may be remarkably well preserved, those of Pharoah Rameses II being an example. As a boy, the author saw such a thing in Long Beach, California, a cadaver "on tour" of the United States, reportedly the mummy of John Wilkes Booth.

22. Consult Thomas Sugrue, *There is a River: The Story of Edgar Cayce*, Henry Holt & Co., New York, 1942.

23. Consult Harold Sherman and Sir Hubert Wilkins, *Thoughts Through Space*, Fawcett Publications, Greenwich, Conn., 1951.

24. Sheila Ostrander and Lynn Schroeder, *Psychic Discoveries Behind the Iron Curtain*, Prentice-Hall, Englewood Cliffs, New Jersey, 1970; also, *The ESP Papers*, by the same authors, Bantam Books, New York, 1976; or David St. Clair, *Drum & Candle*, Bell Publishing Company, New York, 1971.

25. Known as Alladin in English.

GLOSSARY OF FOREIGN WORDS AND GUIDE TO PRONUNCIATION

auto-da-fé (act of faith) (autó da fay):   The act of burning a heretic at the stake during the Spanish Inquisition and at other assizes presided over by the Dominican and Jesuit orders.

balalaika (bala-líe-ka):   Russian triangular guitar.

bhakti (báak tee):   In the Hindi language of India, the way to salvation.

borzoi (bor-zóy):   The Russian wolfhound.

devochka (dév-osh-ka):   Girl.

Djipsaya (Gíp-si-ya):   A female Gypsy, identified by the feminine ending.

djizan (jéez-an):   Life.

Duma (Dóo-ma):   Legislative assembly during the last phase of the reign of Tsar Nikolai II.

durak (dur-óc):   Fool.

hara-kiri (háhra-kíree):   Japanese ritual suicide with a consecrated knife.

Hermanos Penitentes (Air-máanos Penee-tén-tais):   Brothers Pentitent, a Mexican religious cult.

Hetman (Hét-maan):   Cossack chief.

isba (éez-ba):   Peasant hut.

iurodivye (ee-oo-ro-déev-ya):   Holy idiots. Severely handicapped or insane people traditionally believed to be touched by God.

lingam (leen-gáam):   Stylized phallic symbol of Hindu India.

malodushni (malo-dúsh-nee):   Coward.

milochka (mée-losh-ka):   My dear.

muzhik (moo-zhéek):   Peasant.

pantaloni (pan-ta-ló-nee):   Trousers.

podpol'nik (pod-pól-neek):   Underground man. A religious mendicant wandering from village to village and often sleeping in cellars.

poilu (pwáhl-you):   Vernacular for the French infantryman.

Roskolniki (Ros-kól-nih-kee):   The Old Believers, a religious sect.

salazki (sa-láz-kee):   Horse-drawn sleigh.

samadhi (sa-máad-hee):   Illumination. The Hindu approach to the godhead.

stránnik (strá-neek):   Religious mendicant. The term is virtually synonymous with *podpol'nik.*

suttee (sút-tee):   Suicidal widow burning in India. A part of Hindu ritual before outlawed by the British Raj.

svinya (sveén-ya):   Swine.

uchast (oo-cháast):   Destiny.

uiti v stranstvo (ooéetee va stráanst-vuh):   Wandering.

vozhd (vózhd):   Leader.

Walpurgisnacht (Vaal-púr-gees-nacht):   Witches' Night. The Witches' Sabbath.

zlaya zhenshina (zlý-yah zhén-sheen-a):   Vixen. Said of a shrewish or ill-tempered woman.

BIBLIOGRAPHY

Aleksandr, Grand Duke (Aleksandr Mikhailovich Romanov). *Once A Grand Duke*. New York: Garden City Publishing Co., 1932.

Bach, Marcus. *Strange Sects and Curious Cults*. New York: Dodd, Mead & Company, 1961.

Blanch, Lesley. *The Sabres of Paradise*. New York: The Viking Press, 1960.

Churchill, Winston. *The World Crisis* (one-volume edition). New York: Charles Scribner's Sons, 1923.

Fülöp-Miller, René. *Rasputin: The Holy Devil*. Leipzig: Grethlein & Co., 1927. New York: The Viking Press, Inc., 1928. New York: Garden City Publishing Company, Inc., date not given.

Gilliard, Pierre. *Thirteen Years at the Russian Court*. New York: Doran and Company, 1921.

Goerlitz, Walter. *History of the German General Staff*. New York: Frederick A. Praeger, Inc., 1953.

Hart, B. H. Liddell. *Strategy*. New York: Frederick A. Praeger, Inc., 1954.

Karpovich, Michael. *Imperial Russia, 1801–1917*. New York: Henry Holt and Company, 1932.

Kluchevsky, V. O. *History of Russia* (5 volumes). London: J. M. Dent and Sons, Ltd., 1911–1931.

Koenig, William. *Epic Sea Battles*. Secaucus, New Jersey: Chartwell Books, Inc., 1975.

Lamb, Harold. *Genghis Khan the Conqueror: Emperor of All Men*. New York: Doubleday edition, 1952.

Liepman, Heinz. *Rasputin and the Fall of Imperial Russia*. New York: Rolton House, Inc., 1959.

309

Massie, Robert K.. *Nicholas and Alexandra*. New York: Atheneum, 1967.

Middlebrook, Martin. *First Day on the Somme*. New York: W. W. Norton & Company, Inc., 1972.

Moorehead, Alan. *The Russian Revolution*. London: William Collins, Sons & Co., Ltd., 1958.

Ostrander, Sheila and Schroeder, Lynn. *Psychic Discoveries Behind the Iron Curtain*. Englewood Cliffs, New Jersey: Prentice-Hall, Inc., 1970.

Pares, Sir Bernard. *The Fall of the Russian Monarchy*. London: Jonathan Cape, Ltd., 1939.

Rasputin, Maria (Maria Grigorievna Rasputina) and Barham, Patte. *Rasputin: The Man Behind the Myth*. Englewood Cliffs, New Jersey: Prentice-Hall, Inc., 1977.

Robbins, Rossell Hope. *The Encyclopedia of Witchcraft and Demonology*. New York: Crown Publishers, Inc., 1959.

Romanovna, Anastasia Nikolaevna. *I Am Anastasia*. New York: Harcourt, Brace & Company, 1959.

Sava, George. *Rasputin Speaks*. London: Faber & Faber, Ltd., 1941.

Sherman, Harold and Wilkins, Sir Hubert. *Thoughts Through Space*. Greenwich, Connecticut: Fawcett Publications, Inc., 1951.

Shub, David. *Lenin: A Biography*. New York: Doubleday and Company, Inc., 1948.

Spiering, Frank. *Prince Jack: The True Story of Jack the Ripper*. New York: Jove Publications, Inc., 1978.

St. Clair, David. *Drum and Candle*. New York: Bell Publishing Company, 1971.

Stevenson, Robert Louis. *Dr. Jekyll and Mr. Hyde*. New York: Airmont Publishing Company, Inc., 1964.

Sugrue, Thomas. *There is a River: The Story of Edgar Cayce*. New York: Henry Holt & Co., Inc., 1942.

Summers, Anthony and Mangold, Tom. *The File on the Tsar*. New York: Harper and Row Publishers, Inc., 1976.

Voltaire, François Marie Arouet de. *The History of Charles the Twelfth, King of Sweden*. New York: Leavitt, Trow & Co., 1848.

Vyrubov, Anna (Anna Aleksandrovna Virubova). *Memories of the Russian Court*. Toronto: Macmillan and Co., Ltd., 1923.

Wilson, Colin. *Rasputin and the Fall of the Romanovs*. Secaucus, New Jersey: The Citadel Press, 1964.

Yussupov, Prince Feliks. *Rasputin*. New York: Dial Press, 1927.

INDEX

Abdul Hamid II (Sultan of Turkey), 205
Ahmed III, Sultan (Turkey), 87
Akulina Nikichkina, 144–145, 151, 156, 237, 261, 279; preparation of Rasputin's body for burial by, 293
Albert, Prince, 117
Alcibiades, 159
Aleksandr, Grand Duke, 92
Aleksandr I, Tsar, 56
Aleksandr II, Tsar, 89, 90–91, 102, 164, 211
Aleksandr III, Tsar, 90–94, 108, 115, 179; death of, 81, 91, 95, 102, 104, 194; funeral cortege of, 108; godson of, 149; unveiling of statue of, 175
Aleksandra Feodorovna (Alix, Sunshine, Sunny), Tsaritsa, 6, 81, 102–103, 172; and assassination of Franz Ferdinand, 222; and celebration of reign of Romanov Dynasty, 206–209; children of, 83, 105, 116, 117, 118; courtship of, 92–95; her devotion to Rasputin, 138, 163, 179, 192–193, 194, 211–212, 247, 260, 261–262; and Dzhunkovsky, 237, 243; efforts to depose, 212; and events following Rasputin's assassination, 288, 290, 291, 293, 294; first meetings with Rasputin, 105–106; gossip about Rasputin and, 193–194, 238–239; health of, 173, 179; Iliodor's attempt to blackmail, 196; isolation of, 247, 277; her letter to Rasputin, 193–194; marriage of, 95; misery suffered by, 117–118, 208; murder of, 297; and Rasputin's daughter Maria, 148, 296; Rasputin's journal edited by, 173, 174; and Rasputin's last letter to Nikolai II, 268; Rasputin's telegram to, 190–191, 192, 194; as scapegoat, 265; and son Aleksei's injuries, 119–120, 184, 185–188, 263; and son Aleksei's miraculous recoveries, 120–124, 134, 188–192, 263–265; and Stolypin, 175; and tragedy of Khodynka Meadow, 107–108; and Anna Virubova's train accident, 240–242
Aleksei I, Tsar, 45, 46
Aleksei Nikolaevich, Tsarevich, 118, 148–149, 150, 212, 230; his devotion to Rasputin, 260; and events following Rasputin's assassination, 294; hemophilia suffered by, 105, 116–117, 119–120, 122, 186–187; injuries to, 119–120, 184, 185–188, 263; miraculous recoveries of, 122–

Aleksei Nikolaevich, Tsarevich, *(cont)*: 124, 134, 135, 155, 188–192, 263–265, 303
Aleksei Petrovich, 87, 89
Aleksei Mihailovich, Tsar, 58
Alicia, Grand Duchess, 93, 117
Allegri, Gregorio, *Miserere*, 17
Ambrose, Saint, 138
Anastasia, Grand Duchess, 148, 195
Anastasia, Tsaritsa, 84
Anastasia Nikolayevna (Stana), Grand Duchess, 84, 97, 100–101, 120–122, 164, 216
Andronikov, Prince Nikolai Petrovich, 266
Anthony, Marc, 54
Anthony (Metropolitan of St. Petersburg and Ladoga), 211
Antoni (strannik), 149
Asceticism, religious, 53–55
Augustine, Saint, 29, 138, 140
Augustus II, King (Poland and Saxony), 86
Avvakum, 46

Bach, Marcus, 54–55
Badmaev, Pyotr Aleksandrovich, 149, 155, 192, 236
Baghdad Railway, 204
Balanchine, Georg, 132
Balk (Prefect of Police), 290–291
Balkan War: First (1912), 215; Second (1913), 215
Barham, Patte, 300–302
Batu Khan, 5
Beatrice, Princess, 117
Beatty, Sir David, 220
Becket, Thomas à, 54
Bekyeshova, Dunia, 11, 60–63, 72, 73, 74; and abuse of Rasputin's daughter Maria, 126–127; and attempt to blackmail Rasputin, 168; and attempt on life of Rasputin, 223, 224; departure from St. Petersburg of, 179; and events following Rasputin's assassination, 293, 295; and meetings between Rasputin and Yussupov, 255–256; parting between Rasputin and, 261; with Rasputin and Maria in St. Petersburg, 138, 150, 193; and Rasputin's wife's illness, 130; her

Bekyeshova, Dunia, *(cont)*: relationship with Rasputin, 128, 167–168, 182, 225, 232–233, 237–238, 255; religious event experienced by, 224–225; and Anna Virubova's train accident, 240–241, 242
Beletski (assistant to Interior Minister), 260
Belisarius, 3
Bentley, B. Allen, 3
Berchtold, Count Leopold von, 223
Berdyaev, Nikolai, 17
Berlin, Treaty of, 205
Bernadette, Saint, 134
Bismarck, Prince Otto von, 204
Black Hand, 206, 221
Black Mass, 66–71
Blanch, Lesley, *The Sabres of Paradise*, 17, 131
"Bloody Sunday" (1905), 104, 113–114
Bogrov, Mordka, 176, 177–178
Bolshevik Revolution, *see* Russian Revolution
Bolsheviks, 135, 137–138, 178, 193, 297, 299; and letter from Aleksandra to Rasputin, 194; proletarian support of, 203–204; reassertion of, 243; rumors spread by, 230; and strikes, 229
Booth, John Wilkes, 221
Borodin, Aleksandr, 132
Borodino, Battle of, 184
Botkin, Eugene, 119, 122, 179, 184, 186
Boxer Rebellion, 109, 110
Brusilov, Aleksei Alekseyevich, 258
Brutus, Marcus Junius, 3, 54, 270
Bucharest, Treaty of (1913), 215
Buddhism, 29
Bulba, Taras, 24

Caesar, Julius, 3, 10, 270
Cagliostro, Alessandro, 4, 156–157, 282
Calpurnia, 10
Calvin, John (Jean), 47, 138
Casanova de Seingalt, Giovanni, 4
Cassius Longinus, Gaius, 54, 270
Castration, 55. *See also* Emasculation
Catherine II, Empress, 55, 87, 121, 157, 208
Catholicism, 43, 47
Cayce, Edgar, 303
Chekhov, Anton, 17, 132

Chaliapin, Feodor, 64
Charles XII, King (Sweden), 85–87
Cheka, 299
Chinese Eastern Railroad, 110
Chino-Japanese War, First (1894–1895), 110, 111
Christian IX, King (Denmark), 102
Christianity, 43–45
Churchill, Winston, 249
Church of Satan, 70
Civil War, American, 228–229
Cleopatra, 54
Clitoris, 44; removal of, 55
Code of Bushido, 54, 113
Congress of Vienna, 184–185
Convent of Saint Tikhon, 144
Cossacks, 24, 46, 86, 176, 207
Crimean War, 81
Crowley, Aleister, 47
Cult of the Assassins of Alamút, 29–30
Cult of Thugee, 29

Dagmar, Princess, *see* Maria Feodorovna, Dowager Empress
Damien de Veuster, Father Damien, 4
Davidsohn (agent of Iliodor), 220–221
Dematerialization, 156–157, 171–172, 282
de Seversky, A. P., 250
Diaghilev, Serge, 132
Disraeli, Benjamin, 94
Dmitri Pavlovich, Grand Duke, 243, 288, 292, 294; and Rasputin's assassination, 269–270; his relationship with Prince Yussupov, 160, 213, 214, 215, 251, 269
Dobrovolsky (Rasputin's secretary), 268
Donskoy, Dmitri, 56, 57
Dostoevski, Fyodor, 17, 132, 301
Dreadnaught (battleship), 205
Dueling, 133
Duma, 210, 265, 296; in dismissal, 250–251; hatred of Rasputin in, 246, 259; president of, 194, 209, 211
Dumas, Alexandre, *The Man in the Iron Mask*, 91–92
Dyerevyenko (Aleksei's guardian), 119
Dzerzhinsky, Feliks (chief of Bolshevik Cheka), 299
Dzhunkovsky (police chief), 237, 242, 243

Edward VII, King (England), 94, 159
Ehrlich, Max, *Shaitan*, 6
Einstein, Albert, 304
Elizaveta Feodorovna (Elizabeth, known as Ella), Grand Duchess, 92, 94–95, 104, 212, 213–214
Elizaveta Petrovna, Empress, 121
Elston, Feliks, 158
Emasculation, 283, 293
Encaussé, Dr. ("Papus"), 149
Ernst, Grand Duke, 94
Exorcism, 144–145, 156
Extrasensory perception (ESP), 303–304

Falkenhayn, Erich von, 217, 235
Fedorov (doctor), 187
Feliks, Father, 42
Filipich, Danila, 57–58
Flagellation, 54–55
Fox, George, 18
Francis, Saint, 3; Third Order of, 55
Franciscans, 43
Franz Ferdinand, Archduke (Austria), 206, 221–222, 223, 224
Franz Joseph, Emperor (Austria), 206
Frederick IV, King (Denmark), 86
French Revolution, 84
Friedrich III, Holy Roman Emperor, 157
Friedrich Wilhelm, Crown Prince (Germany), 257
Fülöp-Miller, René, 140, 145, 160, 167, 173, 198; on location of Rasputin during assassination of Stolypin, 176, 177; *Rasputin, The Holy Devil*, 12, 58
"Fundamental Laws," 115

Gapon, Father Georg, 113
Gautama Buddha, 29, 134
Genghis Khan, 5
Gilliard, Pierre, 185, 192
Glinka, Mikhail, 132
Godunov, Boris, 179
Gogol, Nikolai, 17, 132
Golos Moskvy (*Voice of Moscow*), 194
Golovina, Madame, 155, 156, 160, 171, 252, 277
Golovina, Maria Evgeniya (Munia), 155, 156, 160, 161, 171, 277; and events following Rasputin's

Golovina, Maria Evgeniya (Munia), *(cont)*:
assassination, 288, 290; and Prince Yussupov, 252
Goremykin, Ivan Longinovich, 115, 164, 218, 259
Gorki, Maxim, 211
Great Awakening, 54
Great Northern War (1699), 86
Greek Orthodox Church, 43
Grey, Lord, of Fallodon, 224
Grigoryev (police chief), 289–290, 291, 292
Guchkov, Aleksandr, 194, 211, 265
Gunther, John, 18
Gurko, Vasili, 265
Guseva, Chionya, 219, 221, 246, 256, 278; stabbing of Rasputin by, 11, 222–223
Gustavus Adolphus, 85
Guynemer, Georges, 250
Gypsies, 9, 21–24, 166, 233, 276, 279, 280

Habsburgs, 157, 204, 205, 206
Haig, Sir Douglas, 258
Hara-kiri, 54
Harbin, 110
Hasan ben Sabbáh, 29
Hélène, Princess, 93–94
Hemophilia, 105, 115–117, 119–120, 186–187; Aleksei's recovery from attacks of, 122–124, 134, 135, 155, 188–192, 263–265, 303
Henry II, King, 54
Hermanos Penitentes (Brothers Penitent), 54–55
Hermogen (Bishop of Saratov), 82, 98, 148, 151, 163, 193; banishment by Tsar, 150, 211; his hatred of Rasputin, 143–144, 147; and Iliodor, 138, 139, 143; and nomination of Rasputin to Union of True Russian Men, 140, 141
Hindenburg, Paul von, 217, 234
Holy Synod, 147, 163, 171
Homosexuality: of monks, 41, 43; Yussupov's, 9, 159–160, 162, 213–214, 251, 255, 256
Hus, Jan, 138
Hypnotism, 253–254, 303

Iliodor (Sergei Trufanov), 82, 138–139, 156, 171, 212; assassinations planned by, 218–219; his attempts to destroy Rasputin, 143, 151, 155, 193–196, 218–222; banishment by Tsar, 150, 211; and letters from Imperial Family to Rasputin, 193–195; his relationship with Rasputin, 139–142, 146–148
Innocent III, Pope, 3
Inquisition, Spanish, 44
Iosif, Father, 41, 42, 43
Ippolitov-Ivanov, Mikhail, 132
Ivan IV (Ivan the Terrible), 57, 64, 84, 89
Ivan of Kronstadt (Ivan Sergeiev), 81–82, 98, 140
Ivanov, Kondrati, 55–56
Ivanova, Katya, 61, 62, 73, 74, 130, 263–264; and events following assassination of Rasputin, 292, 293, 294; and Rasputin's depression, 262; her relationship with Rasputin, 10, 198, 233; visit to Petrograd of, 260
Izvestiya, 114

Japanese Navy, 111, 112
Jerome, Saint, 29
Jesus Christ, 63–64, 150, 151, 169–170, 171; death of, 287; miracles of, 172; Sermon on the Mount of, 139
Joan of Arc, 194, 216, 245
Joffre, Joseph, 257
John the Baptist, 150, 172
Jones, Jim, 47
Justinian I, 3

Kali, 29
Karsavina, Tamara, 132
Kazakov (airman), 250
Kemal, Mustapha, ("Ataturk"), 205
Kerensky, Aleksandr, 202, 296, 297, 299
Khlisti sect, 40–41, 42, 65, 73, 77, 135; appeal of beliefs of, 56–57; history of, 56, 57–58; on marriage, 198; orgies of, 49–53, 64, 97, 200; Rasputin's membership in, 48–49, 62, 143, 183, 211; and Skoptzi, 47–48, 55–56
Khodynka Meadow, tragedy of, 107–108

Khristos, 67, 150, 170, 281
Khvostov, Aleksandr, 176, 260, 277
Kipling, Rudyard, 6
Knox, John, 138
Kokovtsov, Vladimir, 165, 175, 176, 178, 218
Koliava, Mitya, 147, 149
Krishna, 67
Kronstadt Monastery, 80–84, 100, 105, 138
Kschessinska, Mathilde, 92, 93, 132
Kubasov, General, 21–22, 60–61
Kubasova, Irina Danilova, 21–22, 23, 25, 60–61, 122, 172
Kutuzov, Mikhail, 184, 245

Ladislaus II King, (Poland), 109
LaVey, Anton Szandor, 70
Lawrence, T. E., 18
Lazovert, Stanislas, 269–270, 271, 285, 294
Lenin, Nikolai (Vladimir Ulyanov), 114, 164, 251, 294, 297, 299; exile of, in Switzerland, 202–203, 250
Lentulus, Publius, 63–64
Leonidas I, King, 159
Leopold (Duke of Albany), 117
Lermontov, Mikhail, 132
Levitation, 171–172
Liepman, Heinz, *Rasputin and the Fall of Imperial Russia*, 12
Lincoln, Abraham, 172, 221
Lokhtin, State Councillor, 145
Lokhtina, Olga Vladimirovna, 145–148
Louis XV, King (France), 115
Louis Napoleon, Emperor, 84
Ludendorff, Erich von, 217, 234, 235, 245
Lupkin, Prokopi, 58
Luther, Martin, 47, 138
Lvov, Prince, 296, 297

Mackensen, August von, 217, 235
Mai, Princess, 93
Makari (starets), 41–42, 84
Makarov (Minister of Justice), 291
Maklakov (Minister of Interior), 250, 265, 268, 269, 270, 283
Mamai, Khan, 56
Manasevich-Manuilov (manipulator/spy), 260

Mangold, Tom, 299
Mannock (airman), 250
Margaretha, Princess, 94
Maria, Grand Duchess, 148, 178, 294
Maria Feodorovna, Dowager Empress, 102, 118, 184, 192, 215, 252
Mary of Burgundy, 157
Mary Magdalen, 3
Massie, Robert K., 165, 176, 177, 245; *Nicholas and Alexandra*, 12
Maximilian I, Holy Roman Emperor, 157
Mazeppa, Ivan, 86, 87
Melville, Herman, *Moby Dick*, 31
Mensheviks, 114, 243
Menshikov, Prince, 86
Militsa Nikolayevna, Grand Duchess, 97–98, 100, 105, 130, 136, 137
Miliukov, Pavel, 296
Mohammed, 29
Moltke, Helmuth von, 235
Montenegrin sisters, 97–98, 105, 120, 121, 164, 216. *See also* Anastasia Nikolayevna (Stana); Militsa Nikolayevna
Mordvinov, Nikon, 45–46, 47, 57
Moussorgsky, Modeste, 132; *Boris Godunov*, 64; *Khovantschina*, 46–47; *A Night on Bald Mountain*, 2–3
Mozart, Wolfgang Amadeus, 17
Mukden, Battle of, 111
Mutilation, sexual, 55, 293, 302, 303
Mysticism, 119; Russian fascination with, 132

Nagorny (Aleksei's guardian), 119
Napoleon Bonaparte, 85, 112, 208, 233, 257; and Battle of Borodino, 184; Pitt the Younger on, 98
Narodno Obrana, 206
Natalya, Tsaritsa, 58
National Geographic Society, 12
Nefedov (Yussupov's valet), 269–270, 290, 294
Nelson, Horatio, 205, 258
Nevsky, Aleksandr, 109
Nijinsky, Vaslav, 132
Nikita, Prince, 97
Nikolai Nikolayevich, Grand Duke, 97, 98, 120, 216, 219; dismissal of, 244–245; his hatred of Rasputin, 164,

Nikolai Nikolayevich, Grand Duke,
  (cont):
  220, 244; martial talent of, 245; his
  treasonous conversation with
  Rasputin, 217–218
Nikolai I, Tsar, 81, 244
Nikolai II, Tsar, 6, 81, 90–92, 107,
  172; abdication of, 296; and alliance
  between France and Russia, 108–109;
  and assassination of Franz Ferdinand,
  222; and attempt to blackmail
  Rasputin, 168–169; and celebration
  of reign of Romanov Dynasty, 206–
  209; children of, 83, 84, 116, 118;
  courtship of, 92–95; "dark star" of
  reign of, 102–105, 106–107; dismissal
  of Grand Duke Nikolai Nikolayevich
  by, 244–245; and Duma, 250–251;
  and events following Rasputin's
  assassination, 293, 294; first meetings
  with Rasputin, 105–106; hunting by,
  183–185; indecisiveness of, 203–204,
  216; and Kokovtsov, 218; marriage
  of, 95; murder of, 297; and October
  Manifesto, 114; and Pavlovich, 213;
  Rasputin's final letter to, 267–268;
  his relationship with Rasputin, 148,
  150–151, 179, 230–232, 247, 264–
  265; relatives of, 158, 160; and
  Rodzianko, 211; and Russian
  intervention in Balkans, 215–216;
  and son Aleksei's injuries, 119–120,
  184, 186–188, 263; and son Aleksei's
  miraculous recoveries, 120–124, 134,
  188–192, 263–265; and Stolypin, 175–
  177; and tragedy of Khodynka
  Meadow, 107–108; and Anna
  Virubova's train accident, 240–242;
  and Witte, 115; and World War I,
  229, 239, 247
Nivelle, Robert, 257
Nizier-Vachot, "Doctor Philippe," 149–
  150
Nostradamus, 156

Occult phenomena, 131, 132, 156, 216
October Manifesto, 104, 114–115, 178
Okhrana, 64, 167, 213, 219; reports of,
  on Rasputin's activities, 143, 165;
  surveillance of Rasputin by, 261,

Okhrana, *(cont)*:
  269; warnings of, to Rasputin, 220,
  260
Old Believers, *see* Raskolniki
Olga, Grand Duchess, 148, 177, 194,
  195
Omar Khayyám, 29, 133–134
Onate, Don Juan de, 55
Opium War, 110
Order of the Golden Dawn, 47
Order of St. Andrei, 104, 106–107
Orlov brothers, 55
Ossipova, Darya, 149
Ostrander, Sheila, 303–304
Oyama, Iwao, 111

Paléologue, Maurice, 228
Parapsychology, 2, 118–119, 132
Pares, Sir Bernard, 145, 268
Paris, Comte de, 93
Pasteur, Louis, 192
Paul, Father, 18, 23, 32, 77
Paul, Saint, 3
Paul, Tsar, 208
Pavel Aleksandrovich, Grand Duke, 160
Pavolva, Anna, 132
Peace of the Pruth (1711), 87
Pétain, Henri, 257
Peter, Father, 77–78, 182–183
Peter I (Peter the Great), Tsar, 3, 89,
  115, 121, 230; birth of, 58; and
  Charles XII, 85, 86–87; founding of
  St. Petersburg by, 87, 154; and
  Kronstadt, 80, 81; social revolution
  of, 85; and Yussupov family, 157
Peter III, Tsar, 55
Petersburg Soviet of Workers'
  Deputies, 114
Petipa, Marius, 132
Petrov, Andrei, 58
Pitt, William, the Younger, 98
Pizarro, Francisco, 44
Plehve, Vyacheslav Konstantinovich,
  104, 114
Pobedonostsev, Konstantin, 218
Poe, Edgar Allan, "The Masque of the
  Red Death," 88–89, 133
Polakova, Nastiya, 279
Polivanov (War Minister), 250
Port Arthur, 110; Japanese attack on, 111

Portolá, Gaspar de, 54
Portsmouth, Treaty of (1905), 113
Potëmkin (battleship), 112–113
Predestination, 31, 131, 197
Princip, Gavrilo, 206, 221–222
Prokofiev, Sergei, 132
Protestantism, 43, 93
Protopopov, Aleksandr, 9, 259, 266, 277, 287–288; and events following Rasputin's assassination, 292, 293
Pugachëv, Yemelyan, 55
Purichkevich, Vladimir Mitrofanovich, 266–267, 268–270; and assassination of Rasputin, 282–285; and events following assassination of Rasputin, 289, 291, 294
Pushkin, Aleksandr, 132, 209
Pyotr Nikolayevich, Grand Duke, 97, 98, 105, 130

Rachmaninov, Sergei, 132
Radaev, 58, 62, 138, 143
Raskolniki (Old Believers), 45–46, 53, 56, 57, 89
Rasputina, Anna Egorovna (mother), 13–14, 72
Rasputin, Dmitri (Mitya, son), 34, 72–73, 183, 260–261, 293, 294
Rasputin, Efim Akovlevich (father), 22–23, 63, 72, 74–76; and Rasputin's early life, 13, 14, 16–17, 19
Rasputin, Gregori Efimovich: abuse of daughter Maria of, 126–129; and Aleksei's miraculous recoveries, 120–124, 134, 135, 155, 188–192, 263–265, 303; assassination of, 275–286; and assassination of Stolypin, 176–177; attempted assassination of, 11, 16, 222–223; attitude toward women of, 25, 254–255; and Dunia Bekyeshova, 60–63, 128, 167–168, 182, 225, 232–233, 237–238; birth of, 12; birth of children of, 34; Black Mass experienced by, 66–71; his call to St. Petersburg, 78–79, 80–84, 88; carousing by, 166–167, 232–233, 242–243, 262–263; and celebration of reign of Romanov Dynasty, 206–209; change in appearance of, 162–163,

Rasputin, Gregori Efimovich,*(cont)*:
207; characterized, 2, 4, 35, 199–200; charges against, 77–78; as Christ, growing belief in, 63–66; clairvoyance of, 4, 16–17, 32–33, 148, 151, 176–177, 189, 196, 303; "court" of, 137, 142, 155, 197–200, 230, 237, 261; with daughter Maria in St. Petersburg, 130–131, 132, 134, 135, 166, 193; as deliverer of Jews, 245–246; and demon-possessed nun, 144–145; departure from St. Petersburg of, 179–180; depression of, 259–260, 262; desecration of body of, 296–297; destiny of, 172, 196–197; dual personality of, 25–26, 37, 73; early life of, 13–20; enemies of, 142, 143–144, 155, 163–165, 167, 174, 193, 195, 210, 212, 213, 237, 246; failure of healing powers of, 236–237; faith healing by, 4, 14, 16, 32–33, 63, 64, 67, 134–135, 172, 303; fear of, 33; his final letter to Nikolai II, 267–268; first meetings of, with Tsar and Tsaritsa, 105–106; funeral of, 293–294; holy vigil of, 74–76; house built by, 34–35, 126; and Iliodor, 138–142; illness of, 171–172, 174, 229–230, 238, 263; his influence in church and secular politics, 163, 165, 176, 193, 196, 216; journal of, 173–175; at Kronstadt Monastery, 80–84; last remaining days of, 261–265; letters from Aleksandra and daughters to, 193–195; life of Anna Virubova saved by, 241–242, 245, 247, 260; light found by, 18, 23, 27–28, 33, 36, 71, 97, 123; light lost by, 30; and Olga Lokhtina, 145–148; marriage of, 32, 33–34; as member of Khlisti sect, 39–43, 48–53, 62, 143, 183, 211; and Nikolai Nikolayevich, 217–218; out-of-body experience of, 156–157, 171–172, 174; pacifism of, 216, 224; physical descriptions of, 24, 32, 48, 136, 163; pilgrimage of, to Jerusalem, 169–171; plan to entrap and compromise, 165–169; power of, 58–59; precognition of, 16, 197; his predictions about World War I, 224,

Rasputin, Gregori Efimovich,*(cont)*:
231, 233, 243, 258; his premonition
of death, 4, 267; press's attack on,
178–179; and Purichkevich, 266, 267;
religiosity of, 17, 18–20, 28–31, 35–
37, 58–59; and Rodzianko, 209–210,
250; and royal family, *see* Aleksandra
Feodorovna, Aleksei Nikolaevich,
Nikolai II; at Russian court, 96–101,
148–151; sexual activities of, 2, 21–
24, 49–53, 61, 67–69, 71, 142–143,
166–167, 182, 196, 197, 198–200;
sexual organ of, 200, 293, 302; social
gatherings attended by, 162, 163; and
Stolypin, 164–165; his telegram to
Aleksandra, 190–191, 192, 194; his
trips to Pokrovskoye, 71–78, 126–
129, 130, 179–180, 182–183, 188–
190, 219–221, 222; underground
chapel of, 73–74; at Verkhoture
Monastery, 39–43; and Anna
Virubova, 136–138; his wife's illness,
130; writings about, 1; and
Yussupov, 9–11, 154–162, 251–257
Rasputin, Maria (daughter), 13–14, 61,
62; abuse of, by friend's father, 126–
127, 129, 130; on Akulina, 145; and
attempt on life of Rasputin, 220, 224;
on Dunia Bekyeshova, 168, 224–225;
on Black Mass, 69–70; departure
from St. Petersburg of, 179; and
events following Rasputin's
assassination, 287–288, 291–295; and
Grand Duchess Maria, 178; on
Iliodor, 218–219; and Kubasova
incident, 25; on Olga Lokhtina, 145;
marriage of, to Boris Solovyov, 297–
300; on meeting between Rasputin
and Prince Yussupov, 161–162, 253,
255–256; her mother's illness, 129,
130; *Rasputin, The Man Behind the
Myth*, 12, 18, 142, 300; with
Rasputin in Pokrovskoye (1911–
1912), 183, 188–189; with Rasputin
in St. Petersburg, 130–131, 132, 134,
135, 138, 166, 193; on Rasputin's
clairvoyance, 16; on Rasputin's
house, 35; Rasputin's last letter to,
262, 292; on Rasputin's out-of-body
experience, 171–172, 174; on
Rasputin's religiosity, 30, 37; on

Rasputin, Maria (daughter), *(cont)*:
Rasputin's reunion with family, 72–
73; on Rasputin's sexual activities,
142–143, 200; on Rasputin's spiritual
transcendence, 18–19, 28; at Russian
court, 148, 150; and Anna Virubova,
136, 177, 240–242; her warning to
Rasputin, 10, 11–12, 276, 278, 280
Rasputin, Mischa (Mikhail, brother),
13, 15, 34, 183
Rasputin, Praskovia Feodorovna (wife),
11, 61–63, 260, 261; and attempt on
life of Rasputin, 223, 224; birth of
children of, 34; and events following
assassination of Rasputin, 292, 293,
294; illness of, 126, 127, 129–130;
marriage of, 32, 33–34; and
Rasputin's holy vigil, 74–76; and
Rasputin's relationship with Dunia
Bekyeshova, 182; religious experience
of, 224–225; her reunion with
Rasputin, 71–73; her separations
from Rasputin, 36–37, 78–79
Rasputin, Varya (daughter), 10, 34, 62,
72, 73, 183; and events following
assassination of Rasputin, 291, 292,
295; with Rasputin in St. Petersburg,
193; and Yussupov, 255, 256
Rasputin and the Empress (film), 2–3
Razin, Stenka, 24
Reformation, 47
Religious fanatics, 138
Rennenkampff, Pavel, 234
Repin, Ilya Yefimovich, 96
Retz, Gilles de, (or de Rais), 194
Richthofen, Manfred von, 250
Rimsky-Korsakov, Nikolai, 132; *The
Invisible City of Kitezh*, 132; *Le Coq
d'Or*, 132; *Sadko*, 132; *The Snow
Maiden*, 132; *Tsar Sultan*, 177
Rodzianko, Mikhail, 209–210, 211–212,
218, 250, 265; his hatred of
Rasputin, 202, 220
Rozhdestvensky, Zinovi, 111–112
Russian Navy, 111–112
Russian Orthodox Church (religion),
43, 45, 47, 49, 93, 119; attitude of,
toward Rasputin, 164; and Iliodor,
139, 196; subordination of, to
Crown, 89
Russian Red Cross, 266

Russian Revolution (1917), 56, 113, 194, 296
Russian roulette, 133
Russo-Japanese War, 109–113, 159, 216, 229

Saborevski, Mileti, 35, 40
Sade, Marquis de, *Justine*, 70
St. Clair, David, 304
St. Petersburg: aberrant sex in, 132–133; description of, 87–89; founding of, by Peter the Great, 87, 154; Rasputin's call to, 78–79, 80–84, 88; Rasputin's home in, 106, 135–136, 138, 166, 193, 197, 217, 230, 237, 253; salon life in, 118; spiritualism and the occult in, 131, 132
St. Petersburg's Theological Academy, 82
Samsonov, Aleksandr Vasilievich, 54, 234
Sarasate, Pablo de, 276
Sardanapalus, 54
Sasanov, Grigori Pyotrovich, 106, 134, 135–136, 142, 147
Sasanova, Marusa, 135, 219, 240
Satanism, 69–70
Saul, King, 54, 170
Savonarola, Girolamo, 138
Sazonov, Sergei, 224
Schlieffen, Alfred von, 206, 235
Schlieffen Envelopment (Plan), 206, 228, 235
Schroeder, Lynn, 303–304
Séances, 98–100, 119, 149, 216
See of Tobolsk, 163
Self-immolation, 47, 53–54
Self-sacrifice, martial, 54
Selivanov (Kondrati Ivanov), 56
Semonovsky Regiment, 103
Serbia, 204, 205–206, 215, 223–224; declaration of war against, 224, 228
Serge Aleksandrovich, Grand Duke, 92, 95, 104, 213
Sergeiev, Ivan (Ivan of Kronstadt), 81–82, 98, 140
Sergius, Father, 43
Serra, Fray Junipero, 54
Sex, aberrant, in St. Petersburg, 132–133
Shakespeare, William, 95
Shamanism, 5, 64, 132

Shamyl, Murid emir; the "Lion of Daghestan,"17
Sherman, Harold, 303
Simanovich, Aaron, 268
Simeon the Just, Saint, 40
Simeon Stylites, Saint, 54
Skoptzi sect, 47–48, 55–56
Social Revolutionary Party, 104, 243
Solomon, King, 53, 197, 198
Solovyov, Boris, 297–300
Sophie, Archduchess and wife to Archduke Franz Ferdinand (Austria), 222
Spengler, Oswald, *The Decline of the West*, 227
Spiritualism, 131
Stalin, Joseph, 203
Stanislaus I, King (Poland), 86
Starets, defined, 5–6
Stepanova, Natalya Petrovna, 22–23, 25, 27, 147
Stevenson, Robert Louis, *Dr. Jekyll and Mr. Hyde*, 3
Stolypin, P. A., 105, 155, 164, 167, 169, 218; assassination of, 175–178, 208; his efforts to discredit Rasputin, 211; his encounter with Rasputin, 164–165; premiership of, 175; reforms of, 178
Stravinsky, Igor, 132
Stürmer, Boris Vladimirovich, 259
Suicide: mass, 46, 47; rate, in St. Petersburg, 133
Sukhomlinov, Vladimir, 244, 250
Sukhotin, Ivan, 269–270, 285, 294
Sumarokov, Count, 158
Sumarokov-Elston, Count, 158
Summers, Anthony, 299
Suslov, Ivan, 50–51, 58
Suvorov, Aleksandr, 55, 208, 245

Tamerlane, Timur-i-Leng; Mongol Khan, 157
Taneev, Aleksandr, 136
Tansin, Lisa, 166–167, 170, 230
Tatiana, Grand Duchess, 148, 177
Tchaikovsky, Peter, 132, 251
Teach, Edward (Blackbeard), 303
Theofan, Archimandrite, 82, 98, 105, 122, 140, 141; and Iliodor, 138, 139, 143

Third Order of St. Francis, 55
Tiberius Caesar, 63
Togo, Heihachiro, 111, 112
Tolstoy, Aleksei, *Ordeal*, 211
Tolstoy, Leo, 17, 131–132; *Anna Karenina*, 131
Trans-Siberian Railroad, 92, 109, 110, 129
Trotsky, Leon, 114, 164, 297, 299
Trufanov, Sergei, *see* Iliodor
Ts'u Hsi, Empress, 110
Tsushima Strait, Battle of, 137
Turgenev, Ivan, 17, 132

Ulyanov, Vladimir, *see* Lenin, Nikolai
Union of True Russian Men, 140, 143, 163, 164, 171; plan of, to entrap Rasputin, 165–167

Varnava (Bishop of Tobolsk), 163
Verkhoture Monastery, 39–43, 84
Victoria, Queen, 92, 93, 94, 117, 209
Villeneuve, Pierre de, 54, 112
Virgin of Kazan, 36, 78, 83, 237, 280; Rasputin's vision of, 28, 97, 123, 172, 190, 264; weeping, 225
Virubov, Boris, 137
Virubova, Anna Aleksandrovna, 122, 150, 176–177, 179, 297; and Aleksei's injury and miraculous recovery, 185–186, 188, 189, 191, 192; apartment found for Rasputin by, 136, 138; and events following Rasputin's assassination, 288–289, 290, 293–294, 295; Rasputin's saving of life of, 241–242, 245, 247, 260, 303; her relationship with Rasputin, 136–138, 238–239; train accident of, 239–241
Vishniakova, Maria, 119
Voltaire (François Marie Arouet), 86
Voronikhin (architect), 207

Wilde, Oscar, 162, 251
Wilhelm II, Kaiser (Germany), 94, 108, 109
Wilkins, Sir Hubert, 303
Wilson, Colin, 14, 145, 176–177, 224, 268; *Rasputin and the Fall of the Romanovs*, 12, 17–18
Witchcraft, 70
Witte, Count Sergius, 91, 164, 175,

216, 218, 231; death of, 247, 268; October Manifesto of, 114–115, 178
World War I, 30, 196, 227–229; Battle of Lemberg (Lvov) in, 233–234; Battle of the Masurian Lakes in, 234; Battle of Tannenberg in, 234–235; casualties in, 235–236; chaos in Russia during, 249–250, 258–259; First Battle of the Marne in, 234, 249; First Battle of the Somme in, 257–258; First Battle of Ypres in, 249; impact on Europe of, 227; prelude to, 221–225; Rasputin's predictions about, 224, 231, 233, 243, 258; Second Battle of Ypres in, 257; and Verdun, 257, 258
World War II, 257
Wyclif, John, 138

Yeats-Brown, Francis, *The Lives of a Bengal Lancer*, 30–31
Young Turks, 205
Yussupov, Prince Feliks Feliksovich, 9–11, 160, 171, 302; assassination of Rasputin by, 275–285; characterized, 156, 158, 212–213; conspiracy of, 267–271; early life of, 158–159; and Elizaveta, 213–214; and events following Rasputin's assassination, 287, 288–291, 292, 294–295; homosexuality of, 9, 159–160, 162, 213–214, 251, 255, 256; marriage of, 215; meetings between Rasputin and, 160–162, 251–257; at Oxford, 162, 212; and Dmitri Pavlovich, 159–160, 213, 214, 215, 243, 251, 269; his planned seduction of Rasputin, 251–257; and Purichkevich, 267, 268–269; *Rasputin*, 12–13, 160–161, 214; and Rodzianko, 212; wealth of, 154–155, 156, 157–158, 212
Yussupov, Nikolai, 155, 158, 159, 252
Yussupova, Princess Irina Aleksandrovna, 10–11, 271, 277, 280, 288; beauty of, 9–10, 158, 214; birth of her daughter, 251; marriage of, 158, 214–215
Yusup Mursa, 157

Zenaidye Nikolayevna Yussupova, Princess, 158, 212

236